The **Institute of Southeast Asian Studies (ISEAS)** was established as an autonomous organization in 1968. It is a regional centre dedicated to the study of socio-political, security and economic trends and developments in Southeast Asia and its wider geostrategic and economic environment. The Institute's research programmes are the Regional Economic Studies (RES, including ASEAN and APEC), Regional Strategic and Political Studies (RSPS), and Regional Social and Cultural Studies (RSCS).

ISEAS Publishing, an established academic press, has issued more than 2,000 books and journals. It is the largest scholarly publisher of research about Southeast Asia from within the region. ISEAS Publishing works with many other academic and trade publishers and distributors to disseminate important research and analyses from and about Southeast Asia to the rest of the world.

First published in Singapore in 2013 by
ISEAS Publishing
Institute of Southeast Asian Studies
30 Heng Mui Keng Terrace
Pasir Panjang
Singapore 119614

E-mail: publish@iseas.edu.sg
Website: <http://bookshop.iseas.edu.sg>

All rights reserved. No part of this publication may be reproduced, stored in a retrieval system, or transmitted in any form or by any means, electronic, mechanical, photocopying, recording or otherwise, without the prior permission of the Institute of Southeast Asian Studies.

© 2013 Institute of Southeast Asian Studies

The responsibility for facts and opinions in this publication rests exclusively with the authors and their interpretations do not necessarily reflect the views or the policy of the publishers or their supporters.

ISEAS Library Cataloguing-in-Publication Data

Encountering Islam : the politics of religious identities in Southeast Asia / edited by Hui Yew-Foong.
1. Islam and politics—Southeast Asia.
2. Religion and politics—Southeast Asia.
3. Islam and secularism—Southeast Asia.
4. Muslims—Southeast Asia.
I. Hui, Yew-Foong.
BP173.7 E561   2013

ISBN 9789814379922 (soft cover)
ISBN 9789814379939 (PDF)

Cover photograph: Attack on participants of a rally promoting religious tolerance at the Indonesian National Monument in Jakarta on 1 June 2008. Photo, courtesy of the National Integration Movement.

Typeset by Superskill Graphics Pte Ltd
Printed in Singapore by Oxford Graphic Printers Pte Ltd

CONTENTS

Acknowledgements vii

Contributors ix

Part I: Introduction

1. Introduction — Encountering Islam 3
   Hui Yew-Foong

Part II: Islam across Borders

2. Religious Elites and the State in Indonesia and Elsewhere: Why Takeovers are so Difficult and Usually Don't Work 17
   M.C. Ricklefs

3. "I was the Guest of Allah": Modern Hajj Memoirs from Southeast Asia 47
   Eric Tagliacozzo

4. The Aurad Muhammadiah Congregation: Modern Transnational Sufism in Southeast Asia 66
   Ahmad Fauzi Abdul Hamid

Part III: Malaysia

5. Legal-Bureaucratic Islam in Malaysia: Homogenizing and Ringfencing the Muslim Subject 103
   Maznah Mohamad

6. The Letter of the Law and the Reckoning of Justice
   among Tamils in Malaysia — 133
   Andrew Willford

7. Islamization and Ethnicity in Sabah, Malaysia — 158
   Regina Lim

Part IV: Indonesia

8. Natsir and Sukarno: Their Clash over Nationalism,
   Religion and Democracy, 1928–1958 — 191
   Audrey Kahin

9. Religious Freedom in Contemporary Indonesia:
   The Case of the Ahmadiyah — 218
   Bernhard Platzdasch

10. Religion and the Politics of Morality: Muslim Women
    Activists and the Pornography Debate in Indonesia — 247
    Rachel Rinaldo

Part V: Muslim Minorities

11. Malay Muslims and the Thai-Buddhist State: Confrontation,
    Accommodation and Disengagement — 271
    Ernesto H. Braam

12. Identifying with Fiction: The Art and Politics of Short Story
    Writing by Muslims in the Philippines — 313
    Coeli Barry

13. Issues on Islam and the Muslims in Singapore Post-9/11:
    An Analysis of the Dominant Perspective — 335
    Noor Aisha Abdul Rahman

Index — 377

ACKNOWLEDGEMENTS

This volume is based, partly, on proceedings of an international conference on "Religion in Southeast Asian Politics: Resistance, Negotiation and Transcendence", held on 11–12 December 2008 at the Institute of Southeast Asian Studies, and grateful acknowledgement is due to the Konrad Adenauer Stiftung for generous funding of the conference and Cornell University's Southeast Asia Program for co-sponsorship.

Chapter 9 was first published as "Religious Freedom in Indonesia: The Case of the Ahmadiyah", ISEAS Working Paper, Politics and Security Series No. 2 (2011).

An earlier version of Chapter 13 was published as "The Dominant Perspective on Terrorism and Its Implication for Social Cohesion: The Case of Singapore", *The Copenhagen Journal of Asian Studies* 27, no. 2 (2009): 109–28.

CONTRIBUTORS

AHMAD FAUZI Abdul Hamid	Universiti Sains Malaysia, Malaysia
Coeli BARRY	Princess Maha Chakri Sirindhorn Anthropology Center and Mahidol University, Thailand
Ernesto H. BRAAM	Utrecht University, The Netherlands
HUI Yew-Foong	Institute of Southeast Asian Studies, Singapore
Audrey KAHIN	Cornell University, USA
Regina LIM	Birmingham University, UK
MAZNAH Mohamad	National University of Singapore, Singapore
NOOR AISHA Abdul Rahman	National University of Singapore, Singapore
Bernhard PLATZDASCH	Institute of Southeast Asian Studies, Singapore
M.C. RICKLEFS	The Australian National University, Australia
Rachel RINALDO	University of Virginia, USA

Eric TAGLIACOZZO   Cornell University, USA

Andrew WILLFORD   Cornell University, USA

PART I
Introduction

1

INTRODUCTION — ENCOUNTERING ISLAM

Hui Yew-Foong

This volume evolved out of a conference with the theme "Religion in Southeast Asian Politics: Resistance, Negotiation and Transcendence", held on 11–12 December 2008. Part of the proceedings of the conference has been published in a Special Focus Issue of *Sojourn: Journal of Social Issues in Southeast Asia* (April 2010), with the theme "Religion and Politics in Southeast Asia", edited by Terence Chong. The articles that are related to the politics of Islam or the politics of religion in countries where Islam is the dominant religion are collected in this volume. Along the way, other chapters that fill the gap in terms of pertinent issues related to the theme of the volume were also commissioned.

The premise for the conference was the observation that, religion, whether institutionalized or otherwise, has an uncanny tendency to intervene in the political life of nation-states from time to time. The conference sought to address the following questions:

> How is it that religion, which ostensibly espouses transcendental worldviews, cannot seem to avoid intervening in the profane world of politics? Can the boundary between religious and political space be clearly

marked, or is it bound to be constantly negotiated and transgressed? How do we account for and characterize the potential of religion to transcend both the authority and boundaries of the state?

In raising these questions, there are two implicit assumptions. First is the assumption that what religion is is apparent. This is not the case. In fact, the more we reflect on the question, "What is religion?", the more the concept becomes intractable (see de Vries 2008). Is it to be defined as a set of beliefs, a worldview, cosmological orientation, and/or ontological disposition articulated through rituals and institutions? Clifford Geertz, in defining religion as a "system of symbols" (1973, pp. 90, 125), was limited to introducing an anthropological approach to the study and understanding of religion rather than defining the concept. It does not say how this "system of symbols" is different relative to other systems of symbols. It also does not account for motivations that are yet to be signified within such a system. As such, questions such as how religion can play primary roles in some societies and secondary roles in others, or how it can be both transcendental and effect this-worldly consequences, are inadequately addressed. Inasmuch as religion, as a phenomenon, haunts our everyday lives, it remains elusive as a concept.

Secondly, in speaking of religion today, we cannot ignore the flip side of the coin, that is, secularism, which is often taken as apparent. The tendency is to frame issues in such a way as to assume an ideal boundary between the religious and secular, relegating the former to the private sphere and associating the latter with modern public life. But religion and the secular have always implied each other, entwined in a politico-historical process without necessarily being dichotomized (Asad 2003). It is more reasonable to recognize that religion and religious identities do play powerful roles in public life, albeit under the arbitration of secular states (Butler et al. 2011; Willford and George 2005).

In the diverse national contexts of Southeast Asia, the line between religion and politics is not always clear. In encompassing all aspects of life for major populations of Southeast Asia, the moral and institutional foundations of religion were often bases from which these subjects were mobilized to articulate their political aspirations and form their sense of political consciousness.[1] It is no wonder then that religion, in whatever form, often has an important role to play in the life of the nation-state. Moreover, religion, in assuming an authenticity and authority that transcends the this-worldly orientation of the state, often serves as the source of substantive critique against the state. In turn, the state finds it useful to co-opt religious elites, institutions and ideas to shore up its legitimacy and authority.

Although every major world religion is represented in Southeast Asia, one cannot avoid encountering the prominence of Islam in this part of the world. One major reason is none other than the demographic composition. That is, Islam is the religion of the majority in three countries, namely Indonesia, Malaysia and Brunei, and of substantial minorities in the rest of Southeast Asia. In 2010, the Muslim population stands at 257,715,000, or 12.0 per cent of the population in Southeast Asia. This is projected to grow to 307,256,000, or 12.9 per cent of the population in Southeast Asia, by 2030 (Pew Research Center 2011, p. 72).

But perhaps a more substantive reason is the othering of Islam in public and geopolitical discourse, from the days of colonial exploration (Said 1979) to the more recent experience of 11 September as a global event. The proliferation of books and institutions involved in the production of knowledge concerning Islam over the course of the last century, and the media's projection of Islam as a socio-political phenomenon and force more recently, is testament to a fixation that has intensified. Islam, then, has been represented as a vestige of the feudal past embedded in an irrational exceptionalism that lacks compatibility with the secular modern nation-state. It is through the space created by such othering and its counter-discourses that Islam looms large in debates surrounding religion and politics.

In the specific context of Southeast Asia, Islam has been prominent in the public life of nations in multiple ways. In Muslim-dominant countries such as Indonesia and Malaysia, Islam is an integral part of the founding ideologies of these nations, and ideological elements of Islam are drawn upon by both political parties and organizations in civil society (Nagata 1984; Hefner 2000). In countries where Islam is considered the religion of a minority that nevertheless belongs to a transnational milieu, these minorities have to negotiate their position and seek an accommodation within a non-Islamic national imaginary. In countries such as Thailand and the Philippines, their engagement with the state or differential vision of nationhood, sometimes resulting in violence, has often thrown them into the national and international limelight (McCargo 2008; Abinales 2000). But it is not only in countries where Muslims are minorities that they may be marginalized and embroiled in violence, whether real or symbolic. In Malaysia and Indonesia, Islamic groups have also been subject to state violence and/or co-optation as well. In all cases, the debate concerning what constitutes authentic or orthodox Islam remains a perennial one. Islam, as encountered in public life, has come to encompass multifarious experiences associated with multiple religious identities.

However, recent work engaging with the political dimension of Islam tends to be cast under the neo-orientalist shadow of 11 September as an event. This volume seeks to move beyond such apprehension of Islam as a singular phenomenon, and thereby goes beyond narrow concerns with what is recognized as militant Islam and its attendant security issues. That is, the volume seeks to convey an understanding of Islam that is not limited, figuratively speaking, to the impressions of a single encounter. In *encountering* Islam, we seek to linger beyond the summary moment and reflect on the multiple impressions, suppressions and repressions, whether coherent or incoherent, associated with Islam as a socio-political force in public life. To this end, it is not adequate simply to represent the divergent identities associated with Islam in Southeast Asia, whether embedded in state-endorsed orthodoxy or Islamic movements that contest such orthodoxy. It is also important to examine other religious identities that have been inflected by the dominance of Islam in public discourse. By situating these religious identities within their larger socio-political contexts, this volume seeks to provide a more holistic understanding of what is encountered as Islam in Southeast Asia.

The rest of the volume is organized into four sections. The first consists of chapters that consider religious identities across political boundaries, while the rest of the volume addresses more specific national contexts. Quite inevitably, a book of this nature would give more attention to the countries of Malaysia and Indonesia, where Muslims form substantial majorities. (In Malaysia, the Muslim population stands at 17,139,000, or 61.4 per cent of its population, while in Indonesia, which is currently home to the largest Muslim population in the world, there are 204,847,000 Muslims, constituting 88.1 per cent of its population (Pew Research Center 2011, p. 156).) As such, the second section focuses on Malaysia, while the third deals with Indonesia. The last section examines Muslim communities in national contexts where they are minorities, specifically, in Thailand, the Philippines and Singapore.

Chapter 2 by Merle Ricklefs aptly dwells on that intractable boundary between religion and politics. Through examining the role of religious elites in politics, Ricklefs argues that even when states are weak and religious elites are strong, religious elites find it difficult to assume political power.

This is because the basis and exercise of power are essentially different for political and religious elites, in terms of asymmetrical capacities for action and differing bases of authority. While Ricklefs's chapter draws extensively on his understanding of Islam and politics in historical and contemporary Indonesia, he also examines examples beyond Islam and Southeast Asia to elicit more general conclusions.

One fundamental conceptual concern is the secular nature of modern statehood, such that it is difficult for religious agendas to gain traction within state bureaucracies without being diluted, even when religious elites are on the ascendant. In fact, the question is also whether religious elites can assume secular instruments of power without being secularized. The other conceptual concern is the nature of authority. Religious authority, by nature, draws on transcendent sources, and as such what is at stake is more existential, and embedded in an unlimited time-space, while political authority is rather more limited to the here and now. It is because of this and what Ricklefs calls the "epistemological uncertainty of religious authority", that what constitutes religious orthodoxy and orthopraxy remains an arena for perennial contests between religious elites. These issues are to emerge repeatedly in this volume.

For colonial governments, the Islamic pilgrimage to Mecca and Medina known as the Hajj, in crossing borders and thereby transcending the authority of states, had often generated cause for concern and surveillance (Laffan 2003; Ho 2006). Eric Tagliacozzo, in discussing the Hajj through the memoirs of Islamic pilgrims in Chapter 3, gives us a glimpse of the sojourning Muslim subject. From the experiences of Hang Tuah in the fifteenth/sixteenth centuries, to the ruminations of Munshi Abdullah in the nineteenth century, one reads of Muslim subjects negotiating between political and religious authorities. In the accounts examined, the journey is not only marked by a topography of sacred sites, but is also an inner journey that refracts the identities of the pilgrim, whether it be geographical provenance, occupation or gender. For the Muslim subject, this journey also marks transitions between the sacred, which bestows the gift of contemplating death, and the profane, that is, between authority that is transcendental and authority that is worldly.

Another way in which Islam transcends the boundaries of states is through transnational Sufi movements. In Chapter 4, Ahmad Fauzi Abdul Hamid relates the beginnings, diffusion and evolution of one such Sufi movement, namely, the Aurad Muhammadiah, in Southeast Asia. While Aurad Muhammadiah's main chapters are based in Singapore and Malaysia, it remains very much a transnational movement with religious, business and kinship links across national boundaries. When the movement in Malaysia, in the form of Darul Arqam, became embroiled in political and theological controversies and was banned in 1994, it evolved and survived in the form of transnational business concerns, first as Rufaqa' Corporation, and subsequently as Global Ikhwan. In this case, there are limits to how much political authority can determine religious orthodoxy, not only because the religious movement subscribes to a different school of religious thought, but also because it subscribes to different geographical limits.

Where the specific case of Malaysia is concerned, the state had actively engaged in the governance of the religious sphere through the co-option and outlawing of "deviant" Islamic movements. This active intervention in the Islamic institutions of the nation continues through what Maznah Mohamad (Chapter 5) describes as the rise of legal-bureaucratic Islam, that is, the expansion of the bureaucracy and legal institutions in the administration of Islamic matters, and the adjudication of Islamic law through the Syariah Court. By taking up the mantle of Islamic administration, the state seeks to assume the authority of religion, and in turn the power to define the Islamic subject. This erosion of the private sphere of religion, coupled with the Islamization of the public sphere, threatens the normative notion of the secular, such that it is no longer certain that the state would continue to protect what is understood as the "freedom of religion".

Indeed, it is in protest against the failure of the state to protect the rights of Hindus that led more than 30,000 Hindu Tamils to demonstrate under the banner of the Hindu Rights Action Force (Hindraf) in late 2007. In Chapter 6, Andrew Willford weaves together the different threads that contributed to the emergence of this movement, such as the demolition of Hindu temples, the symbolic appropriation of a Tamil national hero that Syariah officials claimed had secretly converted, and the marginalization of the Tamil working class. The perceived injury upon the Hindu Tamil body politic led to memoranda submitted to Malaysian leaders to no avail, and so in a final sensational move, a memorandum was presented to the British who were seen as being historically responsible for the Tamils' plight in Malaysia. This unveils the vacuity and opaqueness of the law, as embodied in the state and its apparatuses, which drives the Tamils towards a source of justice that is not only foreign, but transcends foreign sovereigns and governments. Eventually, Willford argues, the Tamil community becomes aware that justice is not to be found in the law, but in its transgression, and this justice is rooted in desire for "a re-entangling of Tamil and Malay historicities". Ultimately, by investing justice with transcendental authority, justice in turn possesses and haunts the Hindu Tamil subject.

Regina Lim (Chapter 7) draws our attention to Sabah in East Malaysia to examine the effects of statist Islamization. The ethnic and religious constitution of Sabah, whereby a large proportion of indigenous people is non-Muslim, makes it more difficult to legitimize the dominant position of Islam in the public sphere, as is the status quo in West Malaysia. Nevertheless, the federal government was able to import pro-Islamist politics and policies into Sabah through compliant state governments and transforming the religious demographics of the state via mass conversions and the assimilation of Muslim immigrants. However, the state, in so doing, is perceived as abandoning its normative secular mandate, thus risking the alienation of its non-Muslim constituency, which in turn limits the extent of its legitimacy.

The section on Indonesia opens with Audrey Kahin's examination of debates over the role of Islam in politics during the formative years of the Indonesian nation. In particular, Chapter 8 looks into the ideas of Mohammad Natsir, leader of Masjumi (then Indonesia's largest Muslim political party), and Sukarno, Indonesia's first president, concerning the place of religion in the political life of the nation. Sukarno was inclined towards the separation of state and religion, with religion remaining in the private sphere, while Natsir propounded the use of Islam as a moral yardstick for ordering the new nation-state. For Natsir, it was not sufficient merely to include belief in God among the "Five Principles" or Pancasila that became Indonesia's state ideology. He had advocated for a country where the practice of democracy was guided by Islamic values, while Sukarno's vision was a secular one whereby nationalists, Muslims and Marxists coexisted in harmony. As we shall see, this tension between the desire for "Islamic morality" and support for a secular state that guarantees religious pluralism would continue to characterize the political life of contemporary Indonesia.

In Chapter 9, Bernhard Platzdasch looks into the case of the Ahmadiyah, an Islamic sect deemed deviant by conservative Muslims that, nevertheless, had thrived in Indonesia. However, the sect had, in more recent years, been further marginalized by mainstream Islamic organizations and even suffered assault by a militant Islamist group. In the midst of this controversy, the Indonesian state had taken an equivocal stance, sanctioning the sect without banning it outright. At the same time, what is at stake is, on the one hand, the contest over what constitutes Islamic orthodoxy and, on the other hand, the state of religious pluralism and tolerance in Indonesia. In the final analysis, Platzdasch suggests that the state had remained irresolute in the face of this crisis because the legal basis for the relationship between the state and religion, in particular, Islam, had not been unambiguously resolved.

Rachel Rinaldo (Chapter 10), in exploring how different Islamic women's groups approach the controversy over the anti-pornography bill, brings us the gendered dimension of the debate over the role of religion in the political life of Indonesia. One key proponent for legislation on pornography was the Prosperous Justice Party, and its women's division articulated support for the bill in terms of safeguarding the morality of the nation. On the other hand, Fatayat, a women's group of the Nahdlatul Ulama, opposed the legislating of morality, asserting that this might not necessarily protect the rights of women and children victimized by the sex industry, while at the same time privileging certain religious interpretations of morality. Both groups view Islamic morality as important, but differ on whether such issues should inform legislation and the public sphere, or be confined to the private domain of everyday life. There are here echoes of the debate between Natsir and Sukarno.

In the foregoing chapters on Malaysia and Indonesia, where Muslims are in the majority, the debate tends to revolve around the role of Islam in politics and its interface with secular statehood in the context of multicultural and multi-religious imagined communities. With the ascendency of Islam in the national public sphere, the danger is that certain religious communities, whether Islamic or otherwise, may be sidelined. In the case of Malaysia, with the appropriation of Islam by the state, which in turn actively takes on the mission of Islamizing the nation, secular space is eroded and, in fact, put on the defence (Yeoh 2011). As for Indonesia, with the democratization of politics in the post-Soeharto era, Islamic groups have increasingly shaped public discourse and, in some cases, led to more aggressive claims to Islamic orthodoxy. These developments are traceable to the global Islamic resurgence of the 1970s and 1980s (Hefner and Horvatich 1997), and states have employed different strategies to manage their Muslim constituents depending on their strength. In countries where Muslims are in the minority, the political issues that emerge are quite different. In these political contexts, Muslim minorities have to contend with the dominant political culture, whether it is shaped by majority religious or secular sensitivities. Often, the neo-orientalist vision of the state, in constituting the Muslim minority as an internal other, relegates Muslim communities to the periphery of the national imaginary. In instances where they are associated with separatist movements or, more recently, terrorist networks, these communities are put under surveillance, policed, or even treated as enemies of the state.

While the Islamic Deep South of Thailand tends to attract attention as the bedrock of terrorist violence and separatist ambitions, Ernesto Braam (Chapter 11) paints a rather more complex picture of how Malay-Muslim subjects relate to the Thai-Buddhist state. Braam demonstrates that even the violent confrontations vary in character, showing us the subtle differences between the suicidal Krue Se incident, the tragic Tak Bai incident and the enigmatic Al Furqan incident. But besides these violent episodes, Thai Muslims have engaged the state at different levels, including participation in formal politics and accommodating Thai officialdom, in order to maintain Muslim political representation and protect the Islamic religious space. At the same time, there are also others who choose to disengage with the political conditions they are embedded in by participating in the piety movement of the Tablighi Jamaat, traipsing the rural landscape to answer the call of a higher authority and engage in a fraternity that transcends limited nation-states. Even as a minority, there are multiple ways of being Muslim and living the Islamic experience.

One window into the Islamic experience is literature, and Coeli Barry (Chapter 12) draws us in through the short stories written by Muslims in the Philippines. These short stories, written in English, tell the tales of boundary crossing, from the Muslim village to the Christian city, from the nostalgic confines of tradition to the jarring allure of modernity, even as they are narrated, not in the vernacular, but in the language of the colonizer. The stories also reflect the historical consciousness of Muslims, depicting, from the 1950s, the experience of rupture under American rule, in the 1970s, the conflict between the Catholic state and Muslim South, and in more recent years, conflicts within Muslim communities as they seek to define Muslim identity. Through this survey of Muslim short fiction, Barry's essay argues for a nuanced reading of Muslim-Filipino identities and demonstrates how these stories, from the margins, constitute part of the "artistic and literary life of the nation".

The final chapter dwells on how the secular state of Singapore manages its Muslim minority. In Chapter 13, Noor Aisha Abdul Rahman shows the limits of the culturalist approach to managing ethnic relations, whereby an overly-essentialized understanding of Islam shapes public discourse and policies. Not only does such an approach fail to capture the diverse religious opinions held by different segments of the Muslim community, it also does not adequately account for the socio-political factors that influence the social behaviour of Muslims. As such, a more holistic approach is needed to facilitate cross-cultural understanding.

The chapters of this volume, whether focusing on Islam exclusively or otherwise, give us a deeper understanding of Islam and its role in politics as encountered in different political contexts, eschewing the neo-orientalist approach that has informed public discourse in recent years. In transnational contexts, we have seen that the transcendence of political boundaries often translates into the transcendence of political authority. In contexts where Islam is the dominant religion, we observe the marginalization of minor Islamic sects, minority religions, and even secular space. In polities where Muslims constitute minorities, they are often subject to dominant national discourses that do not take into account their divergent subject positions. At the same time, whether Muslims are in the majority or minority in a country, what constitutes authentic, orthodox or legitimate Islam remains very much a contested arena. Such struggles tend to be more intense in the former, presumably because more is at stake politically. Here, the struggles also involve negotiation between religious and political elites, and it is not always clear which is the stronger. In any case, in the entanglement between religion and politics in Southeast Asia, Islam will continue to play a key role.

Note

1. Consider, for example, the emergence of Sarekat Islam as the first Indonesian nationalist organization (Kahin 2003, pp. 65–70; Shiraishi 1990). See also Laffan (2003).

References

Abinales, Patricio N. *Making Mindanao: Cotabato and Davao in the Formation of the Philippine Nation-State*. Quezon City: Ateneo de Manila University Press, 2000.

Asad, Talal. *Formations of the Secular: Christianity, Islam, Modernity*. Stanford, CA: Stanford University Press, 2003.

Hefner, Robert W. *Civil Islam: Muslims and Democratization in Indonesia*. Princeton, NJ: Princeton University Press, 2000.

Hefner, Robert W. and Patricia Horvatich, eds. *Islam in an Era of Nation-States: Politics and Religious Renewal in Muslim Southeast Asia*. Honolulu: University of Hawai'i Press, 1997.

Ho, Engseng. *The Graves of Tarim: Genealogy and Mobility across the Indian Ocean*. Berkeley: University of California Press, 2006.

Kahin, George McTurnan. *Nationalism and Revolution in Indonesia*. Ithaca, NY: Cornell Southeast Asia Program, 2003.

Laffan, Michael. *Islamic Nationhood and Colonial Indonesia: The Umma below the Winds*. New York: Routledge, 2003.

McCargo, Duncan. *Tearing Apart the Land: Islam and Legitimacy in Southern Thailand*. Ithaca, NY: Cornell University Press, 2008.

Nagata, Judith. *The Reflowering of Malaysian Islam: Modern Religious Radicals and their Roots*. Vancouver: University of British Columbia Press, 1984.

Pew Research Center. "The Future of the Global Muslim Population: Projections for 2010–2030" <http://pewforum.org/uploadedFiles/Topics/Religious_Affiliation/Muslim/FutureGlobalMuslimPopulation-WebPDF-Feb10.pdf> (accessed 21 March 2011).

Shiraishi, Takashi. *An Age in Motion: Popular Radicalism in Java, 1912–1926*. Ithaca, NY: Cornell University Press, 1990.

Vries, Hent de. "Introduction: Why still 'Religion'?" In *Religion: Beyond a Concept*, edited by Hent de Vries. New York: Fordham University Press, 2008.

Willford, Andrew C. and Kenneth M. George, eds. *Spirited Politics: Religion and Public Life in Contemporary Southeast Asia*. Ithaca, NY: Southeast Asia Program Publications, Cornell University, 2005.

Yeoh, Seng Guan. "In Defence of the Secular? Islamisation, Christians and (New) Politics in Urbane Malaysia". *Asian Studies Review* 35, no. 1 (2011): 83–103.

PART II
Islam across Borders

2

RELIGIOUS ELITES AND THE STATE IN INDONESIA AND ELSEWHERE: WHY TAKE-OVERS ARE SO DIFFICULT AND USUALLY DON'T WORK

M.C. Ricklefs

> *The present age is really the same old age:*
> *It is either the men of prayer or the politicians who are in charge.*
> — Muhammad Iqbal[1]

This chapter argues that Iqbal was correct to identify two major kinds of elites — the "men of prayer" and "the politicians" — but that a scholarly rather than poetic consideration leads to the conclusion that "men of prayer" find it very difficult to be "in charge". Rather, state-controlling elites — "the politicians" — typically maintain primacy. And — remarkably — this seems to hold true across times and cultures, despite social, cultural, political, economic and technological differences. Here we ask how such consistency can be explained. I will argue below that the answer is to be found in (1) an asymmetry of capacities between religious and state elites and (2) the different epistemological standing of the authority of those "men of prayer" and "politicians".

In a consideration as full of slippery areas as this, we must be clear about our definitions at the outset. By *religious elite*, I mean here those who are defined, legitimated and inspired by their religious standing. They are the priests in religions that have priests, the ordained theologians in others, or — of particular relevance in the Indonesian and other Islamic cases — the learned scholars of the faith, the respected interpreters of scriptures, recognized as such by their community. This can be a problematic category in Islam, where formal processes by which one becomes such a person are few. By *political elite* or *state-controlling elite*, I mean those who control the state, its apparatus, institutions and symbols, or those who are in competition with other similar figures to do so. So these are the politicians of our day, the kings and emperors of previous days and their colleagues. In some states, this state-controlling elite includes the military.

In our present age, we see cases of such *religious elites* aspiring to control or to exercise decisive influence over states in order to carry out their religious, moral and legal agendas. Yet historically we rarely see such aspirations succeeding. It is necessary therefore to ask why that might be so, for the historical experience may shed light on contemporary circumstances.

The consistency mentioned above — that of the primacy of the "politicians" over the "men of prayer" — may not at first be obvious. Looking at the past, one might think that a distinction between religion and the state was moot. Precolonial states often had kings who claimed supernatural powers, were reputed to be shadows of God upon the earth and were surrounded by supernatural sanctity. Panembahan Senapati Ingalaga (r. c.1584–1601), Sultan Agung (r. 1613–46) and other monarchs of Java's Mataram dynasty were reputed to be the supernatural husbands of the Goddess of the Southern Ocean, who controlled the spirit armies of Java. Pakubuwana II (r. 1726–49) — or, more correctly, his influential Sufi grandmother Ratu Pakubuwana — sought to make Javanese kingship a subset of Islamic kingship, with Pakubuwana II eventually presenting himself as the conquering king of Holy War (Ricklefs 2008). Those who did not rule, but rather rebelled against the monarchs of Java, normally invoked supernatural authority on their behalf. So the boundaries between religion and politics often seem obscure, perhaps even meaningless, in precolonial sources.

If religious and state authorities sometimes appear tangled together in precolonial times, they may seem differently related in more modern times, where state legitimacy tends to be secular in nature. Yet here again the picture is complicated. In the circumstances of contemporary Indonesia, there has been no shortage of people wishing to take over the state so as to impose *shari'ah* law, or to capture specific institutions as a means to impose their views on society and to suppress the contending views of other Muslims. We will discuss several of these below. Here, a distinction between state authority and those religious activists who seek to take it over seems obviously relevant, as is the wish of the activists that the distinction should not exist. The slippery element here is this: many of these religious activists are not to be considered members of the religious elite. They are typically products of secular educational institutions and, however profound their personal piety (or not, in the eyes of many a cynic), few are recognized as learned scholars of the faith or respected interpreters of scriptures. There are few recognized *ulama* (learned scholars of Islam) to be found among them. These Islamists are more commonly people aspiring to political control or influence, using Islam as their source of legitimacy and/or inspiration; they are thought of as politicians, and sometimes quite effective ones.

Despite such evident differences, however, here I will argue, based on both historical and contemporary Indonesia, and with consideration of examples from elsewhere, that across time and cultures there is in fact a similar relationship between state authority on the one hand and religious authority on the other, and that this sheds light on the nature of authority itself.

INDONESIAN HISTORIES

In 1613 there came to the throne the greatest of Mataram's kings, Sultan Agung. He continued his predecessors' wars against coastal states, culminating in the fall of Surabaya in 1625. This left Agung as the dominant force in the Javanese heartland of Central and East Java as well as Madura. In the west of Java, however, the Dutch East India Company (VOC) had established its headquarters at Batavia in 1619, thereby threatening Agung's ambitions in the west of the island. In 1628–29 Agung attacked Batavia. His first siege seriously threatened the Company but failed in the end. His second was a disaster from the beginning.

It seems that Sultan Agung's failure before Batavia called into question his invincibility and the supernatural sanctions that he claimed. The Goddess of the Southern Ocean's spirit armies had proved no more successful than Agung's mortal troops in expelling the VOC. Agung was now at his weakest, for if he was truly the protégé of the Goddess, the shadow of God upon the earth, the spiritually qualified owner of the supernaturally endowed royal regalia (*pusaka*) and the invincible conqueror of all who stood against him, how could he have failed against Batavia?

With the loss of his aura of invincibility and supernatural authority, Agung found himself facing challenges from new Javanese opponents (Ricklefs 2006, pp. 36–50). The greatest of these challenges was evidently religiously justified and based at the holy grave at Tembayat of Sunan Bayat, the semi-legendary bringer of Islam to South-Central Java. According to the VOC officer Pieter Franssen, who visited the court of Mataram at this time, twenty-seven villages joined this anti-Agung rebellion, its leaders having gone from village to village dressed as mendicants to recruit followers. The rebellion was crushed and Franssen witnessed captured rebels being brought to the capital for interrogation — and, we may be sure, various brutal forms of torture and execution.

The rebellion was put down, but now Agung faced a need to domesticate the potential of Islam to challenge his authority and to inspire resistance. He had to co-opt that supernatural power and its attendant elite which might otherwise destroy his fragile kingdom. So in 1633 he went on a pilgrimage to Tembayat. Agung undertook several spiritually significant steps, either while still at Tembayat or at least at around the same time, that boosted his Islamic credentials and served to co-opt the political and supernatural potential of Tembayat to his cause. According to Javanese traditions, he met with the spirit of Sunan Bayat, who instructed Agung in "the hidden mystical sciences". He erected a ceremonial gateway there that still stands, inscribed with a record of the King's visit. Agung decreed a change in the Javanese calendrical system around this time, abandoning the Hindu lunisolar era which was still being used for court purposes, adopting instead the Islamic lunar months, but continuing the Śaka enumeration of years which became the unique Anno Javanico era. The King also achieved a rapprochement with the defeated princely line of Surabaya, descended from one of the first bringers of Islam to Java (the semi-legendary nine *walis*). Agung also introduced at least three literary works into the court canon that were of more specifically Islamic inspiration. These were a tale elaborated from the Muslim version of the legends of Alexander the Great, *Carita Sultan Iskandar* (based on Qur'an 18: 82–98); another romance developed from the Qur'anic account of Joseph in Egypt, *Serat Yusuf* (from Qur'an 12); and a third concerning major figures of Islamic tradition, but of no known Middle Eastern source, entitled *Kitab Usulbiyah*. Supernatural powers were ascribed to all three books.

Agung seems probably also to have inspired a fourth work, entitled *Suluk Garwa Kencana*, which is of particular interest for our discussion of religion and the state, for it seems to be Agung's personal political philosophy. Here Javanese kingship was seen as a form of Sufism, its martial traditions as equivalent to the Sufi *al-jihad al-akbar*, the "greater holy war" to control one's own passions. It is possible that these teachings represented what Agung is said to have learned from the spirit of Sunan Bayat. For example:

> Let that which serves as your citadel be
> constant struggle;
> that which serves as your weapon
> the exalted contemplation (of God);
> as your vehicle: steadfast trust in God.
> Take care and battle firmly.
> Let the scriptures (*sastra*) serve as your subjects.
> Let piety serve as your bow;
> let *dhikr* (the repetition of divine formulae) serve as your quiver,
> and the *Qur'an* as your arrows.
> Draw your bow on the field of battle.
> Truly heroic are you, Your Highness,
> surrounded by virtue and firmness.
> ....
> When you are consecrated as king,
> don your royal garb:
> let *Khak* (Reality) serve as your crown,
> with *tarekat* (the mystical way) as its crest.
> Struggle constantly,
> *sarengat* (the law) serving as your lower garment.

Thus were the traditions of Javanese martial kingship evidently reconciled with the demands of Islamic mystical piety.

We may reasonably presume that something else followed from this. That is, the *ulama* — in Javanese more commonly called *kyai* — gained greater influence at court in an Islamizing period such as this. It may be in these circumstances that we can see the roots of what followed Agung's death.

In 1646 Agung was succeeded by his son Amangkurat I (r. 1646–77), who presided over the greatest slaughter of Muslim divines in Javanese history. Amangkurat I stands in Javanese historical traditions as the ultimate tyrant, who ruled by murder and, at the end, probably went mad (de Graaf 1961; 1962). He did not use the title Sultan but instead called himself by the Javanese royal title Susuhunan, perhaps a token of his intention to distance himself from Islamic influence. After suppressing opposition from a brother, who seems to have had support from Muslim divines, Amangkurat I moved to eliminate the religious elite. He summoned the prominent religious leaders of the kingdom to the court where, upon his signal, 5,000–6,000 Muslim leaders and their families were slaughtered. The Dutch ambassador Rijklof van Goens still observed unburied bodies from this massacre on his visit to the court in 1648.

The Javanese saw this slaughter of Muslim leaders as a dreadful event. The chronicle *Babad ing Sangkala* contains a passage that was probably composed during Amangkurat I's reign itself, which describes the slaughter in the following terms:

> When disappeared the teachers upon the road,
> men departed from the [rightful] path.
> As if dimmed was the lustre of the kingdom;
> rain fell heavily; the king constantly cherished a grim
> hatred and ordered the troops.[2]

From this time onward, for nearly eighty years there is little evidence of *kyai* being influential in royal affairs. Indeed, over those decades Islam is more likely to appear in the sources as the rallying cry of rebels who opposed the dynasty and denounced it for its alliance with the *kafirs* of the VOC. The VOC alliance thus offered military support to the dynasty while at the same time inspiring opposition to it.

A second major reconciliation of the court — as the main definer of Javanese cultural identity — and Islamic sensibilities took place in the reign of Susuhunan Pakubuwana II (1726–49). Early in the reign, the King's formidable Sufi grandmother Ratu Pakubuwana (b. c.1657, d. 1732) wielded influence over a new Islamizing process in the court, inspired by the example of Sultan Agung a century before (Ricklefs 1998). The King himself was just sixteen years old on ascension and an inconstant, unreliable and weak character. Indeed, he was arguably the most disastrous king in the dynasty's history, so that the two major episodes of Islamization in the court were presided over a century apart by the dynasty's greatest king (Agung) and its least (Pakubuwana II).

An Islamizing clique in the court led by the elderly Ratu Pakubuwana endeavoured to turn Java into a pious Sufi kingdom. A 1728 court command (ibid., p. 26), among other provisions, imposed stoning to death as the punishment for adultery by a royal official. If the chief religious officer (Pangulu) failed to teach a true teaching, he would be banished to the wilderness. These were not just theoretical punishments. In 1738 the son of the Pangulu and a royal concubine were put to death for committing adultery. The Pangulu's wife was then accused of teaching "scandalous histories and ditties", with the result that she, the Pangulu and all their family were banished from the court to the wilderness in 1739 (ibid., p. 221). In 1731 a royal order outlawed gambling on pain of death — with the culturally potent exception of cock-fighting (ibid., p. 166), which governments today still find difficult to abolish. In 1732 Pakubuwana II attended public worship in the great mosque at the capital city of Kartasura, a very rare event for kings, who usually carried out their religious duties in the privacy of the court itself (ibid.). Despite there being evidence that the King himself had homosexual relations, he denounced homosexuality — as did works inspired by Ratu Pakubuwana on Qur'anic authority — and in 1739 banished his homosexual brother Prince Blitar for eight months to the mosque at Imogiri, where he was imprisoned with only women in attendance. When Blitar had demonstrated satisfactorily that he had reformed his ways, he was allowed back to court, where he soon reoffended. Thereupon his lover was killed and his head impaled on a stake in the marketplace. Blitar reacted with violence and sought to kill another prince, whereupon he was again banished from the court (ibid., pp. 222–23).

Ratu Pakubuwana revived the three supernaturally powerful books introduced to the court in Sultan Agung's time, *Carita Sultan Iskandar*, *Serat Yusup* and *Kitab Usulbiyah*, which were rewritten with introductory passages praising the religious standing of Ratu Pakubuwana. *Suluk Garwa Kencana* was also rewritten at this time. Another work, the *Serat Wulang Pakubuwana II*, was ascribed to the King himself and said to be his teachings. This condemned the use of opium, called for a life of piety and morality and emphasized Islamic mystical doctrines. Other courtiers who opposed the Islamizing clique were sidelined.

This Islamizing trend peaked in the "Chinese War" (1740–43). Pakubuwana II sided with the Chinese who were fighting the VOC and in July 1741 attacked the VOC garrison at the court. Several VOC officers were killed and others were forcibly converted to Islam and circumcised. Pakubuwana II was now the conquering Sufi king, the victor in Holy War against the infidels. But the Chinese side began to collapse as the VOC regained the military initiative. At this stage Pakubuwana II — inconstant to the very end — sought reconciliation with the Company, which had of course little inclination to trust him. This attempted reconciliation was sufficient to turn those Javanese who had joined the rebellion against the King. They captured the court, sacked it and put the King to flight in June 1742. Madurese forces ostensibly allied with the VOC drove the rebels from the court in December 1742, sacked what remained to be sacked, and refused the King access to the ruins of his court. He was restored to his throne in 1743 only because the VOC supported him, for in his abject condition the Company at last saw what it had always wanted, a king that would be entirely dependent on the VOC. Thereafter the pious, Islamizing Sufism of the past was seen no more. Figures who had opposed the Islamizing clique dominated court affairs thereafter. And within three years began the Third Javanese War of Succession (1746–57) which would partition the Javanese state.

With regard to the relationship between state and religious authority, these episodes suggest the primacy of political authority in precolonial Java. It was those who controlled the state — in this case, we mean those who controlled the court — who determined the success or failure of efforts to Islamize the court and the society. These episodes enable us to distinguish those who exercised what we recognize as political authority from those whose authority rested on claims to being pious, learned and/or divinely protected Muslims, and who did not control the state. The relationship varied; it was sometimes harmonious and sometimes antagonistic, even violent.

These episodes also suggest that those who sought a more pious Islamic state had their greatest prospects of winning influence when the monarchy was at its weakest. Thus, it was Sultan Agung's failure before the walls of Batavia and the ascension to the throne of the weakest and most dismal failure among Mataram's kings, Pakubuwana II, that opened possibilities for greater Islamization.

We should note also that winning influence in a weakened state did not mean an ability to implement a pious religious agenda or that a religious elite was now in charge. Arguably it was Agung who, in his need to renew his legitimacy and supernatural aura, co-opted the supernatural legitimacy offered by Islam. When Agung's state recovered, it was handed to Amangkurat I who implemented the greatest slaughter of Muslim divines in Javanese history. Similarly disastrous was the final stage of the Islamizing thrust of Pakubuwana II's time: the double fall and sacking of the court, the exiling of leading Islamizers, further VOC intervention and further rebellion.

Let us turn now to more modern episodes from Indonesia's first decade of independence.[3] In this period, an Islamist[4] agenda was represented by the Masyumi party, which wished to see a more Islamic state and society. At least to some extent, Masyumi was influenced in this by the writings of the Pakistani Islamist thinker Abul A'la Mawdudi.[5] Masyumi's most prominent leader was Mohammad Natsir (see Kahin, this volume), who later became personally acquainted with Mawdudi. Before independence, Natsir emerged as a major figure in the Persatuan Islam organization, a fairly extreme and puritanical version of Modernist Islamic thought. Later, after 1967, he became the lead figure in the Dewan Dakwah Islamiyah Indonesia and the Middle East–funded Rabithah al-Alam al-Islami (Muslim World League), major channels for the introduction of Wahhabi and Muslim Brotherhood thought into Indonesia. But Natsir and his leading Masyumi colleagues — men whose commitment to Islam was strong — were not regarded as being among the learned scholars of the faith or the respected interpreters of scriptures. In the terms set out later in this chapter, these were *zu'ama'* rather than *'ulama'*: Iqbal's "politicians" rather than "men of prayer".

In the 1950s, Indonesia faced many difficulties. It had major war damage, a poorly educated and mostly illiterate populace, unfavourable world economic circumstances (except for a brief Korean War boom), a bloated and often incompetent bureaucracy, an army that was searching for its role in a peacetime nation, a major Islamic rebellion from 1948 in the Darul Islam movement and a society polarized along lines of religious and cultural identity, particularly in Java. The government was hardly able to manage any of these issues. Indonesia was, in other words, very much what we mean when we think of a weak state.

In the first Cabinet (September 1950–March 1951) Natsir was Prime Minister and Masyumi dominated with support from the small Socialist

Party. From then until March 1956, during the heyday of this first experiment in parliamentary democracy, Masyumi was either the major party or one of the major parties in all five Cabinets. Masyumi held the Prime Ministership in four of those governments.

So, with Islamist politicians holding power in a weak state, how much Islamising of state and society was implemented? Effectively none. There was an anti-Communist sweep in August 1951 under the Masyumi Prime Minister, Sukiman Wirjosandjojo, but it had little effect and all the people arrested were released by the subsequent government, where Wilopo of the Nationalist Party (Partai Nasional Indonesia, PNI) was Prime Minister but Masyumi was also in the Cabinet. The main demand of Islamists in this period was the restoration of what was known as the "Jakarta Charter" — a constitutional curiosity dating from the 1945 constitution that seemed (in the eyes of some) to require the state to implement Islamic law amongst Muslims, which had disappeared with the implementation of the interim constitution of 1950. Even Masyumi probably realized that making any aspect of *shari'ah* compulsory — fasting, payment of alms, attendance at mosque services, female dress codes or such like — would have further polarized an already volatile society.

Thus, Islamist politicians held power in a weak state and could do nothing — or at least did do nothing — with that state to pursue an Islamizing agenda. In other words, commanding a weak state did not bring with it an ability to implement a pious agenda. And those who did the commanding were pious politicians, not the religiously defined elite.

TWO KINDS OF ELITES

In the discussion of Indonesia so far we have been distinguishing two kinds of elites. Repeating the definitions set out at the beginning of this discussion, these two are:

- those who control the state, its apparatus, institutions and symbols (the political elite), as against
- those who are defined, legitimated and inspired by their religious standing (the religious elite).

The question properly arises as to whether such a distinction is reasonable and defensible. In practice, the two kinds of elite may seem to become muddled together. Sultan Agung gained a reputation as a "holy" king. In the 1950s, a religiously inspired group of politicians (Masyumi) controlled the state while another religiously defined movement (Darul Islam) sought to overthrow it but failed. So to some extent, or in some circumstances, the state elite and the religious elite seem to become mixed together.

It is worth noting that similar distinctions were made by people involved at the time. Kyai Haji Wahid Hasyim, one of the leaders of the traditionalist organization Nahdlatul Ulama (NU), said the following to a propagation (*dakwah*) conference in 1951:

> Within the Islamic community there are two kinds of leadership groups. There is the group of political leaders who use the brand or stamp of Islam: they usually consist of clever people with Western education. The second group consists of the religious experts who really master Islamic religious knowledge widely and are called *ulama*. These have great influence among the populace and occupy greatly honoured positions[6] [but — we might add — did not control government, as did the Masyumi leaders].

Precedents for such a distinction are found in Islamic thought. There we find a difference between the *'alim* (pl. *'ulama'*) — the scholars, the doctors of religious sciences — and the *za'im* (pl. *zu'ama'*) — chiefs, leaders, military commanders and politicians — or the *amir* (pl. *umara'*) — the commanders, governors, princes.

In 1951 Wahid Hasyim was drawing a distinction between the *zuama* politicians who led the Masyumi party and the *ulama* religious elite of the Nahdlatul Ulama. In 1952 these wings split, with NU becoming a political party in its own right — the most direct Indonesian example of a religious elite seeking dominance in the Indonesian state.

But Indonesia's religious elite had limited political influence in the 1950s, however much social respect they may have received from devout Muslims. A congress of *ulama* and propagators of Islam in 1953 published a legal opinion (*fatwa*) that it was "incumbent upon every Indonesian citizen who embraces Islam … to go to the polls and elect only candidates who will fight for the realization of Islamic teaching and law in the state" (quoted in Hosen 2007, p. 66). This admonition had limited effect. In the 1955 parliamentary elections, Masyumi won 20.9 per cent of the vote and NU 18.4 per cent, and many people undoubtedly voted for these parties for reasons other than a wish to see Islamic law imposed by the state.

But is Indonesia, or perhaps Islam, somehow special in this regard? Perhaps Indonesia has a particular history of tension over the relationship between religious and state authority. Conversely, is it perhaps the case — as has been suggested to me on several occasions — that a distinction between religious and state elites is really a modern, Western concept, reflecting the distinction between Church and state in Western Christian societies? Betrand Badie has analysed persuasively how these two kinds of authority — the political and the religious — evolved in European history and draws distinctions between that experience and the history of the Islamic Middle East with regard to the evolution of the state (Badie 1997). But does the history of the non-West also reflect the idea of two distinguishable forms of elites and their authority?[7] To deal with this question, we must look further afield historically and geographically.

We may turn to non-Indonesian and non-Islamic cases, such as Hinduism in India. Here, too, we find a differentiation between what we may call "political" and "religious" elites. Ignoring multiple complexities, we may observe that in theory the caste system distinguishes the Brahmins — the religious elite, priests — from the Kṣatriyas — the warrior elite, i.e., the politicians. In principle, kingship in ancient India was religious or supernatural in the sources of its authority and was consecrated by the priesthood. But the religious elite was distinct from the ruling elite, the Brahmins were distinct from the Kṣatriyas, rather as the *'ulama'* were different from the *zu'ama'* or *umara'* in Islam.

Such ideas were probably quite widely held in ancient times, but the matter is complex. Jan Gonda, studying "Ancient Indian kingship from the religious point of view" observes: "We shall not err in maintaining that ancient Indo-European kingship was, in important aspects, a sacred institution" (Gonda 1966, p. 141). He points out that "the Homeric king was *theios* and *dios*" and that recognizably similar ideas were found elsewhere, referring even to the Archbishop of Canterbury's ritual role in anointing the English monarch. Nevertheless, Gonda comments, "There can … be no doubt that the sacred nature of kingship assumed, in India, a much more definite character than may be assumed to have existed in prehistoric Indo-European antiquity" (ibid., pp. 141–43).

We should note that this is not a case of a religious elite (the Brahmins) becoming kings. Rather, the religious elites validated, legitimated and supernaturally endowed the Kṣatriya rulers with religious power and authority. So we may say that this is religion in the service of the ruling elite — a kind of "co-optation" in more modern parlance.

Kṣatriyas and Brahmins were mutually dependent but in principle power was in the hands of the Kṣatriyas. Brahmins were not kings. Here we may note again the primacy of the political, just as in the Indonesian examples above. In pre-modern India, at least in theory, there should be no question of a religious elite taking over the state. Rather, the governing elite (the Kṣatriyas) governed and mobilized the religious elite to serve its power through religious ideas, which presumably the Kṣatriyas also believed in. The religious elite (the Brahmins) ritually validated the supernatural power of government but did not govern.

Buddhism offers an even clearer distinction between religious and political elites. Here the central religious institution is not a priesthood but rather the monastic order (sangha). In principle, the sangha was supposed to be entirely non-political, even if in practice that theory was ignored from time to time, such as when rebellious monks sought to become kings, as in eighteenth-century Siam. With regard to Buddhism in South Asia, Heinz Bechert comments: "Doubtless for kings the promotion of Buddhism had the advantage that the monks generally could not become as much of a threat to their power as the Brahminical priesthood could to Hindu kings, because the monks were obliged by the prohibitions of their religion to refrain from direct involvement in politics" (Bechert 1966, p. 22).

In principle, Buddhism was so devoid of a political role that it was unable to offer legitimating rituals to kings. Hence, state rituals tended to remain largely Brahminical in South and Southeast Asia, Confucian in China and Korea and Shinto in Japan, regardless of how Buddhist the state and society were in other respects.

The ultimate paradigm of the Buddhist king was the emperor Aśoka (third century BCE). After a bloodthirsty start to his reign, he converted to Buddhism. Thereafter inscriptions attest to his piety. He sent missionaries, for example, to Sri Lanka, to promote Buddhism. He was concerned with the reformation of the sangha and his compassion for all beings led to the establishment of hospitals. Aśoka, the ideal Buddhist monarch, is thus presented in the sources as the patron and protector of religion. His royal authority was undoubtedly validated by its consistency with Buddhist ethics but it was unmistakably clear that the emperor governed while the sangha was dependent upon him.

Although of course we cannot know what deep feelings may have inspired Aśoka, his example raises another possible relationship between state authority and religious authority that is of interest to us. That is, a powerful state authority that decides out of its own religious conviction to embrace a religious agenda may thus admit religious elites to positions of authority. In such a case, clearly the political authority still retains primacy and is the one that chooses to open the doors of power to the religious.

Theravada Buddhism in Thailand also offers valuable examples. Craig Reynolds writes of "the king, who needed the sangha as an emblem of his right to command allegiance, and the monks, who needed the king to maintain an ascetic standard and provide the material for glorification of the religion" (Reynolds 1972, p. 23). The Chakri dynasty played a religious role from the start. King Rama I (r. 1782–1809) convened the Ninth Buddhist Council in 1788 to revise the canonical scriptures of Theravada Buddhism (the Theravada Tripitaka).

Rama I's descendant King Mongkut (Rama IV, r. 1851–68),[8] the most dramatic figure in this story, spent twenty-seven years from the age of twenty living as a Buddhist monk. He was a learned man, who studied a range of both Asian and Western foreign languages. He is credited with having studied Sanskrit, Pali, Lao, Khmer, Vietnamese, Mon, Burmese, Malay, Hindi, English and Latin, as well as history and modern disciplines of various kinds, including science and technology.

As a monk, Mongkut established the reformist Dhamayuta sect as a means of returning to a purified understanding of the Pali canon. He acquired a printing press to disseminate his ideas. We see here a Thai version of a classic "modernist" reform movement that is also seen elsewhere in the nineteenth and twentieth centuries: a return to what is thought of as an "original" culture or faith combined with modern, Western learning to produce a stronger civilization that is indigenous — indeed more purely so — while also being modern. Similar ideas may be seen in the Self-Strengthening Movement in China, in the Meiji Restoration in Japan and in Islamic Modernism in the Middle East and Asia. Mongkut's reformed Dhamayuta differed from the Mahanikaya sect (still the larger of the two today) in the way the robe is worn and other practices. Mongkut's reforms were ahead of such developments in other Theravada lands, leading Bechert to call him "one of the most spiritually significant personalities of his century in Asia" (Bechert 1967, p. 199). Mongkut's son Chulalongkorn (Rama V, r. 1868–1910) also supported the reform of Buddhism as did the latter's brother, the head of the sangha (the Sangharaja) Vajirañāna (1860–1921). Thus the intimate links between Thai royalty and the sangha are clear.

It is obvious in the Thai case that initiative lay in the hands of royalty and that the sangha reacted to that, responding positively or resisting. If we think of the royals as being the political for our purposes, then again we see the primacy of the political elites.

There is an interesting comparison with Burma, where there were contemporaneous episodes of the Buddhist sangha being politically active.[9] The British colonial rulers abolished the Burmese dynasty and thereby removed also the royal structure that had patronized and disciplined the sangha. In the absence of such indigenous political authority, sangha discipline declined and political activism rose. The religious objectives of the sangha were thereby undermined. Here we may observe the consequences of the primary political authority being unable to function.

An interesting precolonial South Asian case is that of Shah Sibghat Allah (d. 1606), a fervent Shattari reformer (Eaton 1978, pp. 112–17). In his time, Bijapur was governed by Sultan Ibrahim II (r. 1580–1627), a man of eclectic religious tastes, and there was much Hindu-Islamic syncretism (ibid., p. 107). Shah Sibghat Allah arrived there in CE 1591 — the Muslim year AH 1000 — which may have inspired millennial expectations in Bijapur. In any case, Shah Sibghat Allah was determined to reform the Sultan and his society. He admonished the King to give up Hindu singing, to "take up the road of repentance and the true faith, clean your heart of false beliefs, and be a believer in the One." Sultan Ibrahim II responded that he was just trying to improve his voice. Shah Sibghat Allah also denounced the local Shi'ites, who included many nobles and officials. This was a most sensitive matter for there was a history of violent Shi'a-Sunni conflict in Bijapur.

At a Friday sermon, Shah Sibghat Allah declared that prayer was no longer possible in Bijapur so long as the Sultan continued to stray from the rightful path. He demanded that prostitution and the sale of wine be stopped and that Shi'ites be barred from power. In 1596 he sent his students to attack a Shi'ite group celebrating 'Ashura, which produced a bloody riot. The Sultan thereupon put Shah Sibghat Allah under house arrest. The reformer was given money to go away on the hajj for a second time. He gave his entire travel allowance to the poor and left Bijapur for Arabia, where he ended his days.

The tale of Shah Sibghat Allah demonstrates again the primacy of political authority. This was of course an experience shared by many a religious leader, in all traditions. We may also think of Archbishop Thomas à Becket, Henry II, and the latter's reputed question, "Who will rid me of this meddlesome priest?" — a query answered by the four knights who murdered the Archbishop in Canterbury Cathedral in 1170. Or, in a more modern but similar vein, we might recall Stalin's famous response when asked whether he could not be nicer to Catholics, which would win favour with the Pope, "Oho! The Pope? How many divisions has *he* got?" (quoted in Churchill 1948, p. 135).

But what of the most prominent modern example which seems to represent a religious elite taking over the state — Ayatollah Khomeini's 1979 Iranian revolution? Here the preceding regime of the Shah was seriously weakened and, when the army turned against the Shah, it was terminally so, enabling Khomeini's revolution to prevail. Yet the Iranian picture is more complicated than a simple religious takeover of a state.

Said Amir Arjomand argues that Khomeini's revolution overturned conventional Shi'ite political thought (Arjomand 1993). This posited that since the twelfth Imam disappeared in occultation (in the ninth century), the infallible political authority of the Imams was lost. It was only their authority as teachers and interpreters of the law that devolved on subsequent Shi'ite jurists. In declaring his "Mandate of the Jurist" (*velayat-e-faqih*), however, "Khomeini took the radical step of claiming that the imams' right to rule also devolved upon the religious jurists and, further, that if one of them succeeded in setting up a government" — as Khomeini had done — "it was the duty of the other jurists to follow him". This was an explicit demand that the religious elite serve the state rather than the reverse. This, argues Arjomand, "was a sharp departure from the traditional Shi'ite principle that no religious jurist has any authority over other religious jurists" (ibid., p. 89). Thus was established the personal dictatorship of Khomeini as the Leader of the Islamic Republic, a leadership genuinely exercised as those opponents who were imprisoned and executed came to realize.

In 1988 Khomeini declared that his government represented a divinely ordained "absolute mandate", "the most important of the divine commandments" and that it had "priority over all derivative divine commandments, even over prayer, fasting and pilgrimage to Mecca". The President, Ayatollah Sayyid 'Ali Khamanei, agreed that "[t]he commandments of the ruling jurist [i.e., Ayatollah Khomenei] are primary commandments and are like the commandments of God" (quoted in ibid., pp. 96–97). Thus, all governmental regulations carried the authority of the Leader, who governed on behalf of the Hidden Imam (whom some thought

Khomeini indeed to be) and thus on behalf of God. There were some who resisted Khomeini's idea of leadership, claiming that it constituted the sin of *shirk* (ascribing partners to God), but Khomeini prevailed.

Arjomand observes that Khomeini's doctrine "required a drastic transformation of Shi'ite Sacred Law. From a 'jurists' law' it had to be transformed into the law of the state" (ibid., p. 100). Further, "[t]he institutionalization of the Mandate of the Jurist into a monistic authority structure of the nation-state was directly detrimental to the traditional pluralism of the institution of the religious leadership of the sources of imitation [the Shi'ite jurists]" (ibid., p. 101). He continues,

> This story is not without irony. I believe that Khomeini, who outsmarted all opponents, was eventually defeated by the cunning of history. The practical consequence of Khomeini's statements and of the amended constitution has been the strengthening of the actual authority of the bureaucratic state rather than the hypothetical authority of the jurist. ... We were told by Khomeini that obeying petty bureaucrats, who derive their authority from the sacred Mandate of the Jurist, is more important than prayer and fasting.
>
> Well over a century ago, de Tocqueville noted that, in France, the paradoxical consequence of revolution was the strengthening of the state it sought to destroy. There can be little doubt that de Tocqueville has once more been vindicated. The state, which Khomeini initially intended to wither, not only has grown enormously in size but has expanded in the legal sphere, too, and has emerged as the unintended victor of the Islamic revolution, making its clerical masters also slaves to its logic. (ibid., p. 105)

Thus religion became whatever the state (i.e., Khomeini) said it was and whatever the state did. The traditional definers of religious orthodoxy were sidelined, leaving the state and bureaucracy to dominate. A revolution whose appeals had been in large part religious thereby became a personal dictatorship with detrimental outcomes for the Shi'ite religious elite. This is, thus, hardly a religious elite taking over a state but rather a state taking over a religious revolution. It would be hard to claim that the hopes of the original jurist supporters of the 1979 revolution had been achieved.

In the cases we have examined here, the distinction between elites who control the state, its apparatus, institutions and symbols (whether or not they are personally religious) on the one hand and elites who are defined, legitimated and inspired by their religious standing on the other seems valid. And we see repeatedly the primacy of the former.

CONTEMPORARY INDONESIA

Let us now return to Indonesia in present times,[10] where there are plenty of Islamist groups who seek to control the state so as to carry out their political, religious, social and legal agendas. But it is remarkable that in the public political arena few of such groups consist of persons who would be recognized as *ulama*. The main case of *ulama* politics involves the non-Islamist[11] *kyai* of NU, who are discussed below.

We find Islamist political parties who compete within the political system, the main ones being Parti Bulan Bintang (PBB) and Partai Persatuan Pembangunan (PPP). To date the Islamist parties have done poorly in elections and have no prospect at all of winning government. PBB gained just 2.6 per cent of the national vote in 2004 and only 1.9 per cent in 2009, below the threshold required to gain a seat in the national parliament. PPP, which has a history going back thirty years in Indonesia, did better at 8.2 per cent, the fourth-largest share of the vote, in 2004, but fell to 5.3 per cent in 2009.

There is also Partai Keadilan Sejahtera (PKS), which is apparently evolving from an Islamist party to a semi-Islamist and more centrist party. PKS (then called just Partai Keadilan) did poorly in the 1999 elections, gaining only 1.4 per cent of the national vote. In 2004 it dropped its public Islamism and improved dramatically to 7.3 per cent of the vote — a significant figure in Indonesia's multiparty democracy and just behind President Susilo Bambang Yudhoyono's Partai Demokrat. In 2009, however, it achieved only a small advance on that figure, winning 7.9 per cent, whereas Partai Demokrat bolted ahead to win the largest share of the national vote at 20.9 per cent. In recent times, PKS has also been pursuing growth strategies at civil-society level. It is an increasing influence particularly within the Islamic Modernist organization Muhammadiyah (with tens of millions of adherents).

There are also Islamist parties that operate outside the electoral system, refusing to stand candidates in an election process that they label un-Islamic but nevertheless desiring state power. These are notably Hizbut Tahrir Indonesia and Majelis Mujaheedin Indonesia. These parties have no prospect of gaining power in Indonesia or implementing their aim of a universal caliphate. They are, however, having some success in infiltrating large mass-based socio-religious organizations, particularly Hizbut Tahrir Indonesia which has been infiltrating the Traditionalist NU (with its tens of millions of followers).

There is a great variety of civil-society organizations — some of which behave distinctly uncivilly — the most prominent for our purposes being Front Pembela Islam (FPI). FPI has managed to intimidate local societies and both local and national governments by using violence against "immorality" (discotheques, prostitution, gambling and such like), non-Muslim places of worship (especially informal, technically "illegal" churches) and what it regards as deviant forms of Islam, particularly Ahmadiyah (an international movement; see Platzdasch, this volume) and Lembaga Dakwah Islam Indonesia (a local one).

Outright terrorist organizations are also found, the most famous being Jemaah Islamiyah and its offshoots. These remain a significant concern for police and intelligence agencies, but their murderous violence has alienated Indonesians of all social classes and (along with much foreign government pressure) has motivated national and local-level governments to act. Indonesia probably has the best record in the world at identifying, disrupting, killing, arresting, trying and imprisoning or executing its domestic terrorists. They have no prospect whatever of gaining power.

Many of these organizations have advisory boards on which *ulama* are named, but there is hardly a member of the *ulama* to be found among their actual leaders or activists. This has in fact always been true. The greatest figure in Masyumi in the 1950s, Muhammad Natsir, was well educated and articulate, and won the respect and admiration of many — Muslims and non-Muslims, Indonesians and foreigners alike — but was not thought of as one of the *ulama*. In contemporary Indonesia, Hidayat Nur Wahid, the very effective PKS figure who led it successfully through the 2004 elections and went on to become chairman of Indonesia's upper house People's Consultative Assembly (MPR), was educated in Islamic institutions in Indonesia and Saudi Arabia. But he is not thought of as an *alim*. As an exception to this rule, the head of the religious school at Ngruki, Abu Bakar Baasyir, who has been accused of being the spiritual leader of the Jemaah Islamiyah terrorists (which he denies), is accorded the religious elite titles of *kyai* and *ustad* and is regarded — certainly at least by his followers — as one of the *ulama*.

The distinction we observe today is thus the one already noted above in the 1951 comment by Wahid Hasyim: that between "the group of political leaders who use the brand or stamp of Islam" and "the religious experts who really master Islamic religious knowledge widely and are called *ulama*". Thus, even within the Islamist side of politics, it is the political elite that holds the initiative in most circumstances. These are the *zuama* at work.

Amongst the nation's *ulama*, many of NU's *kyai* are politically active, with somewhat curious outcomes. The party which is most clearly the successor to the NU political party of the 1950s is Partai Kebangkitan Bangsa (PKB), but its platform has remained non-Islamist, indeed secularist. Whereas NU won 18.4 per cent of the vote in the 1955 parliamentary elections, in 1999 PKB gained 12.6 per cent, in 2004 only 10.6 per cent, and in 2009 only 4.9 per cent. This last figure was partly the consequence of deep splits among the *kyai* that spawned a rival NU-based party (Partai Kebangkitan Nasional Ulama) which, however, gained only 1.5 per cent of the vote and thus failed to win a seat in the national parliament. More fundamentally, the outcome of elections since 1998 demonstrates that this religious elite's capacity to influence voter behaviour is limited and declining. At grass-roots levels, their social standing is also under some challenge because their political and financial affairs raise questions about their commitment to religious values. We see here an example of the religious elite's comparative weakness in its capacity for political action, a topic to which we return below.

In Indonesia there are also religiously defined elites working within state structures. This has been facilitated by the existence of a Ministry of Religious Affairs from the beginning of the country's independence — a case of the founding political elite deciding to allow a place within government for religious figures.

The most important state-sponsored institution where such leaders are found is the Indonesian Ulamas Council (Majelis Ulama Indonesia, MUI). This was established in 1975 by the Soeharto regime as a means to manage Islam. Its membership is full of men (and a few women) with both modern academic titles and designations as *kyai*. Its judgments (fatwa) have been generally conservative — indeed, many would say reactionary. Its most famous were the July 2005 fatwas declaring that liberalism, pluralism and secularism were forbidden to Muslims, that Muslims should not marry non-Muslims (despite specific Qur'anic approval for a Muslim man to marry a Jewish or Christian woman, as indeed had the Prophet

Muhammad himself), that Muslims must not engage in joint prayers with non-Muslims (a not-unusual occurrence in multi-religious Indonesia) and (renewing an older fatwa) that the Ahmadiyah is a deviant form of Islam. What is most remarkable is that the decisions of the MUI — which has no constitutional foundation in Indonesia — are commonly disregarded by the general populace but often treated by police and local governments as if they had the force of law.

The national government under President Susilo Bambang Yudhoyono itself acts as if MUI fatwas had the power of legislation. Any present-day government in Jakarta is inherently weak because of the decentralization of many vital governmental functions to regions. Furthermore, Susilo Bambang Yudhoyono has shown himself to be generally weak and indecisive. It is possible that he is himself inclined to the Islamist cause. In any case, he said the following at the opening of the MUI national congress on 26 July 2005:

> We open our hearts and minds to receiving the thoughts, recommendations and *fatwas* from the MUI and *ulama* at any time, either directly to me or the Minister of Religious Affairs or to other branches of government. We want to place MUI in a central role in matters regarding the Islamic faith, so that it becomes clear what the difference is between areas that are the preserve of the state and areas where the government or state should heed the *fatwa* from the MUI and *ulama*.[12]

While this comment preserved the primacy of the state by asserting that it would decide in what areas to act, the President went further to depict his government as the agent of MUI fatwas in criminal and moral issues. With the national head of the police among his audience, Susilo Bambang Yudhoyono said to the MUI congress:

> I am happy that the Head of Police is with us. The task entrusted by the *ulama* to the government that I lead is not just to wipe out evil, but to fight all forms of evil and immorality. God willing and with the blessing and support of the *ulama* — the various forms of wickedness and immorality, whether it is narcotics, gambling, pornography or pornographic actions, and other things connected thereto, we'll have to face up to firmly in order to save our future, to save our generation.[13]

While one may be uncertain just what the President intended in these comments — an uncertainty generally appropriate with regard to the pronouncements of politicians, of course — it seems that the religious elite in Indonesia has the greatest prospect of winning influence over or capturing the state in one of two circumstances. Either (1) a weak state (at either national or regional level) allows them to take over state functions or (2) a willing state invites them to do so. In either case, the primacy of the political is preserved, for it will be the actions and circumstances of the state elite that determine what the religiously defined elite is able to do.

All of these elites and their agendas operate within a fundamentally weak Indonesian state. A nice example arises in a recent doctoral thesis that has examined, *inter alia*, the desire of Indonesian Islamists for the state to collect the obligatory religious alms (zakat) (Fauzia 2008). This occurs in a state so organizationally weak that it cannot even collect all of the obligatory income tax. So, we must ask, how much of the Islamists' zakat agenda could be implemented even if they could take over the state's revenue-collecting capacity?

THE GENERAL PATTERN

It is time to ask what the discussion above tells us about the general pattern of relations between the state and religion. In particular — repeating what was said above — we have considered here the relationship between two kinds of elites:

- those who control the state, its apparatus, institutions and symbols, or compete to do so (the political elite), as against
- those who are defined, legitimated and inspired by their religious standing (the religious elite).

We have seen that this distinction between different sorts of elites has precedents in the great philosophies of Asia. We see it in Islam (*'ulama'* vs. *umara'* or *zu'ama'*), Hinduism (Brahmins vs. Kṣatriyas) and in Buddhism (monks vs. monarchs). This is, in other words, not simply a relatively modern, Western separation-of-church-and-state idea.

The cases discussed above suggest that it is extremely difficult for a religious elite to take over a state or to gain major influence in it. Its best chances are when the state is weak, as it was under Sultan Agung after his failure before Batavia, under Pakubuwana II — that weakest, most dismal of Javanese kings — or in Iran as the Shah's regime disintegrated. The irony, however, is that a state weak enough to be taken over is also one that is usually too weak to implement an agenda effectively, including a religious one. The other circumstance in which a religious elite gains influence in or takes over a state is when the political elite is willing to allow such influence, as was presumably the case in the time of Aśoka.

Thus, political authority usually determines the outcomes — as it did bloodily for the *kyai* murdered by Amangkurat II in 1648, more benignly for the monastic order reformed by Thai royals, and painfully for Shah Sibghat Allah as he was expelled from Bijapur.

The curious case of the Ayatollah Khomeini's Iran is instructive. Here the religious leader effectively became the state itself: self-legitimating, self-regulating, unchallengeable and the ultimate authority in a state-controlling elite. The Iranian state and its bureaucracy dominated and the religious elite (the jurists) was sidelined, commanded to obey a state whose orders were declared to have divine authority.

THE QUESTION

A large question now arises. Most analysts of how religion functions in human societies would, I believe, accept the following generalizations:

- Religion is fundamental in many individual lives and human societies.
- For many people, religion is the source of meaning, the measure of truth and justice.
- In many religious traditions, there is a suspicion of governing political elites and a perceived need to find means of restraining their potential for tyranny.

Moreover, believers are open to claims of authority by religious elites. This is true almost by definition and can be observed in many contexts. Like Arjomand above, we might invoke the observations of Alexis de Toqueville, describing the young American nation in 1831:

> It is evident that all the naturally religious minds among the Protestants, the grave and proud souls whom the Protestant vogue wearies and who at the same time deeply feel the need of religion, are abandoning the search for truth in despair and throwing themselves again under the sway of authority. Their reason is a burden which weighs on them and which they sacrifice with joy. They become Catholics. (Quoted in Pierson 1996, p. 156)

Now, if all that is true, why is it not easier for religious elites to dominate a state?

A DOUBLE ANSWER

I suggest that there are two reasons why religious elites find it so difficult to gain great influence in or to take over a state if the political elite resists their influence.

The first reason arises from an asymmetry of capacities. The religious elite needs the state's capacity for implementation and action because religious elites typically lack such a capacity themselves. That is, they are inherently weaker in their capacity for action. This supports the primacy of the political elite, who can allow or deny access to the state's capacities. They may allow access willingly, particularly if the state-controlling elite is itself of a strong religious persuasion: Aśoka has been our prime example here and Susilo Bambang Yudhoyono may incline the same way. Or they may do so out of weakness, as we saw in Sultan Agung in his darkest hour, or in Pakubuwana II — or, again, perhaps in the case of Susilo Bambang Yudhoyono. But in either case it is the political elite who determines the outcome of the relationship.

Peter Beyer writes of "systems": economic, political, legal and so on. He observes that,

> Unlike states, religious authorities do not have at their disposal effective religious mechanisms to enforce their orthodoxies/orthopraxies. Instead, they tend to rely on the capacities of other systems, notably but not exclusively the political, legal or educational where such resort proves possible; and on the family socialization of the young. (Beyer 2006, p. 95)

Furthermore, he argues,

> One of the more frequent features of the contemporary world is the intermittent but frequent attempts to politicize religion: that is, to use the power of the state to enforce one or more religious orthodoxies.... The only limits that the functionally differentiated structure of global society seems to put on it is that theocracies, or the thorough de-differentiation of religion and state, are just as difficult to maintain as radically "atheistic" states. (Ibid., pp. 105–6)

Thus, this first answer says that the primacy of the political arises because religious elites need the state's capacities for action, since religions usually do not have command and enforcement structures of their own. There is something of an exception in Roman Catholicism, where the Pope heads a formal global hierarchy, but social reality suggests that his actual capacity to shape what people think and do has its limits.

We may also note in passing that when politicians with a religious agenda manage to take over a state — sometimes bringing with them openness to the advice and influence of religious elites — it typically does not work very well. This is the irony of takeover that we have identified earlier, an example of which we saw in the Masyumi-dominated Indonesian governments of the 1950s. Marty and Appleby comment that,

> While zeal and increasing political sophistication have carried fundamentalist groups to power in several nations, these groups have not yet proven themselves capable of actually governing effectively....
>
> [The BJP in India, Islamic, Jewish, Christian, Sikh and Buddhist fundamentalists] ... have proven themselves skilled at discerning the problems of society and naming the perpetrators, but they have been far less impressive in posing workable solutions.
>
> Along with the impressive qualities of the fundamentalist political imagination ... comes a severe limitation. Fundamentalists find it difficult to govern without resorting to the services of professional politicians and nonfundamentalist allies. ... [This] can lead ... quickly to the politics of compromise and the distillation[14] of the fundamentalist sociomoral message.... Or, conversely, rule by political or military professionals can lead to a despotic hardening of fundamentalist injunctions as a justification for the imposition of a police state. (Marty and Appleby 1993, pp. 630–31)

Therefore it is the religious elite's comparative weakness in its capacity for political action or enforcement that leads to the comparative primacy of the political or state elite.

A second reason may be less obvious but more fundamental: that the authority of a state-controlling elite and the authority of a religious elite are epistemologically different. This is true whether we think that religion deals with genuine realms beyond normal human cognition or is no more than sophisticated make-believe, and whether we are discussing the third century BCE, the seventeenth CE or the twenty-first.

We should assume that all forms of authority are normally subject to challenge, disputation and conflict. But the epistemological difference between the two kinds of elites means that challenge or conflict has different outcomes.

In the case of a political elite, conflict or challenge can be resolved in epistemologically robust ways. It is possible to know and to prove who has succeeded his father upon a throne, or won a civil war, or successfully carried out a coup, or won an election or can give an order that the military will follow.

Among such political elites, dispute, discord and conflict may be endemic and long-running, but in principle it is capable of resolution — even if that takes a long time. We are capable of knowing what the outcome is because some person or some party commands the state's means of violence, orders the bureaucracy, and so on. And we can observe and test whether that is so. Even the losers in a contest can recognize the outcome — and decide whether to accept it or to try again.

But in the case of religious elites — as defined above, the priests in religions that have priests, the ordained theologians in others, or the learned scholars of the faith and respected interpreters of scriptures — conflict or challenge cannot be resolved in epistemologically robust ways. It is not possible to know or to prove who teaches an interpretation of theology that is indisputably true, or has a divinely granted right to determine orthodoxy or orthopraxy, or is in fact the messiah or *mahdi* or Maitreya, or knows when the world will end or who will be saved or damned. For any such claim will be disputed by other religious authorities.

Dispute in religion is certainly endemic and long-running, but in principle it is not capable of resolution — no matter how long it goes on. Muslims have been disputing the meaning of Islam for 1400 years. Christians have been contesting the meaning of Christianity for 2000 years. Buddhists have differed about the Buddha's teachings for 2.5 millennia. Hindus and Jews hold the disagreement record among major world religions, with a history of approximately 3.5 millennia.

Furthermore, in the case of disputation among contending religious elites, we are not capable of knowing what the outcome is, for no person or party commands unchallenged authority to interpret the faith or an enforcement structure that can in fact impose an interpretation.[15] In religious disputes, the losing elites (if they survive, which is rather more likely in today's world than in the blood-soaked past) commonly do not recognize the outcome. That, indeed, is why religious conflict is so endemic and long-running. If the losers believe that they are in the right, that their ideas represent a cosmic truth and divinely imposed obligation, they typically feel obliged to struggle on.

It is in principle a problem for political elites with religious agendas — the *zuama* of Indonesia's present-day Islamist parties — that the epistemological uncertainty of religious authority may rub off on them in the eyes of the electorate. Perhaps here we see the ultimate roots of the poor electoral showing of Islamist parties and, conversely, the improvement achieved by PKS between 1999 and 2004 when it moved away from its visible Islamist stance towards a more centrist public platform.

We may therefore think that the elite who control the state (or compete to do so), who know the extent of their control and the extent of whose control is known and verifiable by others, may be reluctant to yield influence and authority to a religious elite because the religious elite's claims are unverifiable and always open to contest and challenge by persons who also claim religious authority. Indeed, acceding to such claims would be a recipe not only for the loss of influence but also for division and discord, for challenges to the integrity of the state system that the political elite seeks to continue to dominate.[16]

So we may suggest that in relations between religiously defined elites and elites who control the state, the religious elites need to capture the state if they wish to impose a religio-moral-legal agenda, but it is extremely difficult for them to do so. The political elite typically maintains primacy and determines the outcome of the relationship in its own favour. Where religious elites manage to dominate a weak state, that state is a poor instrument for the imposition of their agendas.

A fundamental reason for this primacy of the political — I am suggesting — lies in the different epistemological status of religious and political authority. Person A and his co-believers may be convinced that doctrine X is true, while person B and his fellows may believe that doctrine Y is true — and each side may be quite unable to persuade the other of the truth of its doctrine — but both can agree that Barack Obama was elected President of the United States.

Hence, I argue that:

- political elites controlling strong states may co-opt religion to serve their purposes, or may allow influence to religious elites on the grounds of their own religiosity, but are unlikely to allow the state to be taken over by a religious elite; and
- religious elites may gain great influence in or take over weak states, but because of this very weakness, such states are unlikely to be

able to fulfil the religiously defined social, political, moral or legal agendas sought by the religious elites.

And I am arguing that this is true because of two things:

- the asymmetrical capacities of religious and political elites, with the latter having primacy; and
- the epistemological difference between religious and political authority, with only the latter being demonstrable in epistemologically robust ways.

Notes

1. "Mastership" in Mir 2007, p. 99.
2. *Babad ing Sangkala* I:60 in Ricklefs 1978.
3. The classic study of the period remains Feith (1962). For a briefer overview, see the relevant chapters in Ricklefs, *History of Modern Indonesia*.
4. In Indonesia a political party may be considered Islamist if it aims to reintroduce the "Jakarta Charter", to make the Qur'an the constitution of the state and/or to make *shari'ah* the positive law of the country.
5. See the comments by A. Syafi'i Ma'arif (b. 1935, one of Muhammadiyah's foremost leaders and head of the organization 1998–2005) in his autobiography (Maarif 2006, pp. 192–95).
6. Quoted in Choiratun Chisaan 2008, p. 99.
7. While Badie argues that in the Islamic Middle East a different concept of sovereignty evolved, he also recognizes the existence there in modern times of two kinds of authority represented by the *ulama* and the modern state — what he calls "deux rationalités contradictoires" (ibid., p. 192).
8. See Reynolds, "Buddhist Monkhood", for an authoritative analysis. See also the valuable account to be found in Bechert 1967, pp. 198–201.
9. See the comments by Bechert 1966, p. 25.
10. My research on recent and contemporary Indonesia, focusing on the Javanese ethnic group, was conducted with the support of Singapore Ministry of Education Academic Research Fund Tier 2 grant no. T208A4107. See Ricklefs 2012.
11. In the sense that political parties with roots in NU do not support reintroducing the Jakarta Charter, making the Qur'an the constitution of the state or making *shari'ah* the positive law of the country.
12. <www.presidenri.go.id/index.php/pidato/2005/07/26/370.html> cited in International Crisis Group 2008, p. 8.

13. <www.presidenri.go.id/index.php/pidato/2005/07/26/370.html>. It should be noted that a controversial bill outlawing *pornografi* and *pornoaksi*, with provision for civil society groups to act on their own in this respect — an implicit licence for FPI and other such organizations — was passed by the parliament in late 2008 and quickly signed into law by President Susilo Bambang Yudhoyono (see Rinaldo, this volume).
14. A curious choice of word: "watering-down" seems to be meant, but that is not what distillation actually is.
15. The Roman Catholic Church — despite the Papal pretension to infallibility — is no exception here, for its history is replete with dissent and schism, including of course the bloody Wars of Religion in Europe and an ongoing inability to reconcile with either Orthodox or Protestant versions of Christianity.
16. Readers may sense echoes of Weber's distinctions between bureaucratic and traditional authority, or charismatic versus institutional authority. But Weber is more interested in explicating how various types of authority work than how they compare when in competition for power.

References

Arjomand, Said Amir. "Shi'ite Jurisprudence and Constitution Making in the Islamic Republic of Iran". In *Fundamentalisms and the State: Remaking Politics, Economies and Militance*, edited by Martin E. Marty and R. Scott Appleby. Chicago: University of Chicago Press, 1993.

Badie, Betrand. *Les deux États: Pouvoir et société en Occident et en terre d'Islam*. Paris: Fayard, 1997.

Bechert, Heinz. *Buddhismus, Staat und Gesellschaft in den Ländern des Theravāda-Buddhismus*, vol. 1: *Grundlagen; Ceylon*. Frankfurt am Main & Berlin: Alfred Metzner Verlag, 1966.

———. *Buddhismus, Staat und Gesellschaft*, vol. 2: *Birma, Kambodscha, Laos, Thailand*. Wiesbaden: Otto Harrassowitz, 1967.

Beyer, Peter. *Religions in Global Society*. London: Routledge, 2006.

Chisaan, Choiratun. *Lesbumi: Strategi politik kebudayaan*. Yogyakarta: LKiS, 2008.

Churchill, Winston S. *The Second World War*, vol. 1: *The Gathering Storm*. Boston: Houghton Mifflin, 1948.

Eaton, Richard Maxwell. *Sufis of Bijapur, 1300–1700: Social Roles of Sufis in Medieval India*. Princeton: Princeton University Press, 1978.

Fauzia, Amelia. "Faith and the State: A History of Islamic Philanthropy in Indonesia". PhD dissertation, University of Melbourne, 2008.

Feith, Herbert. *The Decline of Constitutional Democracy in Indonesia*. Ithaca, NY: Cornell University Press, 1962.

Gonda, J. *Ancient Indian Kingship from the Religious Point of View*. Reprinted from *Numen III* and *IV*; Leiden: Brill, 1966.

Graaf, H.J. de. *De regering van Sunan Mangku-Rat I Tegal-Wangi, vorst van Mataram 1646–1677*. 2 vols; *VKI* vols. 33, 39. 's-Gravenhage: Martinus Nijhoff, 1961, 1962.

Hosen, Nadirsyah. *Shari'a and Constitutional Reform in Indonesia*. Singapore: Institute of Southeast Asian Studies, 2007.

International Crisis Group. *Indonesia: Implications of the Ahmadiyah Decree* (Asia Briefing no. 78). Jakarta/Brussels: International Crisis Group, 7 July 2008.

Maarif, Ahmad Syafii. *Titik-titik kisar di perjalananku: Otobiografi Ahmad Syafii Maarif*. Jogjakarta: Ombak and Maarif Institute, 2006.

Marty, Martin E. and R. Scott Appleby, eds. *Fundamentalisms and the State: Remaking Polities, Economies, and Militance*. Chicago: University of Chicago Press, 1993.

Mir, Mutansir, ed. and trans. *Tulip in the Desert: A Selection of the Poetry of Muhammad Iqbal*. Lahore: Iqbal Academy Pakistan, 2007.

Pierson, George Wilson. *Tocqueville in America*. Baltimore: Johns Hopkins University Press, 1996.

Reynolds, Craig James. "The Buddhist Monkhood in Nineteenth-century Thailand". PhD dissertation, Cornell University, 1972.

Ricklefs, M.C. *Modern Javanese Historical Tradition: A Study of an Original Kartasura Chronicle and Related Material*. London: School of Oriental and African Studies, 1978.

———. *The Seen and Unseen Worlds in Java, 1726–49: History, Literature and Islam in the Court of Pakubuwana II*. St. Leonards NSW: The Asian Studies Association of Australia in association with Allen and Unwin; Honolulu: University of Hawai'i Press, 1998.

———. *Mystic Synthesis in Java: A History of Islamisation from the Fourteenth to the early Nineteenth Centuries*. Norwalk: EastBridge, 2006.

———. *A History of Modern Indonesia Since c.1200*. 4th ed. Basingstoke: Palgrave Macmillan; Stanford: Stanford University Press, 2008.

———. *Islamisation and Its Opponents in Java: A Political, Social, Cultural and Religious History, c.1930 to the Present*. Singapore: NUS Press; Honolulu: University of Hawai'i Press, 2012.

3

"I WAS THE GUEST OF ALLAH": MODERN HAJJ MEMOIRS FROM SOUTHEAST ASIA

Eric Tagliacozzo

One of the more important ways that accounts of the hajj have been transmitted is through memoirs — the conscious act of people setting down their memories to pen and paper, in order to have these memories preserved as a record of their journeys. Few experiences, in fact, have been deemed more worthy of a written account than those activities involving a spiritual quest of one sort or another, a state of affairs commented upon in some detail by scholars of this genre of writing (Hutch 1997). Yet the memoir as artefact, as nearly everyone would agree, is not a dyed-in-the-wool record of actual events, preserved in complete veracity with "what happened". It is, rather, a construct, with "truth passing toward art" in the words of one prominent critic (Barrington 1997). Distortion, whether intended or unconscious, is always a part of this morphogenesis, and is in fact part and parcel of translating one's lived experiences into a format ready for the reading of other people (Conway 1998). As such, memoirs can and should be dissected, to see what their writing can tell us about how such stories are generated, and what their very inscription means as an act of intent (Hart 1970, pp. 485–511). Some scholars have noted that memoirs have their own rhythms and patterns as a genre, often following certain themes in their quest to lay out and explain lived experience (Fletcher 1966). These critical dimensions of gauging the worth of memoirs are useful and instructive in thinking through the value of such accounts, and perhaps especially so in the telling of a journey as large (and as diverse) as the hajj, which allows millions of people to undertake a voyage in many of the same ways.

In the pages that follow I set out some of the ways in which hajj memoirs can be read. These memoirs nearly all come from the past fifty or so years (that is to say, the postcolonial period in Southeast Asia), when pilgrims were making hajj from independent nation-states in the region. Nearly all of these narratives have been written in Indonesian or Malay. An initial subsection of the chapter looks at hajj memoirs that were crafted earlier than this period, to provide something of a limited genealogy to these accounts throughout the centuries before our own. After these accounts have been examined, we turn to the notion of place (*topos*) in the pilgrimage, as Southeast Asian pilgrims narrate their experiences in a variety of important locales in the Hejaz. Jeddah (the disembarkation point in Arabia), Mecca, the plain of Arafat, Mina and Medina are all briefly studied. The second half of the piece looks at the hajj and the self, that is to say, where the haji or hajah fits into his or her conception of the hajj based on their own provenance, whether this is geographic, occupational, gender-specific, etc. I argue that these sorts of considerations play a large part in the narration of hajj memoirs as well, as can be shown from literally dozens of accounts on these topics. The chapter then ends with a look at the notion of introspection in the memoir, as well as the idea of "the return" to Southeast Asia, after a successful pilgrimage has been undertaken. Throughout the piece we will focus on the published memoirs of a wide variety of regional Muslims, whose autobiographical accounts constitute en masse an impressive and under-studied body of literature on the past age of the Southeast Asian hajj as a whole.

THE FADED TEXT: HAJJ MEMOIRS FROM THE PRE-INDEPENDENCE PERIOD

We know that a small number of Southeast Asians were making the hajj from a very early date, and that these numbers increased over the course of the centuries, until in the nineteenth century the numbers started to reach into the thousands year after year. Yet for the pre-modern era before this time, the number of actual accounts available to be studied is even smaller than the small trickle of hajis who were actually able to ply back and forth across the Indian Ocean on these distant maritime routes. One of the first of these memoirs, if it can indeed be called such, is the *Hikayat Hang Tua*, or Tale of Hang Tuah (Ahmad 1997). Hang Tuah was a subject of the Malay Sultan of Melaka, and this account refers to events in the fifteenth and sixteenth centuries, though it was probably written later in the mid-seventeenth century. Hang Tuah's pilgrimage to Mecca is mentioned in this "memoir", but interestingly only as an aside to his journey: his real destination was Rum, or what might now be called Ottoman Turkey. He undertook this long, dangerous voyage in order to make political contact with the Ottoman court, and to bring cannon back to the "lands beneath the winds" so as to help his sultanate fight off local military challenges, including those of the first European invaders (Braginsky 2004, pp. 284, 467). As he was en route to Rum, Hang Tuah saw Jeddah, and he was persuaded to drop anchor and perform hajj while on his way towards his diplomatic mission. Though Hang Tuah's description of the hajj processionals stretching from Jeddah to Mecca is opulent, his language in general on the hajj is curt and rather muted. One theorist has suggested that this was because a Malay's allegiance at the time was to be solely towards his or her sultan, and that any superfluous descriptions of other powers and allegiances — especially spiritual ones, as would have been the case with the Holy Cities — was to be carefully avoided on shrewd political grounds (Errington 1975, p. 159).

If the *Hikayat Hang Tuah* was constructed in the seventeenth century, then by the mid to later eighteenth century other Southeast Asian authors were also leaving occasional memoirs which touched on their activities in the Middle East while performing the hajj. Abd as-Samad of Palembang was one of these men: he was a prolific Sufi author who wrote both in Arabic and in Malay, and he penned a number of important tracts in Mecca in the 1760s, including memoirs of his time while on pilgrimage (Braginsky 2004, p. 653). A few decades on the other side of the eighteenth/nineteenth century divide, men like Syaikh Daud of Sanur were also appearing in Mecca, and they too left notices of their time on hajj. Syaikh Daud implored other archipelago Muslims to come to the Hejaz to sharpen their religious understanding, so that their knowledge would become "sharp as a straight thorn" (Braginsky 2004, p. 229). We know from the prodigious collecting work of Annabel Gallop of the British Library, working on both the "Malaysian" and "Indonesian" sides of the Straits, that the art of letter writing became very important around this time as well, so that formal, highly-stylized letters were being sent back and forth across the Indian Ocean, often with news on a particular archipelago eminence's time while on hajj (Gallop 1993 and 1994). In all of these ways, and through these various kinds of media, memoirs of the pilgrimage trickled into the consciousness of Southeast Asian Muslims as a whole, shaping perceptions of the possibilities of a journey to Arabia in numerous ways.

By the second half of the nineteenth century, much more rounded and full accounts of the hajj as memoirs had started to appear, even if they were still comparatively few in number. The *Tuhfat al-Nafis* (or "Precious Gift") was written at this time (1860s, in Penyengat, Riau), and though it described earlier events, in its pages we get something of the sensibility of the age. In this memoir, Raja Ahmad, the son of the Bugis hero Raja Haji, performs the hajj after travelling to several places in Southeast Asia to raise funds for the voyage. The main thrust of his memoir, however, is less about his hajj, and more on the houses and land he buys in the Hejaz for the use of archipelago pilgrims, as well as other acts of charity he performs and then notarizes in his text (Matheson and Andaya 1982). Munshi Abdullah, writing as a Malay from the Peninsula around the same time that the *Tuhfat* was penned, actually died in Mecca while completing his hajj. Yet his memoir, written in temporal proximity to the *Tuhfat*, bears a different *Geist* altogether in its qualities as a memoir: Munshi Abdullah uses the first-person "I" in narrating his journey, one of the first people to do so in all of "traditional" Malay literature. There is something hauntingly modern about his text: his allegiance is no longer to his Malay sovereign, critics have pointed out, but rather to Allah as Supreme Being and Creator. He is now a member of the global *umma*, and less a subject of a Malay *kerajaan*, or polity (Matheson and Milner 1984, pp. 21–23; Hill 1970). Other Malay-language memoirs of this period also start to show evidence of this change in perspective among writers — the hajj starts to be seen around this time as something that all Muslims might share, regardless of their political affiliations within the Malay world. The breakdown in the tension between a local political life and a larger, even global religious one seems to have been a hallmark of this late colonial age, at least among the memorialists of Southeast Asia's seas (Syair Mekah 1869; Syair Mekah 1873; Syair Mekah 1885; Syair Makkah 1886; Syair Negeri 1888; Syair Negeri 1889).

This notion of "modernity" coming to hajj memoirs as a genre is an interesting one, and is given further weight as a literature-based phenomenon by published accounts of the 1920s. In 1925, the Regent of Bandung, Raden Adipati Aria Wiranata Koesoema, had a memoir of his pilgrimage published in the *Algemeen Dagblad de Preangerbode*, but there was enough interest in it subsequent to this that it was eventually reissued as a small book. The regent talked of his spiritual journey while on hajj, but he also made careful notes about the trip by sea and his fellow passengers, the colonial quarantine station at Kamaran, the architecture of a number of religious buildings, palaces, and libraries, as well his journey through the rugged mountain interior of Yemen. It is, in effect, a modern travel narrative; it would not be out of place in one of our own contemporary bookstores (van Bovene 1925). A year later Haji Abdul Majid, a Malay Muslim from the Peninsula, published his own account of his hajj in the *Journal of the Malay Branch of the Royal Asiatic Society*. Majid's narrative was remarkably similar in many ways to the Javanese regent's, only Majid came from the British-controlled Malaya rather than Dutch-controlled Java. He also described his approach and entrance by sea to Jeddah, which appeared "very pretty to look at from the sea and from a distance", but which he found to be squalid and disorganized upon his disembarkation. Majid was full of admiration for his fellow pilgrims, realizing the sacrifices that many of them had made to get to the Hejaz, and he pointed out that 15 per cent of his fellow Malay hajis died while he was there, a number in keeping with the last few years' statistics of mortality rates for the Malay pilgrimage as a whole (Majid 1926, pp. 269–70, 287). The hajj as an entire social-religious-medical-political-economic phenomenon was starting to be fleshed out at this time, in other words, by archipelago pilgrims who were coming from an increasing variety of places, and in larger and larger numbers. This modern idiom of reportage in the religious memoir would be continued after independence in the middle decades of the twentieth century, and it is to that topic that we now turn.

TOPOS: SEEING SACRED SITES

One of the ways that modern hajj memoirs are often organized is through the lens of visiting sites, or "place"; this emphasis on *topos* (geography) is a common organizational focus for these accounts, and is repeated again and again in modern Southeast Asian narratives of a voyage to the Hejaz. Almost invariably, the first place mentioned is Jeddah, which as we know is the feeder port for the holy cities, historically by sea but now much more so by air. Pilgrims writing home in the 1970s told of long, segmented journeys from the archipelago to Jeddah, often stopping in several cities such as Medan and Colombo (Sri Lanka), before the aircraft touched down in Jeddah (Hasjmy 1979, p. 9). This was in the day of writing letters while on hajj in the Hejaz; once we get to accounts from the 1990s, communication would just as likely be by cell phone (or email) rather than by post, and the flights were now more likely direct and not in a trunk line (Hadiluwih 1990, p. 9). Jeddah fascinated many pilgrims and continues to do so, with hajis and hajahs writing in astonishment of the numbers of planes coming from all over the world, emblazoned with the logos of many countries, but particularly the rich gulf states (Daud 1992, p. 22). One pilgrim remembered that even in the midst of all of these impressive aircraft descending into Jeddah's airport, that chaos was the rule from the outset: large numbers of pilgrims could not read Latin characters, so the arrival and departure procedures in the King Abdulazziz airport could take a very long time (Hassan 1975, p. 41). Others noted that Jeddah was not just an embarkation and disembarkation point, but interesting in its own right as well, with a number of important historical mosques (such as the Masjid Madinatul Jujijaj, the Masjid bin Mahfudh, and the Masjid Syarafiah) littering the city's skyline. The fact that the city was outside of the "haram zone" meant that its cosmopolitan character was even enriched by crowds of non-Muslims, who lived and worked there or otherwise made the city function through commerce or through the service industries, often in conjunction with the hajj (Roham 1992, p. 63).

If Jeddah is the near-universal arrival point for pilgrims, then Mecca is the place all of these global religious travellers are hoping to reach. In most memoirs, Mecca looms as the main geographical "goal" of the hajj, if there is indeed one *topos* to be named. The chaos of the city is palpable in these narratives, as a huge ribbon of humanity winds its way from Jeddah on the coast into the blasted interior of the Arabian desert. Mecca finally appears almost as a mirage. The very old religious buildings, mixed in with newer buildings (but the latter mostly constructed of the same sand-colour to maintain a kind of architectural uniformity), give Mecca a very different flavour from its littoral cousin on the Red Sea shore (Hasjmy 1979, p. 9). The crowd conditions are intense, not just in the religious sites but also in the streets and in the markets. People constantly call out to the pilgrims "Haji!, Haji!", and try to sell small amounts of fruit, cooked meat, or merchandise, often through a mix of sign-language, gestures, or phrases of Arabic and Malay combined (Hadiluwih 1990, p. 40). These congested conditions also make Mecca something of a dangerous place vis-à-vis fire and other concerns, as has been commented upon regularly by a number of memorialists (Zaini 1975, pp. 75, 81). Yet one can also read of finding tiny places of silence in the city to pray, whether in the great mosques or elsewhere, and of the helping hands of strangers leading one slowly to the correct places for this, when so many people are all trying to get to required stations to perform their religious duties all at the same time (Sabary 1996, p. 39; Katianda 1996, pp. 67–68). The phrase "I was swimming in an ocean of humanity" in Mecca is uttered again and again in these accounts to describe the shock of encountering so many pilgrims at entering the city during the hajj season. Yet it seems this designation is not entirely a negative attribute, at least to many of the people who do cross huge expanses of the globe to get to the Hejaz to perform their pilgrimages (Bisri 1993, p. 135).

From Mecca the pilgrims eventually make their way out onto the plain of Arafat. Arafat is laced with memory for the pilgrim in his or her writing — this is where Abraham and Hajar and Isma'il walked; this is where the tears, trials and tribulations of the ancients can still be felt (Navis 1994, pp. 132–35). The plain of Arafat has been described in some of these memoirs as a city without buildings. Rather, it is a city of tents, all of them white and sinuous, looking like so many sails of stationary dhows beached in neat rows in the desert (Hasjmy 1979, p. 185). On Arafat the air temperature in the heat of the day and in direct sunlight can reach fifty-five degrees Centigrade, which is simply too hot for human beings to withstand for more then a few minutes at a time (Saleh 1990, p. 92). With pilgrims overnighting in Muzdalifah nearby, the extremes of moving between this kind of heat and cold in the middle of the night can be a serious health risk (Darwis 2005, p. 151). The hajis and hajahs are in *ihram*, after all, clad only in a simple white cloth garment, which the dictates of the pilgrimage requires to ensure a state of non-distinction before God. The white cloth is of little use on Arafat against the blazing sun or against the chill. Yet it is precisely because of this isolation in the desert, coupled with the chaos of the exact opposite of this "aloneness" (millions of co-Muslims, all experiencing the same things together on that plain of hard scrabble rock) that the intensity of Arafat is written about so prominently in these memoirs. "My thoughts were only on Allah", writes one pilgrim, "there was a direct connection between us" (Machfudz 1993, p. 105). Authors of such narratives say again and again that it is very difficult to experience this same kind of feeling anywhere else, a kind of spiritual charge that is apparent on Arafat, regardless of whom the pilgrim may be or where he or she is from.

Arafat leads to Mina. Mina is where the stone pillars are set, which every pilgrim must stone with small rocks in order to symbolize the casting out of the devil. This act is described somewhat matter-of-factly in a number of memoirs, yet video footage of the hajj shows that this *topos* is actually fraught with an intense energy, as large crowds of pilgrims try to get close enough to the pillars to throw their stones, while other pilgrims are simultaneously trying to leave (Roham 1992, pp. 141–45). Though Arafat and Mina are mostly flat, and have in fact been described as being part and parcel of a large plain with a number of very broad and well-constructed roads (the Nazca lines in Peru are evoked in some of these descriptions, interestingly enough), the bottleneck conditions of this station of the hajj have caused serious problems in the past (Saleh 1990, pp. 140–41). Best known, perhaps, was the immense crush of bodies and the ensuing panic and stampede that occurred in 1990, when a very large number of pilgrims (1,426) lost their lives at Mina. In a number of memoirs these events have been described in painstaking detail, including by eyewitnesses who saw huge amounts of breathing space just adjacent to the fenced avenues if pilgrims had just been able to climb the barriers (Hadiluwih 1990, pp. 59–89). Other memoirs mention the tragedy as a rumour which whipped through the assembling crowds, though pilgrims were witnesses to pockets of weeping hajis and hajahs who had just heard the news of what had happened (Sumarni 1996, pp. 189–90). The Saudi state intervened soon after this and rebuilt sections of the Mina site, all in an effort to ensure that a tragedy such as this one would not occur again. Yet the events had already entered into memory, and memoirs of pilgrims who were there are one of the best ways to get at the actual particularities on the ground as to what actually happened. This was especially so as state explanations of how the disaster happened were rarely convincing, as a number of officials tried to disassociate themselves and their respective bureaus from responsibility for what had occurred.

The last important *topos* of the pilgrimage is Medina, the Prophet's city, which is situated at some distance from most of the other holy sites that together collectively make up the stations of the hajj. Many Southeast Asian memorialists talk about the stretch of desert that must be crossed to get to Medina — the desert here is not necessarily hotter than what has already been traversed, but the distances are longer and pilgrims are already tired from their journeys. One writer spoke of this terrain as being "true" desert, and completely barren:

> [I]t is not beautiful like our own environment in the archipelago — no green, trees, or rivers, there is only blasted earth. But you feel very small here against nature; you have a sense of your place in the universe. (Hassan 1975, p. 41)

Many cars and buses in fact break down on the road to Medina, so that there is a kind of topography of failed vehicles on the roads leading into the city (Sukarsono 1975, p. 207). But once inside, the sense of chaos and confusion reigning there is apparent, as many narrators stress in their accounts. Things seem noticeably less coordinated than in Mecca; it is almost as if even the pilgrimage officials and all infrastructure, even the state itself, is exhausted at this point from having to deal with so many millions of hajis (Alawaiyah 1996, pp. 214–19). Street culture rules the city. Most buying and selling, and indeed almost all transactions generally, take place between cart vendors and pedestrians, a steady stream of humanity coming towards the end of their spiritual duties (Esmara 1993, p. 61). There are still mosques to be visited, and still prayers to be intoned, but the chaos of everyday life begins to course through the crowds again, just as the worst of the desert is being left behind. Medina in these narratives almost exudes a sense of relief — it is not the end of the journey, but the horizon towards return is visible from here. Mecca will be entered again by most pilgrims, and Jeddah almost certainly, but in Medina the sense of the spiritual *topos* being visited for the first time begins to come to an end. Medina, at least as far as Southeast Asian hajj memoirs are concerned, feels like the tower on the hill that one must ascend, therefore, before returning to one's own individual life.

THE HAJJ AND THE SELF

The above places figure prominently in Southeast Asian memoirs of the pilgrimage, but the hajj is an inner journey too, irrespective of which sites are being visited by an individual traveller. It is a noticeable feature of these memoirs that identity is given a prominent place in discussing one's pilgrimage, whether this is identity defined in terms of gender, occupation, or a number of other self-representations. In premodern times the identity ascribed to most hajj memorialists — when we have this information, which is by no means always — has tended to be aligned to the sovereign or elites with whom the pilgrim travelled. In modern times this issue has tended to be far more diffuse.

One of the most common and important of these signifiers is geographical provenance — the pilgrim from "x" on hajj. Many of these accounts seem to intentionally play up the provenance of the author/haji, likely as an attempt to connect him or her to an audience of fellow pilgrims who either have already (or are likely in the future) to make hajj as well. In the terms of Benedict Anderson's "print capitalism" rationale, there may be an economic rationale too, in that the publishing industry seems to have wagered that potential hajis are often likely to buy accounts of other pilgrims who are seen as "co-locals", that is to say, "much like me or us" (Anderson 1983). Thus we get pilgrims such as Haji Danarto discussing the hajj "from the perspective of a Javanese", as the author says in his Forward. Other Indonesians will know immediately that Javanese are supposed to be *halus* or "refined" in their behaviour, so this self-identification means something in terms of the kind of hajj one is expecting (Danarto 1984, p. v). By contrast a Sundanese account (West Javanese, as opposed to Central or Eastern Javanese) is cartoonish by comparison: on the cover of M.S. Maman's memoir, the author is sketched in lampooned lines, but acting as a tour guide, with his hands raised and an over-wide smile on his face (Maman 2004). A Batak account (North Sumatra) is different again; Batak are stereotyped as *kasar* ("coarse") and blunt, and the back jacket of the book even tells the reader to expect a different approach to hajj here: "What happens when a Batak goes on Hajj? This is different from a Javanese, with the emphasis there on esoteric and mystical experience" (Aritonang 1997). These are only Indonesian examples. One can read through the literature on these memoirs and notice variances as you go across the Muslim arc of Southeast Asia, from Singapore to Brunei to Sarawak, each author claiming a different brand of religious experience based on their own geographical-cultural roots (Green 2006; Anon. 1995; Daud 1992, pp. 22–29).

This is one construct of the hajj and the self. Another important one concerns occupation — one's job helping to define what kind of pilgrimage the traveller will have as a truth-seeker in the Holy Land. Here again, as with geographic provenances, much is made in the memoir literature about one's occupation in life affecting very much the kind of hajj one will have in the Hejaz. Some of these accounts are fairly prosaic, for example by doctors, who describe their pilgrimages but also pay special attention to medical matters in their narratives, such as the physical well-being of pilgrims, sanitary conditions, etc. (Ramali 1969; Kamajaya 1993, pp. 118–23). A number of such accounts are anything but prosaic, however. Rock stars, film actors, imams of prestigious (and sometimes very unpretentious) madrasas or mosques, artists, novelists, government officials, and even football coaches and players have all gotten in on the act (Petet 1993, pp. 87-92; Benyamin 1996, op. 34–35; Muchtar 1993, pp. 130–33; Widayat 1993, pp. 225–31; Dunia 1996, pp. 183–84; Wong 1996, pp. 45–46). They describe the hajj from their point of view, often mentioning special aspects of their journeys that touch on their experiences as specialists in any one thing. Politicians and royalty are no different: the Sultan of Brunei, one of the world's richest men, had a glossy memoir-book made up out of his visit to the Holy Cities, replete with numerous photographs of him both in repose and having his hands shaken (and sniffed, in Southeast Asian custom) by a bevy of well-wishers (Anon. 1999). The former dictator of Indonesia, Pak Harto or Soeharto, did the same, though his memoir-book (befitting his Javanese roots, perhaps) was careful to depict him as pious and quiet while on his hajj, as befitting an elected President rather than a member of hereditary royalty (Anon. 1993). Famous politicians (and those aspiring to be famous) have followed suit, like Amien Rais and many others (Rais 1993, pp. 30–37; Saleh 1996, pp. 114–15; Sudirman 1993, pp. 64–71). Yet even housewives have a sub-rubric of this well-established market, with a number of titles on "A Housewife Makes the Hajj" available both in libraries and (more importantly) in local bookstores in the region (Cholifah 2006, p. 25). This last sub-category of memoirs is especially important because women from Southeast Asia are making the pilgrimage more and more often now, and there is a huge and ever-expanding market on how to cater to their needs while on hajj, as well as how to prepare them for the journey.

Gender — and not just in the form of "housewives on Hajj" — makes a strong appearance in many Southeast Asian memoirs across the board. This is true from places like Malaysia, where women can often be integrated into the tales pilgrims tell about their time in Arabia (even in the tales of men), but it is particularly true in Indonesia, where women have a higher social standing than in many other places in the Muslim world (Nasron 2002, pp. 83, 116). Women's concerns make up a small but growing percentage of this literature. Some women — even wealthy ones, such as the TV/film star Ida Leman — have talked about the initial conversations which took place in order to convince their husbands that a pilgrimage to far-away Arabia should be undertaken (Leman 1993, pp. 94–95). Other women have talked at length about very prosaic matters, such as the bringing of panty-liners to the Hejaz to cope with menstruation, or other health-related issues (including praying for the health of loved ones, particularly those in distress) as part of their journeys (Cholifah 2006, p. 25; Arifin 1996, pp. 63–64). A number of accounts even talk about babies being born in the Holy Cities to pilgrims, a great blessing if it happens, but one can surmise a rather enormous matter to arrange so far from one's home, and in a language not one's own (Jutin n.d., p. 112). There is often a didactic tone in many of these gendered memoirs as well, as women tell other women what to expect, what to do, and what not to do (for example, with regards to the correct wearing of ihram, or prohibitions against perfume, the anointing of hair or the cutting of nails, and talk of [or engagement in] sexual activities (Daud 1992, pp. 22–29). Yet a number of accounts by women also deal with the emotional issues of the hajj, and in this they are little different from male-authored accounts, except that "heroines of Islam" (such as Hajar) are given stronger mention in female narratives than in male ones (Arnaz 1996, pp. 35–36). Statements by the well-known female singer Camelia Malik about her breaking into tears upon arrival in the Hejaz are emotive and uttered by a woman, but just as easily could have been penned by a man, given the circumstances and the context of the narrative (Malik 1993, p. 83).

It is this element of introspection which forms a crucial component of the memoir; it is the kernel in some ways of the connection between the "hajj and the self", the title of this subsection. The pilgrimage is a time for introspection, and for inner knowledge — though provenance, occupation, and gender are all important in crafting these narratives, at the height of the spiritual awakening of the hajj, one is alone with God and alone with one's own self. This is the time when you deal with your own ego, and your own battle with yourself and the inner demons you find there (Navis 1996, pp. 92–93). The authors of hajj memoirs deal with this silence within rather differently. One way has been to describe the dream-like state of the hajj, and this notion is constantly evoked in many memoirs, and played upon in this literature a great deal (Noer 1996, pp. 185–86). Narrating the journey as a dream allows it to be reachable again at other points in one's life, since sleep is always with us, and memory comes to us in sleep on a regular basis, usually in the form of dreams. Yet another, and somewhat altered method of dealing with this vast silence of the time for introspection during the time of the hajj has been to weave one's life with death — the great space before and after one's time on earth. Death is ever-present in Southeast Asian hajj memoirs: it appears with an uncanny regularity in the scores upon scores of accounts that I have read. Central here is the question that Yusuf Hasyim, an "average" haji, asks himself in his own memoir: "Is this the end of my life?" (Hasyim 1993, p. 233). Or as H. Ismail Saleh said in his own account, "Is there a reply after death?" (Saleh 1996, p. 114). Our lives are so cluttered and frantic and busy that having the time to merely sit and think in silence for several weeks (even with millions of our co-religionists surrounding us) is beyond life or death — it is precious. It is introspection of the sort that we may only hope to achieve once in our adult lives. The hajj gives this gift.

Then there is the return. By the time most hajis are ready to depart the Hejaz to come back to Southeast Asia, these moments of introspection (penned so emotionally and often so beautifully in memoirs) are long over. This is palpable in the majority of these accounts. The Holy Cities have been left behind: Southeast Asia and home beckon over the horizon, with all of the complications of a return to day-to-day life (job, family, struggle) this implies. The airport in Jeddah is now the last reality of this journey. Memorialists often talk about the difficult conditions of embarkation from the Hejaz: the huge delay in waiting for one's appointed aircraft, for example, which always seems to be hours late, and made later still by waiting behind other, late-arriving aircraft as well (Sukarsono 1975, p. 231). Ferocious lines are de rigueur, many of which are constantly being cut and re-cut by pilgrims who got on the wrong line to begin with, having rushed onto a queue because Bahasa Indonesia was heard, without noting that the plane was en route to Surabaya instead of Jakarta (Zaini 1975, p. 163). There are inevitably problems with luggage as well, and with visas, as well as with the immigration authorities more generally: a huge phalanx of officialdom which must be negotiated, whether it is the pilgrim or his or her belongings that are being scrutinized before being let out of Saudi Arabia's desert kingdom (Darwis 2005, pp. 243–58). It is not all bad. One pilgrim described, in what may perhaps be a backhanded complement, the conditions which enfold all of this chaos: "I felt like I was in a dream when I was leaving from the King Abdul Aziz Airport in Jeddah: luxury goods everywhere, and spotless clean; clean, crisp air-conditioning — it felt like Changi Airport in Singapore" (Esmara 1993, p. 143). Yet it is clear that by this time the pilgrim's thoughts seem to be on other things. The moment has passed, though it lingers in the consciousness; for the memoir itself, though, departure is a time for "coming back to this world", not remaining in the special one that the pilgrim has been inhabiting for the past few weeks. Only one memoir I read dwelled philosophically on this moment, holding onto a kind of lassitude: Emo Kastama described a "romantic return to *tanah air*" (our land and water, i.e., the archipelago). As the Red Sea fell away beneath his aeroplane, he mused that this body of water astride the desert was "strange and mysterious, and full of secrets" (Kastama 1997, pp. 318–19).

CONCLUSION

Memoirs — of the hajj or any other time or experience of one's life — are important social documents that narrate many things, some of them intended, and some of them unintended. They are discourses in the fullest sense of the term: dialogues between the self and an intended audience, with all of the friction that such a meeting of viewpoints potentially implies (Marcus 1994). James Olney has argued that memoirs allow the self to be put forward as a metaphor for other things, essentially for processes that concern the individual, but which are seen through the individual's lived experience as a human being on a journey in this life (Olney 1972). While all memoirs may have this underlying characteristic in common, the many forms and formats of this genre allow the self to be brought across in a number of different ways (Spengermann, 1980). What is one person's value in telling the story of their own life? How are they set apart, or made special? When are they just part of a larger crowd's concerns, such as when millions of people perform a journey such as the hajj all at the same time, year after year after year? (Weintraub 1978) The presentation of the self in such circumstances tells us much about the pilgrim as an individual human being, but in viewing larger patterns in the vast corpus of such memoirs we also see the role of culture and the interplay of social norms writ large in the genre (Folkenflik 1993). The passage of time and memory itself change in memoirs, but they both can be used, constructed, and played with in well-worn channels of written exegesis (Birkets 2008).

The Southeast Asian hajj memoirs we have examined here reveal these processes in interesting ways. Narratives of the pilgrimage from this part of the world stretch back hundreds of years, all the way to Hang Tuah via the Malay Annals, though there are a number of other authors who also wrote on this journey over the course of the centuries. Rare *jawi* and *rumi* texts began to give way to printed accounts in the later nineteenth century, but it is only after independence and the mid-twentieth century that large numbers of these narratives began to appear. These latter memoirs are creations of the independent nation-state period in the region. Print capitalism and the condensation of regional languages into discrete reading publics ensured that there was a ready market for such accounts, both as pieces of emotional literature and as valuable "how-to" kits of undertaking the hajj for subsequent pilgrims. The holy sites of the Hejaz were laid open to inspection by those yet to make the trip, and successful hajis and hajahs themselves were able to keep a record of the fulfilment of their religious duties as Muslims. Yet the self is always evident in these accounts as well, which are not just narratives confined to a particular time (the pilgrimage season) and a particular place (the Arabian Peninsula). Pilgrims undertook this journey as doctors, housewives, imams, and heads of state; they also undertook it as denizens of Brunei, West Java, the Batak districts of Sumatra and of Singapore. They travelled as Chinese converts and as bumiputras, as women and as men. In their collectivity these memoirs show us something of the hajj as an individual quest, but also certain lines of culture that seem to pervade their writing as a corporate enterprise of co-religionists. It is this complexity that makes them so fascinating to study as artefacts of Muslim life.

References

Ahmad, Kassim. *Hikayat Hang Tuah*. Kuala Lumpur: Yayasan Karyawan dan Dewan Bahasa dan Pustaka, 1997.

Alawiyah, Dra. Hj, Tuty. "Saya Ketemu Yasser Arafat". In *Haji Sebuah Perjalanan Air Mata* by Anon. Yogyakarta: Bentang, 1993: 214–19.

Anderson, Benedict. *Imagined Communities: Reflections on the Origin and Spread of Nationalism*. London: Verso, 1983.

Anon. *Haji Sebuah Perjalanan Air Mata*. Yogyakarta: Bentang, 1993.

———. *Perjalanan Ibadah Haji Pak Harto*. Jakarta: Departemen Agama, 1993.

———. *Al-Mu'min Menjadi Tetamu Allah*. Bandar Seri Begawan, Jabatan Pusat Sejarah Kementerian Kebudayaan, 1995.

———. *As Guest of Allah: With Members of the Brunei Royal Family, a Memoir*. Bandar Seri Begawan: Brunei History Centre, 1999.

Arifin, Ny. Hj, Setiati. "Zamzam yang Membawa Berkah". In Nurdin, E. Syarief and E. Kosasih, *100 Keajaiban di Tanah Suci Pengalaman Unik Jamaah Haji*. Bandung: Pustaka Hidayah, 1996.

Aritonang, Baharuddin. *Orang Batak Naik Haji*. Jakarta: Gramedia, 1997.

Arnaz, Hajja Eva. "Tangan Besar yang Menyelamatkan Jiwaku". In Nurdin, E. Syarief and E. Kosasih, *100 Keajaiban di Tanah Suci Pengalaman Unik Jamaah Haji*. Bandung: Pustaka Hidayah, 1996.

Barrington, Judith. *Writing the Memoir from Truth to Art*. Portland: Eighth Mountain, 1997.

Benyamin, H.S. "Kepasrahan". In Nurdin, E. Syarief and E. Kosasi, *100 Keajaiban di Tanah Suci Pengalaman Unik Jamaah Haji*. Bandung: Pustaka Hidayah, 1996.

Birkets, Sven. *The Art of Time in Memoir: Then, Again*. St. Paul, MN: Graywolf, 2008.

Bisri, K.H. A. Mustofa. "Saya Merasa Diwelehke Tuhan". In *Haji Sebuah Perjalanan Air Mata* by Anon. Yogyakarta: Bentang, 1993.

Bovene, G.A. van. *Mijne Reis Naar Mekka: Naar het Dagboek van den Regent van Bandoeng Raden Adipati Aria Wirantakoesoema*. 1925.

Braginsky, Vladimir. *The Heritage of Traditional Malay Literature*. Leiden: KITLV Press, 2004.

Cholifah, Hajja Saida. *Ibu Rumah Tanga Naik Haji*. Yogyakarta: Pustaka Marwa, 2006.

Conway, Jill Ker. *When Memory Speaks: Reflections on Autobiography*. New York: Knopf, 1998.

Danarto. *Catatan Perjalanan Haji Danarto, Orang Jawa Naik Haji*. Jakarta: Penerbit PT Grafiti, 1984.

Darwis, Ir. H. Avicenia. *40 Hari Mencari Cinta: Kisah Nyata Berhaji di Tanah Suci*. Bogor: Ar-Rahmah, 2005.

Dunia, H. Gazali. "Hanya GBpounds 60". In Nurdin, E. Syarief and E. Kosasih, *100 Keajaiban di Tanah Suci Pengalaman Unik Jamaah Haji*. Bandung: Pustaka Hidayah, 1996.

Errington, Shelly. *A Study of Genre: Meaning and Form in the Malay Hikayat Hang Tuah*. PhD dissertation, Cornell University, 1975.

Esmara, Hendra. *Aku Datang Memenuhi Panggilanmu Ya, Allah*. Jakarta: Penerbit PT Gramdeia, 1993.

Fletcher, Ian. "Rhythm and Pattern in Autobiographies". In *An Honored Guest: New Essays on W.B. Yeats* edited by by Denis Donoghue and J.R. Mulryne. New York: St. Martins' Press, 1966.

Folkenflik, Robert, ed. *The Culture of Autobiography: Constructions and Self-Representation*. Stanford: Stanford University Press, 1993.

Gallop, Annabel Teh. *Golden Letters: Writing Traditions of Indonesia*. London: British Library, 1993.

———. *The Legacy of the Malay Letter*. London: British Library, 1994.
Green, Anthony. *Our Journey: Thirty Years of Haj Services in Singapore*. Singapore: Majlis Ugama Islam Singapura, 2006.
Hadiluwih, R.M. H. Subanindyo. *Ibadah Haji: Perjalanan Spiritual 40 Hari*. Medan: Penerbit Dhian-Doddy, 1990.
Haji Daud, Haja Maimunah. "The Haj — A Personal Experience". *Sarawak Gazette* 119, no. 1521 (1992): 22–29.
Hamba. *Itu Dia Hadji Mabrur*. Jakarta: Kantor Pusat Perdjalana Hadji Indonesia, 1971.
Hamka, H.M. Jusuf. *Engkoh Bun Naik Haji*. Jakarta: Penerbit Pustaka Panjimas, 1985.
Harmoko. *Naik Haji Hanya Untuk Ibadah*. Jakarta: Pustaka Kartini, 1994.
Hart, Francis. "Notes for an Anatomy of Modern Autobiography". *New Literary History* 1, no. 3 (1970): 485–511.
Hasjmy, A. *Surat Surat Dari Tanah Suci*. Jakarta: Penerbit Bulan Bintang, 1979.
Hassan, Fuad. *Genglalaman Seorang Haji*. Jakarta: Bulan Bintang, 1975.
Hasyim, K.H. Yusuf. "Inikah Akhir Hidup Saya?" In *Haji Sebuah Perjalanan Air Mata* by Anon. Yogyakarta: Bentang, 1993.
Hill, A.H. *Hikayat Abdullah: An Annotated Translation*. Kuala Lumpur: Oxford University Press, 1970.
Hutch, Richard. *The Meaning of Lives: Biography, Autobiography and the Spiritual Quest*. London: Cassell, 1997.
Jutin, H.A. *712 Mudjahid Gambela Jang Menggembarkan*. Malang: Penerbit UB Milan, n.d.
Kamajaya, H. Karkono. "Tidak Awur-awuran Atau Asla Haji-hajian". In *Haji Sebuah Perjalanan Air Mata* by Anon. Yogyakarta: Bentang, 1993.
Kartono, Mohammad. "Kalau Mereka Tahu Saya Membawa Buku-buku dari Israel". In *Haji Sebuah Perjalanan Air Mata* by Anon. Yogyakarta: Bentang, 1993.
Kastama, Emo. *Catatan Harian Seorang Jemaah Haji*. Jakarta: Cita Putra Bangsa, 1997.
Katianda, I I.A. Gozali. "Tiba-tiba Tangan Saya Ada yang Membimbing". In Nurdin, E. Syarief and E. Kosasih, *100 Keajaiban di Tanah Suci Pengalaman Unik Jamaah Haji*. Bandung: Pustaka Hidayah, 1996.
Leman, Ida. "Allah Mengundang Hajiku Dengan Tiba-tiba". In *Haji Sebuah Perjalanan Air Mata* by Anon. Yogyakarta: Bentang, 1993.
Machfudz, Drg. H. Ircham. "Saya Mengangis, Nikmat Sekali". In *Haji Sebuah Perjalanan Air Mata* by Anon. Yogyakarta: Bentang, 1993.
Madjid, Nucholish. "Haji Itu Transformasi Hidup". In *Haji Sebuah Perjalanan Air Mata* by Anon. Yogyakarta: Bentang, 1993.
Majid, Haji Abdul. "A Malay's Pilgrimage to Mecca". *JMBRAS* 4, no. 2 (1926): 269–87.

Malik, Camelia. "Ada yang Menakut-nakuti Saya". In *Haji Sebuah Perjalanan Air Mata* by Anon. Yogyakarta: Bentang, 1993.
Maman, M.S. *Orang Sunda Munggah Haji*. Bandung: Penerbit Kiblat, 2004.
Marcus, Laura. *Auto/biographical Discourses: Theory, Criticism, Practice*. Manchester: Manchester, University Press, 1994.
Matheson, V. and Milner, A.C. *Perceptions of the Haj: Five Malay Texts*. Singapore: Institute of Southeast Asian Studies, 1984.
Matheson, Virginia and Barbara Watson Andaya, eds. *The Precious Gift (Tuhfat al-Nafis)*. Kuala Lumpur: Oxford University Press, 1982.
Muchtar, K.H. A. Latif. "Haji Bukan Ibadah Puncak". In *Haji Sebuah Perjalanan Air Mata* by Anon. Yogyakarta: Bentang, 1993.
Nasron, Haji Mazlan. *Air Mata: Di Pintu Baitullah*. Kuala Lumpur: Progressive, 2002.
Navis, A.A. *Surat dan Kenangan Haji*. Jakarta: Penerbit PT Gramedia Pustaka Utama, 1994.
Navis, H.A. A. "Penampilan Ego yang Tak Bertuah". In Nurdin, E. Syarief and E. Kosasih, *100 Keajaiban di Tanah Suci Pengalaman Unik Jamaah Haji*. Bandung: Pustaka Hidayah, 1996.
Noer, H. Arifin C. "Tuhan Menidurkan Saya". In Nurdin, E. Syarief and E. Kosasih, *100 Keajaiban di Tanah Suci Pengalaman Unik Jamaah Haji*. Bandung: Pustaka Hidayah, 1996.
Olney, James. *Metaphors of Self: The Meaning of Autobiography*. Princeton: Princeton University Press, 1972.
Petet, Didi. "Allah Sekana Mengundang Saya ke Makah Setiap Tahun". In *Haji Sebuah Perjalanan Air Mata* by Anon. Yogyakarta: Bentang, 1993.
Proudfoot, Ian. *Early Malay Printed Books*. Kuala Lumpur: Academy of Malay Studies and University of Malaya, 1993.
Rais, Amien. "Saya Mina Keturunan, Dikabulkan Allah". In *Haji Sebuah Perjalanan Air Mata* by Anon. Yogyakarta: Bentang, 1993.
Ramali, Ahmad. *Perdjalanan Hadji: Naik Hadji dan Hubungan Sebagai Dokter Djemaah Hadji*. Jakarta: Tintomas, 1969.
Roham, A. *Abujamin, Aku Pergi Haji*. Jakarta: Media Da'wah, 1992.
Saleh, H. Ismail. "Balasan Setelah Mati". In Nurdin, E. Syarief and E. Kosasih, *100 Keajaiban di Tanah Suci Pengalaman Unik Jamaah Haji*. Bandung: Pustaka Hidayah, 1996.
Saleh, Ismail. *Penglalaman Sebagai Amirul Hajj*. Jakarta: Pustaka Kartini, 1990.
Sobary, Mohamad. *Tamu Allah*. Jakarta: Pustaka Firdaus, 1996.
Spengermann, William. *The Forms of Autobiography: Episodes in the History of a Literary Genre*. New Haven: Yale University Press, 1980.
Sudirman, Mayjen. (Purn.) H. Basofi. "Seumanya Merupakan Paket". In *Haji Sebuah Perjalanan Air Mata* by Anon. Yogyakarta: Bentang, 1993.

Sukarsono, H. *Liku-Liku Perjalanan ke Tanah Suci*. Jakarta: P.T. Pranadaya, 1975.
Sumarni, Hj. Sri. "Bayangan Putih di Balik Tragedi Mina". In Nurdin, E. Syarief and E. Kosasih, *100 Keajaiban di Tanah Suci Pengalaman Unik Jamaah Haji*. Bandung: Pustaka Hidayah, 1996.
Sutarmo, H. "Perjalanan Saat Tragedi Mina". In Nurdin, E. Syarief and E. Kosasih, *100 Keajaiban di Tanah Suci Pengalaman Unik Jamaah Haji*. Bandung: Pustaka Hidayah, 1996.
Syair Makkah al-Musyarrafah Madinah al-Munawwarat. Singapore: Publisher Ibrahim, Kampung Gelam, 1886.
Syair Mekah Madinah. Singapore: Tuan Syaikh Haji Muhammad Ali b. Haji Mustafa bala(d) Berbalingga Makam Cahaya, Lorong Masjid, Kampung Gelam, 1869.
Syair Mekah Madinah Jiddah Araafat dan Sekalian Tanah Arab dan Menyatakan Peri Hal Ihwal Orang yang Pergi Haj dan Keeolokan. Singapore: Ofis Cap Haji Sirat Press, 1885.
Syair Mekah Madinah; Syair Mekah Syair Madinah. Singapore: Tuan Haji Muhammad Nuh b. Haji Ismail ahl al_Jawi bil(d) Juwana namanya tempat Dusun Kajian, 1873.
Syair Negeri Makkah al-Musyarrafah dan Madinah al-Munawwarat. Singapore: Haji Muhammad Sidik, 1889.
Syair Negeri Makkah al-Musyarrafah dan Madinah al-Munawwarat; Syair Macam Baru peri menyatakan Orang yang Pergi Haj dari Negeri Bawah Angin sampai kepada Negeri Atas Angin seperti Jiddah dan Mekah dan Madinah dan seperti lain-lainnya. Singapore: Tuan Haji Muhammad Taib, 1888.
Trotskii, Leon. *My Life: An Attempt at Autobiography*. New York: Scribners, 1930.
Weintraub, Karl. *The Value of the Individual: Self and Circumstance in Autobiography*. Chicago: University of Chicago Press, 1978.
Widayat, H. "Saya Bertemu Malaikat". In *Haji Sebuah Perjalanan Air Mata* by Anon. Yogyakarta: Bentang, 1993.
Wong, H. Johnny. "Ingin Seperti Presiden". In Nurdin, E. Syarief and E. Kosasih, *100 Keajaiban di Tanah Suci Pengalaman Unik Jamaah Haji*. Bandung: Pustaka Hidayah, 1996.
Zaini, H. Azkarmin. *Pengalaman Haji di Tanah Suci: Sebuah Reportase Lengkap Tentang Menunaikan Ibadah Haji*. Jakarta: Gramedia, 1975.

4

THE AURAD MUHAMMADIAH CONGREGATION: MODERN TRANSNATIONAL SUFISM IN SOUTHEAST ASIA

Ahmad Fauzi Abdul Hamid

The rising profile of Southeast Asia as a prosperously developing and yet passionately Islamic region necessitates a study of the dynamic interaction between its domestic political imperatives and transnational variables. While transnational factors in themselves may be insufficient to explain the shifting contours of contemporary Islam in Southeast Asia, their presence has arguably been crucial in the continual flourishing and resilience of autonomous Islamism in the face of relentless pressure from the state.[1] Although Islamist movements have over the years become more focused on domestic issues and discourses, none has denied the utility and need to retain transnational dimensions. Notwithstanding the vast diversity of Muslim populations worldwide, as long as the concept of an *ummah* (global Muslim community) is given credence, the emergence of transnational political entities predicated on relations among the Muslim brethren if not among Islamists, cannot be underestimated.[2]

This chapter seeks to address Sufism[3] as another side of transnational Islamism which has flourished without attracting as much attention as has the modernist-reformist variants of Wahhabi-Salafi[4] doctrinal parentage, some of whose protagonists have expressed aversion to Sufism as a kind of "Islam which is not Islam" (Howell 2001, p. 706). The place of Sufism within the rubric of Islamism and Islamist literature has been made uncertain by the hostility shown to it by Islamist ideologues themselves. For example, Abul A'la Maududi (d. 1979), founder of Jamaat-i-Islami party in the Indo-Pakistan subcontinent, exhorted aspiring Muslim revivalists to "shun the language and terminology of the Sufis; their mystic allusions and metaphoric references, their dress and etiquette, their master-disciple institution and all other things associated with it" (Maududi 1981, p. 113). The present contribution argues that Sufism as an Islamic revivalist movement in Southeast Asia has thrived amidst manifold challenges presented by globalization, lack of sympathy from Islamist quarters, and resentment in the case of Malaysia, from a state wary of the possible threat that Sufi groups pose to its self-acclaimed legitimacy as guardians of Islam in a postcolonial national setting. Our object of investigation is the Aurad Muhammadiah congregation (Jemaah Aurad Muhammadiah), which has spread its wings throughout Southeast Asia through several formal and informal organizations, most notably Darul Arqam, banned in Malaysia since 1994.

TRANSNATIONAL SUFISM IN SOUTHEAST ASIAN ISLAM: A HISTORICAL OVERVIEW

Transnational linkages, taking the form of transmission of ideas, finances, logistical support and manpower; is ingrained in the history of Islam in Southeast Asia. The terms "Malaysia" and "Indonesia" were laden with transnational connotations, having been originally used by scholars to denote the whole Malay world or *Nusantara*, encompassing the Malay-Indonesian archipelago, including present-day southern Thailand and the Philippines (cf. Fatimi 1963, p. 3; Naoki 1998, pp. 23–24). Interregional mobility among Malay-Indonesian peoples of varied ethnocultural backgrounds extended well into the eve of full British control of the administration of states in the Malay Peninsula (Khoo 1974, pp. 183–84). While Islam gained an indelible foothold among Malays and other indigenous Southeast Asians from the end of the thirteenth century to the fifteenth century, their encounters with

Muslim traders date back to as early as the ninth century (Al-Attas 1969, pp. 11–17). At the helm of this process of gradual but virtually uninterrupted Islamization were Sufi missionaries coming from or passing through such diverse places as Arabia, Gujarat, southern India, Bengal, Persia and China (Fatimi 1963, pp. 8–36; Ahmad Fauzi 2002, pp. 473–76). Sufi orders in Southeast Asia have invariably Meccan and Medinan provenances (Al-Attas 1963, p. 32; van Bruinessen 1994). While the role of Indian Sufi missionaries should not be discounted, many Southeast Asian–based scholars have lamented the tendency of Western authors who exaggerate the extent of Indian influence, so as to caricature Southeast Asian Islam as being syncretic — a watered-down version of Islam concurrently shaped by local animist, Hindu and Buddhist traditions and practices (Al-Attas 1969, p. 25; van Bruinessen 1999, pp. 159–61).[5] Even in the Middle Eastern heartlands of Islam, there arguably exists a prevailing impression of Islam in the Southeast Asian periphery as being overtly popular and less pure as a consequence of undue incorporation of pre-Islamic cultures, as opposed to the scriptural and orthodox Islam of the Arabs (von der Mehden 1993, p. xi; Johns 1993, pp. 46–47). Developed through centuries of inequitable interaction, such a lopsided view has been accentuated by the dearth of research institutes in the Middle East devoted to the study of Islam and Muslims in Asia (Abaza 2007, pp. 428–34).

Sufi-conditioned Islamization radically transformed the intellectual and cultural outlook of Malay-Indonesian society, as can be inferred from the dominance of mystical and metaphysical themes in scholarly debates and literature of the time (Al-Attas 1963, pp. 21–29; Al-Attas 1969, pp. 2, 26–32). An oft-mentioned achievement of the wholesale Islamization process was the sheer use of peaceful means such as persuasion and preaching, with barely any employment of compulsion or violence (Arnold 1961, pp. 367, 369, 409; Meuleman 2005, pp. 29–30). Malacca, whose sultans Mansur Shah (r. 1459–77) and Mahmud Shah (r. 1488–1511) were known to have developed a penchant for Sufi theosophy, became a springboard for the Islamization of Java at the hands of the legendary *Wali Songo* (Nine Saints), some of whom had earlier studied Islam in Malacca (Osman Bakar 1991, pp. 265–68). Scholars have differed on modalities of their introduction and dissemination of Islam via Sufi networks. Those brought up in the orientalist tradition were inclined to stress utilitarian aspects related to the expansion of maritime trade networks, post-Crusade Muslim-Christian rivalry and the building of strategic alliances via transnational royal marriages (Alatas 1985, pp. 167–70). More recent research, however, has emphasized Suficum-intellectual networks, whereby Sufi sheikhs (mentors) would bequeath the *ijazah* (right) to teach their particular *tariqahs* to favoured students from the *Jawi* (Southeast Asian Muslim) community who congregated around the famous learning centres in the Middle East. The students, upon returning to Southeast Asia after many years of tutelage, played the simultaneous roles of *khalifah* (vicegerent) of a *tariqah* and *ulama* (religious scholars: sing. *alim*) who founded boarding schools called *pesantrens* and *pondoks* which often acted also as Sufi *zawwiyyahs* or *khanqahs* (hospices or hermitages) (Johns 1993, pp. 53–59). Such Sufi luminaries as Hamzah al-Fansuri (d. *c*.1600), Shamsuddin al-Sumatrani (d. 1630) and Nuruddin al-Raniri (d. 1666) were sought for their advice and wisdom by successive rulers of Acheh (Osman Bakar 1991, pp. 283–86).

In the colonial era, consistent interaction between Malay-Indonesians and their Muslim brethren in the Middle East, for instance through the annual pilgrimage to Mecca, returning graduates of Middle Eastern institutions of higher learning, and the migrant Arab communities who had intermarried with Malay-Muslims, had been a source of apprehension to British and Dutch imperialists (cf. Roff 1967, pp. 40–43; Reid 1967, pp. 270–71; von der Mehden 1993, pp. 4, 10, 15). Well-known Sufis partook in the anti-colonial agitation. In Terengganu, for example, religious leader Ungku Sayyid, popularly known as Tukku Paloh of the Naqshbandiyyah order, provided a haven for insurgents fleeing from colonial forces quelling Dato' Bahaman's Pahang uprising (1891–95), thus lending Islamic legitimacy to what had begun as a Malay chieftain's personal crusade (Linehan 1936, pp. 161–62, 166–67; Andaya and Andaya 1982, pp. 169–70). In areas of present-day Indonesia, the Qadiriyyah-Naqshbandiyyah order was involved in anti-Dutch rebellions in Banten, West Java, in 1888, in Lombok in 1891 and in East Java in 1903 (van Bruinessen 1994).

In the Malay Peninsula, Sufis contributed to early stirrings of Malay nationalism, conceptualized around the transnational ideals of a Greater Malaya (*Melayu-Raya*) which amalgamated Pan-Islamism and Indonesian-imported anti-colonialism.[6] Outlasting independence in 1957, transnational Islam ala-*Melayu-Raya* reached a crescendo in 1965 with the Internal Security Act (ISA) detention without trial of opposition Islamic Party of Malaysia (PAS: Parti Islam SeMalaysia) president Dr Burhanuddin Al-Helmy for alleged involvement in a high-level conspiracy to set up a pro-Indonesian government-in-exile in Karachi, Pakistan.[7] Dr Burhanuddin was renowned for his eclectic formulation of Malay nationality as a non-racial concept, a political category encompassing people willing to profess allegiance to the Malay nation, thus providing an avenue for the absorption of non-Malays as definitive Malaysian citizens, parallel to what is presently termed as *bumiputra* (sons of the soil) (Kamarudin Jaffar 1980, pp. 13, 112–21). Such an accommodative ideological outlook could arguably be traced to Dr Burhanuddin's strong grounding in Sufism, to which he returned after a brief flirtation with Islamist modernism in his younger days (Funston 1980, pp. 118, 122; Kamarudin Jaffar 1980, p. 17).

THE BEGINNINGS AND EARLY DIFFUSION OF THE AURAD MUHAMMADIAH IN SOUTHEAST ASIA[8]

The Aurad Muhammadiah order was founded by a peripatetic Sufi of Javanese-Arab ancestry, Sheikh Muhammad Abdullah As-Suhaimi (hereafter Sheikh Suhaimi), who was born in AD 1843 (AH 1259 of the Islamic calendar) in Kampung Sudagaran, a village in the mountainous district of Wonosobo, Central Java. Through the lineage of his father, Abdullah bin Umar, a wealthy merchant of respectable standing, Sheikh Suhaimi claims to be the thirty-third descendant of the Prophet Muhammad, whose progeny left Arabia in droves following the thirteenth century Mongol invasions and again after the Wahhabi conquests of the Hijaz.[9] Sheikh Suhaimi's family was thus part of the migrant Arab community mostly hailing from Hadramawt, Yemen, but which retained intellectual and cultural links with their original motherland in spite of intermarriages with local Malay-Indonesians. This community, active mostly in the Straits Settlements of Penang and Singapore, rapidly won the admiration of local Malay-Indonesians for their enterprise, socio-welfare services and religious knowledge, adding to the respect accorded to the *sayyids* and sheikhs as descendants of the Prophet Muhammad (Roff 1967, pp. 40–43). Hadramis were responsible for the importation of many reformist ideas into Southeast Asia, but they were not monolithic. Intra-Arab cleavages were revealed by the protracted conflict between the conservative Alawis and reform-oriented Irshadis on issues such as the legality of marriages of a *sharifah* (female equivalent of a *sayyid*) to a non-*sayyid* and the conservative practice of religion of the Alawis, as indicated by their maintaining an exclusive *tariqah* of their own (Al-Attas 1963, p. 32; Kostiner 1984, pp. 211–18). As Sheikh Suhaimi had admitted to being a member of the Alawiah order prior to practising the Aurad Muhammadiah (As Suhaimi 1995, p. 1), it can safely be assumed that his family were Alawis. But differing from many typical

Alawis, Sheikh Suhaimi's parents exhibited reformist inclinations, as shown by their refusal to attach the honorific titles of *sayyid* and *sharifah* to their children's names, as befits descendants of the Prophet Muhammad. For them, honorable ancestry was not a source of pride and was no guarantee for success in the world and the hereafter.

From an early age, Sheikh Suhaimi was sent to various *pondoks* around Java to pursue religious education. But instead of yielding to his father's wishes for all his offspring to become involved in the business and trading worlds, Sheikh Suhaimi requested to further religious studies in Mecca, where he studied under such venerable teachers-cum-Sufis as Nawawi al-Bantani and Abdullah az-Zawawi.[10] But after several years of accumulating knowledge of the outer Islamic sciences, Sheikh Suhaimi assumed the life of a wandering dervish (ascetic) in search of spiritual enlightenment. An important segment of his travels throughout Arabia were visitations to graves of prophets, *auliya* (saints), companions of the Prophet Muhammad and members of the Prophet's household. A town called Suhaim in present-day Syria apparently featured in Sheikh Suhaimi's itinerary and inspired him to adopt the appellation "as-Suhaimi". In Egypt, he finally achieved what he wanted — intuitive knowledge (*ilmu kasyaf/ladunni*) kindled by divine inspiration, after a dedicated period of experiencing life as a recluse under the guidance of an initially reluctant spiritual mentor. After twelve hard years of sojourning in Arabia, Sheikh Suhaimi returned to Southeast Asia, settling down in Singapore with his wife, Nyai Qaniah Abdul Rahim, who had accompanied him for part of his overseas journeys. He occasionally returned to Java; one of his trips back to his ancestral homeland was for the purpose of bringing over his parents to reside in Singapore.[11]

In Singapore, Sheikh Suhaimi became *imam* (prayer-cum-community leader) at the Ma'ruf Mosque, built by the Javanese community, in Clyde Street, off North Bridge Road.[12] As word rapidly spread of Sheikh Suhaimi's innovative teaching methods and *karamah* (miraculous feats), his followers rose in number, especially among pockets of Javanese settlements along western coastal routes of the Malay Peninsula. That Sheikh Suhaimi was of respectable scholarly standing within Malay religio-intellectual circles is shown by the fact that his views are authoritatively quoted in religious *kitabs* (textbooks) used in *pondoks* and later madrasas[13] throughout the region.[14] Nonetheless, he was unable to unite his swelling congregation in one *tariqah* as he himself was simultaneously practising *dhikr* (remembrances of God) and other forms of religious chanting systematized by several spiritual genealogies, including those of Al Ghazali (d. 1111).[15] Scrutiny of the contents of Sheikh Suhaimi's treatise entitled *Futuhat al-Ilahiyyah* has led some to conclude that he was a member of the Ghazaliyyah order, not known to have a large following in Southeast Asia (cf. Farahwahida 2007, pp. 46–47).[16] The rather muddled state of spiritual affairs, coupled with increasing leadership responsibilities, prompted Sheikh Suhaimi to pray for God's guidance, after which he received inspiration to enter the Kaabah in Mecca to receive the practice called "Aurad Muhammadiah" directly from the Prophet Muhammad. It is unclear, however, if Sheikh Suhaimi had physically travelled to Mecca or merely performed a spiritual journey to meet the Prophet's spirit in person (Muhammad Taha Suhaimi 1994, p. 23). Thus began the Aurad Muhammadiah congregation, which rapidly burgeoned upon his return to Singapore, attracting thousands of adherents from Malay, Javanese, Arab and Indian Muslim communities who came from all over Southeast Asia. Around the turn of the century (1900), Sheikh Suhaimi bought a piece of land in Teluk Pulai, Kelang, Selangor, where he raised a family as well. Travelling back and forth between Malaya and Singapore, Sheikh Suhaimi oversaw the diffusion of the Aurad Muhammadiah along the route and appointed *khalifahs* to hand down the practice to the Muslim populace.

As a *tariqah*, the Aurad Muhammadiah consists of the recitation, individually after each daily prayer and preferably in congregation on Thursday nights, of seven verses in the correct order, preceded by reading the first chapter of the Qur'an. These verses, four and three of which are to be read ten and fifty times respectively, are together a collection of Qur'anic verses, the twin attestation of faith to Allah and the Prophet Muhammad (*kalimah shahadah*) and a salutation of peace upon the Prophet Muhammad (*salawat*) (Ashaari Muhammad 1986, pp. 58–63).[17] Practitioners are also urged to supplement this practice with the chanting of five more Qur'anic verses (*Ayat Lima*), of *tahlil*[18] and *maulid*[19] on Thursday and Sunday nights, specific supplications for avoidance of contagious diseases, repentance and jihad after daily prayers; and a specific pre-prayer *salawat* coined by Sayyid Ahmad al-Badawi (d. 1276), a famous Egyptian saint (Ashaari Muhammad 1986, pp. 64–66, 109–42). Later, when leadership of the congregation in Malaya passed on to Sheikh Suhaimi's son, Muhammad Khairullah Suhaimi, the *Silat* or *Pencak Sunda* exercise, involving elements of Malay martial arts preceded by the invocation of Sheikh Suhaimi's name, was added to the list of supplementary practices (Ashaari Muhammad 1986, pp. 151–52; Mohd Taha Suhaimi 1996). Strictly speaking, all supplementary practices are not part of the Aurad Muhammadiah, yet they form an important segment of the Aurad Muhammadiah culture. *Ayat Lima* and *Pencak Sunda* would be offered to practitioners who have diligently practised the Aurad for an amount of time until they are deemed by the *khalifah* to be fit for "promotion", after which the daily recitation of the Aurad is not annulled.

Although Sheikh Suhaimi apparently breathed his last and was interred in Kelang in 1925, many within his family insist that he actually went into occultation to prepare for his reappearance as Imam al-Mahdi (hereafter Al-Mahdi), the final deliverer who would restore Islam's glory and implement justice on earth. This postulation is based not only on circumstantial evidence regarding Sheikh Suhaimi such as a pedigree reaching to the Prophet Muhammad and a name and physical features which accorded with the description of Al-Mahdi in Hadiths (traditions of the Prophet Muhammad) (Ashaari Muhammad 1986, p. 178; 1989, pp. 48–49), but also from spiritual communication between Sheikh Suhaimi and chosen descendants. However, both the Singapore and Kelang branches of the family preferred to keep the belief a secret lest it courted unwarranted controversy.[20] It was not until the 1980s, when the Malaysian-based *dakwah* (missionary) movement Darul Arqam became embroiled in several theological disputes with the country's Islamic officialdom that the messianic conviction, considered to have departed from Sunni orthodoxy, suddenly became the subject of intense debate, eventuating in the banning of Darul Arqam in 1994 (Ahmad Fauzi 2005). In Singapore, however, such beliefs as harboured by Sheikh Suhaimi's descendants are not suppressed, even if not wholeheartedly endorsed. This is because religious pluralism within Islam is tolerated in Singapore, where the Islamic Religious Council of Singapore (MUIS: Majlis Ugama Islam Singapura) does not monopolize the meaning of Islamic orthodoxy, as does its Malaysian counterpart, the Islamic Advancement Department of Malaysia (JAKIM: Jabatan Kemajuan Islam Malaysia), which regulates fatwas (legal edicts) via the National Fatwa Council (NFC: Majlis Fatwa Kebangsaan).

Hence, in a 1980 book published in Singapore on the question of Al-Mahdi, for instance, the author discloses how, after discovering "a book entitled Manakib asy-Syeikh as-Saiyid Muhammad bin Abdullah as-Suhaimi, founder of the Suhaimi [sic] sufi order famous in the Malay world", he concludes that the possibility that Sheikh Suhaimi "will reappear and assume an important position as decided by the Council of Saints.... as the awaited Imam Mahdi" cannot be rejected altogether (Muhammad Labib Ahmad 1980, p. 44). Notwithstanding all the problems that have beset their Aurad Muhammadiah brethren in Malaysia, the congregation in Singapore has never been chided as heterodox by the Islamic authorities (Muhammad Taha Suhaimi 1994, pp. 38–43). Moreover, it continues to contribute to the social and educational well-being of Singapore's Muslim community, functioning as part of a religious minority within the context of a secular state. Indeed, despite Singapore's Aurad Muhammadiah chapter being indirectly implicated by the polemic surrounding Darul Arqam and Aurad Muhammadiah in Malaysia, the highly regarded reputation of Sheikh Suhaimi's family has helped to obviate any similar social ostracism and political harassment in Singapore. Eschatological beliefs have not resulted in a challenge to a non-Muslim-dominated state.

THE AURAD MUHAMMADIAH CONGREGATION IN SINGAPORE: MADRASAH AL-MA'ARIF AND PERSATUAN ISLAM DAN PENCAK SILAT SINGAPURA (PERIPENSIS)

In Singapore, the Aurad Muhammadiah congregation's main contribution has been in the field of Islamic education. After Sheikh Suhaimi's era, the congregation's leadership passed on to his son, Muhammad Fadhlullah Suhaimi (d. 1964), a respected *alim* in his own right. At a young age, he had accompanied his father on the latter's travels to Malaya and Thailand, and stayed in Bombay, Mecca and Medina before furthering his education in Cairo's Al-Azhar University in 1911 (Ni'mah 1998, pp. 4–11). Fadhlullah distinguished himself as chief editor of *Al-Ittihad*, the first ever Malay journal published in Egypt, and went on to set up the *Al-Ittihadiyyah* publishing house which published, among other things, works by Sheikh Suhaimi and the first manual on practising the Aurad Muhammadiah (Muhammad Taha Suhaimi 1994, pp. 6–7; Md. Sidin and Mohammad Redzuan 2000, pp. 64, 67). The multilingual Fadhlullah wrote prolifically; he was the first to produce a biography of the Prophet Muhammad in Malay and a biography of his father in Javanese (Darlan Zaini 2003, p. 147). A younger brother, Muhammad Ataullah Suhaimi, was chairman of the organizing committee of commemorative celebrations to honour founders of *Seruan Azhar*, an avowedly anti-colonial journal launched in 1927 by Indonesian and Malay students in Cairo (Roff 1970, p. 85, fn. 37). On the whole, Sheikh Suhaimi's sons' intellectual outlook exhibited a pragmatic synergy between the best of both Sufism and modernist-inclined reformism. While it was true that they were exposed to Salafi ideas whilst in Egypt (Ni'mah 1998, p. 12), where Ataullah eventually passed away, the extent to which they imbibed the thoughts of Muhammad Abduh and Rashid Rida is uncertain. Their father, in any case, had early on shown reformist inclinations as a Sufi master.

Returning to Singapore in 1914, Fadhlullah's politico-intellectual activities were a thorn in the flesh of the British colonial authorities. He therefore relocated his movements to his father's homeland in Java, where he cooperated with leaders of the Sarekat Islam and Persyarikatan Muhammadiyah reform movements to ignite Indonesian nationalism, and founded a Madrasah Al-Ma'arif — prototype of its namesake in Singapore a few years later — in his parents' birthplace of Wonosobo (Ni'mah 1998, pp. 13–18). He was compelled to come back to Singapore in 1925 to assume leadership of the now leaderless Aurad Muhammadiah congregation. Fadhlullah brought the congregation to new heights by establishing the Madrasah Al-Ma'arif in Tanjung Katong in 1936.[21] The Madrasah has since been at the forefront of reformism in Islamic education in Singapore (cf. AlJunied and Dayang Istiaisyah 2005, p. 253). It pioneered many advancements hitherto thought of as unfeasible or even Islamically improper, for example the formal education for Muslim girls in Singapore, the introduction of English language as a subject along with Arabic and Malay, the introduction of a modern curriculum which included modern subjects often associated with secular education, the making of Sundays instead of Fridays as public holidays, the streamlining of term holidays with those of public schools, and the levying of school fees — unprecedented for madrasa education (*Inspiration* 1987, pp. 21–25; Ni'mah 1998, pp. 40–45, 61–73). Today, Madrasah Al-Ma'arif has emerged as one of the most competitive madrasas in Singapore, preparing students for primary, secondary and pre-university levels of education with similar accreditation criteria as in public schools (Alatas 2005, p. 217). Its management committee is still helmed by Sheikh Suhaimi's descendants and members of the Aurad Muhammadiah congregation, who also form a large part of the teaching staff. Students are not necessarily inducted into the Aurad Muhammadiah, but some of the Aurad's auxiliary practices are incorporated into their daily activities.[22]

As a public figure, Fadhlullah was instrumental in the founding of many other Islamic educational and missionary institutions in Singapore and

Malaya (Ni'mah 1998, pp. 20–23). He staunchly advocated the unification of religious administrations of Malay states and chaired a conference of *ulama* which was instrumental towards the eventual formation of PAS (Safie Ibrahim 1981, pp. 17–18; Mohd Fadli 2008). Politically, however, he remained neutral and was concerned solely with Islamic reforms and advancement of Malay-Muslim society. Hence, while maintaining a traditionalist stance in line with his Sufi background,[23] he was not fearful of proposing radical changes so that Malay-Muslims were not left behind in the modern world, and therefore supported *ijtihad* (independent reasoning) (Ni'mah 1998, pp. 83–89). His penchant for reforms was continued, though to a lesser extent, by his son Muhammad Taha Suhaimi, who led the Aurad Muhammadiah congregation in Singapore until his death in 1999. Muhammad Taha's social contributions included being the first President of the Shariah Court of Singapore and the first preacher to recite sermons in English during Friday prayers. It was during his time that the Islamic and Martial Arts Association of Singapore (PERIPENSIS: Persatuan Islam dan Pencak Silat Singapura) was established, originally to legalize the gathering of *Pencak Sunda* players but which later evolved into a business entity with indissoluble connections to Madrasah Al-Ma'arif (Muhammad Taha Suhaimi 1996, pp. 35, 38–39). Among PERIPENSIS's activities are annual visits to Sheikh Suhaimi's ancestral shrines in Wonosobo (cf. Darlan Zaini 2003, p. 198).[24]

Having a few works on comparative religion to his credit, Muhammad Taha is however better remembered for putting the Aurad Muhammadiah and related messianic convictions into public limelight, especially after the Darul Arqam controversy in Malaysia had purportedly brought the congregation in Singapore, as practitioners of the same *tariqah*, into disrepute as well. In any case, Muhammad Taha was responsible for rewriting the Malay-language biography of his grandfather, Sheikh Suhaimi, based on but not constricted by the original Javanese version authored by Fadhlullah Suhaimi. It is to this allegedly adulterated version that Ustaz Ashaari Muhammad, leader of Darul Arqam, is said to have relied on in declaring his conditional belief in Sheikh Suhaimi as the awaited Al-Mahdi (Ashaari Muhammad 1986, pp. 95, 178, 184; Farahwahida 2007, pp. 69–75). Since Muhammad Taha's demise, leadership of the Aurad Muhammadiah congregation and PERIPENSIS has passed on to his son, Muhammad Hafiz (Darlan Zaini 2003, pp. 149–53). According to Muhammad Hafiz, the number of Aurad Muhammadiah followers has dramatically risen in recent times, coming from all over Southeast Asia.[25] One estimate puts the congregation's membership at 18,000 (Darlan Zaini 2003, p. 199). This does not include those who took the Aurad's *bay'ah* (pledge of allegiance) at the hands of Ashaari Muhammad and his appointed *khalifahs* in Malaysia.

THE AURAD MUHAMMADIAH CONGREGATION IN MALAYSIA: DARUL ARQAM, RUFAQA' CORPORATION, GLOBAL IKHWAN

Darul Arqam was founded as a study group by religious teacher Ashaari Muhammad (b. 1937) in 1968. Born to Aurad Muhammadiah–practising parents in Kampung Pilin, Rembau, Negeri Sembilan, Ashaari was initiated into the order at the age of sixteen by his maternal uncle, Lebai Ibrahim, who studied directly under Sheikh Suhaimi and whose sister was married to Kiyai Syahid, Sheikh Suhaimi's *khalifah* who purportedly gave Ashaari his name (Ashaari Muhammad 1986, pp. 13, 78; Khadijah Aam 2006, pp. 24–26; Farahwahida 2007, p. 47). Ashaari's spiritual genealogy has since been an issue of contention within the larger congregation, some of whom, including Muhammad Taha Suhaimi (1994, p. 36), head of the Singapore chapter, have questioned whether Lebai Ibrahim was legitimately authorized to hand down the Aurad. Ashaari calls Lebai Ibrahim a *"khalifah*'s representative" who wields such authority, and whose name is mentioned by Ashaari's followers in the genealogical recitation prior to commencing reading the Aurad (Ashaari Muhammad 1986, p. 79; Khadijah Aam 2006, p. 49). In any case, Ashaari was said to have renewed his *bay'ah* from Muhammad Abdullah, son of Muhammad Khairullah and head of the Kelang chapter, whom Ashaari had befriended during his studies at Maahad Hishamuddin, Kelang, in the mid-1950s (Ashaari Muhammad 1986, p. 14; Khadijah Aam 2006, pp. 68–69). This latter version, however, added messianic insinuations missing from the original version plus *Pencak Sunda*, allegedly authorized by Sheikh Suhaimi himself via spiritual communication (Muhammad Taha Suhaimi 1994, pp. 36–37; Farahwahida 2007, pp. 48–49).

Disillusioned with PAS, in whose programmes he actively participated in 1958–68, Ashaari resolved to mould his Sufi thought and practice into a distinctive movement of its own, prodded by a spiritual vision he had had of Sheikh Suhaimi (Khadijah Aam 2006, p. 97). He had never shirked reading the Aurad throughout his years in PAS, but the practice was not imposed on Darul Arqam members from the outset. Darul Arqam's early programmes, then conducted within the vicinity of a house in the Kuala Lumpur suburb of Dato' Keramat, were mainly Sufi-style self-purification (*tazkiyah al-nafs*) efforts, involving intensive spiritual training and material sacrifice, conducted in congregation to nurture brotherly love. The Aurad Muhammadiah was communicated privately within the expanding congregation. In 1973, Ashaari and his disciples pioneered Darul Arqam's first model Islamic village on a five-acre piece of land in Sungai Penchala, a remote area twenty kilometres from its birthplace of Kuala Lumpur. Later, this new settlement served not only as a retreat towards personal salvation, but also as a base for socio-welfare services, economic projects, educational initiatives and medical facilities (Mohd. Rom 1992, pp. 192–96). Taking into account his Sufi worldview and eschatological beliefs, Ashaari's penchant for transnational Islam was far from surprising.[26] In the 1970s, Ashaari once led his followers in joining a Jamaat Tabligh[27] *dakwah* tour to Singapore in a learning mission (Abdul Rahman 2007, p. 6). But he then apparently decided that trade served as a more subtle and effective medium of *dakwah*. As demand for Darul Arqam products, services and publications rose in the 1980s, Darul Arqam swiftly expanded overseas, especially in Southeast Asia (Darul Arqam 1989, pp. 2–18, 26–102).

In the 1980s, Darul Arqam was effectively transformed into Malaysia's Aurad Muhammadiah congregation, eclipsing the Kelang chapter which had been left leaderless after Muhammad Abdullah's death. Ashaari's leadership was given huge credibility by the testament of one Kiyai Mahmud, who claimed to have heard in person Sheikh Suhaimi's prediction of the weakening of the Aurad Muhammadiah congregation following his occultation, only to be revived by a man named "Ashaari Muhammad" (Ashaari Muhammad 1989, p. 84; Khadijah Aam 2006, pp. 2–3, 27–28). In 1986, Ashaari successfully overcame internal rebellions to his leadership instigated by his deputy Mokhtar Yaakob, an Al-Azhar University-trained practitioner of the Nashbandiyyah *tariqah*, who had questioned the theological validity of the Aurad (Amirullah Mohamed 1994, pp. 56–62). The withdrawal of Mokhtar and his loyalists effectively made Darul Arqam a single-*tariqah* organization. By 1988, Ashaari was bold enough to proclaim the emergence of Darul Arqam as the Aurad Muhammadiah congregation. Internal and external pressure, exerted by the Islamic Affairs Division of the Prime Minister's Department, had the opposite effect of stiffening Ashaari's messianic convictions; not only did he openly predict Sheikh Suhaimi as the awaited Al-Mahdi, but he also specified seven years from 1988 as the upper time-limit for Al-Mahdi's appearance (Ashaari Muhammad 1988, pp. xi, 257; Farahwahida 2007, pp. 46, 78, 147–50). Having encountered problems with the religious authorities which had banned some of his treatises, Ashaari travelled abroad for extensive periods,[28] incidentally steering Darul Arqam into the realm of transnational economics, and later, politics.

By 1993, Darul Arqam had established thirty-seven communication centres in sixteen countries.[29] Through trade missions, Darul Arqam set up investment subsidiaries abroad; for example, a restaurant and a tailor shop in Tashkent, Uzbekistan, an animal husbandry project in Ningxia, China, catering and perfume industries in Pakistan, a double-decker executive tourist coach in Thailand, a food packaging and distribution company in Singapore, and in Indonesia, a private school in Pekan Baru, soya sauce and shoe factories in Tasek Malaya, and a hairdressing saloon, groceries and tailor shops in Jakarta and Medan (Darul Arqam 1993*a*, p. 198; Muhammad Syukri Salleh 1994, p. 44). On 7–8 August 1993, in Chiengmai, Thailand, in conjunction with Darul Arqam's First International Economic Conference, Ashaari Muhammad inaugurated the formation of the conglomerate Al-Arqam Group of Companies (AGC), which consisted of twenty-two business sections. Darul Arqam declared that profits made by economic projects under the AGC would be "channelled towards social welfare service, financing…. Darul Arqam's da'wa [*sic*] missions around the globe" (Darul Arqam 1993*a*, supplement; 1993*c*). Such accomplishments were invariably attributed to the *barakah* (blessings) of the Aurad Muhammadiah, which was by then practised by "practically every member of Darul Arqam" (Ashaari Muhammad 1989, p. 203; Darul Arqam 1993*a*, pp. 101–3).

Darul Arqam's well-documented transnational economic forays were by then becoming a source of attraction to Malay-Muslim business elites, whose National Economic Policy (NEP)-driven[30] economic advancements had hitherto been very much assisted by the extent of their connectedness to the United Malays National Organisation (UMNO) — the Malay ruling party. Darul Arqam had reportedly tapped into influential elements within UMNO, thus potentially drawing Malay middle-class support away from the party (Nagata 2004, p. 110; Ahmad Fauzi 2004, p. 172).[31] The government became increasingly alarmed by the rising tempo of Ashaari's critique of the political establishment, authored from his peripatetic overseas bases but produced by Darul Arqam's home-grown publication arm (cf. Ashaari

Muhammad 1991, Chapters 5–6; 1993*a*, Chapters 9, 14; 1993*b*, Chapter 14; 1993*c*, pp. 88–92). He supplemented rebuke of politicians at home with open advice to foreign Muslim leaders (Darul Arqam 1993*b*, pp. 29–34). Large sections of Darul Arqam publications were increasingly devoted to colourful coverage of overseas visits by Darul Arqam delegations and their meetings with journalists, intellectuals, government officials and political leaders from other countries (Nagata 2004, p. 109; cf. Ashaari Muhammad 1993*d*, pp. 43–52, 69–84).

In mid-1994, the Islamic authorities publicly accused Darul Arqam of operating a 313-men "suicide squad" codenamed the "Badr army" based in Bangkok in its desire to take over power in Malaysia through militant means.[32] Attacks against Darul Arqam thereafter proceeded to focus on the disputable theological legitimacy of the Aurad Muhammadiah and Ashaari's prediction of Sheikh Suhaimi as the awaited Al-Mahdi. A national ban was imposed on Darul Arqam following a NFC-issued fatwa pronouncing its heterodoxy in August 1994 (Ahmad Fauzi 2005). In a transnational war of words, the Malaysian Government sought for cooperation from neighbouring governments to help suppress Darul Arqam.[33] Darul Arqam retaliated by breaking its media silence and vocally speaking out to foreign journalists.[34] From his shifting overseas sanctuaries, Ashaari lambasted the "corrupt" Malaysian Government and boldly challenged the Prime Minister to a "popularity" referendum.[35] The government's high-handedness culminated in the forcible extradition of Ashaari and a group of followers from Thailand in a joint Malaysia-Thai security operation and his subsequent detention under the ISA. Malaysia's rough treatment of Darul Arqam and the Thai Government's complicity in what was widely dubbed as Malaysia's "political game" was roundly reproved by the Thai press, academics, human rights organizations and Muslim groups (Ahmad Fauzi 2006*a*, pp. 103–5). Subjugated by inter-movement rivalry and a predominantly Wahhabi-Salafi ideological outlook, fellow Islamists in Malaysia generally welcomed the proscription although some cautioned against the government's overbearing treatment of Darul Arqam followers (Ahmad Fauzi 2003).

There were varied responses from Southeast Asian Muslim communities.[36] Singapore's Acting Community Development Minister-cum-Minister of Muslim Affairs, Abdullah Tarmugi, while backing cooperative efforts between the Singapore and Malaysian governments in checking Darul Arqam's influence in Singapore, insisted that action was taken on internal security grounds, not on the "basis of faith." A fatwa issued by MUIS, advising Singaporean Muslims against joining Darul Arqam or practising its teachings, was motivated by social rather than religious reasons. Darul Arqam was frowned upon, for example, for allegedly condoning polygamous marriages with lax requirements, thus contributing to family break-ups. But MUIS refrained from implicating the Aurad Muhammadiah (Mohd Taha Suhaimi 1994, p. 78, S.M.M. 1994). In his capacity as PERIPENSIS chairman, Muhammad Taha Suhaimi challenged MUIS to a debate to "further the cause of truth" and dubbed the Malaysian Government's actions against Darul Arqam as "politics". He did not, however, endorse Darul Arqam either. Dissociating PERIPENSIS from Darul Arqam, he defended the authenticity of the Aurad Muhammadiah but expressed reservations for the way Ashaari had spread the Aurad and his millenarian beliefs.[37] In Indonesia, despite the Fatwa Commission of the national Indonesian Ulama Council (MUI: Majlis Ulama Indonesia) coming out with an edict whose wording amounted to condemnation of Darul Arqam as "deviant", the MUI presidency never promulgated it (Meuleman 1996, p. 58). MUI, and for that matter the Malaysian Government, was dealt a severe blow when Indonesia's largest Islamic organization, the Nahdlatul Ulama (NU: Renaissance of Ulama) — long-time patron of many Indonesian *tariqas* (Howell 2001, pp. 709, 714), issued an opposite fatwa which exonerated Darul Arqam's teachings from charges of deviationism. Until the official disbandment of Darul Arqam, following its detained leaders' forced repentance in front of NFC members on 20 October 1994, Brunei was the only other country to have banned it on a national basis.

In April 1997, organizational remobilization of former Darul Arqam members took place with the founding of Rufaqa' Corporation, a private limited company with Ashaari as its executive chairman and Bandar Country Homes, Rawang, a non-Muslim majority township in Selangor where he had been residing under restrictive residence regulations since 1994, as its headquarters. Starting with the manufacturing and distribution of herbal-based health products, Rufaqa', capitalizing on Darul Arqam's well-known enterprise spirit and close-knit networks, quickly captured national and regional markets.[38] Rufaqa' successfully spread its wings to Southeast Asia and the Middle East through Zumala Group, a joint-venture company between Rufaqa' Corporation and Hawariyun Group of Companies, a conglomerate owned and operated by Darul Arqam members in Indonesia.[39] The phenomenally successful Hawariyun, subsequently renamed Rufaqa' Indonesia, continued to produce books promoting Ashaari's messianic thought for distribution in Malaysia (cf. Atta' 1998;

Taufik Mustafa 2002; Effendi and Puspita 2003). It was hardly surprising that in July 2000, the media flashed out headlines declaring Jakarta to be the new hub of activities in reviving Darul Arqam, prompting instant denials by Rufaqa' officials that it was linked in any way to the defunct Darul Arqam.[40] In truth, Darul Arqam's adeptness in applying transnational Islam to encompass the economic and socio-welfare domains rendered the national ban on Darul Arqam practically ineffectual. During the immediate post-banning period, material and morale backing from its overseas chapters, all of whom pledged loyalty to their Malaysian leadership, was instrumental in perpetuating Darul Arqam's nexuses and ideals in spite of the stringent surveillance on its former members in Malaysia. Darul Arqam's strategic use of transnational marriages between its Malaysian and non-Malaysian nationals, facilitated by the wide practice of polygamy among its leadership (Nagata 2004, p. 108),[41] compelled the immigration authorities to allow the strategic flow of former Darul Arqam members across international borders.

On 25 October 2004, his health acutely deteriorating after ten years of virtual house arrest, Ashaari was finally released from restricted residence requirements while in Labuan, an island off the coast of Sabah state in Borneo, where he had been banished since February 2002. Freedom was granted by the administration of Abdullah Ahmad Badawi, who had replaced Dr Mahathir Mohamad as Prime Minister on 31 October 2003. In the early phases of Abdullah Badawi's era, Rufaqa' appeared to have arrived at some kind of peaceful modus vivendi with the government.[42] By then, benefiting from transnational economies of scale, Rufaqa' had burgeoned into a conglomerate boasting 500 to 700 outlets specializing in small and medium size industries, covering operations in Malaysia, Indonesia, Singapore, Thailand, Australia, Jordan, Syria, Egypt, France and Germany (Asaari Mohamad 2005, pp. 62, 68; Khadijah Aam 2006, pp. 14, 126, 235). In fact, so diversified and successful were Ashaari's post–Darul Arqam business ventures that he was rumoured to have reached millionaire status (Muhammad Syukri Salleh 2003, pp. 142–48, 156–58).[43]

Nonetheless, when some in Rufaqa' attempted to publicly resurrect transnational millenarianism ala Darul Arqam, it was deemed to have overstepped political boundaries. Khadijah Aam's[44] controversial hagiography, *Abuya Ashaari Muhammad Pemimpin Paling Ajaib di Zamannya*, was auspiciously launched in October 2006 in Phuket, Thailand, after Malaysian authorities blocked attempts to launch it in Kuala Lumpur.[45]

What was politically sensitive in the book were assertions that Ashaari was worthy of the titles of *mujaddid* (reformer) and *Al Fata At Tamimi* (youth of Bani Tamim), who, according to prophetic Hadiths, would act as the precursor to Al-Mahdi (Khadijah Aam 2006, p. 222).[46] Malaysia was portrayed as the hub of a global movement which would climax with the handing over of political power from *Al Fata At Tamimi* to Al-Mahdi, ushering in inexorable Islamization which would encompass Muslim reclamation of Jerusalem (Khadijah Aam 2006, pp. 212–17). In August 2007, claims of Ashaari's destined role as the anointed *Al Fata At Tamimi* were published and freely distributed to influential sections of the Malaysian public, including government ministries.[47] Minister in the Prime Minister's Department in charge of Islamic affairs, Abdullah Md. Zin, reacted to the renewed messianic pretensions by sternly warning Rufaqa' to give up its quest to establish a "Bani Tamim government".[48] As soon as states passed fatwas pronouncing Rufaqa"s heterodoxy, religious officials sporadically raided business premises of Rufaqa', confiscated paraphernalia which allegedly proved ominous intentions to revive Darul Arqam, arrested alleged ring-leaders and charged them in the Syariah Court for subscribing to and propagating false Islamic doctrines.[49]

Under sustained pressure in 2006–7, Rufaqa' directors de-registered the company and established an apparently new entity called Global Ikhwan, the new appellation reflecting the integral role that transnational Islam occupies in the restructured entity.[50] Global Ikhwan exploits economic connections that had been pioneered by Darul Arqam and bequeathed to Rufaqa'. Global Ikhwan hardly differs from Rufaqa' in its concerns, activities and relational networks. But living up to its name, Global Ikhwan has intensified links with the Middle East, as can be seen by the constant stream of foreign businessmen and Sufis, with whom Ashaari cemented linkages during his travels abroad in 1988–94, who pay courtesy calls on the bedridden Ashaari upon visiting Malaysia. For example, in July 2008, two Sudani sheikhs from the Tijaniyyah order visited Malaysia and pledged allegiance to Ashaari. Other Sufi sheikhs who continue to send delegations of followers to pay courtesy visits to him are Sheikh Abdul Nasser Al-Husaini Al-Shadhili of Saudi Arabia, Sheikh Abdussalam Harras of Morocco, Sheikh Abdul Khalid Al-Syammar of Jordan, Sheikh Abd al-Jabbar of Iraq, Sheikh Mahmud Effendi and Sheikh Haydar Bas, both of Turkey.[51] These are also sheikhs whom Ashaari has named as forming part of Al-Mahdi's Cabinet (Farahwahida 2007, pp. 203–8). Such

Sufi networks thrive on similar doctrinal worldviews as conditioned by a curious synergy between Sufism, messianism and economic activism (Ahmad Fauzi 1999). Transnational contacts built on such fundamentals are not uncommonly concretized by the erection of transnational familial nexuses, as when Ashaari took Dr Mahmood Marglani, right-hand man of Sheikh Abdul Nasser Al-Husaini Al-Shadhili and a practitioner of the Shadhili *tariqah*, to be his son-in-law in 2006 (Khadijah Aam 2006, pp. 148–49). Dr Mahmood has been actively deciphering Shadhili Sufi ideas for a Malay-Muslim audience and maintains an Arabic-language website on the "science of *tasawwuf*" (Marglani 2006, pp. 52–87).[52] Global Ikhwan's credentials as a modern transnational Sufi movement are underscored by its global Internet connectivity; in disseminating Ashaari's ideas and the Aurad Muhammadiah, Global Ikhwan maintains websites and weblogs in Malay, Indonesian, English, Thai, Japanese and French.[53]

CONCLUDING ANALYSIS

In spite of persistent pressure exerted by the state and intermittent glitches in the form of internal dissension, the Aurad Muhammadiah congregation continues to expand throughout Southeast Asia, with its strongest representation in Malaysia and Singapore. Malaysia-based Darul Arqam and its organizational successors are an acknowledged force within regional Islamism,[54] maintaining self-sufficient communities around Indonesia,[55] and a healthy following in Thailand with its greatest presence in Phuket.[56] In parts of southern Thailand, both Jamaat Tabligh and Darul Arqam, in their competition for influence, have been "successful in attracting considerable numbers of new followers", thus providing a bulwark against Wahhabi-Salafi influences (Horstmann 2006, pp. 73–74). In Singapore, Rufaqa' maintains a peaceful if sometimes edgy coexistence with its co-*tariqah* brethren from PERIPENSIS. However, lest it be misconstrued as a security threat to a Singaporean state increasingly wary of terrorism, it officially denies linkages with Malaysia.[57] Lately though, Global Ikhwan Singapore has actively ventured into commercial enterprises in the neighbouring Malaysian state of Johor, whose government has voiced uneasiness over the presence of active elements seeking to bring back "practices of Aurad Muhammadiah" in Johor.[58] Such transnational business connections are innately built into Sufi networks, and hence are very difficult for governments of modern nation-states to monitor on the basis of religion alone. For example, in fact, in the 1980s and 1990s, Madrasah Al-Ma'arif's cook admits getting her raw food supplies from Darul Arqam in Johor (*Al-Istiqamah* 1997, p. 43).

The Aurad Muhammadiah congregation's proclivity in maintaining economic independence within a non-Muslim dominated economy has meant that there is low possibility of their cooptation into and dependence on a state-managed polity which often exploits distribution of economic resources to the ruling elites' political advantage. The attempt by some state governments in Malaysia to regulate *tariqahs* by requiring their registration belies an inability to understand the fluid and dynamic nature of Sufism,[59] which has flourished in history on the basis of informal and popular approaches of presenting Islam, as opposed to the rigid and uncompromisingly legalistic methods adopted by Islamists of Wahhabi-Salafi orientation. If they persistently utilize confrontational methods suited to neutralize political challenges within the context of nation-states, governments will continue to encounter problems handling transnational Sufi movements whose worldview is predicated on *ummatic* rather than national loyalty. It is hardly surprising therefore, that since 1994, when the fatwa pronouncing the Aurad Muhammadiah as deviant was gazetted, news of attempts to revive the Aurad keep emerging from time to time.[60] In reality, it never disappeared, and its continual existence is not conditional upon the survival of any organization affiliated to it. In its practitioners' transnational worldview, the fatwa was religiously irrelevant as it exhibited a Wahhabi-Salafi bias and was politically motivated (Ashaari Muhammad 1989, pp. 41–44; Ahmad Fauzi 2000). Moreover, no similar fatwa prohibiting the Aurad has been passed in other countries. Scholarly works condemning the Aurad have invariably adopted Wahhabi-Salafi theological positions (cf. Mohd Lazim Lawee 2004; Farahwahida 2007), rendering them less than credible in the eyes of Sufis. As long as the practice of a *tariqah* survives, a congregation will naturally come about sooner or later, clustering around a master, irrespective of whether he is legitimately or illegitimately appointed, in the eyes of the state. In fact, Aurad Muhammadiah practitioners have congregated around two separate chapters in Malaysia and Singapore. It is effectively a *tariqah* of two congregations rather than one. Its followers around the world pledge *bay'ah* to either one, discounting other splinter groups whose following, however, is negligible.

For the Aurad Muhammadiah congregation, transnationalism goes hand in hand with modernity. Instead of displaying a reactionary approach to religion, the congregation manifests reformist credentials which startled traditionalists of the time. Benefits of modernization have never been discarded for the purpose of *dakwah*, as comprehensively demonstrated in Darul Arqam's calibrated yet relatively liberal use of musical instruments and female troupes in its hugely popular cultural performances. In fact, since most of the top Islamic bands in Malaysia have a history of involvement in the Aurad Muhammadiah congregation,[61] it would not be exaggerating to attribute the emergence and rapid development of the *nasyid* (Islamic song) industry in Southeast Asia to the Aurad's entertainment-friendly culture, as powerfully ingrained in its melodic chantings (cf. Tan 2007; Barendregt 2008). Such creativity, while being frowned upon by legalist Muslims, captures the heritage of Sufi missionaries of olden days when Islamizing a Southeast Asia deeply steeped in indigenous traditions. Clearly, the Aurad Muhammadiah congregation does not perceive Sufism as an otherworldly discipline to be pursued for its innate spiritual value and mystical experiences. It ingeniously integrates the saintly aspects of traditional Sufism with an intellectual pragmatism akin to modernist-reformism. As such, it would be apposite to categorize the Aurad Muhammadiah as a neo-Sufi order comparable to the reform-oriented North African Tijaniyyah and Ahmadiyyah-Idrisiyyah orders founded by Ahmad ibn Muhammad al-Tijani (d. 1815) and Ahmad ibn Idris (d. 1837) respectively (van Bruinessen 1994). Undergirding this classification is the similar claim advanced by all three of the orders' founders: that they received the *tariqahs* directly from the Prophet Muhammad, thus short-circuiting their spiritual genealogies (cf. Tomai 1989; Wan Mohd. Saghir 2000, p. 125). Needless to say, such a claim elicited opposition from not only modernists but also traditional Sufis. Eschatological predictions advanced by Ashaari Muhammad in Malaysia have relied as well on such direct audience with the Prophet and Sheikh Suhaimi,[62] as have comparable messianic claims once projected by the virulently anti-colonial Sufi, Muhammad ibn Ahmad al-Mahdi (d. 1885) of the Sudan (Hopwood 1971, p. 154).

Notes

1. Autonomous or non-state Islamism is understood here as sustained political action designed to establish Islam as the supreme creed of a polity and social order, separately conceived and executed from any form of state-driven Islamization.
2. For a recent discussion of the concept of the *ummah* from both Islamic and Western perspectives, and its link with the politics of transnational Islam, see

Akram (2007). For a contrasting view — that the concept of an *ummah*, as far as contemporary Islamic politics is concerned, is nothing but a myth — see, for example, Syed Zainal Abedin (1994, p. 31).

3. The term "Sufism" is used here interchangeably with the Arabic *tasawwuf* to denote the branch of the Islamic doctrine associated with spirituality, mysticism and expression of Islam's inner (*batin*) essence and esoteric aspects as distinguished from its external (*lahir*) and exoteric aspects, as manifested in absolute love of the Divine. Practitioners of Sufism are called "Sufis", irrespective of whether they have attained or not their goal of the ultimate knowledge of God termed as *ma'rifah* (gnosis) and *haqiqah* (the truth), which are preceded by the elementary stages of shariah (revealed law) and *tariqah* (the way — often used to denote a particular Sufi order or brotherhood). For a detailed explanation on the origins and usage of this jargon by classical and contemporary scholars, see Anjum (2006, pp. 222–31).

4. The term "Wahhabi" is derived from the name of the reformer of Nejd in present-day Saudi Arabia, Muhammad ibn Abd al-Wahhab (d. 1787), who struck a strategic alliance with a local warrior, Muhammad ibn Saud (d. 1765), in 1744. Tribal and religious forces thus united and expanded territories under their control to lay the basis for the first Saudi state. Wahhabi puritanism strove to cleanse the Islamic faith from *shirk* (idolatry) and *bid'ah* (innovations), which were almost always blamed on the undesirable influence of Sufism, and equated heretical Muslims with belligerent infidels. Defeated by the Ottomans in 1819, the Saudi-Wahhabi alliance re-emerged in the 1820s, but was defeated again in 1891. The third Saudi state could be dated back to 1926, when Abd al-Aziz ibn Saud and pro-Wahhabi warriors called the Ikhwan conquered the Hijaz. In 1932, the Kingdom of Saudi Arabia was proclaimed. Essentially a Saudi-derived reincarnation of Wahhabism, Salafism is the contemporary movement to reassert the ideals of the pious generations of the first 300 years following the death of the Prophet Muhammad in 632. Salafism traces its roots to the reform movement initiated by the Egyptian modernist Muhammad Abduh (d. 1905) and his disciple Rashid Rida (d. 1935). Being strict monotheists, Salafis deplore the use of the term "Wahhabi" to describe their movement of reform. In any case, the employment of such terms is highly contestable, but they have increasingly gained currency in Western analyses of Islamism. See Husain (1995, pp. 46–48, 100–2).

5. Despite the "Indian origin" theory having been discredited within Southeast Asian scholarly circles, some contemporary Western academics have adamantly clung to the supposed relationship between Sufism and Southeast Asian Islam's tolerance of Indianized folk accretions; see for example the interview with Mark Mancall, Professor of Southeast Asian history at Stanford University, in Shih (2002, p. 114).

6. On pre–World War II Malay nationalism, see Soenarno (1960, pp. 8–10) and Roff (1967, pp. 87–89).
7. Dr Burhanuddin, who died shortly after regaining his political freedom in 1969, strenuously denied these allegations of treachery, as recently exposed by his private notes during solitary confinement in 1965. See Burhanuddin Al-Helmy (2006), where the official document outlining the alleged plot is appended in pages 122–51.
8. Unless specifically indicated, material in this section is drawn from available biographies of the founder of the Aurad Muhammadiah order: Mohd Taha Suhaimi (1990; 1994) and Darlan Zaini (2003, pp. 110–53).
9. See endnote 3 above.
10. Nawawi al-Bantani (d. 1897) was a prolific author of over a hundred works in Arabic, de facto head of the *Jawi* community in Mecca and member of the Qadiriyyah-Naqshbandiyyah order. His writings displayed a reformist tinge, in a way anticipating the arrival of salafism. Abdullah az-Zawawi (d. 1924) was once Muftis of Mecca, Riau-Lingga and Pontianak in Kalimantan, and a khalifah of the Nashbandiyyah Muzhariyyah order. See further Johns (1993, pp. 57–58) and Wan Mohd. Saghir (2000, pp. 49, 69).
11. Sheikh Suhaimi's father, mother and wife died in Singapore and were buried at the Bukit Wakaff cemetery in Grange Road, near Orchard Road, donated by the famous Aljunied family which pioneered Arab settlements in Raffles' Singapore. The graves have since been relocated to Pusara Aman Muslim cemetery at the Choa Chu Kang cemetery complex. There is little doubt that Sheikh Suhaimi's extended family's pedigree facilitated their entrée into the then thriving community of Arab Muslims in Singapore, noted for their entrepreneurial acumen and philanthropic deeds which transcended ethnic and religious boundaries.
12. The site is now occupied by Parkview Square, just opposite Raffles Hospital, North Bridge Road.
13. Literally, madrasa simply means "religious school". Technically, the madrasa system is a progression from the traditional *pondok* system, after the adoption of organizational reforms such as the incorporation of modern methods of education, modern and vocational subjects, business training and examination-based assessment and promotion. The proliferation of madrasas in early twentieth century Malaya reflected the rising influence of Egypt vis-à-vis Mecca as the primary centre for higher Islamic education in the Middle East. While the establishment of madrasas have usually been associated with modernist *ulama*, Sufi-oriented traditionalists operated distinctive madrasas of their own; see Andaya and Andaya (1982, pp. 233–35), Khoo (1987, pp. 185–89) and Md. Sidin and Mohammad Redzuan (2000, pp. 28–34).
14. Some of the *kitabs* are in fact still in use in the curriculum of Malaysia's religious schools; see for example *Risalah At-Tauhid: Pindaan*, originally drafted in 1907

by Abdul Ghani Yahya and Umar Yusuf (1952), which cites Sheikh Suhaimi's opinions on the attributes of God on pages 19–20. The book, widely used in Johor, is in *jawi* (Malay language written in Arabic script).

15. A Persian scholar widely recognized as *Hujjatul Islam* (Proof of Islam) within Islamic scholarly circles, Abu Hamid Al-Ghazali (d. 1111), is credited with reconciling Sufism with orthodoxy at times of flux when the faith was under onslaught from unfiltered incorporation of Greek philosophical elements, and thus elevating sufism "to an exalted position within the fold of 'orthodoxy'" (Al-Attas 1963, p. 9). In the Malay-Indonesian world, Al-Ghazali's Sufi doctrines had held sway by the eighteenth century, as shown by the widely taught translations and commentaries of his works done by such Malay scholars as Abd al-Rauf Al-Sinkli (d. 1693) and Abd al-Samad al-Palembani (d. 1788) of the Shattariyyah and Sammaniyyah orders respectively. Salafism, however, is inclined to deplore Al-Ghazali's seemingly "excessive inclination towards *tasawwuf*", to quote Maududi (1981, p. 64).

16. In Singapore, such a claim was advanced, for example, by former President of the Shariah Court, Haji Abu Bakar Hashim, but denied by his predecessor, Muhammad Taha Suhaimi, who was also Sheikh Suhaimi's eldest grandson-cum-biographer. See "Aurad Muhammadiah bukan berasal dari Sheikh Suhaimi", *Berita Harian* (Singapore), 17 September 1994, and Muhammad Taha Suhaimi (1994, pp. 1–29).

17. The epistles which together form the Aurad Muhammadiah can be read both in their Arabic originals and English translations at <http://kawansejati.ee.itb.ac.id/book/export/html/18564> (accessed 6 December 2008) — being an English translation of Chapter 17 of the controversial book by Khadijah Aam, *Abuya Ashaari Muhammad Pemimpin Paling Ajaib di Zamannya* (Abuya Ashaari Muhammad the Most Miraculous Leader of His Time) (2006). The chapter's webpage in the book's official website <http://skygate.wordpress.com/2007/07/09/aurad-muhammadiah/> does not spell out the Arabic wording of the verses (accessed 6 December 2008).

18. *Tahlil* refers to religious chantings which testify that Allah is the One and Only God. The *tahlil* of Aurad Muhammadiah, however, supplements these chantings with rhythmic melodies sung in unison under a congregational leader (cf. Ashaari Muhammad 1986, pp. 119–27).

19. *Maulid* refers to melodic renditions of episodes from Prophet Muhammad's life, virtues of which were extolled by Sheikh Suhaimi (As Suhaimi 1995, pp. 2–24). But because Sheikh Suhaimi himself did not write any such biography, Aurad Muhammadiah followers are exhorted to recite the version produced by Jaafar al-Barzanji (d. 1177), a preacher at the Prophet's mosque in Medina.

20. Information related to the author by Abdul Jabbar Suhaimi, son of Muhammad Khairullah Suhaimi and a respected elder among the Aurad Muhammadiah congregation in Kelang (Penang, June 2007).

21. Originally located at the present site of the Church of Our Lady at Tanjung Katong Road, in 1940 the Madrasa moved to Ipoh Lane on land donated by benefactor Sheikh Omar Bamadhaj. Rundown infrastructure forced the Madrasah to be temporarily relocated to Burn Road in 1985. Its new building at Ipoh Lane was reconstructed with financial help from the Islamic Development Bank (IDB), Jeddah, and was inaugurated in 1987 amidst much publicity. However, the Madrasa had to move yet again in 2007 to Lorong 39 Geylang to give way for development plans. See the souvenir books, *Inspiration: Madrasah Al-Ma'arif Al-Islamiah 50th Anniversay and Official Opening Ceremony 15th March 1987* (1987), *Al-Istiqamah: Madrasah Al-Ma'arif Al-Islamiah Sempena ulangtahun Al-Maarif yang ke 60* (1997) and *Madrasah Al-Ma'arif Al-Islamiah Yearbook* (2005).
22. Information gathered from Abdul Khalid Aliman, member of Madrasah Al-Ma'arif's management committee, during the present author's visit to the madrasa (Singapore, September 2007). Mohd. Taha Suhaimi (1996, pp. 35, 37) admitted that Madrasah Al-Ma'arif was the centre of *Pencak Sunda* activities and the venue for the congregational recitation of the Aurad Muhammadiah on Thursday nights.
23. For example, he vigorously defended orthodox Sunni theology against the onslaught of *Wahhabi-Salafism*, as represented for instance by fellow Singaporean, Ahmad Hassan Bandung (d. 1958), leading to a famous debate between them in Penang in 1953. Ahmad Hassan had earlier replaced Fadhlullah as teacher at Madrasah Al-Sagoff, Jalan Sultan; see Mohd Fadli (2008) and "Hassan Bandung: Gigih Tegakkan Syiar Islam" <http://demimasa2.tripod.com/tokoh1> (accessed 6 December 2008).
24. Such tours are now conducted as part of business operations of PERPENSIS subsidiary Murad Travel — Muhammad Murad being a son of Muhammad Taha Suhaimi — based in Tanjong Katong Complex. See pictures of such visits in Mohd Taha Suhaimi (1994, 1996). It is believed that the upkeep of those shrines is financially maintained by PERIPENSIS members.
25. Information obtained from Sheikh Muhammad Hafiz Suhaimi in a conversation with him at a PERIPENSIS function (Singapore, June 2007).
26. Sufism and Islamic eschatology are arguably inherently conducive to an *ummatic* (pertaining to the *ummah*, see endnote 2 above) type of transnationalism; see Ernst (2003) and Akram (2007, pp. 409–10).
27. A transnational missionary movement initiated by Maulana Mohammad Ilyas (d. 1944) among poverty-stricken Muslims in Mewat, India, in the 1920–30s and arriving in Southeast Asia in the early 1950s.
28. Accounts of some of Ashaari's post-1988 expeditions have been recorded by followers and accompanying journalists; see for example Mohd Sayuti Omar (1989), Mohamad Mahir Saidi (1992) and Abdul Halim Abbas (1992).

29. They are Indonesia, Singapore, Thailand, the Philippines, Brunei, Jordan, Egypt, Pakistan, Uzbekistan, the United States, the United Kingdom, France, Germany, Japan, Australia and New Zealand; see Darul Arqam (1993, pp. 41, 181).
30. An affirmative action policy enunciated in the Second Malaysian Plan (1971) following the May 1969 racial riots, designed to uplift the economic status of bumiputra. Officially though, it sought to pursue the goals of poverty eradication and economic restructuring so as to eliminate the identification of race with economic function.
31. "Radical Chic: Islamic Fringe Groups Gain Influence among the Elite", *Far Eastern Economic Review*, 26 May 1994. In the report "A Ban against the 'Messiah'", *Time*, 22 August 1994, a Malay professional is quoted as praising Darul Arqam for having "managed to put into practice what Muslim business should be" without having "to lie or cheat".
32. "Al-Arqam tubuh pasukan bersenjata", *Utusan Malaysia*, 13 June 1994; "Kerajaan pandang serius Tentera Badar", *Utusan Malaysia*, 14 June 1994.
33. Michael Richardson, "Malaysia and Neighbors to Curb Sects", *International Herald Tribune*, 5 August 1994.
34. Cf. "Target: Al-Arqam", *Asiaweek*, 20 July 1994; "Malaysia: Holier than them", *The Economist*, 23 July 1994; "Mahathir opens high-risk crusade against Islamic sect", *Financial Times*, 6–7 August 1994; "Malaysian sect pays penalty of politics", *The Times*, 8 August 1994; "In the Name of Security", *Far Eastern Economic Review*, 11 August 1994; "Premier vs. Preacher", *Far Eastern Economic Review*, 15 September 1994; "Cult of the Father", *Newsweek*, 19 September 1994; "Sect tries to turn away Malaysia PM's wrath", *The Independent*, 4 October 1994; "A Malay Plot? Or Just a Well-Meaning Commune", *The New York Times*, 10 October 1994.
35. "Al-Arqam Leader Hits Out at 'Corrupt' Kuala Lumpur", *The Nation*, 2 July 1994; "Ashaari: Let's hold referendum", *New Sunday Times*, 24 July 1994.
36. Unless specifically indicated, material in this paragraph draws from Ahmad Fauzi (2006a, pp. 99–106, 111). See also Meuleman (2005, p. 37).
37. "Peripensis tiada kaitan dengan Arqam Malaysia", *Berita Harian* (Singapore), 29 October 1994.
38. "Rufaqa' terkenal di seberang laut", *Utusan Malaysia*, 8 February 2000; Joceline Tan, "Former Al-Arqam Redefines Itself: The Movement Now Concentrates on Its Business Enterprises", *New Sunday Times*, 30 April 2000; "Setelah abuya memilih tobat", *Gatra*, nos. 2–3, 6 December 2003.
39. "Zumala bentuk 14 rangkaian runcit", *Utusan Malaysia*, 3 February 2000; "Zumala tinjau pasaran baru di Asia Barat", *Berita Harian* (Kuala Lumpur), 4 February 2000.

40. "Jakarta markas Arqam", *Utusan Malaysia*, 13 July 2000; "Rufaqa' nafi ada kaitan Al-Arqam", *Berita Harian* (Kuala Lumpur), 13 July 2000.
41. The practice of transnational marriages was among Darul Arqam's transnational empire-building strategy, see Abdul Halim Abbas (1991, pp. 30–33). On how Darul Arqam utilized polygamy towards accomplishing wider aims of the Islamic struggle, see Khadijah Aam (1990). Ustaz Ashaari himself, with four wives and close to forty children, has sons-cum-daughters-in-law who are nationals of Indonesia, Thailand and Saudi Arabia.
42. For example, Ashaari praised Abdullah's Islam Hadhari scheme as a "novel and prudent formula.... to make Malaysia and Malaysians truly excellent, glorious and distinctive", resembling his own vision of an Islamic society; see Abu Dzar (2005, p. xi).
43. Cf. "Banned Al-Arqam Cult Thriving under Business Umbrella", *Straits Times*, 9 February 2002.
44. Khadijah Aam (b. 1953) was Ashaari's second wife who together with her husband had been detained under ISA-related restrictive regulations from 1994 to 2004.
45. See <http://skygate.wordpress.com> for contents of the English version of the book (accessed 6 December 2008).
46. For a summary of Ashaari's messianic thought, see Ahmad Fauzi (2006*b*).
47. The claims were made in a book authored by Ashaari's son Mohd Nizamuddin Ashaari and his wife Laila Ahmad, entitled *Abuya Hj Ashaari Muhammad adalah Putera Bani Tamim* (2007). Its contents can be surfed at <http://puterabanitamim.blogspot.com> (accessed 6 December 2008).
48 "Lupakan hasrat tubuh kerajaan Bani Tamim", *Utusan Malaysia*, 17 October 2007.
49. "Banned Al-Arqam Tries to Get Members, 100 Arrested", *New Sunday Times*, 26 November 2006; "JAIS tahan dua pemimpin Rufaqa'", *Berita Harian* (Kuala Lumpur), 2 December 2006; "JAIS tetap dakwa 16 pengikut Rufaqa", *Berita Harian* (Kuala Lumpur), 5 January 2007; "JAIS serbu markas Rufaqa, tiga ditahan", *Berita Harian* (Kuala Lumpur), 2 March 2007; "51 pengikut cuba hidup semula al-Arqam ditahan", *Berita Harian* (Kuala Lumpur), 3 November 2007; "Ashaari's Wife in Syariah Court", *The Star*, 6 November 2007; "43 pengikut al-Arqam dihadap ke mahkamah", *Berita Harian* (Kuala Lumpur), 23 February 2008.
50. "Rufaqa tukar nama kepada Global Ikhwan", *Utusan Malaysia*, 6 July 2008. Global Ikhwan's corporate website can be accessed at <http://globalikhwan.net/index.php> (accessed 6 December 2008).
51. See "Kunjungan Syeikh Thariqat Tijaniyah dari Sudan" and "Kawan-kawan Abuya", http://dijanjikan.wordpress.com (accessed 6 December 2008).
52. See <http://sufiology.com> (accessed 6 December 2008).

53. See respectively, <http://ikhwantoday.com>, <http://ikhwan-daily.com>, <http://ikhwan-insight.com, <http://islampattana.pantown.com>, <http://ikhwankenshiki.wordpress.com and <http://aimedieu.wordpress.com> (all accessed 6 December 2008).
54. See for instance the designation of Darul Arqam as "scriptural-conservative and fundamentalist" among major Islamist groups in contemporary Southeast Asia in the typology offered by Rabasa (2004, pp. 376–77).
55. See for example the special reports "Mimpi Bandar dari Sentul", *Gatra*, 21 May 2004, and "Warna-warni Bandar Rufaqa'", *Gatra*, 9 November 2004, available at <http://www.gatra.com/2004-05-21/artikel.php?id=37396> and <http://www.gatra.com/2004-11-17/artikel.php?id=48890> respectively (both accessed 6 December 2008).
56. See for example the coverage "Sekolah 'Ajaib' untuk Keluarga Poligami", *Pikiran Rakyat* (Bandung), 9 November 2006, available at <http://www.mail-archive.com/media-dakwah@yahoogroups.com/msg09658.html> (accessed 6 December 2008).
57. "Pengarah: Rufaqa' S'pura tiada kaitan dengan Malaysia", *Berita Harian* (Singapore), 16 December 2006.
58. "Deviant Islamic Groups Still Active", *The Star*, 5 December 2008.
59. Cf. "Amalan tarekat di Perak perlu didaftarkan di JAIP", *Utusan Malaysia*, 14 November 2007.
60. For the latest reports, see "Ajaran Aurad Muhammadiah cuba dihidup" and "Mekanisme baru perlu dicari tangani al-Arqam" (editorial), *Berita Harian* (Kuala Lumpur), 25 November 2008.
61. "Raihan, Rabbani dan Hijaz berakar umbi dari al-Arqam..." <http://www.malaysiakini.com/news/93319> (accessed 6 December 2008).
62. See the transcript of Ashaari's purported dialogue with Sheikh Suhaimi in Amirullah Mohamed (1994, pp. 109–11) and his latest claim to have communicated with the Prophet in his open letter to UMNO, "Pilihan raya Tuhanlah yang menang" in Global Ikhwan (2008, p. 11).

References

Abaza, Mona. "More on the Shifting Worlds of Islam. The Middle East and Southeast Asia: A Troubled Relationship?" *Muslim World* 97, no. 3 (2007): 419–36.
Abdul Ghani Yahya and Umar Yusuf. *Risalah At-Tauhid: Pindaan* (in *jawi* script). Johor Baharu: Al-Ahmadiah Press, 1952.
Abdul Halim Abbas, Ustaz. *Meruntuh Berhala di Tiongkok*, Kuala Lumpur: Penerbitan Hikmah, 1992.
Abdul Halim Abbas, Ustaz Haji. *Panduan Membina Empayar Islam di Asia Tenggara*, Kuala Lumpur: Penerbitan Hikmah, 1991.

Abdul Rahman Haji Abdullah. *Gerakan Islam Tradisional di Malaysia: Sejarah Pemikiran Jama'at Tabligh dan Darul Arqam*. Shah Alam: Karisma Publications, 2007.
Abu Dzar, Mejar (B). *Islam Hadhari Menurut Ust. Hj Ashaari Muhammad*, Rawang: Penerbitan Minda Ikhwan, 2005.
Ahmad Fauzi Abdul Hamid. "New Trends of Islamic Resurgence in Contemporary Malaysia: Sufi-Revivalism, Messianism and Economic Activism". *Studia Islamika* 6, no. 3 (1999): 1–74.
———. "Political Dimensions of Religious Conflict in Malaysia: State Response to an Islamic Movement". *Indonesia and the Malay World* 28, no. 80 (2000): 32–65.
———. "The Impact of Sufism on Muslims in Pre-colonial Malaysia: An Overview of Interpretations". *Islamic Studies* 41, no. 3 (2002): 467–93.
———. "Inter-Movement Tension among Resurgent Muslims in Malaysia: Response to the State Clampdown on Darul Arqam in 1994". *Asian Studies Review* 27, no. 3 (2003): 361–87.
———. "Islam, Weberism and Economic Development: An Adjunct to Nagata's Outline of the Arqam Experiment in Malaysia (1969–1994)". *Global Change, Peace and Security* 16, no. 2 (2004): 169–79.
———. "The Banning of Darul Arqam in Malaysia". *Review of Indonesian and Malaysian Affairs* 39, no. 1 (2005): 87–128.
———. "Southeast Asian Response to the Clampdown on the Darul Arqam Movement in Malaysia, 1994–2000". *Islamic Studies* 45, no. 1 (2006a): 83–119.
———. "The Futuristic Thought of Ustaz Ashaari Muhammad of Malaysia". In *The Blackwell Companion to Contemporary Islamic Thought*, edited by Ibrahim M. Abu-Rabi'. Malden: Blackwell, 2006b.
Akram, Ejaz. "*Muslim Ummah* and its Link with Transnational Muslim Politics". *Islamic Studies* 46, no. 3 (2007): 381–415.
Al-Attas, Syed Naguib. *Some Aspects of Sufism as Understood and Practised Among the Malays*, edited by Shirle Gordon. Singapore: Malaysian Sociological Research Institute, 1963.
Al-Attas, Syed Naguib. *Preliminary Statement on a General Theory of the Islamization of the Malay-Indonesian Archipelago*. Kuala Lumpur: Dewan Bahasa dan Pustaka, 1969.
Al-Istiqamah: Madrasah Al-Ma'arif Al-Islamiah Sempena ulangtahun Al-Maarif yang ke 60. Singapore: Madrasah Al-Ma'arif Al-Islamiah, 1997.
Alatas, Syed Farid. "Notes on Various Theories Regarding the Islamization of the Malay Archipelago". *Muslim World* 75, nos. 3–4 (1985): 162–75.
———. "Madrasah Education in Singapore: Continuities and Breaks with Tradition". In *Islamic Education in South and Southeast Asia (Diversity, Problems and Strategy)*, by S. Yunanto et al. Jakarta: The Ridep Institute and Friedrich Ebert Stiftung, 2005.
AlJunied, Syed Muhd Khairudin and Dayang Istiaisyah Hussin. "Estranged from the Ideal Past: Historical Evolution of Madrassahs in Singapore". *Journal of Muslim Minority Affairs* 25, no. 2 (2005): 249–60.

Amirullah Mohamed. *Antara Halal dan Haram Al-Arqam: Jawapan Kepada Ashaari*. Kuala Lumpur: Rodatra, 1994.

Andaya, Barbara Watson and Leonard Y. Andaya. *A History of Malaysia*. London: Macmillan, 1982.

Anjum, Tanvir. "Sufism in History and its Relationship with Power". *Islamic Studies* 45, no. 2 (2006): 221–68.

Arnold, T.W. *The Preaching of Islam: A History of the Propagation of the Muslim Faith*. Aligarh, 1896. Reprinted Lahore: Sh. Muhammad Ashraf, 1961.

As Suhaimi, Muhammad bin Abdullah. *Hembusan Kasturi: Maulid Nabi SAW*, translated by Muhammad Taha Suhaimi, Singapore: PERIPENSIS, 1995.

Asaari Mohamad, Ustaz Hj. *Nasihat Buatmu Bekas Kawan-kawan Lamaku dalam Arqam*, Rawang: Penerbitan Minda Ikhwan, 2005.

Ashaari Muhammad, Ustaz. *Keadilan Menurut Islam*, Kuala Lumpur: Penerbitan Hikmah, 1993*a*.

Ashaari Muhammad, Abuya Syeikh Imam. *Meninjau Sistem Pemerintahan Islam*, Kuala Lumpur: Penerbitan Hikmah, 1993*b*.

———. *Assalamualaikum Dato' Seri PM: Surat-surat Kepada Perdana Menteri Malaysia (jawapan kepada tuduhan-tuduhan)*. Kuala Lumpur: Penerbitan Abuya, 1993*c*.

———. *Presiden Soeharto Ikut Jadual Allah*, Kuala Lumpur: Penerbitan Abuya, 1993*d*.

Ashaari Muhammad, Ustaz. *Berhati-hati Membuat Tuduhan*, Kuala Lumpur: Penerangan Al Arqam, 1989.

———. *Perang Teluk: Islam Akan Kembali Gemilang*, Kuala Lumpur: Jabatan Syeikhul Arqam, 1991.

Ashaari Muhammad, Ustaz Hj. *Aurad Muhammadiah Pegangan Darul Arqam: Sekaligus Menjawab Tuduhan*. Kuala Lumpur: Penerangan Al Arqam, 1986.

Atta', Abu Muhammad. *Pemuda Bani Tamim Perintis Jalan Imam Mahdi Penyelamat*, Jakarta: Penerbit Giliran Timur, 1998.

Barendregt, Bart. "The Sound of Islam: Southeast Asian Boy Bands". *ISIM Review* 22 (2008): 24–25.

Burhanuddin Al Helmy *Hari-hari Aku Dizalimi*. Batu Caves: PAS Gombak, 2006.

Darlan Zaini. *A Study of Sufism: The Aurad Muhammadiah Order in Singapore*. Unpublished manuscript, 2003.

Darul Arqam. *Al Arqam Dalam Media Antarabangsa*. Kuala Lumpur: Penerangan Al Arqam, 1989.

———. *25 Tahun Perjuangan Abuya Syeikh Imam Ashaari Muhammad At Tamimi: 25 Years of the Struggle of Abuya Syeikh Imam Ashaari Muhammad At Tamimi*. Kuala Lumpur: Penerbitan Abuya, 1993*a*.

———. *Message from the East*. Kuala Lumpur: Bahagian Pengeluaran Minda Sheikhul Arqam, 1993*b*.

———. *AGC: Al-Arqam Group of Companies*. Kuala Lumpur: Al-Arqam Information Department, 1993*c*.

Effendi, Ing. Abdurrahman R. and Ing. Gina Puspita. *Abuya Syeikh Imam Ashaari*

Muhammad At Tamimi: Diakah Mujaddid di Kurun Ini? Jakarta: Penerbit Giliran Timur, 2003.

Ernst, Carl W. "Sufism, Islam, and Globalization in the Contemporary World: Methodological Reflections on a Changing Field of Study", 2003 <http://www.unc.edu/~cernst/articles/global.doc> (accessed 3 December 2008).

Farahwahida Mohd Yusof. *Al-Arqam dan Ajaran Aurad Muhammadiah: Satu Penilaian*, Skudai: Penerbit Universiti Teknologi Malaysia, 2007.

Fatimi, S.Q. *Islam Comes to Malaysia*, edited by Shirle Gordon. Singapore: Malaysian Sociological Research Institute, 1963.

Funston, N.J. *Malay Politics in Malaysia: A Study of the United Malays National Organisation and Party Islam*. Kuala Lumpur: Heinemann, 1980.

Global Ikhwan. *Buletin Global Ikhwan Zon Tengah* 1. Rawang: Penerbitan Minda Ikhwan, 2008.

Hopwood, Derek. "A Pattern of Revival Movements in Islam?" *Islamic Quarterly* 15, no. 4 (1971): 149–58.

Horstmann, Alexander. "The Revitalization of Islam in Southeast Asia: The Cases of Darul Arqam and Jemaat Tabligh". *Studia Islamika* 13, no. 1 (2006): 67–91.

Howell, Julia Day. "Sufism and the Indonesian Islamic Revival". *Journal of Asian Studies* 60, no. 3 (2001): 701–29.

Husain, Mir Zohair *Global Islamic Politics*. New York: HarperCollins, 1995.

Inspiration: Madrasah Al-Ma'arif Al-Islamiah 50th Anniversary and Official Opening Ceremony 15th March 1987. Singapore: Madrasah Al-Ma'arif Al-Islamiah, 1987.

Johns, Anthony H. "Islamization in Southeast Asia: Reflections and Reconsiderations with Special reference to the Role of Sufism". *Southeast Asian Studies* 31, no. 1 (1993): 43–61.

Kamarudin Jaffar *Dr. Burhanuddin Al Helmy: Politik Melayu dan Islam*. Kuala Lumpur: Yayasan Anda, 1980.

Khadijah Aam. Ustazah. *Manisnya Madu*. Kuala Lumpur: Jabatan Syeikhul Arqam, 1990.

———. *Abuya Ashaari Muhammad Pemimpin Paling Ajaib di Zamannya*, Rawang: Penerbitan Minda Ikhwan, 2006.

Khoo Kay Kim. "Malay Society 1874–1920s". *Journal of Southeast Asian Studies* 5, no. 2 (1974): 179–98.

Kostiner, Joseph. "The Impact of Hadrami Emigrants in the East Indies on Islamic Modernism and Social Change in the Hadramawt during the 20th Century". In *Islam in Asia (vol. 2: Southeast and East Asia)* edited by Raphael Israeli and Anthony H. Johns. Jerusalem: Magnes, 1984.

Linehan, W. "A History of Pahang". *Journal of the Malayan Branch of the Royal Asiatic Society* 14, part 2, 1936.

Madrasah Al-Ma'arif Al-Islamiah Yearbook. Singapore: Madrasah Al-Ma'arif Al-Islamiah, 2005.

Marglani, Mahmood. *Murid Yang Sejati: Hubungan Murid Dengan Guru Pada Pandangan Tasawwuf*. Rawang: Penerbitan Minda Ikhwan, 2006.
Maududi, S.A.A. *A Short History of the Revivalist Movement in Islam*, fifth edition, translated by Al-Ash'ari. Lahore: Islamic Publications, 1981.
Md. Sidin Ahmad Ishak and Mohammad Redzuan Othman. *The Malays in the Middle East: With a Bibliography of Malay Printed Works Published in the Middle East*. Kuala Lumpur: University of Malaya Press, 2000.
Meuleman, Johan H. "The History of Islam in Southeast Asia: Some Questions and Debates". In *Islam in Southeast Asia: Political, Social and Strategic Challenges for the 21st Century* edited by K.S. Nathan and Mohammad Hashim Kamali. Singapore: Institute of Southeast Asian Studies, 2005.
Meuleman, Johan Hendrik. "Reactions and Attitudes towards the Darul Arqam Movement in Southeast Asia". *Studia Islamika* 3, no. 1 (1996): 43–78.
Mohamad Mahir Saidi. *Memoir Ilham dari Gua Nabi Ibrahim: Singkapan Minda Ustaz Ashaari Muhammad dalam Musafir*. Kuala Lumpur: Penerbitan Hikmah, 1992.
Mohd. Fadli Ghani. "Sheikh Fadhlullah As-Suhaimi: Ulama Pengasas PAS". *Harakah* (*Fikrah* section), 1–15 May 2008.
Mohd. Lazim Lawee. *Penyelewengan Jemaah Al-Arqam dan Usaha Pemurniannya*. Bangi: Penerbit Universiti Kebangsaan Malaysia, 2004.
Mohd. Nizamuddin Ashaari and Laila Ahmad. *Abuya Hj Ashaari Muhammad adalah Putera Bani Tamim*. Kuala Lumpur: Penerbitan Mata Angin, 2007.
Mohd. Rom Al Hodri. "Liku-liku Perjuangan Awal". In *Politik Dakwah*, edited by Ustaz Yusuf Din. Kuala Lumpur: Syeikh, 1992.
Mohd. Sayuti Omar. *Rahsia Ustaz Ashaari Terbongkar di Luar Negeri*. Kuala Lumpur: Prodescom, 1989.
Mohd. Taha Suhaimi, Ustadz Hj. *Sejarah Hidup Syeikh Muhammad Suhaimi*. Singapore: PERIPENSIS, 1990.
———. *Jawapan Bagi Tuduhan-tuduhan Terhadap Sejarah Hidup Syeikh Muhammad As-Suhaimi dan Aurad Muhammadiah*. Singapore: PERIPENSIS, 1994.
———. *Sejarah Pencak Suhaimi (Sunda)*. Singapore: PERIPENSIS, 1996.
Muhammad Labib Ahmad. *Siapa Imam Mahdi?* Singapore: Pustaka Nasional, 1980.
Muhammad Syukri Salleh. "An Ethical Approach to Development: The Arqam Philosophy and Achievements". *Humanomics* 10, no. 1 (1994): 25–60.
———. "Perniagaan Gerakan-gerakan Islam di Malaysia". *Pemikir*, no. 31 (2003): 133–85.
Muhammad Taha Suhaimi, Ustaz Hj. *Tiada Tengkarah Mengenai Aurad Muhammadiah: Jawapan-jawapan kepada Ustaz Hj. Abu Bakar Hashim, Harun Din, Hj. Ashaari Muhammad, Majlis Pusat Islam, Kuala Lumpur*. Singapore: PERIPENSIS, 1994.
Nagata, Judith. "Alternative Models of Islamic Governance in Southeast Asia:

Neo-Sufism and the Arqam Experiment in Malaysia". *Global Change, Peace and Security* 16, no. 2 (2004): 99–114.

Naoki, Soda. *Melayu Raya and Malaysia: Exploring Greater Malay Concepts in Malaya.* Kyoto: The Setsutaro Kobayashi Memorial Fund.

Ni'mah bt Hj Ismail Umar. *Fadhlullah Suhaimi.* Ulu Kelang: Progressive 1998.

Osman Bakar. "Sufism in the Malay-Indonesian World". In *Islamic Spirituality: Manifestations* edited by Seyyed Hossein Nasr. London: SCM, 1991.

Rabasa, Angel M. "Southeast Asia: Moderate Tradition and Radical Challenge". In *The Muslim World after 9/11* by Rabasa et al. Santa Monica: RAND Corporation, 2004.

Reid, Anthony. "Nineteenth Century Pan-Islam in Indonesia and Malaysia". *Journal of Asian Studies* 26, 1967.

Roff, William R. *The Origins of Malay Nationalism.* New Haven: Yale University Press, 1967.

———. "Indonesian and Malay Students in Cairo in the 1920s". *Indonesia* 9 (1970), pp. 73–87.

S.M.M. "Fatwa Yang Berbeza Mengenai Aurad Muhammadiah". In *Tiada Tengkarah Mengenai Aurad Muhammadiah: Jawapan-jawapan kepada Ustaz Hj. Abu Bakar Hashim, Prof. Dr. Harun Din, Hj. Ashaari Muhammad, Majlis Pusat Islam* by Ustaz Hj. Muhammad Taha Suhaimi. Kuala Lumpur: PERIPENSIS, 1994.

Safie bin Ibrahim. *The Islamic Party of Malaysia: Its Formative Stages and Ideology.* Pasir Puteh: Nuawi bin Ismail, 1981.

Soenarno, Radin. "Malay Nationalism, 1896–1941". *Journal of Southeast Asian History* 1, no. 1 (1960): 1–33.

Syed Zainal Abedin. "Minority Crises: Majority Options". In *Islam, Muslims and the Modern State: Case-studies of Muslims in Thirteen Countries*, edited by Hussin Mutalib and Taj ul-Islam Hashmi New York: St. Martin's Press, 1994.

Tan Sooi Beng. "Singing Islamic Modernity: Recreating *Nasyid* in Malaysia". *Kyoto Review of Southeast Asia* 8, 2007 <http://kyotoreviewsea.org/tansooibeng.htm> (accessed 6 December 2008).

Taufik Mustafa. *Pengembaraan Sang Duta Halilintar Muhammad Jundullah: Sebuah Model Memperjuangkan Kasih Sayang.* Jakarta: Penerbit Giliran Timur, 2002.

Tomai, Husain Hasan. *Masalah Berjumpa Rasulullah Ketika Jaga Selepas Wafatnya*, translated by Ustaz Anuar Hj. Abdul Rahman. Kota Bharu: Pustaka Aman, 1989.

van Bruinessen, Martin. "Origins and Development of the Sufi Orders (tarekat) in Southeast Asia". *Studia Islamika* 1, no. 1 (1994): 1–23 <http://www.let.uu.nl/~Martin.vanBruinessen/personal/publications/Sufi%20orders%20in%20Indonesia.htm> (accessed 6 December 2008).

———. "Global and Local in Indonesian Islam". *Southeast Asian Studies* 37, no. 2 (1999): 158–75.

von der Mehden, Fred R. *Two Worlds of Islam: Interaction between Southeast Asia and the Middle East*, Gainesville: University Press of Florida, 1993.
Wan Mohd. Saghir Abdullah, Hj. *Penyebaran Thariqat-thariqat Shufiyah Mu'tabarah di Dunia Melayu*, Kuala Lumpur: Khazanah Fathaniyah, 2000.

PART III
Malaysia

5

LEGAL-BUREAUCRATIC ISLAM IN MALAYSIA: HOMOGENIZING AND RING-FENCING THE MUSLIM SUBJECT

Maznah Mohamad

In Malaysia, the contestation over what was to be the correct and authoritative Islam came to an end sometime in the mid-1990s. The United Malays National Organization (UMNO), the ruling Malay party, had battled the Pan-Malaysian Islamic Party (Parti Islam SeMalaysia, PAS), its rival Malay-Muslim party, over the latter's version of Islam and won. The vanquished also included many other competing non-state Islamic movements. For example, the most powerful Islamic youth movement, the Angkatan Belia Islam Malaysia (ABIM) was inducted into the mainstream with the co-optation of Anwar Ibrahim into UMNO in 1982 (Hussin Mutalib 1993). The Sufi-inspired communal sect, the Darul Arqam, was no less influential than ABIM in attracting scores of followers. But in 1994 it was banned on charges of being a deviant stream of Islam (by the state fatwa councils)[1] and a security threat by the government (Ahmad Fauzi 2003).

When the dust of some of the above episodes had settled, UMNO seemed quite set in having the upper hand in determining the Islamic agenda or at least controlling it from falling into the hands of other contenders. By the late 1990s the UMNO-led state paved a trail for Islam to be absorbed into lawmaking and policymaking and institutionalized it as a wide-reaching state apparatus (Norhashimah 1996; Hamayotsu 2003). While UMNO as a political party was more concerned that this exercise would continue to give the party its legitimacy over the Malay-Muslim constituency, there were other dynamics which were created as well.

UMNO's calculated and expedient manoeuvre had led it to institutionalize Islam within the legal-bureaucratic sphere, exclusive only to the Muslim citizenry, and did not purportedly touch the affairs of non-Muslims.[2] But rather than reform the party internally to imbibe Islamic values and ideologies, UMNO, as the major party within the ruling coalition, preferred to Islamize state institutions, rather than change the party to reflect this new orientation. However, once Islam has been institutionalized within the state apparatus, it would inevitably be the bureaucracy which will inhabit this powerful space. While this class may be patronized by UMNO, state Islamization had become such a successful symbol of UMNO's legitimacy that it would be difficult to suppress the growing influence of this bureaucratic authority even if some of its stances went against UMNO's own image of Islamic moderation. I would also view the process of lawmaking among this class as a form of governance technology which is invoked as a "racial rule, promoting racial categorization and racial identification" (Goldberg 2002, p. 142), or in the Malaysian case, to create a non-ambivalent Muslim subject which would be the object of the law. At the same time, this would also delimit the role of the others (non-Muslims) who would be immune to the law's jurisdiction, but by that token also excluded from having any right to a discursive engagement with the process. One could use Michael Peletz's concept of the "Islamic modern" on these bureaucrats, for although they invoke traditional principles, they could actually only reinvent these traditions through the adoption of a modern and legal-bureaucratic system (Peletz 2002). Ernest Gellner's observation of a "High Culture reverence for law" replacing the trend of a "Low Culture cult of personality" may also be understood as the motivation behind lawmaking by statist Islam today (Gellner 1994, p. 26). The progression of Islam's folk status (Low Islam) into High Islam is seen in its imbibing of modernism, and making change and consolidating power through lawmaking.

The above dynamics indicate that there is an emerging new Islam in Malaysia, or what I would call legal-bureaucratic Islam. By Islamic bureaucratization I mean the multiplication of bureaucratic and legal institutions related to the administration of Islamic matters and the adjudication of Islamic religious laws through the Syariah Court system. Indications of a huge expansion of the Islamic legal-bureaucracy are evident in the growth of administrative departments, personnel and the deployment of resources used. Institution-building also corresponds to the increase in the number of new *syariah* laws legislated or administratively gazetted by the various bodies, from the office of the *Mufti* (where fatwa are issued), to the state assemblies. This is an Islam which has become highly centralized and authoritarian and led by a bureaucratic class, which is potentially becoming an added, defining force (next to civil society) in the assemblage of state-religion relations.

HOMOGENIZATION AND RING-FENCING

One of the most significant consequences of these trends of bureaucratization has been the *homogenization* of Islam and the *ring-fencing* of the Muslim subject. As Islam becomes more and more the purview of the state there is a tendency to subject the religion to an official and codified definition, hence the *homogenization*. On the other hand, *ring-fencing* involves delineating spheres of Islamic authority upon the juridical Muslim subject, the definition of which remains contestable, but coerced through strategies such as preventing the exit of Muslims (as in anti-apostasy laws) or even subjecting the civil rights of the Muslim citizen to the exclusive purview of the *syariah* rather than the stipulations of the national Constitution.

The bureaucratization of Islam thus adds new challenges to governance within a multi-religious nation-state, while also increasing the risk of alienating the non-Muslim constituency by having more Islam in the state.

POLITICAL ISLAM AND STATE-SOCIETY RELATIONS: FROM MARGINALIZATION TO EXPANSION

In order to understand the rise of bureaucratic Islam it would be useful to trace the emergence of this new Islam to some of its antecedents, namely the various phases of Islam as it engages with state and society. I identify at least four phases or waves of these engagements, namely:

1. Marginalization (from colonial to early independence, 1900–1960s): The phase whereby political Islam was at the margins and power bases were largely decentralized.
2. Contestation (1970s to the 1980s): A phase during which the state competed with Islamic civil society to win authority over Islam and define what Islam meant.
3. Centralization (1980s to the 1990s): In this phase the state was successful in capturing Islam by centralizing control over Islamic governance and institutions within the state bureaucracy.
4. Expansion (2000s till currently): It is during this phase that legal-bureaucratic Islamic institutions are multiplied, expanded and enhanced, and ultimately constituting a new challenge to civil institutions.

Marginalization (1900s to 1960s)

This first stage was characterized by a decentralized, marginalized political Islam, where Islamic propagation was limited to the level of the village, *pondok* schools (informal Islamic schools) and independently-run madrasas (learning centres) and neighbourhood locales or home-based circles. Malay political struggles during the colonial and early postcolonial period was more about an overt striving for Malay linguistic and economic-developmentalist rights, with Islam providing a spiritual and transcendental inspiration for the movement. Islam was important in so far as it constituted a part of the definition of what it meant to be Malay. But while Islam was central to this politicization of identity it was not the main pillar of Malay nationalist and developmentalist struggles. The other Islamic-based nationalist movements, with pan-Islamism as its basis, such as the Kaum Muda, had already been sidelined and replaced by nationalism-oriented Malay parties like UMNO and even PAS by the time the struggle for self-rule was taking place (Roff 1974; Ariffin Omar 1993). During PAS early years as a political party, it was striving for a Malay nationalism that was generally secular in that Islam's importance was as an identity marker and symbol for mobilization rather than as the basis for governance or lawmaking (Farish Noor 2004).

Contestation (1970s to 1980s)

This second stage saw the state waging a "war" with Islamic civil society to win control and authority over Islam. The revitalization of Political Islam during this post-nationalist period by non-statist actors can be seen as the direct and almost immediate outcome of the post-1969 state reinvention of itself. The iconic "May 1969 racial riots" had been used to justify the adoption of the New Economic Policy (NEP). But before this, Malay struggles for rights were vociferous about establishing Malay dominance through calls such as the adoption of Malay as the national language, conversion of national schools into Malay medium schools, opening up higher education for more Malay enrolment and restructuring the economy to create more Malay wealth. However, in one fell swoop the NEP seemed to have taken up all of these causes, leaving nothing behind for the array of Malay movements formed in the wake of the 1969 event to appropriate as their own. What was left, really, for Malay non-state activists, was the Islamic cause. The question of Malay economic underdevelopment seemed to have been resolved, or rather, pushed aside to make way for the other struggle, namely, Islam.

When Islam was revived as a cause, in the post-1969 period, the old Malay schism based on the dichotomy between rural Malays of "humble origins and inspired by Middle-Eastern Islamic modernism" and Malays of the "well-born, English-educated, highly anglicized" administrative and aristocratic class (Kessler 1980, p. 6) began to be modified. The new division emerging became one between "devout Muslims who have found and understood the totality of Islam as a way of life" against those who were the "secular Westernized Malays whose priorities lie with modernization and development" (Zainah Anwar 1987, p. 90). Class or the rural-urban divide had become less of a basis for differentiation among Malays. Religio-ideological cleavages were the new source of conflict among Malays as well as between state and non-state actors.

This stage was a much more aggressive period in which Islam's propagation had been extended to the urban centres and penetrated public institutions like schools and universities. The competition for interpretation of meanings, power and adherents was fought along ideological lines, such as whether the practice of Islam implied embracing the concept of Islamic statehood, or was to be limited to the infusion of Islamic values in society, or was to be radically detached from the state altogether, creating a self-sufficient Islamic utopia based on an alternative epistemological paradigm.

There was intense competition between state and civil society to capture the ultimate ground for religious authority and legitimacy. All of these social movements were ultimately in competition with the UMNO-led state. Various strategies were employed by the state to blunt the radical influence of these movements — from co-optation of their leaders (as in the case of Anwar Ibrahim who was courted into joining UMNO) to out-Islamizing the other party (through infusing more Islamic elements into the political system to counter PAS agenda for Islamization) to outright banning of the movement (as in the Darul Arqam case). The state ultimately won as it was able to fashion a statist Islam that would ensure UMNO's relevance, both for Muslims as well as for non-Muslims. For Muslims, the state as represented by UMNO acted as guardian and arbitrator of the "right" Islam. For non-Muslims UMNO held the unassailable position as guardian of Malaysia's ethnic democracy. UMNO was the defender of moderate, accommodating Islam, whose jurisdictional reach would be exclusive to and not exceed the Muslim domain.

Centralization (1980s to 1990s)

The centralization of Islamic institutions by the state marked the third stage of this engagement. It involved the mainstreaming of Islam itself, a phase in which Islam was to be integrated into governance and controlled at the federal level rather than left within the purview of semi-autonomous state governments. At this point, competition among Islamic groups had been reduced, differences had been levelled, and much of the movements' core ideologies had been appropriated by the state. There was a "mellowing of radicalism" and many of these movements such as ABIM, the Jemaah Islah Malaysia (JIM) and even PAS had begun to operate along the lines of "less conflict, more harmony, and systematic implementation of activity culminating in what appears to be a stronger and more peaceful Islam, defined, of course, by the state" (Muhammad Syukri Salleh 1999, p. 45). Islamic groups then evolved to become legitimate pressure groups or legally registered bodies, forming part of a legitimate Islamic civil society that would participate in reforms along procedural constitutional lines. From the late 1990s onwards, we would be more familiar with smaller and more urban-based non-governmental organizations such as the Muslim Professional Forum, the Muslim Lawyer's Association, the Confederation of Muslim Graduates of the Peninsula (GAMIS: Gabungan Mahasiswa Islam Semenanjung) or the coalition body calling itself the Allied Coordinating Committee of Islamic NGOs (ACCIN).[3] Many of the newer Islamic organizations are mosque-based or charitable bodies and do not have the same mobilizational power as the mass movements which grew up in the late 1970s and the 1980s. From another point of view, these new post-2000 Muslim civil society groups were actually offshoots of the previous more potent, anti-state Islamic movements. By this time, Islamization as instituted by the state had already become considerably more extensive. Norms, principles, policies and laws were all being redefined to reflect the new "Islamicized" state. Islam by now had been reduced to what can be seen as a "world-maintaining" process, and although its presence had been institutionalized, its dynamism as a "world-shaking" force had been doused (Billings and Scott 1994, p. 173). Statist Islam became the main definer of Malay religio-cultural identity and constituted the source of Malay normative ethics and morality. A sense of rising but stabilized Islamic piety was felt among Muslims who had by then occupied higher or middle-class ranks in society. The UMNO-led government was firmly in power while the NEP had reached its maximum or optimal reach with no public institutions left untouched by bumiputra/Malay dominance.

Expansion (From 2000s Onwards)

At the fourth stage, all aspects of life related to Islam had effectively been taken over by the state through the expansion of the bureaucracy, which oversaw all Islamic matters, and the strengthening of the Syariah Court as the supreme legal institution for Muslims. Far from adopting a traditionalist stance, the proponents of the *syariah* today are more pragmatic and even strategic at seizing the moment for asserting their power through the infrastructure of modern systems. Indeed the changes in the direction of Islamization through the *syariah* are actually legal modifications to laws and institutions, "suffused with melding, absorption, and sheer syncretism" (Horowitz 1994, p. 254). The *syariah* Islamists are well aware that Islamization should be implemented through constitutional procedures.

Adding to the strength of the Islamic administrative and legal bureaucracy is the rise of the Malay-Muslim middle class and an Islamic civil society. These civil society elements provided their own momentum to the shaping of a bigger Islamic agenda in society. Sporadic in terms of affiliation, these individuals and organizations constitute a ready-made reservoir of idealists and pragmatists that could be tapped for political mobilization. In this milieu of strong Islamic civil society and a swelling Muslim middle class, the Islamic politico-legal elites became confident about testing the strength of the *syariah*, particularly the extent of its jurisdiction. It made sense that they would coalesce around legislative instruments to further their cause because they were in actual fact modernists and had none of the illusions of previous groups such as the banned Darul Arqam which operated on the basis that Islam could be more genuinely activated through non-state, neo-Sufist, or millenarian communal movements detached from statist engagements (Ahmad Fauzi 1999).

EXPANSION, ELEVATION AND EMPOWERMENT OF LEGAL-BUREAUCRATIC ISLAM

Having sketched the transformation of Islamic politics above, I now trace four developments integral to the expansion of the Islamic legal-bureaucracy, namely:

1. The establishment of centralized control over Islam by the creation of federal institutions of Islamic development, which in effect circumvented constitutional provisions establishing Islam under the control of state governments and Malay rulers.
2. The restructuring, multiplication and proliferation of Islamic institutions at the state level to reflect the various arms and functions of Islamic governance, such as the creation of the Office of the Mufti, the Syariah Court system and the various administrative divisions to oversee Muslim matters.
3. The inclusion of more provisions, regulations and laws under *syariah* statutes
4. The "harmonization" of civil with *syariah* systems and laws, including the passing of civil legislations to accommodate Islamic principles.

I will discuss each of the above to illustrate this process of progressive state Islamization achieved through legal-bureaucratic expansion.

Creating Federal-Level Islamic Institutions

Over a span of twenty years in Malaysia the Islamization project concentrated on building and expanding the *syariah* legal system as a showcase of successful state promotion of Islam by UMNO. Although Islamic matters come under the jurisdiction of the state rather than federal government, the expansion of the *syariah* could not have happened if not for central control of the process. Centralization meant that the development of Islamic institutions could be coordinated as well as moderated and curbed (if need be) by the national leadership, specifically the Office of the Prime Minister. This gradual centralization of Islamic institutions occurred most intensively under the Mahathir government (1982–2004), starting from about the mid-1980s onwards. A central body, under the watchful eye of the Prime Minister, was tasked with the role of setting the pace for expanding the *syariah* legal system. This body was the Jabatan Kemajuan Islam Malaysia (JAKIM), or the Department for Islamic Development in Malaysia. JAKIM functions as the de facto Ministry of Islamic Affairs, since constitutionally a federal ministry cannot be created, as Islam is under the purview of state rather than federal government. It originally started as a secretariat in charge of Islamic matters under the Council of Rulers, a body representing the traditional rulers, constitutional monarchs of Malaysia. Later, this became a division responsible for Islamic affairs under the Prime Minister's Office. By 1 January 1997, it was elevated to a department under the Prime Minister's Office. A sprawling new complex called the Islamic Centre was also built to house this department. The function of JAKIM is largely advisory, and the coordination of Islamic activities. But it has much influence and power as it acts as the coordinating body for interstate development of Islam. It is provided with resources for training, education, research, and policy consultation on *syariah* and Islamic knowledge. Besides JAKIM, there were various other bodies and committees, empowered to specifically focus on *syariah* development. For example, to coordinate the *syariah* judicial process and running of courts, a federal body called the Department for the Development of Syariah Judiciary in Malaysia (Jabatan Kehakiman Syariah Malaysia, JKSM) was created. In tandem with this, a federal scheme known as the Common-Use Scheme of the Syariah Administrative Service (Skim Guna Sama Perkhidmatan Pegawai Syariah) was implemented. This facilitated the transfer of *syariah* judges between participating states, hence enhancing their promotional prospects within the *syariah* judiciary (Hamayotsu 2003, p. 62). Since the JKSM is a federal body, it could safely be deduced that emoluments and salaries would also have been paid out from the national treasury rather than from state funds.

    The proliferation of lawmaking institutions can also be said to be quite phenomenal. A Syariah Division was set up within the Attorney General's

Chambers. In 1988, yet another high-powered body was set up in the Prime Minister's Office, called the Syariah and Civil Technical Committee (Norhashimah 1996, p. 218). This is one of the most significant committees as it had prepared the draft laws of almost all of the new or revised *syariah* laws after the 1980s (ibid., pp. 218–19). One of the key persons who led this exercise of reforming the *syariah* institutions, including the drafting of new Islamic laws, was Professor Ahmad Ibrahim, who was formerly from Singapore and became the dean of the first Islamic Law Faculty at the International Islamic University. The groundwork for the Islamization of laws was laid out in publications such as Ahmad Ibrahim and Mahmud Saedon Awang Othman (1988). Hence the intellectual force also emanated from the centre. In a way, constitutional provisions were obviated if not violated by this control over Islamic institutions by the federal government rather than by semi-autonomous state governments. For example, with the establishment of the JKSM, the Syariah Court system was no longer just the domain of states and sultans but had become "nationalized". All of these federal government-funded institutions became the crucial elements or powerhouse of legal-bureaucratic Islam.

Proliferation and Multiplication of Islamic Institutions

At the semi-autonomous, state-level, Islamization of the bureaucracy was enhanced with the systematization of Islamic governance. Previously, the administration of Muslim matters, from case hearings to appeals, to the management of religious schools, all came under a single body, known as the State Islamic Religious department. The functions of these divisions often overlap. For example, the office of the *mufti* would conduct legal prosecution, supervise the running of religious schools, appoint the *kadi* (Islamic judges) to adjudicate in the lower courts, and provide Islamic guidance and teachings to the sultans. The *kadi* also have multiple functions, such as administering mosques as well as try claims of maintenance and settle matrimonial disputes (Abdullah Alwi 1996, pp. 126–219). From the 1980s onwards all these began to change. The different functions were streamlined, divided and elevated. The office of Islamic Religious Affairs evolved into three separate institutions, namely, the Syariah Courts, the office of the Mufti and the Islamic Religious Council. Today, they all have different functions and operate autonomously from one another. The Syariah Court system was expanded from what was considered a lower court (*Kadi's* court) into three levels — the Syariah Lower Court, the

Syariah High Court and the Syariah Appeals Court. The Office of the Mufti now primarily issues fatwa (religious edicts) that can be administratively gazetted as law (rather than be subjected to debates in the state assemblies) (Suwaid 2004, pp. 38–41).

What is most emphasized in this institution-building process is the elevation of the Syariah Courts. There are two ways in which this has been done. The first is to ensure that the civil court has no jurisdiction over any matters deemed to be under the jurisdiction of the Syariah Court. This means that any judgements made by the Syariah Court would not be overridden by the secular or civil courts, as in cases of appeals or in matters of constitutional importance, as was done previously. This was put into effect by the amendment to Article 121(1A) of the Federal Constitution.[4] The purpose of this amendment was to delineate the separate jurisdictions of the Syariah Court and the Civil Court, so as to subject Muslims and non-Muslims to different jurisdictions when it comes to various laws, both family and criminal as long as they apply differently. This clause of allowing only the Syariah Court to have jurisdiction has been persistently invoked in court judgments involving inter-religious applications, such that the civil court is limited in its power to decide on issues that have anything to do with Islam.

Another measure that elevates the Syariah Court is the revision of its powers to mete out punishment. Through the Muslim Court (Criminal Jurisdiction) Act 1965, the maximum penalty that the Syariah Court can impose is six months' imprisonment and a fine of RM1,000. In the 1980s, through pressures from the Islamic lobby, this act was amended with the passage of the Muslim Courts (Criminal Jurisdiction) Act 1984, which gives the Syariah Court powers to impose a punishment of imprisonment up to three years, a maximum fine of RM5,000 as well as six strokes of the whip (Norhashimah 1996, p. 213). Still, this enhancement of court powers was not considered sufficiently severe by the Islamic lobby, since according to scholars on Islamic writings/scriptures, the punishment for illicit sex (*zina*) is purportedly stoning till death, for drinking alcohol, a hundred strokes of the cane (Mahmood Zuhdi 2001, p. 179), and for apostasy, death (Mohd Izani 2005, p. 160).

More Laws under Syariah Statutes

Under British colonial administration there were a variety of laws which were applied to Muslims, but these mainly dealt with matrimonial matters and the administration of Muslim lands and inheritance. Even child custody, whether it be of Muslims or non-Muslims, was within the jurisdiction of the common law court (Abdul Hamid 2008, p. 4). The first effort at rationalizing these various Islamic laws (many of the enactments had the term "Muhammadan" attached to them, such as the Muhammadan Marriage Ordinance 1946, or the Muhammadan Converts [Property] Ordinance) was to have them all included under one legislation, such as the Administration of Muslim Law Enactment 1952, passed in the state of Selangor.

But from the 1980s onwards, these legislations were again subjected to revamp and restructuring. Essentially, the *syariah* lobby wanted the different provisions, such as family laws and Islamic criminal codes, to be contained under their own separate statutes. New laws to govern the functioning and administration of the newly-established Syariah Courts were also necessary. Finally, there were laws that were needed to define Syariah Court procedures, for both civil and criminal cases. The following is a rough typology of the kinds of new *syariah* legislations which emerged out of these new concerns:

1. Laws on Islamic family matters;
2. Laws on Islamic criminal offences;
3. Laws on civil procedures to be used in court adjudication of civil matters;
4. Laws on criminal procedures to be used in court adjudication of criminal cases;
5. Laws on the administration of these Islamic laws.

Table 5.1 explains this trend of legislative multiplication. What is shown in the table are examples of laws under the *syariah*, in two periods, in two states, Selangor and Kelantan — the first is between the years 1950 to 1980 and the second is the period after 1980.

One new area of Islamic law, besides family law, which is only applicable to Muslims, is the law on *syariah* criminal offences. Although there is a common penal code in Malaysia, this does not cover certain crimes that are deemed exclusively Islamic. The first state to have a separate legislation on *syariah* criminal offences was Kelantan, which passed the law in 1985. By 1992, seven out of the fourteen states have separate bodies of laws on *syariah* crimes (*jenayah Syariah*) (Mahmood Zuhdi 2001, pp. 150–54).

TABLE 5.1
Malaysian *Syariah* Laws, before and after 1980: Selangor and Kelantan

Syariah laws in the state of Selangor, 1950–1980	*Syariah* laws in the state of Selangor, after 1980
1. Administration of Muslim Law Enactment 1952	1. Islamic Family Law (State of Selangor) Enactment 2003 2. Administration of the Religion of Islam (State of Selangor) Enactment 2003 3. Non-Islamic Religion (Control Against Propagation Among Muslims) Enactment 1988 4. Syariah Court Civil Procedure (State of Selangor) Enactment 2003 5. Syariah Criminal Procedure (State of Selangor) Enactment 2003
	Syariah Court Evidence (State of Selangor) Enactment 2003
***Syariah* laws in the state of Kelantan, 1950–1980**	***Syariah* laws in the state of Kelantan, after 1980**
1. The Syariah Courts and Muslim Matrimonial Causes Enactment 1966 2. Kelantan Islamic Religious Council and Malay Custom Enactment 1966	1. Control and Prohibition of Propagation of Non-Islamic Religion Enactment 1981 2. The Administration of Kelantan Syariah Courts Enactment 1982 3. Islamic Family Law Enactment of Kelantan 2002 4. Syariah Civil Procedure of Kelantan Enactment 1984 5. Syariah Criminal Procedure of Kelantan Enactment 1985 6. Syariah Court Evidence Enactment 1991

Kelantan also passed an enactment (*Kaedah-Kaedah Hukuman Sebat*) on whipping as a punishment in 1987 to distinguish whipping under Islam from that used in the penal code (Siti Zubaidah 2006a, p. 101). However, by the 1990s, all Syariah Courts were given the power to sentence defendants to public caning (Norhashimah 1996, p. 219). The following are examples of crimes that have been included in or codified under the various *syariah* criminal enactments (Mahmood Zuhdi 2001, p. 140):

1. Offences related to morals, as in offensive conduct (*tidak sopan*) or men who behave like women in public places.
2. Sexual misdemeanours such as fornication, adultery, kissing in public, sodomy, lesbian sex and prostitution.
3. Action or behaviour against the religion such as uttering words offensive to Islam, indulging in immoral activities, alcohol consumption, eating during the fasting month of Ramadan.
4. Inciting others to do evil, such as luring a married woman to leave her husband, or forcing children under one's care into prostitution, or kidnapping and handing them over for adoption by non-Muslims or casting aspersion on the Islamic faith of others.
5. Contravening, opposing or deriding the orders or position of officials within the Islamic establishment, as well as contempt of Syariah Court orders.
6. Complicity in any of the above acts.

Although the above can be considered anachronistic in the modern-liberal context, the enforcement of these new regulations requires modern court procedures. New legislations were needed to outline the procedures for handling civil and criminal cases, such as the issuance of summons, obtaining search warrants, making arrests, or the admission of statements (Mahmood Zuhdi 2004, pp. 188–89; Siti Zubaidah 2006*b*, pp. 208–11). Hence, besides the substantive laws which outline the Islamicness of family laws and penal offences, there is also legislation that can be recognized as procedural laws, referred to as *syariah* civil and criminal procedures. Here the *syariah* basically borrows wholly from the civil laws, making the provisions within the *syariah* criminal and civil procedures almost a carbon copy of procedures used in the common law courts (Abdul Hamid 2008, p. 4). The *syariah* system in Malaysia today is part of a movement which draws on Islamic traditions for its substance but at the same time appropriates elements of a more modern legal system (the English common law) to entrench itself in the modern nation-state.

Harmonization of the Civil Legal System with the Syariah System

Yet another indication of an expanding Islamic legal-bureaucracy is what state authorities refer to as their effort to "harmonize" civil common laws with *syariah*. As noted by the country's Attorney General, Gani Patail, in an opening speech at a conference on the "Harmonisation of Civil Laws and Syariah" in 2007, "the call for harmonisation of civil laws and Shariah forms part of the Islamisation process as initiated by the government" (Gani Patail 2008). This is a serious initiative led by the Faculty of Law of the International Islamic University of Malaysia and the Syariah Section of the Attorney General's Chambers, with the participation of Syariah officers from the Department of Syariah Judiciary of Malaysia (JKSM). At the end of the 2007 conference, it was resolved, among other things, that a Harmonisation Committee be set up in the Prime Minister's Office as well as several relevant ministries, that Syariah Courts be empowered to adjudicate on matters involving Islamic banking and finance, that civil laws which are not *syariah*-compliant be amended to conform to Islamic principles, that a Malaysian common law based on *syariah* be developed to eventually replace the English common law.[5] What are the underlying motives for all these? There are actually two positions on this. The first group, whom I call the *syariah* Islamists, sees "harmonization" as a way of extending the Islamization agenda into the public sphere involving both Muslims and non-Muslims, and they see the strength of Islamic economy and finance as one critical domain of influence. The other group of "harmonizers" reflects the position of the interfaith lobby, who genuinely wish to resolve the conundrum that has arisen out of the dualistic or hybridized system of law in the country, which has divided Muslims and non-Muslims acrimoniously when it comes to resolving inter-religious family matters. For this group, an accommodative family law must be constituted, which would incorporate what is common in both *syariah* and the civil law as one of the ways of resolving the conflict.

The first group, the strong *syariah* and Islamic lobby, would stand to benefit most if they have their way in replacing the English common law system with what they see as an Islamic or a Malaysian "common" law system. These are the advocates of Islamization through legal reform. In fact they are quite comfortable with appropriating any law (substantive or procedural) that is "un-Islamic" and make them *syariah*-compliant. There is a penchant for adding Islamic appellations to banking practices, such as the idea of the *mudarabah* to mean profit-sharing contract, or *musharakah* to mean partnership, or *bay bithaman ajil* to refer to the concept of deferred sale (Norhashimah 1996, pp. 259–64). In fact, "harmonization" here also means the passing of civil legislations that incorporate Islamic elements, such as the Islamic Banking Act of 1983 and the Takaful (Islamic Insurance) Act of 1985 (ibid., pp. 204–5). This lobby is on a mission to make existing civil laws conform to Islamic principles. *Syariah* principles of *ijarah* (lease) and *khiyar* (options) are being touted as possible Islamic features that can be incorporated into major and minor laws alike, such as the National Land Code 1965 and the Contract Act 1950 respectively (Gani Patail 2007, p. 5).

For the second group, "harmonization" could open possibilities towards resolving the problem of overlapping and conflicting laws within the dual-jurisdiction system. The argument for this position says that if a new body of "common laws" could be derived based on some universal principles of justice and fairness, these could then be applied to areas of family laws involving Muslim-non-Muslim relations, such as child custody or the division of matrimonial property in cases of divorce. To resolve issues of inter-religious litigations, a former Chief Justice of Malaysia proposed, under this rubric of "harmonization", that in these cases there should be one common law judge and one *syariah* judge, with the hearing taking place either in a civil court or Syariah Court. As practical and sensible as these ideas may be, this is likely to lead to political controversies due to the required constitutional amendments that must be made before these new legal arrangements can be made possible (Abdul Hamid 2008, pp. 5–6).

Nevertheless, it is obviously the first group which has had an upper hand in determining the direction of this "harmonization" exercise. In fact, the second group has not really articulated their solutions to the interfaith problems, not least because this would involve a complex manoeuvre in the reform of both federal and state laws, since civil laws are under the purview of federal parliamentarians while Islamic laws must be deliberated at the state assemblies. So any "harmonization" of *syariah* and civil laws must actually involve coordination that transcends the political division of powers within this federal system.

HOMOGENIZING ISLAM

In this section, I analyse some of the consequences of this new centralizing and expanding Islamic legal-bureaucracy. First and foremost, it determines the definition of Islam, or the codification of what constitutes legitimate Islam as far as the state is concerned. This process also has the underlying consequence of homogenizing the religion, emptying elements of plurality and diversity within Islam. Deviations from the official norms are considered heretical and are products of skewed teachings (*ajaran sesat*). These would have to be wiped out so that only a dominant and totalizing version of state Islam is allowed legality and legitimacy. The right or authorized Islam according to the national Islamic body JAKIM (which comes under the Prime Minister's Office) is the *Sunnah Wal Jammah* (Sunni Islam). A distinction is made between Sunni Islam and Shia beliefs. A fatwa prohibiting Muslims from following Shia tries to make distinctions between the two "Islams" by providing some definitions of the right and wrong Islam and outlaws the practice of unauthorized beliefs.[6]

Internally, the process of defining Islamic orthodoxy is decided in a vociferous way. The purpose is the circumscription of the Muslim subject and not merely the exclusion of the non-Muslim subject. Many forms of Islamic teaching and practice are not tolerated and are in fact outlawed by the fatwa councils of state religious departments. Table 5.2 shows the number of Islamic teachings and sects that have been banned by the national and various state fatwa councils. As can be seen, many branches of Sufism (*tarekat*) have been outlawed by *syariah* and Islamic bureaucrats empowered by the modern state. The latter can be said to be representing a new urban class, eager to promote High Islam and execute a "massive transfer of loyalty away from saint cults towards a scripturalist, 'fundamentalist' variant of Islam" (Gellner 1994, p. 22).

The power to legitimize or criminalize beliefs among Muslims has remained within the hands of the councils on fatwa set up in each state together with a national council which are at liberty to issue religious edicts. Once a fatwa is pronounced the ruling is gazetted as law under state provisions and is then enforceable. Power over lawmaking (in the *syariah* specifically) thus created a new centre of authority over Muslims, or what David Goldberg (2002) would call a "fantasized homogeneity" over subjects falling within the law's scope.

RING-FENCING THE MUSLIM SUBJECT

In addition to homogenizing what should be considered authentic and authoritative Islam, the second consequence of a powerful Islamic legal-bureaucracy is that it leads to a project of ring-fencing the Muslim subject. Both *syariah* and civil laws delineate the boundaries of group identity by playing a gatekeeping function, defining who should be taken in as

TABLE 5.2
Examples of Religious Practices of Muslims Banned by
Various Fatwa Councils of Malaysia

No.	Name of Sect and/or Leader	Notes/Reasons stated for ban
1	Tarekat Naqsyabandiah (Khalidah Kadirun Yahya)	No reason stated.
2	Tarikat Mufarridah	No reason stated.
3	Tarikat Naqsyabandiah (Tuan Haji Ishak bin Mohd	No reason stated.
4	Kumpulan Al Arqam (Haji Ashaari Muhammad)	No reason stated.
5	Syiah sects of the Al-Zaidiyah and Jaafriah groups	Originally recognized through fatwa made on 24 September 1984, but recognition repealed in the current fatwa.
6	Qadiani/Ahmadiah sect	Those who join this sect are not considered Muslims anymore and will not be entitled to burial in a Muslim cemetery.
7	Azhar bin Wahab	No reason stated.
8	Tok Ayah Hasan	No reason stated.
9	Wahdatul Wujud	No reason stated.
10	Tariqat Naqsyabandiah Al-Aliyah (Syeikh Nazim)	No reason stated.
11	Tarikat Zikrulla (Hassan Anak Rimau dan Ayah Pin)	No reason stated.
12	Tijah @ Khatijah bt Ali	Said to be of the Wahdatul Wujud and Martabat Tujuh sect; adding the name of Saidina Fatimah bt Rasulullah in the *Syahadah* (the avowal of faith in Islam) is considered a deviant practice.
13	Tarikat Ismaniah Ibrahim Bonjol	Among the reasons given is that this sect uses the *Kitab Thabitul Qulub* as the main sacred text instead of the Qur'an. The sect considers the latter as merely a historical text.
14	Tarikat Islam Muhammad S.A.W Habibullah al-Hashim (Syed Muhammad Al-Masyor)	The authentic Qur'an is the *Nur Hakim* according to this group.
15	Islam Jamaah (Haji Nur Hassan al-Ubaidah Lubis)	No reason stated.
16	Ahmadiah/Qadiani	Any follower of this sect is considered an apostate, and not entitled to any special privileges given to Malays under the Federal Constitution.
17	Haji Anuar bin Roslan	No reason stated.

Legal-Bureaucratic Islam in Malaysia

18	Azhar bin Wahab (Al-Mansur Holdings)	No reason stated.
19	Zamree bin Abdul Wahab	No reason stated.
20	Tarikat Al-Hasaniah (Haji Abdul Rahim @ Rajin bin Mandul Hati)	Belief in the power light (Nur Chahaya) and the origin of man from Nur Muhammad; practice of this group includes forty-day seclusion and meditation, which is considered a mystical belief.
21	Sect of Ghulam Hasan Al-Bikangi	No reason stated.
22	Ilmu Tajali Ahmad Laksamana (Hakikat Insan)	No reason stated.
23	Ahmadiah/Qadiani	Was previously banned on 15 December 1953 after leaders were tried at the Kuala Lumpur Istana in front of the Sultan of Selangor but had reappeared with a base at Kuala Jeram, Selangor.
24	Aurad Ismaliah (Mahmud bin Haji Abdul Rahman)	No reason stated.
25	Wahdatul Wujud	No reason stated.
26	Jahar bin Dumain (Ilmu Hakikat)	No reason stated.
27	Tarikat Mufarridah (Syeikh Makmun bin Yahya)	No reason stated.
28	Haji Ghazali bin Othman	No reason stated.
29	Haji Mohd Nordin bin Putih	No reason stated.
30	Naqsyabandiah Kadirun Yahya	No reason stated.
31	Golongan anti-hadith	No reason stated.
32	Al-Arqam	Total ban on group including all printed materials, audio casettes, videotapes, films, logo and other forms of representations of the teachings and followings.
33	Ilmu Salah (Haji Kahar bin Haj Ahmad Jalal)	Five daily prayers not obligatory as long as one does good and avoid evil. Does not believe that the Qur'an is authentic as the real one is said to be in the sky or *Luh Mahfuz*.
34	Martabat Tujuh Pimpinan (Hamzah bin Embi)	No reason stated.
35	Syarikat Rufaqa Corporation Sdn Bhd	Set up by former followers of the banned Al Arqam.
36	Abdullah bin Mohamad Syarif	No reason stated.
37	Haji Ahmad Laksamana bin Omar	No reason stated but order was to ban books and tapes produced by this preacher.
37	Muhammad Nur bin Seman	No reason stated.

continued on next page

TABLE 5.2 — *cont'd*

No.	Name of Sect and/or Leader	Notes/Reasons stated for ban
38	Hasan anak Rimau	No reason stated.
39	Azhar bin Abdul Wahab	Adulates the teachings of Wali Songo and Aurad Muhammadiah.
40	Arifin bin Mohd @Ayah Pin	Had preached that the Qur'an is the creation of Prophet Muhammad (s.a.w) by combining elements from the Zabar, Torah and Bible.
41	Pak Chu Bahrin	Banning of four books produced by the preacher, among which is *Risalah Kesufian Ajaran Baharin Salleh* (Guide on Sufism by Baharin Salleh).
42	Tarikat Naqsyabandiah Kadirun Yahya	This sect believes that Allah has bestowed Nur (light) into the body of Prophet Muhammad. Nur Muhammad is then passed on through his lineage, including the founder Professor Kadirun. Followers can go to Pancabudi in Medan for meditation and seclusion.
43	Amanat Haji Abdul Hadi	Muslims are forbidden from acting on the command of Abdul Hadi.
44	Zamri bin Abdullah	No reason stated.
45	Teachings on budi suci	Contains elements of Wahdatul Wujud. In the Syahadah, the appellation Nur Muhammad and Nur Allah have been inserted.

Source: JAKIM7.

legitimate members of the group (in this case as Muslims) and who should be precluded. The following are some of the ways in which this function is instituted:

- No Muslim can opt out of being subjected to *syariah* laws;
- Exiting Islam is dependent on the permission of the Syariah Court;
- Cultural (Islamic) identity to supercede the identity of citizenship.

Essentially, a Muslim subject could be ring-fenced as a subject of religious law through the diminution of his civic identity, such as by having laws to:

- Affix the identity of Islam on all identification papers for Muslims;
- Criminalize all conversions out of Islam;
- Prohibit Muslim-non-Muslim marriage.

The above provisions lent much scope for Islamic interest groups to seize upon laws as the means to control both private and public freedoms. For example, family litigation has become a site for testing the limits of the dual or hybridized legal system, or where Islamic affirmation is pitted against rising but still marginal liberal voices. There are several cases which show how laws have been used to reify the Muslim subject, emptying the Muslim of his civic identity with the acquiescence of the civil-judicial system. The application by Muslims to disavow Islam has become a catalyst in sharpening inter-ethnic animosities. One of the earliest cases of Muslims applying through the court to convert out of Islam was the case of *Soon Singh A/L Bikar Singh V Pertubuhan Kebajikan Islam Malaysia (PERKIM) Kedah & Anor (1999)*.[8] The appellant, Soon Singh, had appealed to the highest court of Malaysia, the Federal Court, to recognize that he was no longer a Muslim. At the age of 17, Soon Singh, who was born to Sikh parents, had converted to Islam without the consent of his widowed mother. At that time he was still considered a minor. By the time he reached the age of 21, Soon Singh went through a Baptism ceremony into the Sikh faith, thereby renouncing Islam. This was followed by a deed poll and an application to the High Court to declare that he was no longer a Muslim. At this hearing, the Religious Department of Kedah objected on the grounds that the High Court did not have jurisdiction to hear such cases as it involved a Muslim conversion and therefore would fall under the purview of the Syariah Court. The High Court upheld the objection of the Religious Department, while the Federal court rejected Soon Singh's appeal. In arguing for the plaintiff, counsel for Soon Singh referred to Article 12(4) of the Constitution which states that the religion of a person under 18 years of age shall be decided by his parent or guardian. They also referred to Article 11(1) of the Federal Constitution which states that every person has the right to profess and practice his religion. However, these lines of defence did not succeed in convincing the judges that Soon Singh had valid constitutional grounds to revert back to his original faith. What was implied by the judgment was still the issue of jurisdiction in that the Civil High Court could not decide on what was deemed to be under the jurisdiction of the Syariah Court, and it seems that the interpretation of the civil court is dependent on the understanding that the right to renounce Islam is held by the Syariah Court.

This particular judgment in 2007 set the precedence for later cases involving individuals like Lina Joy, who also wished to cross the faith line from Islam into Christianity. Another was the case of Kamariah Ali. From 1992 till 2005 Kamariah Ali and four others had applied to the High Court to declare that they were no longer Muslims. However, they were told to apply to the Syariah Court, where they soon discovered that there existed a "no exit" rule for Muslims.[9] At the Syariah Court, their application to renounce Islam was rejected on grounds that the question of verifying whether a Muslim had become an apostate was a question that could not be resolved as it was an ecclesiastical problem beyond the paradigm of secular or wordly legal rules.[10] In short, there seems to be a legal opinion that the custodians of Islam could not accept any application to renounce Islam by any Muslim as apostasy is not only a crime but a divine sin. In 1992, Kamariah Ali and four others served a jail term imposed by a lower Syariah Court in Kota Baru for apostasy. After her release, she was caught with several others for being a follower of the "sky kingdom" cult led by a self-styled preacher, Ayah Pin. Refusing to repent, Kamariah again declared herself to be an apostate and was charged under Section 7 of the Syariah Criminal Offence Enactment (Takzir) Terengganu (2001) (Murali 2008). After a three-year trial, she was found guilty and sentenced to two years of imprisonment in 2008. Whether it was Soon Singh, Lina Joy or Kamariah Ali, all had to seek licence from the Syariah Court, which criminalized their requests anyway. As one of the dissenting judgements in the Lina Joy case puts it, "to expect the Appellant (Lina) to apply for a certificate of apostasy when to do so would likely expose her to a range of offenses under the Islamic law is in my view unreasonable for it means the Appellant (Lina) is made to self-incriminate" (Haris Ibrahim 2008, p. 46).

Renouncing Islam is thus not a private choice, but must be sanctioned by the guardians of the religion. A Muslim does not have a civic identity, meaning an identity that is rightly given to persons by virtue of their membership within a nation-state. The jurisdiction of the Syariah Court is thus far greater than what it is meant to have. I would say that the *syariah* is acting like a sovereign nation or an autonomous polity, asserting membership rules and defining who should remain within its jurisdictional gate. The Muslim citizen is thus denied his or her civic identity with no recourse to the civil judicial system or the highest court of the land, the Federal Court.

The role of the secular bureaucracy, in furthering Islamization, cannot be emphasized enough. For example, riding on the wave of this legislative phase of Islamization were the passing of new civil laws and regulations to fix the civil definition of the Malay-Muslim. One impediment to freedom of identification is the National Registration Regulations (2001), which makes it mandatory for Malays to declare their religion as Islam in their National Registration Identity Card (NRIC). The Lina Joy case specifically illustrates how this national regulation, which is outside of the *syariah* system, has also acted in tandem with Islamic norms to control and prevent exit by members of the Malay or Islamic community into another religious faith. What is most significant in all of these is that it is the Muslims themselves who have had to bear the brunt of this reformed and prevailing *syariah* as well as a circumscribed civil law system whose power has been considerably curtailed. The purpose is to "racialize" the Muslim through a legal apparatus which opens Islam to all entrants but does not allow anyone already in the fold to exit. As a commentator on the Lina Joy case asserts, "Lina Joy is punished because she dared question the power and authority of the gatekeepers who must, for their own political hegemony maintain a tight rein over the main defining characteristic of the Malay-Muslim majority, that is, all Malays are Muslims" (Azza Basaruddin 2008, p. 62).

Nevertheless, there has been some show of "cautious" tolerance (after much public outcry) by the Syariah Court over the issue of conversions. In May 2008, the Penang Syariah Appeals Court allowed a Chinese woman who had previously converted to Islam upon marriage to revert back to her original religion of Buddhism. There are several discrepancies here. The court allowed for her conversion because it claimed that "she has been living a non-Islamic lifestyle and praying to deities and this clearly shows she never embraced Islam" (Malaysiakini 2008*a*). The lawyer further defended the decision by trying to appease Muslims that the judgement was made not because she was allowed to leave Islam but because the conversion (to Islam) was invalid in the first place (ibid.). Prominent lawyer Haris Ibrahim (2009) questioned the validity of the whole case because "[i]f she was not Muslim when she presented her application to court, did the Syariah Court have jurisdiction to hear her case?... Now, did Tan go to the Syariah Court saying 'I am a Muslim and want to get out' or 'I'm not a Muslim'?" And if it was the latter, he asked, how could the Syariah Court have the jurisdiction to hear her case? He was of the opinion that the Syariah Court did not actually have the jurisdiction to hear Tan's case if the basis of her application was that she was not a Muslim. According to the Federal Constitution (Item 1, List 2, 9th Schedule) the jurisdiction of the Syariah Courts is "only over persons professing the religion of Islam". The decision of the Syariah Court still reflects "cautious" tolerance as it was delivered after the 8 March elections (in which one contributing factor to UMNO's poor performance was its policy of intolerance towards non-Muslim litigants) and also because the court was still wary of Muslim protests over such a decision. After the judgement was delivered, the group Hizbut Tahrir issued a protest memorandum proclaiming the judgement to be going against Islamic law as those renouncing Islam must be punished with the death sentence, according to the group (Malaysiakini 2008a).

CONCLUSION: BUREAUCRATIC ISLAMISTS AS THE DEFINING ISLAMIC VOICE

The groundwork for bureaucratic Islam has been created long before the tenure of Abdullah Badawi or the reinvention of PAS in the run up to the 8 March election. It was created sometime between the 1980s and the late 1990s. The issuance of the fatwa on yoga forbidding Muslims from practising the exercise is one example of the excessive control over what is considered deviant by state sanctioned Islam.[11] The form of Islam that the state subscribes to is known as the Al Sunnah Wal Jamaah, or Sunni Islam. The state Islamic authority is extremely intolerant of the Sufi variety of Islam and has issued countless fatwa to prohibit Muslims from following the teachings of many self-styled preachers, including reading, listening and buying of printed materials, video cassettes or any recordings of these.

Although PAS looms large as an influence in the Islamization of Malaysia, it is the institutionalization of Islam by the UMNO government, through the modernization of the Syariah Court system and the religious offices which includes the Fatwa Council and the Office of the Mufti that has ultimately been responsible for entrenching Islam within the state.

Over the years, there has been the creation of a distinct Malay-Muslim polity, of which the weight of Islam on the personal and public self has been brought to bear. Increasingly, all aspects of the Muslim citizenry are now subjected to laws that are more Islamic in nature; even civil laws are expected to comply with some Islamic norms when it involves a Muslim.

Ironically, the only avenue left for a Muslim to be spared the control of the *syariah* law is when it comes to matters of national security or more specifically when legislation such as the Internal Security Act (ISA) is invoked for arbitrary arrest and detention, or whenever the state wants to selectively persecute a person for political reasons. The Anwar sodomy trial is a case in point. Although sexuality is an area that had come under the jurisdiction of religious authorities, his alleged offence was not charged under the *syariah* system.[12] Similarly, although dissident blogger, Raja Petra Raja Kamaruddin was alleged to have "Insulted Islam" and Member of Parliament Teresa Kok was charged with complaining over the Muslim prayer call (*azan*), it was not the Syariah Court which dealt with them, but the Home Ministry (Malaysiakini 2008*b*). All these are indications that the state is highly arbitrary in how it relates to its own Islamized institutions.

UMNO as the leading Malay party has actually not changed to become more Islamic over the years; it merely used the instrument of the state to put in place an Islamic system. Ideologically and in terms of membership and leadership composition, it does not resemble a strident Islamic party. Hence its survival is dependent on the manipulation of symbols of Islam and Islamization; it has had to walk the tightrope of accommodating and balancing the needs of its Islamic constituency with that of its non-Muslim vote bank. By applying state instruments of Islamization to Muslims only, UMNO pronounces that non-Muslims would be shielded from the Islamization process. However, such a case is only remotely possible, given the rise in inter-religious disputes within the recent decade.

UMNO's nemesis, PAS, on the other hand, is appearing more and more as a political party rather than an ideological institution committed to defending its core religious philosophy and values, as evident in the dropping of the Islamic state agenda in the 2008 election campaign. This was done so as not to alienate moderate Muslims and the non-Muslim constituency, which had eventually paid off with its success in winning some seats that are not in Muslim-majority areas.[13] Although PAS pushed for more Islamization in society, it had never been responsible for laying the infrastructural groundwork for bureaucratic Islam. But while it benefited from all this, the party may not have full control over the Islamic bureaucrats and could even be in conflict with them since most of the bureaucrats see UMNO as their patron.

In conclusion we could say that there is a tripartite arrangement emerging here. In the assemblage of state-society relations, we could place UMNO on one side and PAS on the other, with the Islamic bureaucracy occupying the most secure "middle" position. Both UMNO and PAS know that it is almost impossible to dismantle this structure of institutionalized, legal-bureaucratic Islam. Both political parties must at the same time cultivate an image that is friendly to non-Muslims as well as to a segment of liberal Malays. The Islamic bureaucrats, on the other hand, can still call the shots on most questions related to Islam, as they are not answerable to any constituency or vote bank, although they are controlled by the government of the day. The Islamic bureaucracy and its legal apparatus remain the most formidable authority in *homogenizing* Islamic beliefs and practices and *ring-fencing* the Muslim subject in the modern, plural nation-state. These are what characterize the emerging new Islamization in Malaysia, and something which all political parties (regardless of their stance on Islamization) will have to contend with if they are to capture the seats of ruling power.

Notes

1. Fatwa is a religious edict issued by either a *mufti* (religious authority with specific powers to issue rulings) individually or in the modern context by a committee of learned religious leaders and scholars. In Malaysia, each state has a Fatwa Committee tasked to issue opinions and pronouncements on matters related to Islam. Technically and legally, once a fatwa is issued, it becomes enforceable law in Malaysia.
2. Nevertheless, this is not to deny that this vigorous Islamization drive did not have its deleterious effects on the well-being and freedom of non-Muslims. By the 2000s the marginalization of Hindus led to protests against the government which was seen to be biased against non-Islamic interests. Restricting the use of the term "Allah" exclusively to Islamic contexts also led to controversial lawsuits against the government by the Catholic Church.
3. See, for example, the website <http://www.myislamnetwork.net>, which is the official website of the coordinating body called Organisations in Defence

of Islam (Pertubuhan-Pertubuhan Pembela Islam), for a sampling of Islamic organizations that exist today.
4. Article 121(1A) of the Constitution states that the High Courts of Malaya, Sabah and Sarawak "shall have no jurisdiction in respect of any matter within jurisdiction of the Syariah courts".
5. Resolutions passed on 4 December 2007 at the end of the Third International Conference on the "Harmonisation of Civil Laws and Syariah", jointly organized by the Ahmad Ibrahim Kuliyyah of Laws, International Islamic University Malaysia and the Attorney General's Chambers, Malaysia.
6. For example, in a fatwa issued by the Committee on Syariah of the Perlis Religious Department, the definition of what is considered legitimate Islam, the *Ahlus Sunnah Wal Jamaah*, is spelled out. See <http://www.e-fatwa.gov.my/mufti/fatwa_warta_view.asp?keyID=279> linked website on e-fatwa, www.islam.gov.my (accessed 26 November 2008).
7. This information is compiled from a series of fatwa, which could be accessed through *e-fatwa: rujukan resmi fatwa di Malaysia*, the website of the Malaysian Islamic Development Department (JAKIM) at <http://www.e-fatwa.gov.my/default.asp> (accessed 26 November 2008).
8. This case law is sourced from [1999] MLJ 489. This is the reported judgement from the case. MLJ stands for the Malayan Law Journal and the figure in parantheses is the year of judgement.
9. See *Kamariah Binti Ali and anor v Majlis Agama Islam dan Adat Melayu Terengganu and Anor*, High Court (Kuala Lumpur), [2005] MLJU 595. MLJU stands for Malayan Law Journal Unreported Judgments.
10. See Judgement by Justice Raus Sharif in, *Kamariah Binti Ali and anor V majlis Agama Islam dan Adat Melayu Terengganu and Anor,* High Court (Kuala Lumpur), [2005] MLJU 595.
11. In October and November 2008 two controversial fatwa were issued by the Malaysian National Fatwa Council. The first fatwa was on "tomboys" or prohibition against women who are dressed like men. The second fatwa was on the banning of yoga among Muslims. The first fatwa makes it illegal for women to appear and/or dress like men, as the idea is to criminalize lesbianism. The other prohibits Muslims from practising yoga as the argument is that it is a form of worship involving chanting and meditation and may go against the Islamic *aqidah* (belief).
12. Under Section 25 of the Syariah Criminal Offences (Federal Territories) Act 1997, sodomy (*liwat*) is stated as an offence — "Any male person who commits *liwat* shall be guilty of an offence and shall on conviction be liable to a fine not exceeding five thousand ringgit or to imprisonment for a term not exceeding three years or to whipping not exceeding six strokes or to any combination thereof."

13. PAS won three parliamentary seats in the state of Selangor. In districts that had only 39 per cent (Hulu Langat), 47% (Kota Raja) and 61 per cent (Kuala Selangor) Malay voters, the seats were won by Dr Che Rosli Che Mat, Dr Siti Mariah Mahmud and Dr Dzulkifli Ahmad respectively.

References

Abdul Gani, Patail. "Harmonization of Civil Laws and Syariah: Effective Strategies for Implementation". Keynote address presented at the 3rd International Conference on the Harmonisation of Civil Laws and Syariah, International Islamic University, Kuala Lumpur, 4 December 2007.

Abdul Hamid, Mohamad. "Harmonization of Common Law and Shari'ah in Malaysia: A Practical Approach". Paper presented at the Abd Al-Razzaq Al-Sanhuri Lecture, Islamic Legal Studies Program, Harvard Law School, 6 November, 2008.

Abdullah Alwi, Haji Hassan. *The Administration of Islamic Law in Kelantan*. Kuala Lumpur: Dewan Bahasa dan Pustaka, 1996.

Ahmad Fauzi, Abdul Hamid. "New Trends of Islamic Resurgence in Contemporary Malaysia: Sufi Revivalism, Messianism and Economic Activism". *Studia Islamika* 6, no. 3 (1999): 1–67.

———. "Inter-Movement Tension among Resurgent Muslims in Malaysia: Response to the State Clampdown on Darul Arqam In 1994". *Asian Studies Review* 27, no. 3 (2003): 361–87.

Ahmad Hidayat, Buang, ed. *Fatwa di Malaysia* [Fatwa in Malaysia]. Kuala Lumpur: Jabatan Syariah dan Undang-Undang, Akademi Pengajian Islam, Universiti Malaya, 2004.

———, ed. *Mahkamah Syariah di Malaysia* [Syariah court in Malaysia]. Kuala Lumpur: Penerbit Universiti Malaya, 2006.

Ahmad Ibrahim and Mahmud Saedon Awang Othman. *Ke Arah Islamisasi Undang-Undang Islam di Malaysia* [Towards the Islamization of law in Malaysia]. Kuala Lumpur: Yayasan Dakwah Islamiyah Malaysia, 1988.

Ariffin Omar. *Bangsa Melayu: Malay Concepts of Democracy and Community 1945–1950*. Kuala Lumpur: Oxford University Press, 1993.

Azza Basarudin. "Gatekeeping Will Not Stop Apostasy". In *Religion Under Siege? Lina Joy, the Islamic State and Freedom of Faith*, edited by Nathaniel Tan and John Lee. Kuala Lumpur: Kinibooks, 2008.

Billings, Dwight B. and Shaunna L. Scott. "Religion and Political Legitimation". *Annual Review of Sociology* 20 (1994): 173–202.

Farish A. Noor. *Islam Embedded: The Historical Development of the Pan-Malaysian Islamic Party PAS (1951–2003)*, vol. 1 and 2. Kuala Lumpur: Malaysian Sociological Research Institute, 2004.

Gellner, Ernest. *Conditions of Liberty.* London: Hamish Hamilton, 1994.
Goldberg, David Theo. *The Racial State.* Malden, MA: Blackwell, 2002.
Hamayotsu, Kikue. "Politics of Syariah Reforms: The Making of the State Religio-Legal Apparatus". In *Malaysia: Islam, Society and Politics,* edited by Virginia Hooker and Norani Othman. Singapore: Institute of Southeast Asian Studies, 2003.
Haris, Ibrahim. "One More Unemotional Reaction". In *Religion Under Siege? Lina Joy, the Islamic State and Freedom of Faith,* edited by Nathaniel Tan and John Lee. Kuala Lumpur: Kinibooks, 2008.
———. "Tan's off the Hook, Yes, but Will the Next Person be So Lucky, and the One After?" 16 March 2009 <http://harismibrahim.wordpress.com/category/will-they-defend-our-secular-constitution/> (accessed 23 May 2009).
Horowitz, Donald L. "The Qur'an and the Common Law: Islamic Law Reform and the Theory of Legal Change". *American Journal of Comparative Law* 42, no. 3 (1994): 543–80.
Hussin Mutalib. *Islam in Malaysia: From Revivalism to Islamic State?* Singapore: Singapore University Press, 1993.
Kessler, Clive. "Malaysia: Islamic Revivalism and Political Disaffection in a Divided Society". *Southeast Asia Chronicle* 75 (October 1980): 3–11.
Mahmood Zuhdi, Hj. Ab. Majid, ed. *Pengantar Undang-Undang Islam di Malaysia* [Introduction to Islamic law in Malaysia]. Kuala Lumpur: Penerbit Universiti Malaya, 1997.
———, ed. *Ke-arah Merealisasikan Undang-Undang Islam* [Towards the realisation of Islamic law]. Kuala Lumpur: Thinkers Library, 1988.
———, ed. *Bidang Kuasa Jenayah Mahkamah Syariah di Malaysia* [Jurisdiction of Syariah Criminal Court]. Kuala Lumpur: Dewan Bahasa dan Pustaka, 2001.
Malaysiakini. "Syariah Court Allows Woman to Renounce Islam", 16 May 2008*a* <http://www.malaysiakini.com/news/100296> (accessed 21 March 2009).
———. "ISA Crackdown as Pak Lah Faces Dissension", 13 September 2008*b* <http://www.malaysiakini.com/news/89611> (accessed 13 September 2008).
Mohd Izani, Mohd Zain. *Islam dan demokrasi: Cabaran politik Muslim kontemporari di Malaysia* [Islam and democracy: Contemporary challenges to Muslim politics in Malaysia]. Kuala Lumpur: Penerbit Universiti Malaya, 2005.
Muhammad Syukri Salleh. "Recent Trends in Islamic Revivalism in Malaysia. *Studia Islamika* 6, no. 2 (1999): 39–62.
Murali, R.S.N. "Sky Kingdom Member Jailed for 2 Years for Apostasy". *The Star,* 3 March 2008.
Peletz, Michael. *Islamic Modern: Religious Courts and Cultural Politics in Malaysia.* Princeton, NJ: Princeton University Press, 2002.

Roff, William. *The Origins of Malay Nationalism*. Kuala Lumpur: Penerbit University Malaya, 1974.

Siti Zubaidah, Ismail. "Undang-undang jenayah Islam dan pelaksanaan jenayah Syariah di Malaysia" [Islamic criminal law and the implementation of syariah in Malaysia]. In *Mahkamah Syariah di Malaysia* [Syariah Court in Malaysia], edited by Ahmad Hidayat Buang. Kuala Lumpur: Penerbit Universiti Malaya, 2006a.

———. "Undang-undang prosedur jenayah Syariah di Malaysia: satu penilaian" [Syariah criminal procedural law in Malaysia: An assessment]. In *Mahkamah Syariah di Malaysia*, edited by Ahmad Hidayat Buang. Kuala Lumpur: Penerbit Universiti Malaya, 2006b.

Suwaid, Tapah. "Perundangan dan penguatkuasaan fatwa". In *Fatwa di Malaysia* [Fatwa in Malaysia], edited by Ahmad Hidayat Buang. Kuala Lumpur: Jabatan Syariah dan Undang-Undang, Akademi Pengajian Islam, Universiti Malaya, 2004.

Zainah Anwar. *Islamic Revivalism in Malaysia: Dakwah among the Students*. Petaling Jaya: Pelanduk, 1987.

6

THE LETTER OF THE LAW AND THE RECKONING OF JUSTICE AMONG TAMILS IN MALAYSIA

Andrew Willford

The transformation of land usage in Malaysia has been inextricably linked to a politicizing of Islam and Malay rights. In short, the development of the prime industrial and, hence, subsequent residential heartlands of this nation have taken on an ethno-nationalistic urgency, given the politics of identity within this nation. More specifically, the transformation of key lands in and around Kuala Lumpur, Selangor, and the entire Klang Valley, has not only been crucial for economic reasons, but has also figured large in symbolic intent. For these lands, formerly populated mainly by Tamils and Chinese (Kahn 2006), have become the symbolic heartland of a new and politically unified Malay identity (King 2008; Kahn 2006; Bunnell 2004; Hoffstaedter 2008). The developments of Putrajaya and Shah Alam, in particular, have been focal, not only in creating a large urban (and suburban) Malay populace, a key goal of Malaysian developmentalism spearheaded by former Prime Minister Mahathir Mohamad, but also in crafting the semiotics of a new Malay identity. This new Malay identity, as many scholars have noted, is crafted through an emphasis on Islamic modernism fused with nostalgic imaginings for past Islamic civilizations. On the one hand, we see the intense modernity of the Petronas Towers, and the pride for Islam and Malay identity that Mahathir Mohamad sought in their grandiose erection. On the other hand, we witness the neo-Indo-Saracenic splendour of Putrajaya, the new administrative capital, which also incorporates Mughal, Arab, and Ottoman (King 2008) styles liberally into what is supposed to be a Malay icon of the nation. Musings about the alienating aspects of this architecture notwithstanding,[1] the story that is often not told is of the Tamil plantation workers,[2] who, in particular, have been dispossessed of their former lands throughout this process.[3] In this essay, I focus not on plantation ethnography itself (Nagarajan 2004; Bunnell, Nagarajan and Willford 2010), but on the political and psychological effects of plantation retrenchments and dislocations.

The development politics have, in short, brought about a dramatic demographic shift in the ethnic composition of Malaysia's industrial heartland. This was the intended goal all along. To develop the nation's core identity, politically constructed around Malay ethnicity and Islam, the two being increasingly synonymous, Malays, it was argued, had to be united and strong — particularly at the centre. In addition to reforming, and thereby policing Malay identity (Peletz 2002), incentives and privileges created a culture of privilege and, concomitantly, increasing self-rationalization of these purported entitlements. The racializing of urban development, and its troubling potential, is summed up by Joel Kahn in this way:

> [A]lmost exclusively Malay housing estates ... are sprouting up.... In many cases this racial exclusivity is part of the design. One of the first new towns to be built was Shah Alam ... built on plantation land. Its resident population of mainly Tamil estate workers was rehoused elsewhere, or simply evicted to make way for new, mainly middle-class Malay residents. Probably the supreme example of this is the new Federal Capital in Putrajaya (2006, pp. 156–57).

However it would be overly simplistic to state that this process is uniform in intent or circumstances. Indeed, the historical demographics of Malay vis-à-vis Tamil or Chinese communities vary tremendously within the Klang Valley alone. Still, the resentments felt by non-Malays have been tangible and growing, as have the overzealous rationalizations by those designated as "Malays" (many of whom, being of recent immigrant status, or deriving of mixed ancestry, are seen as undeserving by non-Malays), who guard their bureaucratically derived entitlements in the knowledge, albeit probably unconsciously, of their shallow historicity.

It is in this political context that increasing ethnic consciousness is creating fantasies about the Other that are potentially volatile (Willford 2006). Tamils are increasingly resentful of the fact that lands that were developed and populated by their ancestors are now claimed by Malays as their own; and moreover that the land use patterns in these new townships, such as in Shah Alam, are increasingly hostile to the most symbolic vestiges of the Tamil and Hindu presence, the temples. Hindu temples are not only anathema to all that is Islamic and modern within the state-sponsored discourses of reform and orthopraxy, they are also a reminder of both a pre-Islamic past that is always present within certain aspects of Malay culture and identity (but one that is always under siege by Islamic reformers), and a more recent non-Malay presence on the landscapes that are purportedly vaunted as Malay-oriented townships. The compulsive erasure of these sites, as perceived by Tamils, is, in other words, not only a land grab, but also fuelled by a moralizing conscience. It is the combination of demographic transformations, and the political and economic marginalization of Tamils that accompanied this, coupled with the apparently amnesiac hostility that Malays in the newly created townships show to (older) Hindu presences there, that draw the ire of the Tamil community. There is, in short, an awakening of resentment. This, in turn, led to the dramatic events of 2008, the so-called "Hindu Rights Action Force" (Hindraf) rally in Kuala Lumpur that drew thousands of protesters to the streets. In addition to issues pertaining to land, however, legal cases surrounding religious conversion have exacerbated a sense of insecurity among Tamil Hindus.

As Nagarajan (2008) argues, there were several important court cases that brought alarm to non-Muslims in Malaysia, as a "silent rewriting" of the constitution was being done in the name of Islam (see also Maznah Mohamad, this volume); but at the same time, the judgment of prominent federal judges was increasingly revealed to be shaped by religious beliefs. I cite Nagarajan at length on this point, citing but two examples of judicial partiality with regards to conversion law:

> the religious bureaucracy continued to intrude into the lives of the minorities. Islamic authorities forcibly separated V. Suresh from his wife, Revathi Masoosai, and their 16-month-old baby. Revathi was born to Muslim convert parents but was brought up as a Hindu by her Hindu grandmother. She was detained at the Muslim rehabilitation centre

against her will while her child was handed to Revathi's Muslim mother. In another case, P. Marimuth's five young Hindu children were taken from their home by Islamic religious officials who said his wife was technically still a Muslim and therefore their marriage of twenty-one years was invalid.... This worrying trend of Muslim officialdom to ignore the religious sentiments and the rights of non-Muslims only served to fuel more fear and unhappiness among non-Muslims. But they had an even more troubling impact on the Indian Malaysian psyche because most of the affected people are from the community. They not only lost their spouses, but their children were taken away from them and they have no recourse to justice (2008, pp. 390–91).

It is in this context that the actions of about fifty Malay protesters who were protesting a plan to relocate a 150-year-old temple in Shah Alam to Section 23, a "predominantly Malay area", can perhaps be understood. In August of 2009, the protesters marched to the Selangor State Government Secretariat in Shah Alam to protest the proposed relocation of the old temple (which had to be shifted when the plantation had been converted to housing). The protesters, however, carried with them a severed cow head and several banners insulting the Chief Minister of the state as well as his executive councillor.[4] Perhaps, significantly, the Chief Minister, Khalid Ibrahim, and his officers hail from the opposition Parti Keadilan Rakyat (PKR). The cow head was spat upon and kicked, which, in turn, outraged the country's Hindu population and drew angry rebukes from several political leaders, including the Prime Minister himself. The plot thickened when the Home Minister and UMNO Vice President, Datuk Seri Hishamuddin Hussein later appeared in public with the protesters and issued a statement that the protesters "felt victimised" and had only wanted their voices to be heard.[5] Hishamuddin implicitly and apparently sided with the protesters. This, in turn, caused much controversy, as opposition politicians called for his resignation. UMNO leaders kept silent, worried that a rebuke of Hishamuddin would alienate Malay voters. UMNO's silence, in turn, made some suspicious that they were operating behind the scenes, fomenting anti-PKR as well as anti-Hindu sentiment.

This incident, however, sheds light upon the processes of urban change outlined briefly above. The offensive presence of the old Hindu temple in a new Shah Alam neighbourhood is instructive. Shah Alam is a new city. It is built entirely upon former plantation lands, predominantly populated by Tamils. As such, there are dozens of old temples that have been and are slowly being destroyed as this development commenced and continues. The long and drawn out struggle by the temple devotees to have their temple relocated is a story for another day, but it demonstrates the enduring significance these structures hold for communities that have since been relocated and dispersed after their plantation villages have been developed into other land uses. The emotional attachment to the temple runs deep within these communities, and the loss of potentially hundreds of these structures has produced great anxiety for Tamil Hindus in Malaysia. In a very real sense, the landscape where plantations existed is imbued with a sacrality that is now being defiled by the processes of development. On the side of the new residents within Malay-dominated townships, such as Shah Alam, the presence of the older Hindu temple arouses anxiety as well. The temple is a constant reminder of the "immigrant status" of recently arrived Malays to these former plantation areas, their purported claims to bumiputra status, rights and privileges notwithstanding. The demographic evidence suggests that a large percentage of "Malays" are recent immigrants from Indonesia (Kahn 2006), or non-Malays who have married into the community (*masuk Melayu*). The fact that Indians and, in some cases, Orang Asli (indigenous) communities were displaced in order to create the symbolic Malay heartland for the nation is, one could imagine, troubling.

Coupled with the need to erase the presence of the Other as inscribed on the landscape, rationalize privilege, and silence a troubled sense of one's identity's recent historicity, the very vestiges of a so-called Indic or Hindu layer of Malay culture that is constantly and relentlessly being invigilated and purged by state religious apparatuses (Peletz 2002; Hoffstaedter 2008) must also affect how the contemporary Hindu presence becomes an object of avoidance, an *objet petit a*, in Lacan's sense, or that which blocks one's enjoyment or desire. Lacan spoke of the *objet a* in several registers at different periods of his career. In my usage here, I refer to that which remains or is left over after the introduction of a symbolic order. *Objet a* causes anxiety and sets desire in motion in relation to this anxiety. This anxiety, however, is a surplus or excess of the symbolic order itself. In this context, the intractable hold of Malay identity, as a symbolic demand, generates its others through its very impossibility, and also supplements or sutures this lack within the symbolic through avoidance of *objet a*. This avoidance takes ethnographic form through the logic of the supplement: laws, boundaries, and phobic racializations

(Willford 2006). But to qualify, it must be stated that my perspective comes from interactions with and observations of Malaysian Tamils. If this is a dialectical process of identity politics, I am only capturing the minority perspective. But this is valuable, I believe, given the dearth of ethnographic material on this community, and the prioritizing of Malay perspectives in Malaysian studies, more broadly.

HINDRAF (HINDU RIGHTS ACTION FORCE)

On 25 November 2007, thirty to forty thousand Indians demonstrated against the Malaysian Government in the heart of Kuala Lumpur, only to face tear gas, batons, and water cannon. This event, captured by the global media, and spearheaded by Hindraf, surprised many Malaysians, if not other Indians, both in the diaspora and India, in its boldness. But for those familiar with sentiments within the working-class Indian community, the event, while surprising in its scope and audacity, was not entirely shocking. I suggest that the resonance of the movement owes much of its strength to various forms of economic, social, and political marginalization in Malaysia that the working-class Tamils believe they experience.

Hindraf's emergence was the culmination of a host of factors, but I could summarize them briefly here as, (1) the failure of the elected political representatives, the Malaysian Indian Congress (MIC), to ameliorate the perceived economic and political marginalization of the Tamil community relative to the Malay community in particular, which has the aid of special quotas for jobs and education; (2) the belief that Islamization is eroding the rights of non-Muslims, particularly as pertains to conversion laws, inheritance, and the administering of land rights regarding temples, etc. and; (3) the feeling that the Tamil community has been harassed by police and by political proxy groups sheltered by the police, particularly in the fallout of the so-called "Kampung Medan" attacks of 2001,[6] in which no proper investigation, the community feels, was conducted, nor were arrests made, after brutal attacks against Tamil youths and men left five dead and dozens injured (Nagarajan 2004; Willford 2008). In this context, a series of insensitive recent temple demolitions aggravated these already converging sentiments and sparked the movement.

I want to make three broad claims. First, I claim that the Indian awakening or uprising, particularly as realized in the "Hindraf" movement, is gaining resonance as an exorcizing of the law's ghostliness (Derrida

2002). That is, the violent performance and contingency of the law has been increasingly revealed to Malaysian Tamils in recent times, particularly through a series of events that have left them frustrated, angry, and sometimes traumatized. Specifically, the defiling of the temple, the land, and the body by the State, or by private capital working in tandem with it, closely associated in the Tamil-Hindu imaginary of Malaysia, has been a precipitating factor. Secondly, the transgression of the letter of the law has been a means towards realizing a distinction between legality and justice. As communities displaced from plantations, they have utilized tactics of civil disobedience, or have simply become de facto squatters upon the land they have lived intergenerationally, and as such have exceeded the letter of the law in search of compensatory justice. The reasoning of justice, or compensation, being grounded outside of legality, has implications regarding the limits of the law. At the same time, legal redress and precedent is still sought. The dialectic of transgression and re-inscription within the law has Tamil subjects caught between the rails of recognition within the politics of identity and a logic of compensation in Malaysia that confounds legalistic identification. Thirdly, and in relation to the last claim, I suggest that an emergent sense of historicity among Tamils is rising that articulates frustrations over increasing Islamization, and the perceived de-Indianization of Malay culture. The latter point is a source of historical disentangling, Tamils increasingly feel, leaving Malays insecure about their own origins vis-à-vis their Tamil and/or Indian neighbours. Indian fantasies for compensatory recognition imagine a re-entangling of Tamil and Malay historicities, an intimacy that they feel has been disturbed by Islamization and ethnic politics. I will not dwell on this third point of the "re-Indianization" fantasy here, which I have done elsewhere (Willford 2006). Finally, the capricious force of law and the violence of "order" is haunted, I suggest, by its obverse, the sublime and inexplicable fragmentation of memory and experience wrought by the "betrayal" of the state upon the land and the sacred. This sublime horror, a *horror religiosis*, has, paradoxically, a culturally recognizable logic in Tamil Hinduism, though one that does not rest easily within the imagination.

As many scholars have noted, the "Malay" ethnic category is defined and shored up through the Malay language and Islam. That there was no unified Malay culture throughout the peninsula during the nineteenth century comes as no surprise to most students of history who recognize the plurality of groups and the *peranakan* or mixed origins of those who became self-identified as "Malay" (Kahn 2006). What is, perhaps, more surprising is the extent to which the census in the late nineteenth century and early twentieth century reveals just who was living in today's heartland of Malaysia. For example, in Selangor, the industrial heartland of Malaysia today, and former plantation heartland, the census figures in 1911 numbered Indians at 74,067 and Malays and Chinese at 65,062 and 150,908 respectively. By 1931, Indians outnumbered Malays 155,924 to 122,868 in the state. All the more dramatic is the fact that in 1884, only 17,856 Malays were counted as living in Selangor (Gullick 2004; Iyer 1938). The state, in other words, was settled and populated at the turn of the century as the cities of Kuala Lumpur and Klang were developed by Chinese tin mining and business, and through the growth of the plantation industries (Gullick 2004). This is significant, I suggest, because plantation communities, developed and populated by Tamils, date from this period, and are literally inscribed into the landscape in such a way that their descendants today, living within these same plantations (or "estates"), have a growing sense of historicity, and with this, a growing sense of outrage at facing retrenchment and eviction under the pressures of "development" and ethnic politics (Nagarajan 2004). At the same time, however, this historicity increasingly takes the shape of a victim's narrative among the Tamil poor and working class. Moreover, a compensatory narrative is generative of ethnic myths about a lacking and inauthentic Other, the "new Malay" (*Melayu baru*) that is the subject of state-sponsored nationalism. This Other, the ethnic subject of the law (i.e., the so-called bumiputra) is increasingly seen as lacking by Tamils as its claims are revealed as arbitrary, violent, and built upon disavowals of difference within itself. To skip to the punchline, the question that remains is whether this recognition produces deconstructive critique of ethnic subjects as constructed by the state, or whether Tamils, in identifying this lack, in turn identify with this lack, becoming subjects of victimhood.

REGU — HINDRAF LEADER, AND CO-FOUNDER

I met Regu, a leader and co-founder of Hindraf, in a Klang restaurant in late February 2008. He was eager to explain his views, knowing that his compatriots were being held under the Internal Security Act (ISA), which allows for arbitrary detention without charges or legal representation, and that his arrest could come at any time.

Regu began the conversation by stating: "You [the government] pushed us into a corner. There are 27,000 temples in this country. Many of them are

150 to 200 years old. They are threatened with demolition. When we came to this country, our people brought *kallu* (earth) from India with them from their villages in order to start temples wherever they went. The temples they built when they reached Malaya was [*sic*] built upon the earth that they carried from India on the ships, within their own clothing. There is a deep connection to these temples."

Regu continued: "I will tell you the history of Hindraf now. It began with the Moorthy case. This was a terrible injustice. Moorthy was seen offering Deepavali greetings, and two weeks later his body was being claimed. The Syariah Court ignored all of the evidence that was placed before it. We knew we had to do something." Moorthy, it must be explained, was a member of the Mount Everest trekking team, the first Malaysian team to scale the summit. After his tragic death in December 2005, the Syariah officials claimed that he had secretly converted to Islam, unbeknownst to his family and friends. His body was taken from the morgue as his family prepared traditional Hindu prayers. Within the Tamil community, this was seen as an attempt to co-opt a national hero.

Regu said that (then) Deputy Prime Minister and Defence Minister, Najib Razak (currently Prime Minister), had to be acknowledged as the father of Hindraf, as "ten thousand temples had been destroyed under his watch".[7] Moreover, he claimed that it was Najib's attitude towards the Hindus that had allowed this to happen. Finally, Najib had refused to meet the leadership of Hindraf and discuss the problems of the Indian community. While Najib received the lion's share of the blame due to the active role he played as Defence Minister and Deputy Prime Minister, then–Prime Minister Abdullah Badawi was not spared entirely. Though many Indians, including those in Hindraf, saw Badawi as more openminded and democratic than his predecessor (Mahathir), he was accused of being weak, and for allowing his Deputy (Najib) to curry favour with so-called Islamic hardliners and ethnic chauvinists.

I then asked Regu to elaborate a bit on the particular problems that were faced by the Indian community. Regu spoke first about the transformations in the estates that had led to "squatter" areas and projects. In such contexts, there was "no field to play", and this had led to the rise in popularity, among the youths, in video game rooms. These in turn, have become dens of petty urban crime, where protection money is paid to local syndicates to stay in operation. In most cases, these Indian youths act as petty thugs or gangsters for "bosses" and are acculturated into a life of crime. According to Regu, the government failed to invest in "human capital" where and when it was needed most, leading to the rise in urban crime amongst Indian youths.

Regu said a second mistake had been critical. The government had begun to aggressively punish the petty gangsterism of the video game room culture. This, ironically, pushed Indian youths into the hands of yet more violent forms of gangsterism, as economic opportunities were diminished, while urban consumption desires remained great. The drug trade, in particular, came into the scene, in the last five years, making the gangs more violent. Also, theft increased dramatically. This, in turn, led to more police profiling and arrests. A vicious cycle of Indian incarceration had begun. In custody, Indian youths, who are disproportionately represented, often suffer abuse, or even death.

But it was the demolition of a temple in Shah Alam (Padang Jawa), a week before Deepavali in 2007, that outraged the community, particularly after efforts to spare it were ignored. This gave the movement tremendous momentum and popularity. Prior to this, however, Hindraf had distributed literature at the Thaipusam festival at Batu Caves in January 2007, explaining the purpose of the organization. A hundred thousand VCDs were distributed to the large crowds, which showed how temples had been destroyed in other places; these also emphasized the marginalization of Indians. More broadly, this "created awareness", according to Regu.

In the meantime, a memorandum was prepared and presented to the Chief Minister of Selangor, who did not respond. "Then we approached Samy Vellu [President of the MIC], the PM, and even Parliament, but no response. Finally we approached the Agong [King], and no response. At this point, we did not know what to do. But then we thought, the British brought us this problem, why not we present this memorandum to the British Government."

The "Makkal Sakti" (Tamil: "people's power") campaign was not backing any specific political party, but was advocating that Indians should vote against Barisan National (BN, the ruling coalition) at any cost. This would be to punish the United Malays National Organisation (UMNO, the ruling party within the ruling coalition) for its "racist and Islamist agenda", which has led to the demolition of thousands of temples; and to punish the MIC, which has not stood up to UMNO on this issue, and which has failed to deliver economic benefits to the Indian community.

Already, he explained, "Makkal Sakti" has proven its power in organizing against the sheer might of the police and Federal Reserve Units

(FRU), facing down tear gas and water cannon. They also pulled off the amazing boycott of the biggest festival in the Malaysian Hindu calendar, Thaipusam. This normally draws one million visitors to Batu Caves each year. In 2008, as a result of a boycott called for by Hindraf-"Makkal Sakti", the turnout was purportedly only around 275,000. Moreover, 150,000 went to an alternative site in Port Klang as well as other temples in Malaysia to celebrate. Their grievance stemmed from the MIC-backed Batu Caves temple management's tactics on the eve of the 25 November demonstrations. That night, as demonstrators gathered in the temple, they were suddenly locked inside the temple behind the large gates that enclosed the compound. This enraged the crowd. They felt they had been locked in so that they could not demonstrate. While locked behind the gate, some "thugs" began to throw stones at the Hindraf members from outside of the compound; but when those trapped responded in kind, the police intervened, leading to some of the police being hit by stones. This, then, gave the police a pretext for which to arrest and charge those trapped inside with attempted murder, according to Regu's account. Because of this incident, there was tremendous anger towards the Batu Caves temple management, which allowed demonstrators to be locked inside the temple. Moreover, this then led to the stone throwing that injured the policemen, and brought out the water cannon that were fired upon the temple. To many Hindus, this transgression, a sacrilege committed by the law upon a sacred space had further awakened the Indians to the violence of the state directed against Hindu rights. This, in turn, galvanized thousands of Tamil protesters to Kuala Lumpur's streets, in defiance of an "unjust" state and its laws.

RAMAJI, SPIRITUAL ADVISOR TO HINDRAF

Ramaji is a saffron-robed Hindu priest. He offers spiritual counsel to the Hindraf movement, and has a long history of serving with various Hindu organizations in Malaysia. He, like Regu, has been a key organizer and advisor within Hindraf from the start. Ramaji outlined his own version of the Hindraf story.

Ramaji explained that "Islamization was very strong", and had influenced how the police dealt with local communities as well. In 2006 alone, twenty-nine temples were destroyed in the space of three weeks. After these demolitions, memorandums were presented, through their

(Hindraf's) legal counsel, to the Sultan of Selangor, the Prime Minster, and even to the King, but with no response. "We finally said, we had better go to the foreign." Ramaji explained that the decision to file a suit against Her Majesty's Government[8] came only after six letters to the Prime Minister were left unanswered, in addition to the memorandum which had been submitted to the Prime Minister on behalf of Hindraf.

I asked if he thought the movement was headed in the right direction, now that the ISA had detained the leaders,[9] and the government had branded Hindraf a terrorist organization. Ramaji replied:

> We are uniting for the whole of society, not for the self, but for a cause. But we are branded as "gangsters". The youth are motivated. There were no criminal cases at Thaipusam last year. In years past there would always be criminal or gangster elements at Thaipusam.

Hindraf, he maintained, had given them something to believe in.

Ramaji spoke about "harsh chemicals" that were added to the water cannon on the "day of the roses" demonstration.[10] "We wanted to present roses to the Prime Minister, but chemicals were added to the water to hurt us, instead." This, he added, was a very cruel way to treat people who wanted to demonstrate peacefully. Moreover, we "carried the Agong's picture at the rose demonstration to show our loyalty."

I then asked whether the Prime Minister's promise to the Indian community, which came out in a meeting with twenty NGOs, to look into specific problem areas faced by the community, would produce tangible results. Ramaji said, "this is just a 'bluff' to stop our movement ... he has not even acknowledged our memorandum in his promises." That is, his (the Prime Minister's) promises were empty, he (Ramaji) surmised, because they did not respond directly to Hindraf (and thereby failed to give the recognition that the Tamil Indian community sought). Of course, had he responded directly to Hindraf, the political cost among Malay voters would have been terribly consequential for UMNO. But Ramaji did not consider this. Indeed, he sees a dark horizon in interethnic relations brewing in Malaysia which was somewhat ominous, echoing what others had said to me in recent times, "It will happen like Sri Lanka.... We've been tolerant enough for the last fifty years." Indeed, a sense of Tamils being backed into a defensive corner has been a growing chorus in the past seven years or so, particularly after the Kampung Medan attacks. But while Hindraf does not appear, nor admit, to have any Liberation Tigers of Tamil Eelam links, Ramaji did admit to have learned from the Rashtriya Swamysevak Sangh (RSS), and even to have some loose affiliation with the Vishnu Hindu Parishad and RSS in India. His orientation is therefore conservative and Hindu, not Tamil nationalistic. But Hindraf is a many headed hydra and draws support from disparate elements.

Ramaji and Regu then took me to a rally at Padang Jawa, "where it all started". They explained the significance of this sight — "this was a divine event", the awakening of Hindraf. And this awakening happened because of the "breaking" of a specific temple a few days before Deepavali in Padang Jawa, Shah Alam. In this very working-class area, the "ground zero" of the "Makkal Sakti" movement, leaders of the movement have turned the "breaking" of the temple, once a tragic event in the Tamil community, into a rallying point, and even a pilgrimage spot. To underscore its spiritual significance, the temple has been reconstituted within the compound of someone's home, or between two homes, safe from further demolition, for now. Regu said to a crowd of assembled devotees at this site: "We tried every avenue to save this temple, but perhaps, because of this, and how the authorities handled it, something bigger or divine was planned." Ramaji led the group of about one hundred people in chanting and then spoke to the crowd about the "spirit of sacrifice" that was in one woman who had tried to save the temple and who had helped rebuild it. That spirit of sacrifice, he said, was now needed within the whole community. Indian opposition politicians were also called upon to speak.

In this focal point, we can understand Hindraf's power vis-à-vis the force of the law. Though I do not wish to unpack the catastrophic struggle against developers and, ultimately, the state, that led to the traumatizing eventual demolition of the Padang Jawa temple on the eve of Deepavali, an important Hindu festival, I would suggest that this had a profound psychic impact upon the Tamil community. It revealed the state and its laws to be transgressive in a manner more forcefully, if not outrageously arbitrary, than before. This betrayal, in turn, led to a precipitous decline in Indian support for the government. But also, the incomprehensible symbolic violence of demolition, as played out in the Tamil and independent media, awakened an unease, a restless insecurity of faith in both the laws of the land and the powers of the gods, that sought reconstitution in a higher power or reason, in a transcendent source.

In its rebirth, now, the temple itself had been sacrificed for the spirit of community awakening — a "divine event" disseminating the temple's power (or transforming its apparent failure) into the people, now reborn with "people power" (*makkal sakti*). In this instance, the shards of destruction and creative energy (*sakti*) seemed comprehensible, at least in part, in the emergent narrative of the apocryphal birth of Hindraf out of the temple's sacrifice. Still, a violent unease about the future grips the imagination. The spectre of the state, the ghost of "like Sri Lanka", and the fear of future demolitions lurk as an unfathomable horizon.

In Tamil Hindu terms, a violent unleashing of the transgressed goddess (Kinsley 1986; Nabokov 2000) will overwhelm and possess her subjects in response to the arbitrary violence of the law. At the edge of reason, *katavul* (the sacred, God, or, more specifically, "crossing" from the known to the unknown; Nabokov 2000, p. 8) reconstitutes the subject with a sense of power and mastery, but an uncanny residue remains. As Nabokov[11] (2000) has argued for possession and counter-sorcery, more generally, in the Tamil context, a violence inheres in both the attack against the subject that announces itself as possession, as well as in the destruction of the anthropomorphized demonic presence. Nabokov's insightful analysis of several counter-sorcery rituals underscores their unresolved nature. She demonstrates that the destruction of a possessing demonic agent, as achieved through counter-sorcery ritual, is never absolute or complete, as it involves a splitting of the psyche of the Tamil subject. The offending deity, as representative of the subject's forbidden desire, and as translated through the cultural work of symbolization,[12] is subject to external objectification through the work of effigies, which, in turn, are destroyed by decapitation. The literal destruction of one's (alter) self, and the renunciation of desire that accompanies this process, Nabokov argues, produces not only a recapitulation of the law and its violence (in this case, the patriarchal structure of Tamil life), but also the ever-present feeling of suppressed selfhood haunting the conscious subject. Put another way, the transgression of the Other's law is still haunted by the futural recapitulation of the Law, a higher and possessive divine force.

The subject is forced to renounce his/her desire, the aetiology of his/her possession, and to submit to the law, despite the spirited protest by the alien presence, which made itself known at the edge of reason, or in a "crossing" (*katavul*) into the unknown. In the Tamil context, the notion of divine justice is also always already haunted by the force of the law with its arbitrary violence. This Tamil theodicy produces its own version of the sublime, outside, though not entirely dissimilar from its Kantian variant.

As Rodolphe Gasche has eloquently argued, "[w]hat is judged sublime is the mind's capacity to form an apprehension of something that thwarts even the possibility of minimal objectification, and that like the 'wide ocean, disturbed by the storm ... is just horrible'" (Gasche, and Kant cited in Gasche 2003, p. 127). But, arguably, the sublime object, born of a divided and violently suppressed self, is "minimally" objectifiable; however, this objectification, as Freud's notion of the uncanny would have it, possesses the subject, bringing on a restlessness and agitated psychic movement. That is, beyond reason, the force of judgment produces both a futural angst and desirous fantasy about violent outcomes, imagined and figured as justice. Divine justice may mean the destruction of the Other's law, in this case the Malaysian ethnicized state, but in submitting to a higher law, Tamils are still caught by a possessive force, forged, in the context of Malaysia, in reaction to the powers of racial signification.

MALAY UNIVERSITY LEADER

I interviewed the head administrator, of necessity, a Malay, from a leading local university in 2008. He spoke in general terms about the coming elections, stating that "of course, only BN will form the government", when asked. I pressed and asked if he felt it would capture the two-thirds majority, to which he replied, he thought it would be so. Turning to the Hindraf issue, I asked if there would potentially be a Malay backlash against it. He said there already was, pointing out that Malays were a bit annoyed by the image of Gandhi that had been paraded during the 25 November Hindraf demonstration. Moreover, the image of the Queen, evidently, had also been used. To this administrator, and apparently to Malays, the image was insulting, as it connoted loyalty to India, and Britain, respectively, and not to Malaysia. "If they had put an image of our King, that would be better", he said. I mentioned to him then that Gandhi was probably used to indicate non-violence. He replied that it signified loyalty to India in the eyes of Malays.

In another sense, Malays were angered, the administrator claimed, because the Hindraf demands challenged Malay "special rights". Malays perceived the demonstration as being "against Malays". Another professor, present in the room, added that many Malays were worried and upset that their rights to education and economic assistance were being questioned by Hindraf. This, they both concurred, made Malays "against the Hindraf movement", as a whole. But when asked if this perception was entirely accurate or perhaps a misperception of what most Indians seek redress for, they could not say. Moreover, consequences of further Indian discontent, I suggested, might be more assertive civil disobedience campaigns with large public gatherings. To this, the leader of the university answered, "luckily we have our FRU and efficient police to deal with them, so I do not anticipate any problem". In other words, brute force was the correct approach, from his point of view, in dealing with public demonstrations. And, as we have witnessed, this is the very mindset that produces Tamil fantasies about the insecurity of the Other. In other words, to keep the peace and to placate an uneasy public, particularly in the opinion of the Malays, required an iron fist. He confirmed this by stating that the real calming of Malay feelings occurred once the ISA was used to detain the five lawyer-spokesmen for Hindraf.

Regarding the problem of temple relocations and demolitions, the Malay educational leader was not completely sympathetic. He said there was a problem, for certain, but that the problem existed because all of the "Tamils have moved out and the land has been developed in the estates, but only the temple from the plantation is left there". The problem is that, as he argued, "the Indians become upset if you demolish the temple". But at the same time, they do not live there, and this land has to be used for other purposes, he implied. This is an intractable problem of development, in his brief analysis, not a plot to marginalize Hinduism or demolish temples at will. But it did not occur to him to think about the entire process of displacement and development from a larger vantage point, starting with the retrenchment of Tamil labour from the estates that they had lived *in situ* for generations. The sensitivities and emotional attachment to temples arose, I suggested, due to the dispossession these same people felt upon leaving the estates. Therefore, the temple has taken on a magnified importance in their struggles as a semblance of their past community lives. To my comment, he uttered, "yes", but merely stated that the problem of temples was "sensitive" and difficult to resolve as the development process went on, replacing plantation communities with new housing estates that were primarily non-Indian. The point I wanted him to comment upon was whether this replacement itself was just or fair, but he either did not see the point, or thought it mute.

The educationist left me with a final thought to ponder, which seemed to exemplify the government's attitude towards Indians. "Our attitude is that we give the MIC some funding and then let them decide what to do with it. If Indians are not happy with the way the MIC is allocating the resources, it is up to Indians to change MIC. It is not our concern." This attitude is problematic, of course, at several levels. If the government thinks in such a manner, then it is not governing the people, but utilizing political parties as brokers to do their bidding, with little or no oversight. If the performance of the party is "not our concern", then who is to be held accountable? He is implying that it is the ethnic-based party that must be held accountable and not the government as a whole. But what if corruption or mismanagement of resources leaves entire segments of a population marginalized? This washing of the hands by the government empowers the MIC to act as it will, with little concern for the consequences from above, according to some who feel that the party has abused its power at the expense of the people.

My research collaborator and I watched a couple of films about Hindraf made by Malay students of English literature at this university. The films utilized a lot of documentary footage, taken from the Internet, which showed the demonstration on 25 November. The films were, at the outset, somewhat sympathetic, given that the footage showed police manhandling and crowd distress, not to mention the effects of water cannon and tear gas. But when it came time for analysis and interviews, a decidedly non-Indian view came through. One interviewee mentioned that the protesters were simply "against the government, and not against other races", and thus should not be taken as provoking sensitive racial issues. But another Malay interviewee mentioned that the movement had touched on the theme of Malay "special rights", and that they "shouldn't question special rights". Yet another Malay said that they were against the demonstration because "everyone is treated equally in Malaysia, but that Malays should always be given special rights above others". One student filmmaker was very upset with Hindraf, she said, as it had sullied Malaysia's image overseas, adding, "Malaysia is the most peaceful multicultural nation in the world", but the image of the protests would make people think otherwise.

Another Malay said, "This was done just before the election to make people vote for the opposition." The makers of the first film gave their own opinion at the end of their film, stating that it was a difficult assignment. They had gone to Batu Caves to interview people about Hindraf and felt uneasy the whole time, finding it hard to find people to talk to them. I suspect that, as Malays, there was some suspicion that they were reporters or spies for the government. Even saying they were from the university would not be enough to get most Tamil Hindus to open up and talk freely, in my experience. They mentioned, for instance, speaking to taxi drivers around the caves, rather than to Hindu devotees within the caves. They also spoke to policemen in Kuala Lumpur, rather than Hindraf members. The selection of interviewees tells us about the subject-position of the filmmakers and the likely awkwardness of their project at the time of its production. The filmmakers themselves said they initially felt some sympathy with the Indian cause, but felt that the Malaysian Government was basically "fair" to all Malaysians. Furthermore, the "special rights" of bumiputras had to be respected and, therefore, the demands of Hindraf were "unreasonable", they concluded. The Indian grievance or perspective, witnessed in the Hindraf leadership, could not be fathomed.

Though I cannot present a fuller Malay perspective here, I did interview other Malays and saw that Hindraf had the potential of producing a backlash against the Indian community. A debate has erupted within the media amongst Malays about the implications of Hindraf, with those accusing sympathizers of being traitors, and the counter accusation being that Malays have become incredibly insecure in recent years. This is an important point to develop and theorize, but one that I do not have space to take up in this chapter. That is, the notion that a *new and insecure Malay identity* is increasingly brash and assertive, manifesting itself in monocultural policies and Islamist insensitivities to the history of Malaysia, and especially to the sentiments of other communities. This new identity and mindset has been cultivated through exclusive educational institutions, entitlement regimes, and the cognitive dissonance that comes with the partial knowledge that *bumiputraism* (pro-Malay policies and ideologies) is built upon historically shallow notions of ethnic purity that belie recent immigrations from Indonesia, India, etc. That is, Malay identity has always been more fluid (Mandal 2004) and cosmopolitan (Kahn 2006), indeed, Malaysian, than the new brand of ethnic purists want to admit. Hence the new kind of racialism that permeates the landscape of ethnic politics in Malaysia finds its displaced scapegoat in ethnic Others, be they Indians, Chinese, or foreign workers. Indians, in perceiving this lack in the Other, attempt to surmount or supplement it. But in the supplementary acts, the excessive and possessive force of identification also simultaneously alienates the subject from itself (Siegel 2006; Appadurai 2006). The evidentiary base of the archive grows in direct proportion to the sense of self that is forged in the parameters of victimization. The nurturing of spirit (Derrida 1989), or justice, in these terms, carries within it the risk of (temporarily) silencing the haunting double that drives the imaginings of the subject (or, perhaps, of the imaginary subject). As manifested in Hindraf, the call for justice evokes an assertion of higher or divine law, which might even be called a reverse patrimony, as defined against Malay-Islamic nationalism. But achieving this awakening, in turn, required an extensive and feverish archiving of transgressions by the Other against the authenticity of the Tamil Hindu presence. Elsewhere, I demonstrate how this takes place, in particular, within the realm of a meaningful plantation landscape geography that, under the threats of demolition and dispersal, has produced a lore of the miraculous (Willford 2006; Bunnell, Nagarajan, and Willford 2010).

The "powers" and memories associated with temples and shrines within the plantations are, indeed, the animus behind the emergence of Hindraf as a collective force. The benign or protecting powers, associated with the memories of the estate, can turn malevolent too, and that is of concern to devotees, who at some risk to themselves, stage festivals which involve the offerings of meat and beer to potentially violent "guardian" deities (Shulman 1989; Mines 2005; Nabokov 2000). The question that remains is whether ritualized memorializations, protests, or archivization can affect control over the incomprehensible wound caused by the destruction of the sacred space. And more broadly, the question is also whether a particularly dangerous and justice-seeking deity's violence can be contained. Read as an extension of the community, the village gods are explicitly bound to their subjects in an eternal contract of reciprocity. They can equally create or protect against calamity, according to Tamil folklore (Kinsley 1986; Whitehead 1921; Shulman 1989). But against the horrific and sublime reconstitution through ritual control, memories of a landscape that was once theirs are manifest in the focal attention paid to these shrines and temples. Yet even in this repossession of the land, figural or literal, as is often the case in the "social" ritualization of the sacred landscape in Tamil Hinduism, the possession of the devotee that accompanies this process by an unseen and dangerous power that lies outside of oneself becomes partially inexplicable or exceeds the symbolic order (Nabokov 2000). From here, aspiration, divine justice, the miraculous, and the limits of reason coexist. As in Derrida's contrast between the "calculating apparatus" that is the law, and which is subject to the rules of the archive, justice is "infinite, incalculable, rebellious to rule and foreign to symmetry" (Derrida 2002, p. 250). The sublime sacred in Tamil Hinduism haunts the (human) order of the law and exceeds historical reason. Its de(con)structive power to unmask the contingencies of human law proves politically potent, as witnessed in the collective force of Hindraf in the wake of the state's transgression upon sacred spaces.

Through this we can see that the logic of compensation that haunts justice in Malaysia can be witnessed through the optic of Tamil notions of the sacred and its transgression by the law and, by extension, by the actions this might precipitate among devotees. Unlike the reconstitution of the Padang Jawa temple (discussed earlier) into a new pilgrimage spot and, thus, an apocryphal reworking of catastrophic loss into a sacrifice for "people power," the power(s) unleashed by demolition remain undetermined, dangerous, and therefore uncanny in their power to possess (Siegel 2006) and, to an extent, non-cognizable, and perhaps a sublime source of unease (Gasche 2003) as much as a resource for hope through justice.

CONCLUSION

There is a haunting of justice in Malaysia because certain acts of the law are haunted by the force of the decisions that inaugurated them. The instantiation of law is violent in its performative act; but, it is also supplemented in its lack through the sustaining violence of various pieces of juridical evidence (Benjamin 1986; Derrida 2002; De Vries 2002) and further decisions derived from the founding decision, and the archiving of difference circuitously serve as evidence of the law's inviolability. In the case of Malaysia, as in many other postcolonial renderings of juridical difference, identities were created and rendered through the law, supplemented through archival measurements or race and culture but, I am suggesting, these remained haunted by the inability of complete disentanglement or closure. The feverish cataloguing of racial and ethnic difference that distinguished and ossified racialized thinking in Malaysia for decades is a great silencer of legal justice, though it arrives in the name of the law.

That is, an originary lack in the law itself may be haunted by its own violent suppression of its arbitrariness (i.e., a performative founding act). The historicity, and contingency of the state's truth claims, for instance, may require compensatory elaboration in a chain of substitutions, signifiable in time and space as ethnographic others, thus deferring and displacing this originary lack with supplementary violence.[13] As Derrida argues, there is a "mystical" dimension to authority and the law, in its performative utterance, "there is here a silence walled up in the violent structure of the founding act; walled up, walled in because this silence is not exterior to language" (2002, p. 242). He adds, the act is haunted as "its ghostliness deconstructs from within all assurance of presence ... it always maintains within itself some irruptive violence" (2002, pp. 253–56). In this sense, an originary lack inherent in the "irruptive violence" of law is supplemented through the "archive fever" (Derrida 1995) of an ethnographic state (Dirks 2002). Grounding itself "in conventions" provides an aura of retroactive historicity to the violence of the state and law; and the ethnographic archive, in turn, is a critical part of this exercise, and the exercising of the law's ghostliness. That is, the contingency inherent in the violence of the letter of the law, more generally, requires a continuous source of exteriority as a source of authority. This dimension of statecraft, referred to provocatively as "lawfare" by Comoroff and Comoroff (2007), through its very performativity, finds itself vulnerable to hauntings of justice. Racialized thinking and identification in Malaysia has required such feverish archiving (Hirschman 1986; Kahn 2006; Peletz 2002; Mandal 2004); but, I am suggesting, as a consequence, the law (and identity, more broadly) is deconstructible and haunted by the inability of complete disentanglement (Povinelli 2002; Appadurai 2006; Baxtrom 2007; Willford 2006). It is in this sense that a relationship with Lacan's *objet a* becomes apparent.[14] As *objet a* is a source of anxiety generated by the symbolic order that instantiates itself as the subject's law, it generates movement and desire through imaginary realms of substitution and supplementation. Archiving ethnic difference is the form that this supplementation takes in Malaysia.

What can be said, with more circumspection, is that the violence of the law has awakened the Tamil community in ways that it has not been before. This has provoked an awareness that justice, indeed, compensation, is not to be found in the law, but, rather, in its transgression. The delinking of justice and legality has both important theoretical and practical implications for Tamils as they struggle to adjust to a socio-economic reality at the end of the plantation era in Malaysia. And lastly, the emergent sense of justice and compensation is grounded in an equally emergent historicity of cultural recognition, defined against the politics of ethnic exclusivity. Indian fantasies for compensatory recognition imagine a re-entangling of Tamil and Malay historicities, if not identities. The force of law is haunted by the wake of its destruction as well as its inherent deconstructibility (Derrida

2002). But in the fragmentation of memory of experience wrought by state "betrayals" and the violence of displacement, a recognisable logic within Tamil Hinduism has taken hold, both as a political resource, and also as a source of unfathomable unease. Justice in its incalculable and infinite sense is divine. But divinity, too, has the power to violently possess with inexplicable force. The very potential turns the aspiration to justice into its possible haunting.

Notes

1. Several Malays have expressed this view to me privately, including some academics. For instance, some have contrasted the traditional mosque architecture in places like Malacca with that of Putrajaya, noting that the new administrative capital seems to have borrowed more from the Middle East and South Asia than Malay architectural principles.
2. The work of S. Nagarajan (2004; 2008) is a notable exception.
3. The indigenous people, known as Orang Asli, have also been victims of Malaysia's developmental push in Selangor.
4. *New Straits Times*, "Residents Protest Relocation of Temple", 28 August 2009 <www.nst.com.my/Curent News/NST/articles/20090828203330/Article/index.html>.
5. Asrul Hadi Abdullah Sani, "Hisham Defends Cow-head Protesters". *The Malaysian Insider*, 9 February 2010 <www.themalaysianinsider.com/index.php/malaysia/36672-hisham-defends-cow-head-protesters>.
6. Many Indians believed that these attacks were carried out by political proxy "militias" in order to both send a message to the Indian community and to distract attention towards a scapegoat (e.g., Indians) for problems of political disunity within the Malay community. Though the violence was extensive, long-lasting, and brutal, no charges were ever filed against anyone. Furthermore, the government's refusal to conduct a public inquiry aroused further suspicion of a cover-up within the Tamil community (see Nagarajan 2004; Willford 2008).
7. Hindraf literature and legal documents chronicle hundreds of temple demolitions, not thousands. Regu's verbal figures are very likely exaggerated.
8. Hindraf sued the British government in 2007 for abandoning the Indian community in Malaysia at the mercy of the Malay-led government. This was, they admit, more of a publicity stunt than a serious attempt to obtain reparations from the British.
9. The Hindraf ISA detainees were eventually released in 2009.
10. The "day of roses" or Valentine Roses Campaign was organized by Hindraf

to present roses to the Prime Minister to appeal for the release of five Hindraf leaders detained without trial under the Internal Security Act. The rally took place on 16 February 2008, but was broken up when police fired tear gas and water cannon at the demonstrators.
11. Nabokov is now known as Isabelle Clark-Deces.
12. Gananath Obeyesekere (1981) and Sudhir Kakar (1982) have made similar arguments concerning other South Asian contexts.
13. A similar logic is found in Agamben (2005), where he argues that the "anomie" within the heart of Law is shored up through the "state of exception", a figure of displacement.
14. There is a critical difference, however, between Derrida's deconstruction and Lacan's failure of the Law — at least in Derrida's view. In the latter's case, as Derrida argues in several works, there is a paramount Law, the law of the primordial signifier, the phallus. This, Derrida argues, recreates the metaphysics of presence. Derrida, rather, suggests that the Law is always subject to the contingent forces of its creation, without privileging any particular signifier as essential in its constitution.

References

Agamben, Giorgio. *State of Exception*. Chicago: University of Chicago Press, 2005.
Appadurai, Arjun. *The Fear of Small Numbers*. Durham: Duke University Press, 2006.
Asrul Hadi Abdullah Sani . "Hisham Defends Cow-head Protesters". *Malaysian Insider*, 9 February 2010 <http://www.themalaysianinsider.com/index.php/malaysia/36672-hisham-defends-cow-head-protesters>.
Baxstrom, Richard . *Houses in Motion: The Experience of Place and the Problem of Belief in Urban Malaysia*. Stanford: Stanford University Press, 2008.
Benjamin, Walter. *Reflections*. New York: Schocken Books, 1986.
Bunnell, Tim, S. Nagarajan and Andrew Willford. "From the Margins to Centre Stage: 'Indian' Demonstration Effects and Malaysia's Political Landscape". *Urban Studies* 1, no. 22 (2010).
Comaroff, John and Jean Comaroff. "Law and Disorder in the Postcolony: An Introduction". In *Law and Disorder in the Postcolony*, edited by Jean and John Comaroff. Chicago: University of Chicago Press, 2007.
De Vries, Hent. *Religion and Violence*. Baltimore: Johns Hopkins University Press, 2002.
Derrida, Jacques. *Of Grammatology,* translated by Gayatri Chakrovorty Spivak. Baltimore: Johns Hopkins Press, 1974.

———. *Of Spirit: Heidegger and the Question*, translated by Geoffrey Bennington and Rachel Bowlby. Chicago: University of Chicago Press, 1989.

———. *Archive Fever: A Freudian Impression*, translated by Eric Prenowitz. Chicago: University of Chicago Press, 1995.

———. "Force of Law". In *Acts of Religion*. London: Routledge, 2002.

Dirks, Nicholas. "Annals of the Archive. Ethnographic Notes of the Sources of History". In *From the Margins: Historical Anthropology and its Futures*, edited by Brian Axel. Durham, NC: Duke University Press, 2002.

Gasche, Rodolphe. *The Idea of Form: Rethinking Kant's Aesthetics*. Stanford: Stanford University Press, 2003.

Gullick, J.M. *A History of Selangor 1766–1939*. Kuala Lumpur: Malaysian Branch of the Royal Asiatic Society, 2004.

Hirschman, Charles. "The Making of Race in Colonial Malaya". *Sociological Forum* 1, no. 2 (1986) 330–61.

Hoffstaedter, Gerhard. "Muslim Malay Identity Formation and its Articulation in Peninsular Malaysia". PhD dissertation, Latrobe University, Australia, 2008.

Iyer, K.A. Neelakandha. *Indian Problems in Malaya*. Kuala Lumpur: Indian Office in Kuala Lumpur, 1938.

Kahn, Joel. *Other Malays: Nationalism and Cosmopolitanism in the Modern Malay World*. Singapore: Singapore University Press.

Kakar, Sudhir. *Shaman's, Mystics, and Doctors*. Chicago: University of Chicago Press, 2006.

King, Ross. *Kuala Lumpur and Putrajaya: Negotiating Urban Space in Malaysia*. Singapore: Singapore University Press, 2008.

Kinsley, David R. *Hindu Goddesses*. Berkeley: University of California Press, 1986.

Lacan, Jacques. *The Psychoses, 1955–1956*. New York: Norton, 1993.

Mandal, Sumit. "Transethnic Solidarities, Racialisation, and Social Equality". In *The State of Malaysia: Ethnicity and Reform*, edited by Terence Gomez. London: Routledge, 2004.

Mines, Diane. *Fierce Gods: Inequality, Ritual, and the Politics of Dignity in a South Indian Village*. Bloomington: Indiana University Press, 2005.

Nabokov, Isabelle. *Religion Against the Self: An Ethnography of Tamil Rituals*. Oxford: Oxford University Press, 2000.

Nagarajan, S. *A Community in Transition: Tamil Displacements in Malaysia*. PhD dissertation, University of Malaya, Malaysia, 2004.

———. "Indians in Malaysia: Towards Vision 2020". In *Rising India and Indian Communities in East Asia*, edited by K. Kesavapany, A. Mani and P. Ramasamy. Singapore: Institute of Southeast Asian Studies, 2008.

Obeyesekere, Gananath. *Medusa's Hair*. Chicago: University of Chicago Press, 1981.

Peletz, Michael. *Islamic Modern: Religious Courts and Cultural Politics in Malaysia.* Princeton: Princeton University, 2002.
Povinelli, Elizabeth. *The Cunning of Recognition.* Durham, NC: Duke University Press, 2002.
Shulman, David Dean. "Outcaste, Guardian, and Trickster: Notes on the Myth of Kattavarayan". In *Criminal Gods and Demon Devotees*, edited by Alf Hiltebeitel. Albany: State University of New York Press, 1989.
Siegel, James. *Naming the Witch.* Stanford: Stanford University Press, 2006.
Whitehead, Henry. *Village Gods of South India.* Calcutta: Association Press, 1921.
Willford, Andrew. *Cage of Freedom: Tamil Identity and the Ethnic Fetish in Malaysia.* Ann Arbor: University of Michigan Press, 2006.
———. "Ethnic Clashes, Squatters, and Historicity in Malaysia". In *Rising India and Indians in East Asia,* edited by K. Kesavapany, A. Mani and P. Ramasamy. Singapore: Institute of Southeast Asian Studies, 2008.

7

ISLAMIZATION AND ETHNICITY IN SABAH, MALAYSIA

Regina Lim

The normative foundation of the secular state as the separation of religion and the state embodied in much liberal theorizing is becoming untenable in most developing countries. Such perspectives on the ideas of the secular state, it is suggested, underestimate the complexity of the relationship between the religious and the political in many non-Western societies (Bajpai 2002) and, in a curious way, actually privilege a particular Judeo-Christian perspective on the state (Hurd 2008). In contemporary politics, many — if not most — Western countries have subscribed to the norms of secularism. The European/North American "secular age" is characterized by the absence of God in the institutions and practices of the state, followed by the retreat of religious faith into the private sphere (Taylor 2007). God no longer plays a role in governments and politics, and there is an increasing trend towards the privatization of religion in modern societies that witnessed the gradual institutional disengagement or separation of the church and state. Even within this Western context, however, nuanced differences in the interpretation and meaning of "secularism" are evident, as witnessed by the divergence between the U.S. version of secularism, which was originally developed to protect religious institutions from state influence and French laïcité which seeks to protect the state from the influence of religion (Gunn 2004). The history of colonialism and the politics of nationalist movements played important roles in disseminating ideas of secularism, particularly via the dynamics of emerging nation-states (Taylor 2009).

Secularism becomes subject to state negotiation and the interpretation of the public role of religion in society (Yavuz 2009). In the Southeast Asian context, religion remains publicly visible in politics, culture and society but that does not mean that ideas of the secular were never envisaged in the trajectories of state building. The interpretation of the secular and its debates need to be explored in the context of their historical and political contingencies to illuminate contemporary understanding of the state and its relationship with religion. In this chapter, I examine the notions of the "secular" and how its practical relevance as an element of governance in Malaysia is diminishing. Yet in the study of the role of religion in politics, the "secular" cannot be divorced from broader issues of identity and political mobilization in many multicultural states. This chapter examines these debates using the Malaysian State of Sabah as a case study to show how the Malaysian state deploys religious elements in its national development agenda and the extent to which statist Islamization encounters contentious politics emanating from marginalized faiths and ethnicities. The focus on the dynamics of identity politics in Sabah examines how the process of Islamization underscores the complete federal penetration into Sabah's local politics and the extent to which it has become an issue of contestation within the discourse of "endangered identity" (Reid 1997). It aims to illuminate how the politics of Islamization in Sabah generated different kinds of local responses to ideas of citizenship compared to West Malaysia and why the concept of "bumiputra" elicits varied interpretations of "ethnic" rights when Islam is at stake. Sabah is important empirically because the clear dichotomy between Malay-Muslim and non-Malay-Muslim in West Malaysia does not hold in Sabah. We cannot understand the dynamics of Islamization in Malaysia as a whole without reference to East Malaysia and theoretically it gives us a richer understanding of ethnicity and religion beyond the structured ways in which the dichotomies of ethno-religious relations work in West Malaysia.

ISLAMIZATION AND CITIZENSHIP

This section examines the contemporary public role of Islam under the Abdullah administration by tracing the historical process of how the state's institutionalization of Islam contributed to the negation of secular space, particularly for non-Muslims in Malaysia. I want to highlight the unusual process involving the separation of a community of Muslim citizens from the non-Muslim citizens via the Constitutional definition of Malay under Article 160(2) of the 1957 Federal Constitution. Contrary to the norms of the separation doctrine found in a secular state, the rationale for the founding of the 1957 independence of Malaya (subsequently Malaysia in 1963) was driven by the idea of ethnic and religious differences. Islam was introduced to the Malays by Sufi missionaries in the thirteenth century (Hussin Mutalib 1993) and its laws permeated Malay customs (Hooker 1984). Labour migration with its concomitant common law practices under British Malaya during the mid-nineteenth century added a different dimension to the practice of traditional customs in Malaya by circumscribing the scope of Islamic jurisdiction applicable only among Muslims (Horowitz 1994). Despite the existence of other non-Muslim communities in Malaya, the long durée of ethno-religious identification consequently rationalized the essential definition of Muslim-Malay identity, where the Malay leaders and the framers of the 1957 Constitution founded Article 160(2) of the Constitution to define "Malay" as a Malaysian citizen who professes Islam, follows *adat* (Malay custom) and habitually speaks Bahasa Malaysia (Abdullah Saeed and Hassan Saeed 2004).

Despite the secular intention of the Federal Constitution, Article 3(1) of the Constitution provides a public role for Islam, designating it the "religion of the Federation" (Fernando 2006). The Malaysian Constitution elevates the role and status of Islam above all other religions in the country by virtue of its function both as a faith and as a law (Marican Pawancheek and Mohamed Azam Mohamed Adil 2005). The legal provision to elevate a particular religion in the public sphere draws on the issue of neutrality in state practice. Whilst religion is the norm of politics in Malaysia, contemporary political events are beginning to illuminate issues of fundamental concerns with regard to religious liberty and the notion of political equality affecting citizens from minority faith and ethnic backgrounds. The state's departure from the principle of neutrality increases the empirical strengths of religious influence and convictions in fundamental political questions (Audi 2000).

Without delving too much into liberal theorizing, I focus on the normative principle of the separation doctrine found in a secular state which aims to uphold the essences of liberty and basic political equality; and the principle of neutrality in a secular state which imposes essential moral restrictions upon the legitimacy of the state to monopolize the means to violence and unnecessary compulsion upon the liberties of its citizens (Audi 2000, pp. 61–65).

The state defines the duties and obligations of its citizens but is also subject to the moral restrictions of how it derives political legitimacy from society. Tilly maintains that despite the legal interpretations of how citizens should carry out their duties and obligations in return for the rights and protections accorded by the state, "citizenship often comes into being through deliberate exclusion" and therefore seldom reflects the "cumulative sense of common properties" (Tilly 2005, p. 184). The process of exclusion is a function of political boundaries that were historically contingent in identity politics and although these boundaries may appear to shift over time as the result of social mobilizations, Tilly (2005) argues that these boundaries will remain as long as the state and its agents continue to define duties and obligations as the basis of the contractual dimension of citizenship and to deliberate upon citizens' access to rights and benefits in ways that may or may not transform these political boundaries. History played a significant role in the legal provision of a particular ethnic and religious group in Malaysia, but this in theory contradicts the fundamental principle of state neutrality in the separation doctrine (Audi 2000, pp. 32–40; Laborde 2008, p. 33). The Malaysian case provides a strong example that illuminates Tilly's conception of deliberate exclusion because when the state legally exempts itself from the principle of neutrality by favouring a particular community, many questions arise about the issue of political equality enjoyed by citizens from other communities. One related impact of deliberate exclusion can be linked to the phenomenon of the "second-class" citizens whom Gibney defines as "individuals who are nationals of the country in which they are living but who formally lack full (legal) standing in the society" (Gibney 2009, p. 27) The fragile concept of the secular state in Malaysia is increasingly compromised by the expansion of the public role of Islam at the cost of basic political equality among citizens who do not profess the official religion.

Some of the leading causes of contemporary religious inequality can be traced to the Mahathir legacy of statist Islamization in the 1980s

(Hamayotsu 2003; Means 1991). Mahathir proposed the 1988 Constitutional Amendment to Article 121(1A), which stated that "the High Courts in the States of Malaya, Sabah and Sarawak shall have no jurisdiction of the *Syariah* court". It delineates the existing scope of religious liberty and interfaith relations between Muslim and non-Muslim citizens in Malaysian society. Under Abdullah's watch as Prime Minister, there was growing public disenchantment among civil society movements and intellectuals who were critical of the expanded role of Islam in the legal system. Article 11 coalitions, for instance, are civil groups formed in May 2004 that have begun to raise the fundamental issue of the secular state in Malaysia.[1] The growing list of legal cases subjugating the rights of citizens regarding conversion, custodial rights, places of worship, apostasy and other related matters (see, for example, NECF Malaysia 2007) are symptomatic of how the historically dominant religion in Malaysia is at risk of being institutionally embedded by the state to entrench "majority domination" of other minority faiths (Laborde 2008, pp. 80–98). Laborde (2008) observes that the hijab controversy suffered similar ideological supremacy of French *laïcism* as a result of the entrenched majority domination of Western secularism in French politics. In the Malaysian case, the limited legal scope of religious expression among the non-Muslim on the one hand and the institutional expansion of Islamic authority on the other created the space for the majority ethno-religious group to dominate the minority citizens.

Prominent Muslim intellectuals like Farish Noor express deep concern about the future of interfaith relations and dialogue in Malaysia following the amendment.[2] Most cases of legal injustice fell upon non-Muslim citizens who have no legal recourse within *syariah* to resolve matters of dispute with their Muslim counterparts and the legal sanction against the civil courts to interfere effectively maintains the logjam of legal pluralism. Abdullah Saeed and Hassan Saeed (2004, p. 68) argue that the great Hanafi jurist, Sarakhsi Al-Mabsut's political interpretation of the political meaning of apostasy as the "enemy of the state" retains an enduring ideological purchase that divides the modernist and the traditionalist within the contemporary Muslim world, and the Malaysian Government's uncritical acceptance of the traditional interpretation of apostasy influenced the drafting of the Faith Reform Bill 1996,[3] giving the state the ultimate prerogative to measure the faith of individual Muslims. Further, they argue that,

> As a result of the law, the state has become the ultimate arbiter of Muslim faith and belief. It could be said that there are inherent dangers when the

state becomes the ultimate adjudicator of personal faith. This is especially the case in countries like Malaysia where religious institutions and religious officials are subordinated to political authority. (Ibid., p. 143)

The "secular" state came under siege after the 9/11 attacks in the United States when Mahathir declared that Malaysia was an Islamic state.[4] The Deputy Prime Minister, Najib Razak (now Prime Minister) followed suit by claiming that Malaysia has "never been secular".[5] Despite public protests from the opposition parties and civil society organizations, the government banned public discussions of the Islamic state. Former Prime Minister Abdullah gave the assurance that Malaysia was "neither a secular nor a theocratic country, but a country governed on the basis of Islamic principles and observance of the principles of parliamentary democracy grounded in the spirit of social contract within the Federal Constitution".[6] This complemented Abdullah's substantive commitment to Islamic principles when he incorporated Islam Hadhari[7] into the 9th Malaysian Plan as the principal directive policy for national development. The political commitment to Islam as the principal public policy combined with the state's rejection of secular considerations generate what Malik Imtiaz Sawar observes as the existence of irregularity of civil and religious rights by making the non-Muslims second-class citizens in contemporary Malaysia.[8] Citizens in Malaysia hardly bear the commonality of legal rights and religious liberties resulting from the institutional expansion of Islam in the public sphere as this process allows the state to dictate the legitimate space of interfaith dialogue between Muslim and non-Muslim citizens in Malaysia.

When Abdullah became the Prime Minister, he aimed to counter the pathological image of Islamic extremism and was determined to push for a liberal and modern Muslim paradigm for the future of Islamic development in the country.[9] However, the search for a liberal Muslim paradigm did not prevail as the long-standing problems of ethno-religious politics were rehashed into a revision of the historical trajectories of labour migration and ethnic bargain of the 1957 Malayan citizenship to accommodate a rhetorical conception of citizenship called the "social contract". The non-Malay ethnic citizens have been constantly reminded of why the state protects the Malays and other indigenous group rights under Article 153 of the Federal Constitution.[10] Abdullah reiterated these as the foundations of a social contract undergirding the privileging of Malays in Malaysia:

> Perhaps the most significant aspect of the contract was the agreement by the indigenous peoples to grant citizenship to the immigrant Chinese and Indian communities. This changed the character of the nation, from one that originally belonged to the indigenous peoples to one that Chinese and Indian citizens could also call their own. Chinese and Indians now share political power with the Malays, and sit in the Federal cabinet and State executive councils. In return for being granted these political rights, the immigrant communities agreed to special economic privileges for the indigenous peoples given their disadvantaged position. This constitutes the political, economic, legal and moral foundation for the distributive justice policies of the country.[11]

Article 153 extends a provision for the Yang di-Pertuan Agong (The Supreme Ruler) to "safeguard the special positions of the Malays and natives of any of the States of Sabah and Sarawak and the legitimate interests of other communities in accordance with the provisions of this Article".[12] Originally Article 153 was intended for the Malays but was later extended to Sabah and Sarawak when the Malaysian Federation was formed in 1963. Under the new constitutional arrangement, Article 161A was introduced as a way of providing the necessary safeguards for the special interests of Sabah and Sarawak. The reservation of public service, scholarships and educational privileges for the natives of the Borneo States was provided for in Clause 1 of Article 161A. Clause 2 of Article 161A stated that "Article 153 shall have effect with the substitution of references to natives of the State for the references to Malays". Clause 3 of Article 161A provided for the decisive role of the Chief Ministers of Sabah and Sarawak to negotiate these special interests. It is debatable whether Clause 2 of Article 161A would categorically put the rights of the Sabah and Sarawak natives on par with the special position of the Malays, but the statement could have furnished a legitimate point of legal debate for that purpose and it was not a prospect that the Federal government would anticipate. These clauses were repealed in 1971[13] following the 13 May 1969 ethnic riot and the only reasons given by then Prime Minister Tun Abdul Razak were that "Clause 3 of 161A must be repealed in order to rationalize the position of the natives of Sabah and Sarawak with the Malays in West Malaysia, or else it would be inconsistent, and that the special privileges that the Yang di-Pertuan Agong could provide for the natives of Sabah and Sarawak were matters under the jurisdiction of the Federal government."[14]

After the 1969 ethnic riot, the New Economic Policy (NEP) was introduced to restructure the economy. The NEP created a conceptual category known as "bumiputra" (sons of the soil) to be used exclusively in applying affirmative action policies to the Malays in West Malaysia; this umbrella term has also been extended to include other indigenous groups in East Malaysia. Whilst the NEP has been instrumental in addressing the issue of Malay poverty (Ariffin Omar 2004; Faruqi Shad Saleem 2004) and many studies have shown that it contributed significantly to the expansion of the Malay middle class in West Malaysia (Maznah Mohamad 2004; Gomez 2004), the East Malaysian "bumiputra" have not developed as rapidly.

The ruling party of the Malaysian state, the United Malays National Organisation (UMNO), makes exclusive claim upon the political meaning of Malay identity and privileges (Singh 1998). The NEP was designed to alleviate conditions of poverty among the Malays and other indigenous people in Sabah and Sarawak categorized as "Bumiputera". However, UMNO's exclusive claim to uphold Malay special rights exposes the ambiguous and layered meaning of "bumiputra", especially when we consider its purpose and its ideological underpinning vis-à-vis Sabah and Sarawak. Whilst Malay as an ethnic category has constitutional definition, the designation of "bumiputra" and how it is understood in Sabah and Sarawak is less clear. It is questionable whether "bumiputra" has a legitimate status in the Malaysian Constitution and by virtue of its ambiguous status, "bumiputra" remains an academic concept.

UMNO's outright claim to Malay special rights in Article 153 of the Constitution combined with the elevation of Islam as the principle of public policy under Abdullah widened the political scope of majority ethno-religious domination in a multicultural society. The abstract meaning of Islam Hadhari and its concomitant ideological approach to achieving higher moral grounds for Muslims to succeed in multiple global challenges suggests an alternative modernity for Islamic civilization that is authentic. Such political rhetoric is selectively addressed to the Muslim audience with noticeable disregard on how other non-Muslim citizens would be situated and somewhat out of place in this new vision of Islamic civilization. In a society that is multiethnic and religiously diverse, the domineering forces of Islamization in the public sphere tend to circumscribe the secular space where the fundamental question of political equality remains thorny due to the notion of Malay special right as there is less room for other minority groups to coexist on an equal standing. Such political discourse is particularly acute when analysed in the context of the ethnic minorities of the state of Sabah.

THE CONDITIONS OF ISLAMIZATION IN SABAH

The chapter has so far highlighted the recent trends of political contestations emerging from the consequences of the bigger legal role given to the Syariah Court in adjudicating the private domains of conversions and the extent to which this is intertwined with the language of Malay special rights synonymous with UMNO political leadership (see also Maznah Mohamad, this volume). These trends have considerably curtailed the possibility of secular discussions in the public domain, particularly in relation to the normative understanding of citizenship and the idea of democratic participation for citizens from minority backgrounds. In this section, I will use Sabah as an important case to illustrate how the public role of Islam has been strategic in the political co-optation of the local leadership, the manipulation of citizenship and, in some cases, circumventing the local authorities in Sabah. When politics is driven by religion as a factor of political negotiation, all possible avenues for secular political discussions would become insignificant. When such political discourse dictates the layered meanings of "bumiputra", particularly in an ethnically diverse society such as Sabah, the issue of the bona fide versus "second-class" citizens inevitably hinges on the official religion as the endorsement for valid identification.

Sabah was a colony of the British North Borneo Company (BNBC) from 1881 until World War II and became a British Crown Colony before joining the Malaysian Federation in 1963. Unlike Malaya, Islamic influence in North Borneo remained active only in the coastal areas, whereas Christian missions had been successful among the urban Chinese as well as the native communities in rural villages. Official records under the BNBC suggest that Christian missionary work in North Borneo began as early as 1859 and considerable effort was expended in both the religious and elementary English education among the natives in the rural areas as well as the urban Chinese communities. The Christian missionaries were engaged in rural agriculture and their efforts in translating doctrinal texts into the Malay language and other languages of the natives underscored the kind of cultural engagement that took place between Christianity and other traditional belief systems. Their most important historical contribution was in the history of education in Sabah as illustrated by the higher enrolment in secondary mission schools compared to the government and Chinese schools (British North Borneo 1961). During the Japanese Occupation, all the churches and schools were made into military barracks. Rooney (1981) argues that the persecution of Christians under the Japanese Occupation deepened the cultural understanding between these Christian missionaries and the indigenous people, intensifying the understanding of salvation in the Christian faith among the local natives, resulting in the transformation of "old Missionary Church" practice into new patterns of indigenization of the Christian faith. The survival of Christian churches and schools after the war[15] provided the impetus for continued missionary work and educational support, complementing the post-war reconstruction work undertaken by the British Colonial Government until the formation of the Malaysian Federation in 1963.

The ethnic and religious makeup of Sabah, as well as the other Borneo state of Sarawak, was far more complex and less clear cut than Malaya. The potential assimilation of the indigenous Sabah population with the Malays in Malaya was high on the agenda of the Malay leaders in order to offset the large influx of Chinese population from Singapore (Tilman 1963; Stockwell 2004).[16] Initially the leaders of North Borneo were sceptical about the Federation (Luping 1994); even the last governor of North Borneo, William Goode, detested the manner in which Malayan leaders were apathetic to Borneo, "particularly the *Tunku's* ignorance, naiveté and indifference to local resistance to Malaysia".[17] Years later he admitted that the making of Malaysia was,

> [m]erely a desperate political device to enable KL to deal better with Chinese Singapore under the PAP, [it] was not only hopelessly ill-founded and unreal but also most unfair on the happy friendly peoples of North Borneo.[18]

The existence of local resistance to the political union resulted in a number of caveats governing the agreement between Malaya and Sabah (Lim 2008, pp. 40–45). These were meant to prevent the erosion of Sabah's political sovereignty against the odds of what the British politician charged with ascertaining the views of the locals on the possibility of merger, Lord Cobbold, referred to as the threat of "Federal takeover" (Cobbold Commission 1962). Many of these caveats were contained within a document popularly referred to as the "Twenty Points", a list of autonomy related demands submitted to the Inter-Governmental Committee, and freedom of religion was the first priority in the Twenty Points guarantee.

In one of the official interim reports that reviewed the Cobbold Commission, Sir S. Garner identified the lack of consensus between the British members and the Malayan members on the public role of religion in relation to Articles 3, 11, and 12 of the Federal Constitution.[19] Briefly, this report showed the main points of disagreements between the British and Malayan members of the Cobbold Commission: Article 3(1), on whether the position of Islam as the national religion should be extended to the Borneo territories; Clause 4 of Article 11 provides that a state law may control or restrict the propagation of any doctrine or belief among Muslims, and if this provision was to be extended to Borneo territories, it theoretically gives special consideration for Muslims to be treated differently from the rest of the local population; Clause 2 of Article 12 exposes the grey area that underlines federal taxation upon non-Muslims designed to support Muslim institutions or instruction in the Muslim religion. With regard to the last, Sir Garner emphasized that, "since the Federal revenues of Malaysia would in part be derived from the Borneo territories, its application in relation to the Borneo territories might be considered objectionable, as the Malay members of the Commission themselves recognize".[20]

Over the early years of independence, the religious partiality that informed Federal intervention in local Sabah politics was an important source of conflict that was increasingly threatening the political stability of Federal-State relations (Lim 2008). Fractious federal-state relations ensued after Singapore was expelled from the Federation in 1965. When the Chief Ministers of Sabah and Sarawak challenged the constitutional grounds of the expulsion, the federal government embarked on a number of local interventions that resulted in the replacement of Donald Stephens and Steven Kalong Ningkan, who were the leaders of the largest non-Muslim communities in their respective states of Sabah and Sarawak, by local Muslim leaders as Chief Ministers.[21] The ethnic factor that has been suggested by a number of observers (Jawan 1991) seemed to play a lesser role in mediating the early federal-state crises when the federal government interventions in local politics drew on religious association with Islam as an important basis for building stability in political and power relations.

ISLAMIZATION OF LOCAL LEADERSHIP AND SOCIAL TIES

The early life of the Federation told the story of the political marginalization of non-Muslim local leaders under a federal-backed United Sabah National

Organization (USNO) administration. Islamization was carried out by a local organization, the United Sabah Islam Association (USIA), with the support of the Sabah state government, which expelled a considerable number of Christian missionary workers, intensifying the loss of catechist support in many remote villages in Sabah (Rooney 1981). Islamic conversion among elite politicians in the likes of Donald Stephens and Ghani Gilong (Lim 2008, p. 106), as well as wholesale village conversions, became important strategies for USIA to achieve the aims of the Islamic Dakwah movement.[22] Islamic conversion in exchange for Sabah citizenship status is a common story among some older generation Chinese immigrants to Sabah. In a personal interview, one respondent explained the bureaucratic hurdles involved in changing his inherited Muslim name despite having been baptized as a Christian. His father was a Hong Kong immigrant who came to Sabah during the USNO period and was granted citizenship for embracing Islam.[23] These life histories are increasingly difficult to ascertain but they furnish an interesting angle on how instrumental it was for USNO to establish religious ties with Sabah's immigrant community through Islam. In its short political tenure, Islam was the definitive common ground for USNO's political rapport with the federal government. However, when its leader, Mustapha, campaigned for greater political autonomy for Sabah within the Federation, the federal government began to look for a compliant ally through the creation of a new "multi-racial" Berjaya party (Lim 2008, pp. 53–57).

Berjaya's commitment to "multi-racial" principles with the prospect of political comeback for some non-Muslim politicians[24] struck a popular chord among the non-Muslim electorate. However, Muslim leaders under Berjaya began to realize that Islam was the key to establishing political ties with UMNO and weakening USNO's institutional leadership in Islam (Lim 2008, p. 67). Berjaya began to project the Islamic vision of the Federal government through its development policies in Sabah, and the establishment of Majlis Ugama Islam Sabah (MUIS) was strategic in translating the Islamic vision into concrete measures in the propagation of Islam. Islam gradually became associated with state-driven policies in the Sabah State administration, underlining public policies relating to federalization, immigration, even down to the village level by transforming local indigenous religious practices and communities via mass conversions (Lim 2008, pp. 111–17). Throughout the Berjaya administration, certain "exemplars of Islamization" (Roff 1998) became conspicuous, such as the

Malayanization of the professional civil offices (Lim 1997), transformation of the demography as the total Muslim population increased from 40 per cent to 50 per cent within ten years through mass village conversion and large-scale foreign immigration into Sabah, and the Islamization of the indigenous harvest festival by the paying of royal homage to the Malay Supreme Ruler (Lim 2008, p. 117).

Islamization under Berjaya occurred within the ambit of the Mahathir administration and it was during the time when the successful model of the East Asian Developmental states was popular among developing countries as an alternative to the extremes of the American style free-market economy and the Socialist model in Eastern Europe. Mahathir in particular was keen to campaign for the ideals of "Asian values" and was interested in emulating the work ethics of Japanese workers, leading to the "Look East" policy as the way forward to industrialize the country without having to fall into the moral decadence of Western liberal society (Khoo 1995). The Chief Minister of the Berjaya administration, Harris Salleh, shared a similar vision for Sabah, albeit at the price of undermining the political importance of the Twenty Points agreement (Lim 2008; Lim 1997). Berjaya's attempt at espousing the centrality of Islamic leadership in Sabah proved to be unpopular among Sabahans particularly when state-driven Islamization began to penetrate into the social lives of local indigenous communities. These measures were met with critical responses particularly from the non-Muslim grass-roots and local leaders and they provided the decisive groundswell of support for the newly formed Parti Bersatu Sabah (PBS) that toppled Berjaya when it was only registered for two weeks prior to the dissolution of the Sabah State Legislative Assembly in 1985 (Loh 1992; Lim 2008).

As the new Sabah government, the Christian-based PBS attempted to restore the salience of Sabah's Twenty Points Memorandum by readdressing political issues that matter to Sabah; however, this was perceived as a challenge to leadership of the federal government. During the first few years of PBS rule, accusations of high treason and secessionism were repeatedly levelled against PBS top aides (Lim 2008, p. 120). Mahathir employed harsher measures to undermine the economic viability and political stability of the opposition state government.[25] Under Mahathir, development was the key to dent the economic capacity of the local state government (Loh 1997) and one of the most telling measures of control by the federal government was the setting up of the Sabah

Federal Development Department (Jabatan Pembangunan Persekutuan Sabah, JPPS) in 1991, about a year after PBS pulled out from the Barisan Nasional (BN) (Kahin 1992). It was set up under the Implementation Coordination Unit in the Prime Minister's Department during the 6th Malaysian Plan to redirect all federal development allocations into JPPS, effectively circumventing the local authorities under the Sabah government.[26] JPPS was a special federal development agency that had no counterparts in other states, mandated to plan, coordinate and monitor the implementation of federal government development projects, and it completely disabled the economic capacity of the PBS government down to the village level. In 2004, a dozen Sabah BN MPs demanded the abolition of JPPS due to serious flaws associated with the process of implementation of development projects in many rural areas.[27] Some of the Jawatankuasa Kemajuan dan Keselamatan Kampung (JKKK, Village Development and Security Committee) members have noticed how their planning intentions were ignored and sidelined by JPPS contractors.[28] Professional bodies like the Sabah United Chinese Chambers of Commerce had also submitted a joint-memorandum with six other commercial bodies to demand a serious review of the JPPS regarding its overlapping role with the local authorities, particularly with the Public Works Department, and to insist upon giving due consideration for local companies to undertake development projects in Sabah.[29] JPPS was abolished in June 2008 and has been replaced by the Sabah Development Office under the Prime Minister's Department. However, its legacy of circumventing local authorities coupled with the lack of transparency in the process of awarding development projects generated considerable loss of employment and economic opportunities for local contractors and other development agencies in Sabah. It became evident that JPPS failed to transform Sabah's economy when the figures in the 9th Malaysian Plan show that Sabah is the poorest state in the whole of Malaysia.

Since the establishment of the JPPS, PBS's political fortune began to plummet and, as many of its political leaders crossed over to the BN right after the 1994 State Election, UMNO took the reins of government in the state of Sabah in 1995, with the introduction of a two-year rotation system whereby representatives from each major ethnic group could take turns to be the Chief Minister. The rotation system had considerable implications upon the ethno-religious dimension of representative politics in Sabah, particularly when each Chief Minister was chosen by the federal government on the basis of Muslim-bumiputra, Non-Muslim bumiputra and Chinese (see Table 7.1).

FEDERALIZATION OF SABAH POLITICS

The leadership rotation system underscored the Muslim and Non-Muslim political dichotomies in Sabah politics, redefining the Pribumi categorization under the Berjaya administration and further entrenching

TABLE 7.1
Chief Ministers of Sabah by Ethnicity and Party Representation

Chief Minister	Year	Political Party	Ethnicity/Religion	Party Representation
Donald Stephens	1963–65	UPKO	Kadazan/Christian	Kadazan-Dusun
Peter Lo	1965–67	SCA	Chinese/Christian	Chinese
Mustapha bin Harun	1967–76	USNO	Bajau/Muslim	Bumiputera Islam
Harris Mohd Salleh	1976–85	BERJAYA	Brunei Malay/Muslim	Multi-Ethnic
Joseph Pairin Kitingan	1985–94	PBS	Kadazan/Christian	Multi-Ethnic
Sakaran Dandai	Mar–Dec 1995	UMNO	Bajau Murut/Muslim	Bumiputera Islam
Salleh Said Keruak	Dec 1995– May 1996	UMNO	Bajau/Muslim	Bumiputera Islam
Yong Teck Lee	May 1996– Mar 1998	SAPP	Chinese/Buddhist	Chinese
Bernard Dompok	Mar 1998– Mar 1999	UPKO	Kadazan/Christian	Kadazan-Dusun
Osu bin Hj. Sukam	Mar 1999– Mar 2001	UMNO	Bajau/Muslim	Bumiputera Islam
Chong Kah Kiat	Mar 2001– Mar 2003	LDP	Chinese/Buddhist	Chinese
Musa bin Haji Aman	Mar 2003 – today	UMNO	Dusun Indian/Muslim	Bumiputera Islam

the idea of ethnic assimilability under the umbrella term of the "bumiputra". The rotation system exemplified Lord Cobbold's concern with the potential "federal take-over" of Sabah's civil administration and political autonomy. The ideological persuasion of Islamic leadership and the myth of "bumiputra" solidarity in securing indigenous claims to rights effectively sowed the seeds of political acquiescence among the BN leaders in Sabah to allow for UMNO's political ascendancy. Sabah was given a very effective lesson under the PBS opposition government. JPPS and the rotation system were the two interweaving strategies of development and Islamic leadership via UMNO that sealed the federal penetration into Sabah politics. The concentration of political and economic power in the hands of the federal government, and UMNO for that matter, can only mean that politics is tied to UMNO's agenda for national development. UMNO's strategy of federal penetration in Sabah was very successful and led to the entrenchment of UMNO's political supremacy in local politics in Sabah under the Abdullah administration.

The provision of the public role of Islam in the Malaysian Federation has had considerable ramifications upon federal-state relations and the issue of religion has been critical to the political agency of local leaders — from USNO, BERJAYA, PBS and UMNO — when they make decisions for Sabah. This problem has now become acute when it comes to the issue of citizenship and the problem of illegal immigrants in Sabah under the Abdullah administration. Decades of state-endorsed Islamic conversions, the assimilation of Muslim immigrants under USNO and BERJAYA and the inconsistency of statistical representation of the population in Sabah (Lim 2008, p. 114) resulted in the some of the most contentious issues surrounding the problem of illegal "citizenship" in Sabah. Sabah BN MPs like Eric Majimbun, Wilfred Tangau and Abdul Ghapur Salleh have consistently voiced their concerns about the existence of about 400,000 foreigners and the great transformation of the social demography of the local community.[30] They repeatedly made their demands to the Abdullah administration to address the issues of illegal immigration in Sabah, and their pleas for the setting up of the Royal Commission of Inquiry fell on deaf ears. In June 2006, a written reply was given to the question posed in parliament by DAP MP Teresa Kok regarding the percentage breakdown of the ethnic composition in Sabah. The Prime Minister's Department estimated that the population in Sabah as of March 2006 was 2.98 million and Table 7.2 shows the ethnic breakdown of the Sabah population.

TABLE 7.2
Ethnic Composition of Sabah Population as of March 2006

Ethnic Groups	Population (000)	Percentage
Malay	342.5	15.3
Kadazan/Dusun	530.0	23.7
Bajau	399.3	17.8
Murut	98.4	4.4
Other Bumiputra	436.3	19.5
Chinese	287.2	12.8
Other Ethnic	143.5	6.4
Malaysian Citizens	2,237.1	75.1
Non-Malaysian Citizens	743.6	24.9
Total	2,980.7	100

The inconsistency in the ways the census data have been compiled and the changing nature of the "bumiputra" grouping in Sabah contribute to the difficulty in analysing the empirical pattern of population growth by ethnicity. Under the Berjaya administration, there were only "Pribumi", "Chinese" and "Other" categories. The census for the 1990's had nine different categories whereby "Kadazan" was in a different category from "Dusun", with distinct categories for "Indonesian" and "Others". The 2006 ethnic breakdown supplied by the Prime Minister's Department shows a new category of "Other Ethnics" replacing previous categories for "Indonesian" and "Others". There is also no way of knowing who are the "Other Bumiputra" and the "Other Ethnics" and how long the "Non-Malaysian Citizens" population have been staying in Sabah. When the MP for Ipoh Timor, Lim Kit Siang, tabled the motion for the Royal Commission of Inquiry into the problem of illegal immigrants in Sabah, the Deputy Speaker of Parliament, who is an UMNO MP for Beluran in Sabah, rejected the motion on the grounds that it was made in the context of disrespect to the inauguration of the King's speech.[31]

Sadiq (2005) argues that through documentary citizenship the Malay political elites have deliberately enfranchized a considerable number of foreign immigrants for their own political mileage in Sabah by enabling them to participate in Malaysian local elections. The state preference for illegal immigrants over local citizens is only reflected in so far as the issue of religion becomes an important factor in assimilating and transforming

Sabah's electorate for UMNO to remain politically relevant in Sabah. Sadiq argues that the Malaysian case provides a new angle to rethink the conceptual relationship between international politics and the issue of migration in developing countries and the extent to which a "weakly institutionalized state" like Malaysia has failed to monitor the abuse of documentary citizenship in blurring the political right of real citizens from dubious voters. The issue of illegal immigrants in Sabah remains largely a political one. However, to claim that the Malaysian state is institutionally weak in failing to overcome the abuse of documentary citizenship is slightly contradictory, especially when Sadiq also claims that,

> the authorities at the centre collaborate with their regional partners to utilize census practices and documentation to incorporate an illegal immigrant population from the Philippines. The motive for such practices is to use illegal immigrants as voters to assure political control by a Malay/Muslim party such as the United Malays National Organization. (2005, p. 105).

If both the federal and the Sabah state agencies were found to be working together to "abuse" the process of documentary citizenship for UMNO's political gain, then there seems to be a very coherent working structure within the state institutions and a strong political will on behalf of UMNO to grant voting rights to the illegal immigrants in Sabah. Sadiq has usefully illustrated a particularly thorny problem in Sabah politics which implicates the federal government on the issue of citizenship. It is important to draw the difference between competing discourses on citizenship between West Malaysia and Sabah. MP for Tuaran, Madius Tangau, protested that there exists a double standard in the ways the federal government has issued a tougher stance against the Rohingya and Achenese refugees in West Malaysia, whilst at the same time issuing the IMM13 documents to illegal immigrants in Sabah.[32] At the time of the debate, there were five refugee settlements in Sabah with an average of 3,000 people each and one of the solutions to the problem of overcrowding given by the Minister at the Prime Minister's Department, Nazri Aziz, was to send these refugees into isolated villages away from local communities as a preventive measure against the spiralling social problems.[33]

There are clear differences in the way UMNO interprets the issues of contentious citizenships and what "bumiputra" actually means in West Malaysia and Sabah. UMNO in particular has been very protective of

Malay special rights and this is historically linked to their opposition to the proposal of the Malayan Union by the British to grant universal citizenship to the Chinese and Indian migrant communities after the Japanese Occupation in Malaya. Until today, the rhetoric of "Chinese Malaysians as squatters who do not deserve equal rights in the country"[34] remains strong among some UMNO leaders and the idea of an impending threat to Malay special rights and identity is being reproduced in the popular imagination through the Malay dailies.[35] The playing up of the issue of "Chinese squatters" as political threat on the one hand, and the apathy shown towards the problem of illegal immigrants in Sabah on the other hand, demonstrate UMNO's deliberate misrecognition of the difference between what is a real political problem and what is purely imagined. In the end this issue finally prompted one of the Sabah BN allies, the Sabah Progressive Party (SAPP), to pull out from the coalition in September 2008. Yong Teck Lee, the SAPP president, said that "[they] have been wrongly led into believing that the Federal government will take care of things", by which he referred to the worsening state of affairs in the issue of illegal immigrants in Sabah.[36]

How religion becomes involved in the competing understanding of citizenship rights and the interpretation of "bumiputra" underscores the emerging paradoxes of state practice. The 1971 repeal of the special status of Sabah and Sarawak "native" under Article 161(A) constitutes one such paradox of state practice that is indicative of the challenging dynamics of defining the meaning of rights when state neutrality is compromised by an ethno-nationalist political discourse. The 1971 repeal reflected the vindication of the claims of Malayanization in the Sabah civil service (Lim 1997). The intensification of Kadazan nationalism in the 1980's was symptomatic of the political apathy on the part of the federal government to respect religious liberty and fulfil the pledge of Borneonization of the Sabah civil service (Loh 1992). Borneonization of the civil service is now a distant memory as the Sabah government under UMNO executed further Islamization of the public sector such that the proportion of Muslims occupying skilled occupations in the public service has increased by about 8.7 per cent from 1990 to 2000 (see Table 7.3). The persistent lack of Sabahans heading important departments in the civil service constituted the main thrust of political disaffection among PBS leaders and supporters at the time, but PBS's re-entry into the BN coalition in 2003 meant that UMNO has been able to redefine mainstream politics in Sabah.

TABLE 7.3
Proportion of Muslims in Occupational Categories by Employment Sector, 1991 and 2000, per cent

	Public Sector		Private Sector	
	1991	2000	1991	2000
Skilled occupations	54.7	63.4	43.6	44.2
Semi-skilled occupations	70.8	68.4	45.4	55.2
Unskilled occupations	55.4	59.1	63.7	66.3

Note: Occupation skill level defined according to ILO categorization of ISCO occupational codes; "public sector" defined as employment in the following three employment categories: "public administration and defence", "education", and "health and social work".
Source: Author's calculations based on 2 per cent sample of Malaysian census data, 1991 and 2000 (Minnesota Population Center 2009).

As a high-profile civil servant and the current Vice Chairman of SUHAKAM (Human Rights Commission of Malaysia), Simon Sipaun had the opportunity to experience both the pre-Malaysia and post-merger Malaysian administrations in Sabah. Reflecting upon the contemporary dilemma for Sabah "bumiputra", Tan Sri Simon said that prior to Malaysia, there were sixty to seventy Colombo scholarships offered to further the education of local Sabahans on to degree levels in overseas universities, but under the Malaysian Federation, all these awards went to Kuala Lumpur for deliberation.[37] Bernard Dompok, the president of United Pasokmomogun Kadazandusun Murut Organization (UPKO) and Minister in the Prime Minister's Department, is convinced that "people are handicapped by being non-Muslim" and that the NEP did not benefit the "bumiputra" in Sabah and Sarawak in the same ways it benefitted the Malays in West Malaysia.[38]

The public role of Islam has affected the long-standing problems of political economy between the federal government and Sabah, and now the prohibition on use of "Allah" in the Bible and Church sermons has resurfaced since the federal government first issued the ban in 1986.[39] This issue has now been challenged by Pastor Jerry Dusing in court[40] as well as other Christian groups in Kuala Lumpur. On the issue of the sudden termination of the construction of the Goddess of the Sea statue in Kudat,[41] some observers[42] seem to attribute the whole issue to the personality conflicts between Chief Minister Musa Aman and the former Chief Minister, Chong

Kah Kiat.[43] However much these arguments of personality clashes may be believed, the thrust of the issue remains political and there is no denying the fact that practical sensibilities towards basic religious liberties and the right to practise one's religion have been overshadowed by the political abuse of an official religion like Islam. The inability of the Malaysian Government to maintain political neutrality towards religious diversity in the country is precisely why Bishop Vun of the Anglican Diocese in Sabah expresses deep concerns about the diminishing significance of the secular state in Malaysia. In view of the growing cases of interfaith problems in Malaysia, there is a sense of ambivalence over whether the legislation of a particular faith in governmental institutions can really sustain a non-discriminatory public sphere in which the fundamental liberties of every citizen can be equally protected from the abuse of public authority.[44]

CONCLUSION

The paradox of the secular dilemma in contemporary Malaysian politics lies in the state's inability to negotiate effectively a secular space when religious identities are so thoroughly, and increasingly strongly, enmeshed with the ethnic identities that have, since independence, legitimized both the form of political engagement, notably the undermining of democracy, and the content of policy, notably pro-Malay affirmative action. This is historically grounded in the stages of transition from colonial pluralism, the post-war left-wing agitation and, finally, in the competing claims to political self-determination driven by ethnic nationalisms. These episodes furnished the broad historical structure that contextualized the drafting process of the Constitution that originally aimed at establishing a secular foundation for the future of Malayan plural society. The selective narration of national history and the narrow interpretation of the Constitution inevitably compromised state neutrality in the Malaysian case. This has been reflected in the gradual elevation of the role of Islam in the political and public sphere underscoring the ethnic-national discourse in the political construction of the "social contract". In the making of the Malayan nation-state, Islam became the state religion for official and ceremonial purposes. It departs from the norms of separation of religion and the state in that Islam actually plays an important role in protecting the Malay identity. There was no question that the Malayan Constitution originally began as a secular template but the provisions of Islam as the official religion gradually inclined UMNO towards a political interpretation of Malay special rights that gave more significance to religion.

UMNO's political discourse underlines the key elements in defining the political landscape of Malaya and, subsequently, the making of the Malaysian Federation. UMNO's political articulation of Malay rights provided the agency for ethno-nationalist mobilization to undermine the meaning and original intention of a secular constitution. As a result, certain articles that upheld the rights of ethnic Malays in the Constitution have become the focus of UMNO's political discourse that selectively reinterprets their essential meaning and subsequently overwhelmed the harmonious construction of the Constitution as a whole. Hence it can be argued that UMNO's political discourse on Islamizing Malay identity and their claim to championing the special position of the Malays underscore the possibility of differentiating the rights between Muslim and non-Muslim citizens. In this sense it is rather difficult for the state to claim that it is promoting the ideal of universal citizenship rights when closer examination of the Constitution actually reveals otherwise. In empirical terms the Islamic revivalism beginning in the 1980s and the recurrent process of state-driven Islamization in contemporary experience accentuate the fears among non-Muslim civil society groups, human rights groups and individuals about how Islamization will impact secular politics and democratic participation from minority faith and ethnic groups. The expansion of the public role of Islam and the state's departure from "secular" considerations eventually delimits the rights of other non-Muslim citizens in ways that are not immediately discernible but discursively reproduced through the process of deliberate exclusion in the policies of affirmative action and legal pluralism. Differentiating rights in this way will therefore undermine the cumulative sense of common properties usually shared by citizens of a nation-state, vindicating the popular sentiments of "second-class" citizens who do not share the special relationship with the Malaysian state.

The sentiments of the "second-class" citizens are discursively reproduced as the Abdullah administration condones UMNO's brand of politics within the broader context of state-driven Islamization. In recapitulating the style of UMNO politics since the making of the Malaysian Federation in 1963, there is a strong case for an argument that Islamization has transformed local politics in Sabah through the Federal "take-over" of governmental functions and UMNO's penetration in party politics. The strategies of Islamization underlined many issues of political concern in

Sabah and the federal government's success in co-opting local elites and circumventing local authorities only adds to the increasing erosion of political agency among local leadership in Sabah. From the perspective of the minority ethnic state of Sabah, Islamization in the public and political domain has direct ramifications upon fundamental issues of religious liberty and political equality in Malaysia. If the contemporary global experience is a reflection of the normative triumph of secularism, then more research should be done to examine the interpretation of secularism in the Malaysian case. There is a need to address the diminishing significance of the secular state in Malaysia because the critical and objective discussions of the expanded public role of Islam are found to be retreating into the private sphere of Internet bloggers, non-Muslim NGOs, professionals and individuals, where citizens embracing secular ideas avoid colliding with the official sanctity of Islam.

Notes

1. Article 11 of the Federal Constitution states that "Every person has the right to profess and practice his religion" and, subject to Clause (4), to propagate it. In Clause (4) 'State law and in respect of the Federal Territories of Kuala Lumpur, Labuan and Puterajaya, federal law may control or restrict the propagation of any religious doctrine or belief among persons professing the religion of Islam". See <http://www.article11.org/>.
2. Farish Noor, "Religious Freedom in Malaysia", BBC Radio 4, 9 September 2006 <http://www.bbc.co.uk/radio4/news/ram/crossingcontinents_20061116.ram> (accessed 14 October 2009).
3. Rang Undang-Undang Kesalahan Jenayah Syariah (Wilayah-Wilayah Persekutuan) 1996.
4. "Mahathir isytihar Malaysia negara Islam", *Berita Mingguan*, 30 September 2001.
5. "Deputy PM Najib Razak Declared That 'We Have Never Been Secular'", *The Rocket*, 17 July 2007.
6. Malaysiakini, 27 August 2007.
7. Abdullah's vision of "Islam Hadhari" is a step closer towards a mode of Islamic governance that emphasizes the ethics of virtue — that are interpreted in the Holy Qur'an and the Hadith — in the making of a civilized society that is able to withstand the negative forces of globalization. Islam Hadhari is an approach that emphasizes development, consistent with the tenets of Islam and focused on enhancing the quality of life. It aims to achieve this via the

mastery of knowledge and the development of the individual and the nation; the implementation of a dynamic economic, trading and financial system; and integrated and balanced development that creates a knowledgeable and pious people who hold to noble values and are honest, trustworthy, and prepared to take on global challenges. This was the official speech by Prime Minister Abdullah Badawi during the 2004 UMNO General Assembly. Islam Hadhari constituting the ethics of governance is also emphasized in the Ninth Malaysian Plan, 2006–2010. Dewan Rakyat 31 March 2006.
8. Malik Imtiaz Sawar, Malaysian human rights lawyer and President of Hakam, interview with the BBC 7 February 2005.
9. Vatikiotis M. and S. Jayasankaran, "Extremists, Set Aside". *Far Eastern Economic Review*, 5 September 2002.
10. Reservation of quotas in respect of services, permits, etc., for Malays and natives of any of the states of Sabah and Sarawak. 153(2) states that, "Notwithstanding anything in this Constitution, but subject to the provisions of Article 40 and of this Article, the Yang di-Pertuan Agong shall exercise his functions under this Constitution and federal law in such manner as may be necessary to safeguard the special position of the Malays and natives of any of the States of Sabah and Sarawak and to ensure the reservation for Malays and natives of any of the States of Sabah and Sarawak of such proportion as he may deem reasonable of positions in the public service (other than the public service of a State) and of scholarships, exhibitions and other similar educational or training privileges or special facilities given or accorded by the Federal Government and, when any permit or licence for the operation of any trade or business is required by federal law, then, subject to the provisions of that law and this Article, of such permits and licences."
11. Keynote address by Abdullah Badawi, PM Malaysia, "The Challenges of Multireligious, Multiethnic and Multicultural Societies", Asia Media Summit, 19 April 2004 <http://www.un.int/malaysia/PM Statement/PM041904.htm>.
12. Article 153(1), Federal Constitution 2004.
13. Article 161A on the *Special Position of the Natives of Sabah and Sarawak,* Clause (1), (2) and (3) were repealed by Act A30, Section 8, in force from 10 March 1971, read as follows:
    161A. (1) Subject to Clause (2), the provisions of Clauses (2) to (5) of Article 153, so far as they relate to the reservation of positions in the public service, shall apply in relation to natives of any of the Borneo States as they apply in relation to Malays.
    (2) In a Borneo State Article 153 shall have effect with the substitution of references to natives of the State for the references to Malays, but as regards scholarships, exhibitions and other educational or

training privileges and facilities Clause (2) of that Article shall not require the reservation of a fixed proportion for natives.

(3) Before advice is tendered to the Yang di-Pertuan Agong as to the exercise of this powers under Article 153 in relation to a Borneo State, the Chief Minister of the State in question shall be consulted.

Laws of Malaysia (Reprint) Federal Constitution: Incorporating all amendments up to 31 January 2002, The Commissioner of Law Revision, Malaysia.

14. Official Report of the House of Representative, 23 February 1971, column 63 of the *Constitutional Amendment Bill [50]*.
15. Sacred Heart Parish of the Roman Catholic Church in Kota Kinabalu, St. Michael's and All Angels Church in Sandakan.
16. EM West (CO) to Reginald Maulding, 21 March 1962, "The bilateral merger of Malaya and Singapore would have shifted the balance to 45 per cent Chinese and 42.3 per cent Malays. Within 'Greater Malaysia', however, Chinese numbers would have been trimmed as follows: Chinese 42.7 per cent, Malays/Borneo Muslims 38.9 per cent, non-Muslim indigenous peoples of Borneo 5.8 per cent, others (including Indians) 11.7 per cent. The Tunku concluded that the non-Chinese communities of Borneo would go some way towards neutralizing the Singapore threat to the Malay position. Indeed, to be on the safe side he went so far as to demand Malaya's union with the Borneo territories in advance of that with Singapore." *British Documents on the End of Empire*, Series B, Volume 8.
17. Ibid., p. lxxii.
18. Ibid., p. lxxiii.
19. CAB134/2370, OP (62)7, 10 July 1962, "Discussions with the prime minister of the Federation of Malaya on Greater Malaysia. Report by the chairman of the Official Committee": report from Sir S. Garner for the Cabinet Oversea Policy Committee. *British Documents on the End of Empire*, Series B, Volume 8, p. 349.
20. Ibid., Appendix A to 129: Religion: pp. 349–52.
21. The Prime Minister made it explicit in his support for Mustapha the Muslim leader and persuaded Stephens to step down in exchange for a Federal post, whilst Ningkan's dismissal was highly controversial during the 1966 Constitutional Emergency motion in Sarawak (Means 1968).
22. *Dakwah* is generally understood as a movement to intensify the *aqidah* (faith) or the religious practices and beliefs of Muslims. In the context of the Islamic revivalism, such movement affected the Muslim community in Malaysia beginning the late 1970s, particular in terms of pursuing greater piety as part of the Islamic way of life. Missionary activities associated with *dakwah* in various States in Malaysia gradually morphed into a national movement under the purview of JAKIM (Department of Islamic Development Malaysia)

to instill stronger moral foundations for individual Muslims and the Muslim society in Malaysia as a whole.
23. Fieldwork interviews, August 2008.
24. Prominent non-Muslim leaders at the time were Peter Mojuntin, James Ongkili, Joseph Pairin Kitingan, and Chinese leaders like Yap Pak Leong, who was detained without trial under Mustapha, Chong Thian Vui and others (Ongkili 1989).
25. A number of PBS' top aides were detained for alleged political treason (Loh 1997).
26. *Daily Express*, 21 May 2008 The JPPS had four divisions — administration and finance, planning, coordination and implementation and technical support.
27. *Daily Express*, 6 December 2004 Many village development councils were not aware of development projects being carried out in their villages, and cases of incompletion were rampant and local developers were not involved.
28. Fieldwork notes in rubber plantation villages, Kg. Bintangor and Kg. Telipok, Tuaran District.
29. 11 January 2008 <http://www.succc.org>.
30. Parliamentary Debates (Dewan Rakyat) DR22032006; DR27032006.
31. DR22052008, p. 137 "Maknanya Ahli-ahli Parlimen mengucapkan terima kasih ke atas Titah Ucapan Diraja dan adalah tidak sopan bagi kita untuk mengucapkan terima kasih, tetapi memberi syarat kepada raja untuk mengaibkan satu usul yang tidak berkaitan dengan ucapan terima kasih kita kepada raja".
32. DR27062006, p. 13. IMM13 is an official document that classified people as "refugees" in a member country of the United Nations. IMM13 holders are exempted from the Malaysian Passport Act 1966 and they are renewable yearly at the cost of RM90. There were 61,000 IMM13 registered holders in 2006 and they have been allowed to work and given access to public services.
33. DR27032006, pp. 16–17.
34. Penang UMNO division leader Ahmad Ismail made this remark during a by-election campaign in the federal constituency of Permatang Pauh, in the Malaysian State of Penang in September 2008 <http://www.malaysiakini.com>.
35. "Opinion: Does a crisis exist among the Malays?", *Malaysian Bar*, 15 July 2008 <http://www.malaysianbar.org.my>. Other incidents include the Malay-Muslim NGOs protesting against the forum to address issues of conversion and the Malay students demonstrating against reversing the exclusionary policy of UiTM (Universiti Teknologi Mara) to allow 10 per cent inclusion of non-Bumiputera students into the University. August 2008 <http://www.malaysiakini.com>.
36. Personal Interview, 13 January 2009.

37. Personal Interview, 8 January 2009.
38. Personal Interview, 8 January 2009.
39. 1 April 1986, S.59/3/9/A — an official circular given to all Churches in Sabah not to use sixteen words in sermons and publications because these were exclusive to Islam, they include: Al-Kitab, Allah, Firman, Rasul, Syariat, Iman, Kaabah, Ibadat, Injil, Wahyu, Nabi, Syukur, Zikir, Solat and Doa.
40. Pastor Jerry Dusing, leader of the SIB (Sidang Injil Borneo) filed a legal suit against the Internal Security Ministry in February 2008. Case is still pending.
41. The Kudat Town Board approved the Kudat Thean Hou Charitable Foundation's (KTHCF) application to build the thirty-three metre structure in February 2006. But the approval was officially revoked half way through the construction period in November 2007 on the grounds that the project did not comply with the Sabah Town and Country Planning Ordinance. The President of KTHCF, Chong Kah Kiat, took this matter to court to reassert the validity of the approval issued by the Kudat Town Board in February 2006 and to challenge the fatwa issued by the Sabah State Mufti on 7 July 2006 — that the construction of the statue was deemed offensive to Islam — as unconstitutional because it went against Article 11 of the Federal Constitution. This case was dismissed by the federal court in 2010 because the KTHCF was not a legally registered entity. *New Straits Times,* 27 July 2010.
42. Author's personal Interview with local politicians who want to remain anonymous.
43. The president of the KTHCF filed a legal suit against the Sabah government last year but the case was struck out by the Kota Kinabalu High Court on the grounds that the Foundation has no legal status. *The Star,* 5 August 2009.
44. Personal interview with the Bishop of Sabah, the Rt Revd Datuk Albert Vun Cheong Fui on 27 August 2008.

References

Abdullah Saeed and Hassan Saeed. *Freedom of Religion, Apostasy, and Islam.* Aldershot: Ashgate, 2004.

Ariffin Omar. "Origins and Development of the Affirmative Policy in Malaya and Malaysia: A Historical Overview". *Journal of Malaysian Studies* 21, no. 1/2 (2004): 13–30.

Audi, Robert. *Religious Commitment and Secular Reason.* Cambridge: Cambridge University Press, 2000.

Bajpai, Rochana. "The Conceptual Vocabularies of Minority Rights in India". *Journal of Political Ideologies* 7, no. 2 (2002): 179–97.

British North Borneo. *Report on the 1960 Census.* Jesselton: Statistics Department, 1961.
Cobbold Commission. *Report of the Commission of Enquiry, North Borneo and Sarawak.* Kuala Lumpur: Jabatan Chetak Kerajaan, 1962.
Faruqi Shad Saleem. "Affirmative Action Policies and the Constitution". *Journal of Malaysian Studies* 21, no. 1/2 (2004): 31–58.
Fernando, M. Joseph. "The Position of Islam in the Constitution of Malaysia". *Journal of Southeast Asian Studies* 37, no. 2 (2006): 249–66.
Gibney, Matthew J. "Who Should Be Included? Noncitizens, Conflict, and the Constitution of the Citizenry". In *Horizontal Inequalities and Conflict: Understanding Group Violence in Multiethnic Societies*, edited by F. Stewart. Basingstoke: Palgrave, 2009.
Gomez, Edmund Terence. "Affirmative Action and Enterprise Development in Malaysia: The New Economic Policy, Business Partnerships and Inter-Ethnic Relations". *Journal of Malaysian Studies* 21, no. 1/2 (2004): 59–104.
Gunn, Jeremy T. "Under God But Not the Scarf: The Founding Myths of Religious Freedom in the United States and Laïcité in France". *Journal of Church and State* 46, no. 1 (2004): 7–24.
Hamayotsu, Kikue. "The Politics of Syariah Reform: the Making of the State Religio-Legal Apparatus". In *Islam, Society and Politics*, edited by V.M. Hooker and N. Othman. Singapore: Institute of Southeast Asian Studies, 2003.
Hooker, M. B. *Islamic Law in South-East Asia.* Singapore: Oxford University Press, 1984.
Horowitz, Donald L. "The Qur'an and the Common Law: Islamic Law Reform and the Theory of Legal Change". *American Journal of Comparative Law* 42, no. 2 (1994): 233–93.
Hurd, Elizabeth Shakman. *The Politics of Secularism in International Relations.* Princeton: Princeton University Press, 2008.
Hussin Mutalib. *Islam in Malaysia: From Revivalism to Islamic State?* Singapore: Singapore University Press, 1993.
Jawan, Jayum Anak. "The Ethnic Factor in Modern Politics: The Case of Sarawak, East Malaysia". Centre for Southeast Asian Studies Occassional Papers. Kingston-upon-Hull: University of Hull, 1991.
Kahin, Audrey R. "Crisis on the Periphery: The Rift between Kuala Lumpur and Sabah". *Pacific Affairs* 65 (1992): 30–49.
Khoo, Boo Teik. *Paradoxes of Mahathirism: An Intellectual Biography of Mahathir Mohamad.* Kuala Lumpur: Oxford University Press, 1995.
Laborde, Cécile. *Critical Republicanism: The Hijab Controversy and Political Philosophy.* Oxford: Oxford University Press, 2008.
Lim, Hong Hai. "Sabah and Sarawak in Malaysia: The Real Bargain, Or, What Have They Got Themselves Into?" *Kajian Malaysia* 15, no. 1/2 (1997): 15–56.

Lim, Regina. *Federal-State Relations in Sabah, Malaysia: The Berjaya Administration, 1976–1985*. Singapore: Institute of Southeast Asian Studies, 2008.
Loh, Francis. "Modernisation, Cultural Revival and Counter-Hegemony: the Kadazans of Sabah in the 1980s". In *Fragmented Vision: Culture and Politics in Contemporary Malaysia*, edited by J.S. Kahn and F. Loh. Honolulu: University of Hawai'i Press, 1992.

———. "'Sabah Baru' dan pujukan pembangunan: Penyelesaikan hubungan persekutuan-negeri dalam Malaysia". *Kajian Malaysia* 15, no. 1/2 (1997): 175–99.

Luping, Herman J. *Sabah's Dilemma: The Political History of Sabah, 1960–1994*. Kuala Lumpur: Magnus Books, 1994.

Marican Pawancheek and Mohamed Azam Mohamed Adil. "Apostasy and Freedom of Religion in Malaysia: Constitutional Implications". *Yearbook of Islamic and Middle Eastern Law* 11 (2005).

Maznah Mohamad. "Ethnicity and Inequality in Malaysia: A Retrospect and a Rethinking". CRISE Working Papers. Oxford: Centre for Research on Inequality, Human Security and Ethnicity, 2004.

Means, Gordon P. *Malaysian Politics: The Second Generation*. Singapore: Oxford University Press, 1991.

Minnesota Population Center. *Integrated Public Use Microdata Series — International: Version 5.0*. Minneapolis: University of Minnesota, 2009.

NECF Malaysia. *Report on the State of Religious Liberty in Malaysia*. Petaling Jaya: National Evangelical Christian Fellowship (NECF) Malaysia, 2007.

Ongkili, James P. "Political Development in Sabah, 1963–1988". In *Sabah 25 Years Later, 1963–1988*, edited by J.G. Kitingan and J.F. Ongkili. Kota Kinabalu: Institute Development of Sabah, 1989.

Reid, Anthony. "Endangered Identity: Kadazan or Dusun in Sabah (East Malaysia)". *Journal of Southeast Asian Studies* 28, no. 1 (1997): 120–36.

Roff, William R. "Patterns of Islamization in Malaysia, 1890s–1990s: Exemplars, Institutions and Vectors". *Journal of Islamic Studies* 9, no. 2 (1998): 210–28.

Rooney, John. *Khabar Gembira: A History of the Catholic Church in East Malaysia and Brunei (1880–1976)*. London and Kota Kinabalu: Burns and Oates/Mill Hill Missionaries, 1981.

Sadiq, Kamal. "When States Prefer Non-Citizens over Citizens: Conflict over Illegal Immigration into Malaysia". *International Studies Quarterly* 49 (2005): 101–22.

Singh, Hari. "Tradition, UMNO and Political Succession in Malaysia". *Third World Quarterly* 19, no. 2 (1998): 241–54.

Stockwell, A.J. "Introduction". In *Malaysia*, edited by A.J. Stockwell. London: British Documents on End of Empire, HMSO, 2004.

Taylor, Charles. *A Secular Age*. Cambridge, MA: Belknap Press of Harvard University Press.

———. 2009. "What is Secularism?" In *Secularism, Religion, and Multicultural Citizenship*, edited by G.B. Levey and T. Modood. Cambridge: Cambridge University Press, 2007.

Tilly, Charles. *Identities, Boundaries and Social Ties*. Boulder, CO: Paradigm, 2005.

Tilman, Robert O. "Malaysia: The Problems of Federation". *Western Political Quarterly* 16, no. 4 (1963): 897–911.

Yavuz, M. Hakan. *Secularism and Muslim Democracy in Turkey*. Cambridge: Cambridge University Press, 2009.

PART IV
Indonesia

8

NATSIR & SUKARNO: THEIR CLASH OVER NATIONALISM, RELIGION AND DEMOCRACY, 1928–1958

Audrey Kahin

In the closing months of 2008, as Indonesia prepared to hold its third national elections since the downfall of the Soeharto regime, a continuing point of controversy was the growing strength of religion in the country's political life. Discussion of this issue became more heated with the passing of the pornography bill on the national scene (see Rinaldo, this volume) and the increasing number of local initiatives being introduced aimed at strengthening Islam's social and political role. These measures sparked widespread controversy, as they were often seen as aimed at undermining freedoms essential to a democratic society in order to appease some of the stronger Islamic groups (see also Platzdasch, this volume). Similar controversies have been part and parcel of the Indonesian political scene throughout the country's postcolonial history, though they were forcibly suppressed during much of Soeharto's tenure.

Until the final years of his regime Soeharto, like Sukarno before him, had seen the force of political Islam in Indonesia as a threat equal to that of communism and thus needing to be similarly contained. Especially during his first two decades in power, Soeharto attempted to impose the kind of control the colonial government of the Netherlands East Indies had earlier maintained, wherein religion was permitted to play a large role in the country's social and cultural life while it was rigorously excluded from exerting any political influence.

In the late colonial period and in the first decades of independence, Mohammad Natsir, who headed the Masjumi, the country's largest Muslim political party, had been one of the major Indonesian political figures who had fought for the inclusion of religion in the political arena. At the same time, in the 1930s and 1940s, Natsir was in the forefront of the nationalist movement and in the 1950s strove hard to maintain Indonesia as a democratic state. His relationship to Sukarno, Indonesia's first president, and the alliance and disagreements between the two men throw some light on the debates within Indonesia over the form the new state should take and the role of Islam within it.

Conflicts regarding the role of religion in the country's political life had divided nationalist political forces in the Netherlands East Indies long before the declaration of independence in 1945. Already in the late 1920s and early 1930s, leaders of nationalist organizations, both those belonging to specifically Islamic parties and those defining themselves as religiously neutral, were attempting to work out the most viable basis for drawing the people of the Indonesian archipelago into an overarching nationalist movement. The major issue that divided Indonesian nationalists centred on whether Islam, embraced by at least 85 per cent of the population, provided the natural tie among the peoples of the diverse societies making up the Netherlands East Indies or whether the new independence movement should be religiously neutral in order to avoid alienating the country's important minorities of non-Muslims.

In an influential 1925 essay, "Nationalism, Islam and Marxism", Sukarno, Indonesia's foremost nationalist leader and future president, attempted to harmonize the three major streams he perceived in Indonesian society (Sukarno 1969). A few years later, Mohammad Natsir, as a young student in Bandung in the late 1920s, also began to confront some of the basic problems surrounding Islam's role in the struggle for Indonesian independence. At that time he attended the demonstrations mounted by the Indonesian National Party (Partai Nasional Indonesia, PNI) and covered Sukarno's speeches there for *Pembela Islam*, the journal of the Persatuan Islam (Persis), for which he served as editor and correspondent (Federspiel

1970, pp. 12–16).[1] Though strongly attracted to the PNI's condemnation of Dutch colonialism and its demands for an independent Indonesia, Natsir was worried by the growing criticisms voiced by its leaders against aspects of Islamic teachings. As a result, he began to draw a sharp line between a struggle for independence emphasizing nationalism, as was espoused by Sukarno, and a struggle for independence based on Islamic ideals (*Pembela Islam* 1931–1932).[2] Writing under the alias, Is, he emphasized the indispensability of Islam as the major foundation of the nationalist movement.[3] Many religiously neutral nationalist leaders reacted angrily to these articles and accused *Pembela Islam* of trying to split the unity of the independence movement.

The momentum of Sukarno's National Party (PNI) stalled when, fearful of the threat it posed, the colonial government arrested and imprisoned its head in December 1929 and cracked down on other nationalist activities. Police broke up political meetings and arrested the speakers, and under this pressure the PNI finally dissolved in April 1931. The religiously neutral nationalists would never retrieve the unity they apparently enjoyed in the late 1920s, as their leaders increasingly diverged on the strategies to be employed in the face of colonial repression.

After his arrest Sukarno was initially held in Sukamiskin jail in Bandung, where Natsir's mentor, the Persatuan Islam leader Ahmad Hassan, visited him and brought him books. On several occasions Natsir accompanied Hassan on these visits (Rosidi 1990, p. 253).[4] In 1934 Sukarno was exiled to Flores. There, no longer under the pressure of day-to-day politics, he struggled to define his thinking on Islam's current and future role in Indonesia's independence struggle. His efforts were illustrated most clearly in a series of letters he wrote to Hassan between December 1934 and October 1936 (*Surat-Surat Islam dari Endeh*).

In these letters Sukarno analysed the place of Islam in the modern world. He implicitly blamed Muslims themselves for their lack of social and political influence, bemoaning the fact that conservative Muslim groups closed their eyes to modern technological advances and harked back instead to an imagined earlier golden age of Islam. When looking at contemporary society, these Muslims, in his view, tended to focus merely on the restrictions imposed by their religion, ignoring its ability to adapt to changing times:

> How much better it would be if the Islamic community remembered rather what is tolerated and neutral! How good it would be if they

remembered that in worldly matters, in matters of statesmanship, "one may criticize (*berqias*), one may speak heresy (*berbidah*), one may abandon earlier customs, one may adopt new customs, one may have a radio, one may fly in an airplane, one may use electricity, one may be modern, one may be hyper-hyper modern" so long as this is not clearly forbidden or pronounced sinful by Allah and his Prophet. (Soekarno 1959, p. 334)[5]

At the end of the decade, after the Dutch transferred him from Endeh in eastern Indonesia to Bengkulu in southwest Sumatra, Sukarno was still exploring the subject of Islam's place in modern governments and society. He focused on the issue in two 1940 articles published in *Pandji Islam*: "Why Turkey has Separated Religion from the State [Apa Sebab Turki Memisahkan Agama dari Negara]" and "Society in the Age of the Camel and Society in the Age of the Airplane [Masjarakat Onta dan Masjarakat Kapal-Udara]" (Soekarno 1959, pp. 403–45, 483–91). In these essays he again argued for viewing the strictures of the Prophet Mohammad in the context of contemporary society and called on the Muslim community to use their intellect in applying the Prophet's teachings correctly.

As Bernhard Dahm (1969) has noted, these articles provided Natsir with a point of departure for contesting Sukarno's arguments and pointing out what he saw as the inherent dangers in Sukarno's way of thinking. In an article entitled, "Islam's attitude toward Freethinking", Natsir agreed with Sukarno that Mohammad viewed the intellect as an instrument in reaching an understanding of God's word (Natsir 1954*a*, pp. 206–29). But he went on to stress the limits of independent thought:

> He acknowledged that by independent thinking faith could be strengthened and much of the superstition that clung to religion could be eliminated without great difficulties. A free intellect would open the windows of the study and let in the fresh air. But … this gust of fresh air could become a storm, which would throw everything in the study into confusion and which could also shake the foundations of religion. "Freedom without discipline produces terrible confusion; freedom without authority is anarchy". (Dahm 1969, p. 193)

In his later writing Natsir consistently pursued this theme of the dangers posed by unbridled "freedom" or unrestrained action in any sphere, whether in individual thinking or, politically, in the implementation of a democratic order.

At the same time, Natsir never condemned nationalism (*kebangsaan*), as his mentor Hassan did. He rather stressed the need to create a community or society, using whatever tie would help in establishing that unity. He noted Islam's recognition of love of one's native area or land as a natural human characteristic, writing:

> We can be obedient Muslims who with great joy can sing "Indonesia my Native Land [*Tanah Airku*]." How can we eliminate our Indonesian-ness [*ke-Indonesiaan kita*]? Because it is God who created the different peoples who now inhabit the earth. We must be glad and joyful in showing to the outside world that we are the Indonesian people, this is our language, this is our culture, our batik, our carving, our music, and so on. (Natsir 2001, p. 179)

It was only when this natural affiliation was exaggerated into an ideology and assumed the character of racism or chauvinism that it became dangerous. He later clarified the Islamic attitude, when he stated:

> Islam does not agree with racism and except for an anti-colonialist struggle, or struggle for political freedom, it opposes the concept of nationalism, i.e., xenophobia, or the idea of "my country right or wrong".[6]

Thus, in the view of Taufik Abdullah, Natsir emphasized a common nationality, such as portrayed in the Indonesian word *kebangsaan* rather than the concept embodied in the borrowed word *nasionalisme*:

> *Kebangsaan* had a respected place in Natsir's thought. But *nasionalisme* is a different matter. It appears that even though Pak Natsir continued to use the word *kebangsaan*, he strongly differentiated between *kebangsaan* and *nasionalisme*. *Nasionalisme* was an "ideologization" of the ideals of *kebangsaan*. Natsir was rather cool to the process of *nasionalisme*. (Abdullah 2001, p. 53)

In his pre-war writing, opposing the "ideologization" of *kebangsaan* while embracing its anti-colonial characteristics was an integral part of Natsir's attempt to harmonize his view of the need for an independent Indonesian state with his conviction that the movement towards that end had to be based on Islam. In a series of articles in *Pembela Islam* in 1932 he responded to attacks from members of the religiously neutral parties that he and his fellows in the Persatuan Islam were splitting the nationalist movement. In these articles Natsir strove to define what he thought was the essence of *kebangsaan* in Indonesia (Natsir 1932). Recognizing that at that time the peoples of the Indonesian archipelago lacked many criteria often used to define national consciousness (i.e., shared language, physical characteristics, customs, etc.), he sought "the unifying tie" that could not be shattered by "the force of law, constitutions or military arms" (ibid., 1, p. ii). He focused on Ernest Renan's emphasis on "the sufferings that we have together experienced", that connect and unify a people more than their shared joys and happiness (ibid., 2, p. 2). Natsir linked the sufferings of the Indonesian people to "an awareness of our current situation", and "the realization that our self-respect does not accord with that situation [*keinsjafan kepada harga diri sendiri jang tidak tjotjok dengan keadaan itoe*]" (ibid., 3, p. 2). In his view, the Sarekat Islam and other Islamic organizations, such as the Muhammadiyah,[7] had restored the sense of dignity and unity among the peoples of the scattered islands of the archipelago, separated not only by the sea, but also by customs, language and the efforts of the colonial government. These Muslim organizations had raised the consciousness of the diverse peoples of the archipelago so that they "remain closely aligned spiritually [*tetap berbaris rapat dalam kebathinan*], linked by feelings of brotherhood and a yearning to live and die together" (ibid., p. 3). Thus, "these joint ideals became a connection for a group (*kaoem*) spread out (dispersed), with different customs and behavior (*adat dan tabiat*), and differing in the color of their skin and in their languages".[8]

With respect to the relationship between religion and the state, Sukarno often used the example of Mustafa Kemal's Turkey to argue for separation of religion from government. He suggested that independent Indonesia would be faced with two alternatives: "unity of religion and state but without democracy, or — democracy, but with the state separated from religion". He wrote: "I [would] free Islam from the state, so that Islam can be strong and I [would] free the state from religion so that the state can be strong" (Soekarno 1959, p. 406).

In response, arguing forcefully against any possibility that religion could be separated from the governance of a Muslim country, Natsir wrote, also in *Pandji Islam*: "According to our outlook as a Muslim community, Islam is not merely an addition, an 'extra' that has to be incorporated in the state, but in our view it is the state that is the apparatus and instrument for Islam." As consistently in his writings throughout his life, Natsir was then emphasizing that the state was not a goal but an instrument (*staat, bagi kita, boekan toedjoean, melainkan alat*) for achieving the people's ideals (Natsir 1940, p. 8215).

At the same time he did recognize that there were many aspects of a modern state that were outside the Islamic frame of reference. The role of religion, he specified, did not concern factors that alter with time, but was limited to those that are fixed and constant, including,

> the rights and duties between the ruler and the ruled, the principle that certain ills of society be eliminated — such as the drinking of intoxicants, theft, gambling, prostitution, regulations for the harmony of home life, on marriage and divorce and on inheritance; rules to combat poverty, such as to distribute wealth through *zakat* and *fitrah*, to prohibit excessive interest on loans. (Noer 1973, p. 291)

He asserted that such rules would not hamper progress, and in all other matters governance could draw on examples from other countries: "We have the right to adopt good laws from England, or Japan, from Uruguay or Finland if they are not in conflict with our religion" (Natsir 1940, p. 8238). But he disputed Sukarno's portrayal of the Turkey of Mustafa Kemal as a model to be followed by Muslim majority states.

In his series of articles, published under the alias of A. Moechlis in *Pandji Islam* in mid-1940, Natsir focused on refuting Sukarno's idealization of Kemal's rule. He acknowledged the weaknesses of the caliphate in decline in the nineteenth and twentieth centuries, but criticized Soekarno for his willingness to adopt European caricatures of an Islamic regime based on these final decadent years. Rebutting Sukarno's arguments, Natsir contended that, though some of the Caliphs were tyrants, this did not reflect on their religion, for tyrants "can use any philosophy or religion to mask their tyranny". He asserted that once tyranny exists, religion and the state have already been separated and according to Islamic teaching the people then have the right to overthrow the tyrannical government (Natsir 1940).

While acknowledging the virtues of democracy, he also recognized its drawbacks, and contended that an Islamic system had superior characteristics:

> Democracy is good [*bagus*.] But the Islamic state system does not make all matters depend on the mercy of democratic institutions. The progress of democracy from century to century has demonstrated its different good characteristics. But it is also not free from several bad and also dangerous attributes. We Muslims know well enough what is the result when that democracy has eroded to become a "party"-cracy or a "clique"-cracy

complete with games of self-defense and sleights of hand behind the scenes, in which matters Kemal Pasja for instance is himself very skilled and crafty at using in the political game. Because of this, because Islam does not want all its decisions and laws to rest on this so-called democracy, Islam does not want to be labeled democratic. We can surrender that [*itoe terserah*]. Islam is one idea, one understanding, one concept [*begrip*] in its own right that has its own characteristics, Islam is not 100% democracy, it is not 100% autocracy. Islam is.... yes *Islam*. It can be viewed as a synthesis from these two antitheses.... (Natsir 1940, p. 8239)

At the same time, he mocked Sukarno's portrayal of Kemal Mustafa's rule as democratic,

"Democracy" in the country of Kemal Pasha? What is the meaning of democracy in the hands of the dictator Kemal Pasha? What is the meaning of a *vrij spel der krachten* ["free play of forces"] — freedom when all power is in the hands of a single man, the "State president" who is at the same time "Leader" of the only "Volksparty" that exists in his state, or strength in the hand of a "Fuehrer" Mustafa Kemal? What is the meaning of *freedom of the press* in the hands of this "Duce" Kemal Mustafa? (Natsir 1940, pp. 8238–39).

Natsir continued that, though Kemal had replaced Islamic law with laws based on the Swiss and Italian constitutions, "he has asked the people to be patient for ten or twenty years before democracy can be implemented" (ibid.).

Many of the arguments he advanced here against Kemal's government Natsir was to put forward against Sukarno himself in the 1950s when as Indonesia's president Sukarno tried to implement his ideas for a "Guided Democracy". But in contrast to his later stance, in 1940 Natsir strongly advocated an "Islamic" not merely a "democratic" state. He was at the same time, however, in agreement with Sukarno's emphasis on the democratic nature of Islam, asserting, despite what he said above, that Islam is "democratic in the sense that it is anti-despotism, anti-absolutism, anti-arbitrary measures" (ibid.).

The conflict of ideas between Natsir and Sukarno was to continue until Sukarno's fall from power, though, despite their intellectual disagreements, they were able to work harmoniously together during the revolutionary years. The two men did share some common attitudes: both had admiration for Muhammad Abduh and Jamal al-Din al-Afghani; both embraced the progressive and egalitarian nature of Islam; and Sukarno always acknowledged the important role Islam had played in the early nationalist movement, writing as early as 1925:

> Many of our nationalists forget that the nationalist and Islamic movements in Indonesia … had the same origin.… Both originated in a strong desire to resist the West, or, more precisely, Western capitalism and imperialism. So they are really not enemies, but allies. (Soekarno 1969, p. 42)

Both Natsir and Sukarno also opposed certain characteristics of Western democracy, such as government by a fifty-plus-one majority in parliament, stressing instead, though to different degrees, the idea of achieving a consensus among the competing parties.

Sukarno's major emphasis was always on the similarities between, and the need to establish harmony among, the three groups that he saw as making up Indonesian political society — nationalists, Muslims and Marxists. Only through these groups working together, he argued, could a firm basis be laid for an independent Indonesia. Natsir recognized Sukarno's understanding of Islam, acknowledging in 1971:

> Soekarno had a considerable knowledge and understanding of Islam, but was not himself religious, nor attracted to Islam in a positive sense. He saw it as an objective factor operating in Indonesia with which he had to come to terms, this being so both in the period of the nationalist movement and afterwards.[9]

He criticized Sukarno's "deliberate simplifications [of Islam] *in order to find a common denominator*" (Dahm 1969, p. 195). Essentially, for Sukarno religion was an individual matter, while for Natsir, Islam and its laws had the potential for ordering the state and the individuals within it, though within a democratic framework.

Natsir's views diverged from those of many of his educated contemporaries, in both the Islamic and secular political parties, to a considerable extent because of the nature of his education, which, as in the case of Sukarno, he had received exclusively in the Netherlands East Indies. In this he differed from his fellow Minangkabau students, such as Mohammad Hatta and Sutan Sjahrir, who after their schooling in Batavia and Bandung, had continued their education in the Netherlands and had there experienced the political free-for-all of a democratic society. Natsir had little perception of how religion operated in such a context, and disagreed with them in their insistence on avoiding religiously based political organizations. Nevertheless, the Western classical education he received in Bandung had a life-long influence on his way of thinking. It not only had the negative impact of intensifying his fear that the Dutch were using this education to Christianize their students, but also had the more positive influence of opening his mind to some of the most enlightened Western thinkers on human rights and democracy.[10]

At the same time, he also differed from those of his contemporaries who were educated in the Middle East, for he was freed from too strict an adherence either to the modernist stream of teachings in Cairo or the more conservative views being taught in Mecca. Like Natsir, many religious thinkers in the Middle East in the early decades of the twentieth century were searching for an acceptable relationship between nationalism and religion. This was particularly the case in Egypt where, during the struggle against British rule, Muslim nationalists, including such influential teachers as Rashid Rida, were confronting the relationship between their desire for an independent Egypt and their loyalty to a disintegrating caliphate, which lingered on as "a symbol of Islamic internationalism, daily losing ground to the competing ideologies of nationalism and communism" (Laffan 2003, p. 214).

Many students from the Netherlands East Indies, studying at al-Azhar, Cairo's famous teaching mosque, were influenced by Rida's espousal of "the seemingly contradictory goals of both a Muslim community undivided and a new world of independent Muslim countries" (ibid., p. 234). These influences were particularly evident in Natsir's home region of West Sumatra, where al-Azhar graduates founded the Permi party, based specifically on the principles of both Islam and nationalism. Natsir rejected this twin basis of struggle and called on Permi leaders to take Islam as the sole basis of their movement for independence (Natsir 1931).

Despite recognizing ties with his co-religionists throughout the world, Natsir, however, conceived of the Indonesian nation almost exclusively in terms of its colonially defined boundaries. In seeing Islam as a unifying factor for the peoples within the Netherlands East Indies, he did not view the presence of other religions as an obstacle to this unity, for to him an Islamic government was a tolerant government in which Christians and members of other religions were free to follow their own faiths.[11]

Throughout his polemic with Sukarno during the 1930s and early 1940s, as well as in his broader exploration of the relationship of Islam and nationalism, Natsir consistently expressed the belief that Islam was the natural bond among the peoples of the archipelago. He argued that it had always been in the vanguard of Indonesian nationalism and was the appropriate vehicle to unite Indonesian nationalists:

> Long before the Budi Utomo had accepted non-Javanese members, long before the Pasundan movement had given up its provincialism, long before the local movements in West Java, in East Java, in Ambon, and in Central Sumatra looked beyond the boundaries of their own regions, long before there was any mention of an "Indonesian nation," the PSII [Partai Sarekat Islam Indonesia] and the Muhammadiyah had hundreds of thousands of members in their branches throughout Indonesia. These organizations, founded exclusively on the principles of Islam, embodied the concept of Indonesian unity....
>
> It was the Muslim movement that, by breaking down the barriers of provincial thinking, first implanted the idea of Indonesian unity. It was the Muslim movement, holding aloft the banner of Islam, that first inspired a sense of solidarity with the peoples of other colonial countries. (*Pembela Islam* 1931)

With this perception of the ties that bound the peoples of the archipelago, Natsir considered that Sukarno's efforts to evoke earlier Hindu kingdoms such as Majapahit as a basis on which to build Indonesian nationalism were misguided and an extension of Javanism, which would alienate all ethnic groups outside Java.

From 1942 when the Japanese defeated the Dutch in the Netherlands East Indies, the fundamental arguments among Indonesian political thinkers no longer focused on the best way to achieve an independent state and began to emphasize even more the form of government best adapted to that state. During this period tensions were again growing between the religiously neutral nationalists and the Islamic leaders. In the Japanese-sponsored Investigatory Body for Preparatory Work for Indonesian Independence (Badan Penyelidik Usaha Persiapan Kemerdekaan Indonesia, BPUPKI), leaders from both groups began to discuss the basis of a future Indonesian state. In this body, on 1 June 1945, Sukarno first laid out the "Five Principles" or Pancasila that would become Indonesia's state ideology — nationalism, internationalism or humanitarianism, democracy, social justice and belief in God (Nasution 1992, p. 10; Yamin 1960, p. 71; Kahin 1951, pp. 122–27).[12]

Although Islamic leaders did not feel that the Pancasila fully guaranteed their position, they eventually on 22 June reached a compromise expounded in the "Jakarta Charter", which positioned Belief in God as the first principle in the Pancasila and included in the draft constitution a phrase that came to be known as the "seven words": "*dengan kewadjiban mendjalankan Sjari'at Islam bagi pemeluk-pemeluknja*" (with the obligation for adherents of Islam to practice Islamic law). The committee placed these words in the draft constitution's preamble, but at the initiative of Mohammad Hatta, who became Indonesia's first vice president, the words were dropped in the provisional Constitution adopted on 18 August 1945 by the Indonesian Independence Preparatory Committee (Panitia Persiapan Kemerdekaan Indonesia, PPKI), which succeeded the earlier body.

With respect to Hatta's role in removing the seven words from the Constitution, it should be noted that, though he was a pious and devout Muslim, Hatta always strongly opposed political parties being based on religious affiliations. In this instance he intervened to have the seven words omitted, because, according to his own account, a Japanese naval officer (*opsis kaigun*) had assured him that Protestants and Catholics in the eastern archipelago strongly objected to the earlier formulation, viewing it as discriminating against minority religious groups. Fearing that islands outside Java and Sumatra would break from the republic if the phrase were used, Hatta persuaded other members of the committee to remove it (Hatta 1970, pp. 66–70).

Through the later years of Dutch colonialism and throughout the Japanese Occupation, Natsir was known mainly as an educator and a Muslim thinker, while Sukarno became the prime leader of the future independent Indonesia. I do not think Natsir played any role in the PPKI's discussions on the shape of the independent state, though he did attend them, and in the months immediately following the declaration of independence in August 1945 he became a member of the new Indonesian Parliament (KNIP, Komite Nasional Indonesia Pusat, lit. Central Indonesian National Committee). On 3 January 1946, Prime Minister Sutan Sjahrir appointed him to replace Amir Sjarifuddin as the republic's official Minister of Information, a position he held for most of the revolution. As Minister of Information he had to work closely with President Sukarno, who had enthusiastically supported his appointment. In recounting his renewed relations with Sukarno after their pre-war public disputes, Natsir recalled:

> When Sjahrir first proposed to Bung Karno that I become Minister of Information, Bung Karno responded "*Hij is de man.*" [He's the (right)

man]. I didn't meet with him at the time. Then when we did meet in Yogya, we first pretended not to remember what had happened earlier. It was better to confront the current situation and let go of what was in the past, because we were now facing a great struggle. "How about us? We certainly clashed earlier," Bung Karno then said. "Yes," I replied rather jokingly. "Now that serves no purpose, later we can resume it." So from then on we were indeed close. (Natsir 1989)[13]

As Minister of Information, Natsir worked on a daily basis with both Sukarno and Hatta, writing Sukarno's Independence Day speeches and being involved in preparing all the important statements issued by the President and Vice President. The three worked collectively in keeping the people of the new republic informed of the government's policies and activities.

In providing the public face of the republican government, Hatta and Natsir probably exerted something of a brake on the more mercurial Sukarno. It is interesting that each attributed to the other the pivotal role in guiding Sukarno's policies and utterances, Natsir writing:

> Hatta decided everything important. Bung Karno never wanted to issue a statement if Bung Hatta didn't agree. For instance, in facing difficult problems, such as the Madiun affair [the Communist uprising of September 1948] and other affairs, Bung Hatta was the one to decide the policy (ibid.).

For his part, Hatta recalled, "Bung Karno didn't want to sign any government declaration if it had not been prepared by *Saudara* Natsir" (Hamka 1978, p. 320; Roem 1983, p. 176), and he later described Natsir as "Sukarno's golden boy during the revolution" (Abdullah 2009, p. 334).

Natsir apparently retained the trust and confidence of President Sukarno until well after the transfer of sovereignty from the Dutch at the end of 1949. For on 22 August 1950, five days after the new unitary Republic of Indonesia came into existence, replacing the transitory federal United States of Indonesia (Republik Indonesia Serikat, RIS), President Sukarno invited him to form its first government. Natsir thus entered office with the full support of the President. According to one account, when asked by a reporter who should become Prime Minister, Sukarno had replied: "Ya, who else but Natsir of the Masjumi. They have a concept for saving the Republic constitutionally" (Natsir 1989).[14]

Within the next few months, however, their alliance turned into confrontation. To be sure, in the general field of foreign relations Sukarno and Natsir remained broadly in accord. In harmony with Sukarno's attitude and despite Natsir's strong anti-communism, his cabinet espoused "a free and active foreign policy", through which the Indonesian Republic was tied neither to the Western nor the Eastern bloc, displaying this neutrality in its foreign policy decisions.[15] Rather, the clash between Natsir and Sukarno came more narrowly over the role of the President vis-à-vis that of Parliament, and over the republic's ties to the Netherlands.

The two major challenges in the Dutch-Indonesian relationship sprang from the agreements reached at the Round Table Conference held in The Hague in late 1949, where the Dutch agreed to transfer sovereignty to an independent Indonesian state. With respect to the future status of West Irian (Western New Guinea, Papua), the conference had agreed that Dutch authority was to be preserved only for a twelve-month period before the territory's final status was determined. This period would expire on 27 December 1950, little over three months after Natsir assumed office as Prime Minister, and there was no sign that the Dutch would adhere to the agreement. Tied to the West Irian problem was the special relationship between Indonesia and the Netherlands, embodied in the Netherlands Indonesian Union, agreed upon at The Hague talks. As it became increasingly clear that the Netherlands would not in fact reconsider the status of West Irian by the specified date, the Union became a major focus of Indonesian dissatisfaction.

This issue brought to a head the tensions that had been developing between Sukarno and Natsir. When Natsir became Prime Minister, his parliamentary cabinet replaced Hatta's presidential cabinet. In discussions with Sukarno as he took office, Natsir had insisted that in a parliamentary system, responsibility for decision-making lay with the cabinet in agreement with the Parliament, and not with the President. In early December Natsir heard that Sukarno intended to make a speech for Mohammad's birthday, in which he would declare that if "before the cock crows on 1 January 1951 West Irian has not been returned to the Republic, then the Indonesian Dutch Union will be dissolved unilaterally" (Puar 1978, p. 108).

Natsir asked to see the text of Sukarno's statement before he broadcast it and the President reluctantly agreed. Natsir was in accord with the President on the necessity of dissolving the Union but he believed that Indonesia's standing in the world dictated that abrogation of the agreement to form the Union had to be carried out in an orderly manner through a scheduled ministerial meeting between the Dutch and Indonesians and not through a unilateral declaration by the President. Reminding Sukarno of his undertaking to observe Parliament's prime role in decision-making, Natsir proposed that there be joint discussions between the cabinet and the President on the issue. "Flushed with anger", Sukarno reluctantly agreed, and at the cabinet meeting, held in the palace, both he and Natsir presented their views, the President in an eloquent, thirty-minute speech. However, in the ballot that was taken following their presentations, only three of the participants voted to dissolve the Union unilaterally in accordance with Sukarno's demands, while twelve voted for the action to be taken at a joint ministerial session with the Netherlands scheduled several months hence, in accordance with Natsir's proposal.

The President then cancelled his planned broadcast and accepted what he viewed as a major blow to his authority. But he did not forgive Natsir. He renewed the complaints he had been voicing for months that his position as President was no more than a rubber stamp. From then on the personal relationship of respect and cooperation that Sukarno and Natsir had maintained throughout the revolution ended.

The antagonistic relationship that then developed and intensified between the two men after the showdown over West Irian was an important factor in the downfall of the Natsir government. Herbert Feith attributed the original basis of this antagonism not only to the dispute over West Irian but also to the fact that Natsir's cabinet pursued policies that accorded closely with the positions of Hatta and Sjahrir, the pragmatic "administrators" whom he contrasted with the "solidarity makers" epitomized in the leadership style of Sukarno. In addition, the President's misgivings were exacerbated by Natsir's persistent efforts "to confine Soekarno within the bounds of the figurehead President's role, a role to which Sukarno had never resigned himself" (Feith 1962, pp. 170–71). As Feith further noted, after Sukarno was forced to yield over the West Irian issue, "he began to use his influence actively in support of PNI endeavours to bring the cabinet down" (ibid.). This was achieved in March 1951, when Natsir felt compelled to return his mandate to the President.

As the 1950s progressed, Natsir moved from the position of moderate critic of Sukarno to that of outspoken opponent of the President's growing power and of his early steps towards introducing his concept of "Guided Democracy" to the country. The failure of the 1955 general elections to provide a solution to the country's political and economic problems heightened Sukarno's frustration with the parliamentary system. From late

1956 he began to make moves to strengthen his power as President vis-à-vis that of Parliament. These culminated in his February 1957 unveiling of his *"konsepsi"* of a Guided Democracy that he believed was more suited to Indonesian realities than was the Western form of democracy the country had previously been following.

It was as a protest to this proclamation that Natsir began a frontal attack against Sukarno's concept and launched a defence of a democratic system of government. He expressed his views in February 1957 in his "First Reaction to the President's Concept" (Natsir 1957a, pp. 25–27). Responding to the President's criticisms of democracy as a Western concept and unsuitable for Asian peoples, Natsir stated that one could not make a dichotomy between "Western democracy" and "Eastern democracy", affirming instead that "There is only 'democracy and non-democracy' [*jang ada hanja antara 'demokrasi dan bukan demokrasi'*]." It seemed, he said, that the *"konsepsi"* was aimed at creating a "democracy without an opposition". After noting that parallel influences passed from east to west and from west to east, he continued:

> Democracy in my view is a philosophy that is not limited to an administrative system, but democracy is a "way of life" that embraces spiritual and material fields. In this connection the late President Franklin D. Roosevelt formulated an understanding of democracy that I think can be accepted by every true democracy whether of the east or the west. A true democracy gives guarantees for:
>
> 1. Freedom of expression
> 2. Freedom of religion
> 3. Freedom from want
> 4. Freedom from fear.
>
> Democracy can also be divided into political democracy that guarantees freedom of thought, speech, assembly and religion, and economic democracy that guarantees social justice for all members of society. (ibid., pp. 31–32)[16]

Until the debates in the Constituent Assembly in November 1957, Natsir would often stress the virtues of democratic as against authoritarian government and mute any particular advocacy of "Islamic democracy" as such. He did, however, always argue that values based on religion should be the ultimate source of the moral code of policymakers. He contended that authoritarianism was not the answer to the weakness that had become evident in the democratic process in Indonesia. In a country so diverse and extensive, he believed that it was important for people of diverse ethnicities and cultures to recognize that they could bring their grievances to government attention through their representatives, "so that they can really feel that their government is from them, for them and responsible to them.... It is this feeling of belief and love that actually forms the true power that gathers the archipelago of Indonesia into a single state" (Natsir 1956).

But, as in his pre-war writings, he again warned against wild or unfettered democracy (*demokrasi jang liar*), which he thought would result in chaos. Before Sukarno formally presented his own "concept", Natsir had also proposed a

> guided democracy ... not in the sense that this entire democratic system has to be controlled by one or several men who are all powerful and uncontrolled. But guided democracy in the sense that the adherents/ supporters and implementers of this democratic system are guided and led by high moral values and philosophies. (Ibid. pp. 12–13)

By the time he made his major speech to the Constituent Assembly that same month, there appears to have been a major shift in Natsir's thinking with respect to the nature of the Indonesian state. Up to then he seemed to be willing to view the Pancasila as an acceptable philosophy for the state,[17] with the major proviso that belief in God remain the first of its five principles and with the "seven words" of the Jakarta Charter included in the Preamble again. However, in his arguments before the Constituent Assembly that Indonesia should be an "Islamic Democracy", Natsir now contended that the Pancasila was amorphous and essentially secular and thus unsuitable for a Muslim nation such as Indonesia. This change almost certainly was occasioned by two major factors: first, as already mentioned, Sukarno's growing efforts to introduce a more authoritarian order in Indonesia;[18] and second, the growing strength of the Communist Party (PKI) in the 1950s, which became evident in the 1955 elections and even more so in the 1957 local elections. While on a personal basis Natsir was able to maintain cordial relations with the PKI leaders, adhering to his general practice of agreeing to disagree, he opposed and increasingly feared the influence over Sukarno of its philosophy, especially its anti-religion stance.

In his opening speech to the Constituent Assembly, as the major spokesman for the Masjumi party, Natsir made a series of arguments in favour of religion as against secularism, which he now identified with the Pancasila. In doing so, he turned to President Sukarno's speech of 17 June 1945, which had first outlined the concept of the Pancasila. Natsir used that speech to contend that the President's description of religion there, whereby belief in God was irrelevant to later stages of human development, offended the vast majority of Muslims. After quoting extensively from the speech, he said that Sukarno was arguing that "someone who is still at the stage of agrarian life needs God, but when he reaches the stage of industrialism he has no further need of God". Natsir likened this argument to the Marxist position that the economic and social structure of a society determines its religion, culture and philosophy. In contesting this view, Natsir cited Alexis de Tocqueville and others who had, he stated, argued for the merits of religion over secularism in forming the foundation for a state. He further contended that secularism provided a fertile ground for relying on force in the pursuit of power, which he characterized as the standard of fascist regimes such as that of Nazi Germany.

He concluded that secularism does not provide a strong basis for social life, but rather weakens the connections between an individual and the society in which he lives. He then referred back to President Soekarno's assertion that the Pancasila has "five bases or ideas, that are spread throughout the existing groups in Indonesia", and pointed out the contradiction between this statement and the fact that the Communists did not accept the principle of religion included within the Pancasila. He continued that, while no one would argue with the fact that the Pancasila incorporated good ideas, its supporters did not even agree among themselves as to its fundamental character. The reason for this, according to Natsir, was that it was merely an abstraction or concept, trying to stand as neutral above all ideologies, a stance that prevented it having any roots among the people.

There thus appears to be a striking contrast between Natsir's speech to the Constituent Assembly and the positions he had adhered to over the preceding years (and indeed adopted again later), when he had portrayed an Islamic state as an ideal that would take at least decades to realize and when he was willing to compromise with the non-Islamic parties in accepting the fundamental principles of the Pancasila. But the crux of his criticisms lay *not* in the Pancasila itself, but in Sukarno's continuing elucidation of its principles, and Natsir's argument was undoubtedly influenced by his conviction that Sukarno was manipulating these principles in order to maximize his own power. (This would also be the case later under the Soeharto regime, when Natsir opposed that President's insistence on all parties and organizations having the Pancasila as their sole foundation.) And it seems unlikely that Natsir was here actually arguing for an Islamic state, but rather for a state in which there was a convergence between Islamic laws and democratic practices. Such arguments accord with the other distinctions he had frequently drawn between an "Islamic state" and a "Muslim nation", such as Indonesia, with a majority Muslim population, where a democratic form of government would ensure majority Muslim representation in Parliament and militate against any law being passed that contravened Islamic precepts.[19] It seems likely, therefore, that in his speech before the Constituent Assembly he was staking out a position for the Masjumi party that would provide a basis for negotiation with the other groups represented there, most notably the Communist Party, whose growing strength and influence on Sukarno were probably the impetus for many of the arguments he was putting forward.

In interviews fifteen years later, Natsir noted how close to an agreement the different sides came in the later sessions of the Assembly:

> In the closed sessions there were heart to heart talks between the Muslims, *abangan*, Christians, and even the Communists.[20] Prawoto and Osman Raliby spoke for us. Osman Raliby told us that they were just on the threshold of a compromise at the end of 1958.... The Masjumi in the Constituent Assembly was for Islamic teachings forming not the Constitution itself, but to be realized in legislation. However it could not secure two-thirds support for this, and thus ultimately it began to explore possibilities that the Pancasila serve as the basis for the Constitution so long as it included the Jakarta Charter. Before discussion could get underway Soekarno, backed strongly by the army, interrupted and dismissed the Constituent Assembly...[21]

This statement accords with the view of some later scholars, who accepted that, had the President not issued his decree of 5 July 1959, the Constituent Assembly might well have reached an agreement based on a formula wherein Pancasila was infused by the spirit of the Jakarta Charter (Magenda 2008, p. 4).[22]

Throughout 1957 Natsir had been attempting to alert Indonesians to what he saw as Sukarno's determination to destroy democracy and introduce a dictatorship. This he considered to be the major danger threatening the country. He viewed the dissidence that was growing in the regions outside Java that would culminate in the PRRI/Permesta[23] rebellion as stemming from the failure of the central government, and especially the President, to use democratic means to meet the challenges facing the new state. He saw the President's *konsepsi* as aimed at creating a "democracy without an opposition", and argued that this concept was not a cure to the problems the country faced, but a new disease (Natsir 1957*b*).

By this time Natsir stood in strong opposition to Sukarno and his actions, which, in Natsir's view, betrayed the ideals of the nationalist struggle that they had earlier shared. Yet in his growing antipathy towards the President, their long and ambiguous relationship still enabled him to make an insightful assessment of Sukarno's character and motivations in an interview in Jakarta with a British journalist, James Mossman, in November 1957 shortly before Natsir fled the city. Mossman reports him as saying:

> Soekarno is no communist … [n]ot basically. He's a mixture of politician and artist, and he's not always governed by calm reason. He has a sort of psychological complex which seems to urge him to seek the most violent methods he can find, short of war, to represent his country to the outside world. Before 1955 it might have been possible for his gifts and prestige among the people to have been recruited on the side of moderation over New Guinea [West Irian], but once the Dutch refused to negotiate with him over sovereignty, Soekarno veered back to his favourite theme of the need to bang the table. Now he's temperamentally in his element, though he's tired and rather confused and has no plan whatsoever. He's just marking time in the hope that The Hague will make some move to which he could react. (Mossman 1961, pp. 39–40)

During Natsir's years in the jungle after he joined the anti-Sukarno regional rebellion, his views became less nuanced. And his cynicism regarding Sukarno's actions crystallized as the President moved both to impose a more authoritarian regime and to ally more closely with the Communist Party. Natsir's hostility towards Sukarno was reinforced at the end of the rebellion in 1961 when the President reneged on his promise to grant amnesty and pardon to the defeated rebels. Instead, Natsir, together with his civilian and military colleagues, was jailed until after Sukarno's fall from power four years later.

Natsir's long imprisonment must have further convinced him of the tyrannical nature of the later years of the Sukarno regime, and it appears that he welcomed the coup that overthrew it and the ascent to power of

General Soeharto. But his optimism in the wake of the birth of the New Order soon dimmed, as he became aware that the military regime that came to power was opposed as strongly as Sukarno had been both to the political role of Islam and to the institution of a real democratic order in Indonesia. In retrospect, as the new regime ostracized and excluded him from the political process, Natsir seemed to look back with something approaching nostalgia to his earlier relationship with Sukarno, recalling that Sukarno, "whose style was at least elegant",[24] had never barred him from palace functions as Soeharto did, and commenting that Soeharto's treatment of him was "the action of a man with limited education and a limited world view" (Jenkins 1984, p. 185).

Despite the perception that Natsir became narrower and more rigid in his religious beliefs as he grew older (Hefner 2000, p. 105),[25] his fundamental adherence to a democratic form of government for Indonesia never changed and he continued to embrace both Islam and democracy. Even in his final years he strongly and openly expressed his opposition to an authoritarian order, whether of the left or the right, that did not reflect the wishes of the country's population.

Sukarno had died more than twenty years earlier, a broken and disappointed man, but he too had remained true to what was most fundamental in his earlier thinking — the desire that an independent Indonesia should reflect a merging of the major streams in Indonesian society. As John Legge portrayed his closing years, Sukarno rejected Soeharto's willingness to allow the former President "status in return for reduced power", and refused to condemn his erstwhile allies. Legge wrote:

> it might be said that Sukarno's closing years in the presidency were years when he was most clearly standing by principle. He could have condemned the PKI in order to save himself.... He would not take this way out, however, and refused to deny the place of communism in the consensus he had always sought. (Legge 2003, p. 458)

Neither man was able to see the Indonesia he had envisaged — for Natsir a democratic country based on Islam, and for Sukarno a country where nationalists, Muslims and Marxists were brought together in a harmonious entity. But although their conceptions of the roles of Islam and democracy in the political life of the nation evolved with political exigencies, neither ever lost his early vision.

Notes

1. The Persatuan Islam was one of the strictest and most uncompromising Muslim groups of the time. It had been founded by Muslim entrepreneurs mostly from the Palembang region of Sumatra with the aim of exploring the place of modernist ideas in the established religious system. Although members of Persis initially came from both the reformist and traditionalist streams, the traditionalists split off from the organization in 1926.
2. On his attitude towards Sukarno at this time, see his interview with *Editor* (Hakiem 1993, p. 242).
3. In marshalling his arguments for this position, he stated that: (1) Islam is not merely a religion in the sense of only worshipping Allah; (2) Islam opposes colonialism; so it is the duty of the Islamic community to struggle for independence; (3) Islam offers an ideological basis for an independent state; (4) The Islamic community has the duty to organize that independent state on bases that are determined by Islam; (5) This aim cannot be achieved by the Islamic community if they struggle to achieve independence in a merely nationalist party, even more so if this party hates Islam; (6) Therefore the Islamic Community [should] from the beginning enter and strengthen a struggle for independence that is based on Islamic ideals.
4. In his *Editor* interview, Natsir emphasized that while Sukarno was in Sukamiskin jail, it was the Persis members who visited him, not those from the PNI (Hakiem 1993, p. 242).
5. Unfortunately I have not been able to see Hassan's responses, but there is no indication from Sukarno's letters that he reacted too critically. The letters were published by Hassan and later appeared in Sukarno 1959, pp. 325–44.
6. Mohammad Natsir, interview, Jakarta, 24 February 1971. This is one of a series of interviews that George Kahin had with Natsir between January and May 1971. I was present at these interviews and took verbatim notes.
7. Kyai Haji Ahmad Dahlan's aim in founding Muhammadiyah was to promote modernist Islamic thought and to spread adherence to Islam. The organization emphasized social welfare, including education, and during the colonial period its central office advocated non-involvement in politics.
8. In his writings in the early 1930s, *kaoem Muslimin* was the term Natsir used most frequently in describing the Muslim community. He also often used *kaoem* to describe the people of a nation, occasionally as an alternative to *bangsa*. Less frequently he used *oemmat* to describe both the Muslim and national community. See Natsir 1932, passim.
9. Natsir, interview, 28 January 1971.
10. Two of his teachers at the AMS in Bandung personified these differences. While Natsir believed that one of them (Christoffels) sought to undermine the

students' religion, he warmly praised his Latin teacher (Van Bessem), who had protected the students' religious rights, for example opening his classroom to the Jong Islamieten Bond (JIB) to hold meetings that had been forbidden by the school's authorities. Natsir interview, 30 January 1971.

11. George Kahin noted that there was one major difference between the beliefs of Natsir and his mentor, Hassan: "This is their differing stands with respect to religious minorities. Natsir is for full religious freedom to the extent that he feels it is allowable for a Mohammedan to become a Christian if he wishes. Hassan, arguing with historical precedent, condemns this as defection to the enemy." Natsir interview with Kahin, 19 November 1954. Nearly twenty years earlier, in his article "Islam dan Kebudajaan" Natsir (1936) outlined a history of Muslim tolerance towards other religions over the centuries.

12. Adnan Buyung Nasution sees Sukarno's speech as an effort to overcome the conflict between proponents of a secular state and those of an Islamic state.

13. "Dimulai ketika Sjahrir memajukan usul kepada Bung Karno agar saya jadi menteri penerangan.'*Hij is de man* (Dialah orangnya)', kata Bung Karno kepada Sjahrir. Saya belum bertemu dengan beliau waktu itu. Lantas, waktu bertemu di Yogya, kami pura-pura tidak tahu-menahu apa yang terjadi dulu. Lebih baik menghadapi yang ada dan melepaskan apa yang telah terjadi, karena kita sedang menghadapi perjuangan yang besar. 'Bagaimana kita ini, kita dulu'kan cekcok', kata Bung Karno. 'Ya', jawab saya agak bercanda. 'Sekarang tidak usah, nanti saja kita ulangi'. Jadi hubungan kami kemudian memang dekat."

14. "Ya, siapa lagi kalau bukan Natsir dari Masyumi. Mereka punya konsepsi untuk menyelamatkan Republik melalui konstitusi." Mohammad Hatta, the Prime Minister of the RIS, was left with the more prestigious but less powerful position of Vice President of the Republic.

15. Indonesia became a member of the United Nations in September 1950 and participated actively in debates on the Korean War, abstaining on a motion that accused China of being the aggressor. While refusing military assistance from the United States, it did accept American technical and economic aid.

16. He gives the four characteristics of democracy in both English and Indonesian.

17. He had expressed this on many occasions, including in his speech before the Pakistan Institute of World Affairs (Natsir 1954*b*). See also Natsir 1951.

18. Natsir seems to have come to believe that the breadth and flexibility of the Pancasila's principles allowed them to be fashioned into whatever form the President desired.

19 Natsir, interview, 30 January 1971. He continued that an Islamic state "is still an ideal to achieve…. Muslims themselves are not yet living even in a transitional period — the ideal is still very far from the present reality", and

would take decades to achieve. Before a Pakistani audience in September 1954, he explored the differences between an Islamic country and a theocracy (Natsir 1954b).
20. In another part of the interview, he stressed: "In closed debate the Communists were also reasonable — they could respond to logical argument." Natsir, interview, 30 January 1971.
21. Natsir interviews, 30 January and 24 February 1971. This final wording was agreed in a joint interview with Natsir and Osman Raliby on 26 May 1971.
22. Magenda (2008, p. 4) states "such scholars as Endang Saifuddin Anshari and Adnan Buyung Nasution are of the opinion that had there not been the Presidential Decree of 5 July 1959, agreement would have been reached in the Constituent Assembly concerning the basis of the state being the Pancasila with the spirit of the Jakarta Charter."
23. Pemerintah Revolusioner Republik Indonesia/Piagam Perjuangan Semesta Alam, Revolutionary Government of the Republic of Indonesia/Universal Struggle Charter.
24. Natsir, interview, 18 January 1971.
25. Robert Hefner here stressed what he perceived as Natsir's growing rigidity and conservatism, writing that "the Natsir group came to emphasize not merely the shariah-mindedness of Masyumi conservatives but the strict anti-cosmopolitan Islamism of the urban poor and lumpen-middle class", resembling "the stiffly sectarian *Persatuan Islam* (Persis) of the 1930s and 1940s more than the inclusive Masyumi of the 1950s" (Hefner 2000, p. 105).

References

Abdullah, Taufik. *Indonesia towards Democracy*. Singapore: Institute of Southeast Asian Studies, 2009.

———. "Natsir, Seorang Guru yang Perfeksionis Filosofis". In *Pemikiran dan Perjuangan Mohammad Natsir*, edited by Anwar Haryono et al. Jakarta: Firdaus, 2001.

Dahm, Bernhard. *Sukarno and the Struggle for Indonesian Independence*. Ithaca, NY: Cornell University Press, 1969.

Federspiel, Howard M. *Persatuan Islam: Islamic Reform in Twentieth Century Indonesia*. Ithaca, NY: Modern Indonesia Project, 1970.

Feith, Herbert. *The Decline of Constitutional Democracy in Indonesia*. Ithaca, NY: Cornell University Press, 1962.

Hakiem, Lukman, ed. *Pemimpin Pulang: Rekaman Peristiwa Wafatnya M. Natsir*. Jakarta: Yayasan Piranti Ilmu, 1993.

Hamka. "Persahabatan 47 Tahun". In *Muhammad Natsir 70 tahun: Kenang-kenangan Kehidupan dan Perjuangan*. Jakarta: Pustaka Antara, 1978.

Hatta, Mohammad. *Sekitar Proklamasi*. Jakarta: Tintamas, 1970.

Hefner, Robert W. *Civil Islam*. Princeton: Princeton University Press, 2000.

MOHAMMAD NATSIR
1908–93

Born:	17 July 1908, Alahan Panjang, West Sumatra

Education

1916–1923	Hollands Inlandse School (HIS), Solok/Padang
1923–1927	MULO, Padang
1927–1930	Algemene Middelbare School (AMS), Bandung
1931–1932	Teacher training course, Bandung

Career

1928–1932	Head, Jong Islamieten Bond (JIB) Bandung
1932–1942	Director, Pendidikan Islam (Pendis) school, Bandung
1942–1945	Head, Education Bureau, Bandung (Bandung Syiakusyo)
1945	Head of Administration, Sekolah Tinggi Islam (STI, Islamic High School), Jakarta
1945–1946	Member, Komite Nasional Indonesia Pusat (KNIP)
1946–1949	Minister of Information
1949–1958	General Head (Ketua Umum) Masjumi Party
1950–1951	Prime Minister
1950–1958	Member of Parliament representing the Masjumi Party
1956–1958	Member of the Constituent Assembly
December 1957	Fled Jakarta for Padang, West Sumatra
1958–1961	Member of the Revolutionary Government of the Republic of Indonesia (Pemerintah Revolusioner Republik Indonesia, PRRI)
September 1961	Arrested by government forces
1961–1964	In political quarantine, Sumatra and Batu, East Java
1964–1966	Jailed in the RTM (Rumah Tanah Militer), Jakarta
July 1966	Released from detention
1967	Vice President, World Muslim Congress, Karachi, Pakistan
Feb. 1967	Established Dewan Da'wah Islamiyah Indonesia (DDII)
1967–1993	General Head, Dewan Da'wah
May 5 1980	Signed Petisi 50
Died	6 February 1993

Jenkins, David. *Suharto and His Generals: Indonesian Military Politics 1975–1983*. Ithaca, NY: Cornell Modern Indonesia Project, 1984.
Kahin, George McT. *Nationalism and Revolution in Indonesia*. Ithaca, NY: Cornell University Press, 1951.
Laffan, Michael Francis. *Islamic Nationhood and Colonial Indonesia: The Umma below the Winds*. London: Routledge Curzon, 2003.
Legge, J.D. *Sukarno: A Political Biography*. Singapore: Archipelago Press, 2003. (Orig. pub. 1972).
Magenda, Burhan Djabir. "Peranan Bapak M. Natsir sebagai Politisi dan Negarawan". Typescript prepared for Seminar Nasional Satu Abad M. Natsir, Jakarta, 15 July 2008.
Mossman, James. *Rebels in Paradise: Indonesia's Civil War*. London: Cape, 1961.
Nasution, Adnan Buyung. *The Aspiration for Constitutional Government in Indonesia*. Jakarta: Sinar Harapan, 1992.
Natsir, M. *Agama dan Negara dalam Perspektif Islam*. Jakarta: Media Da'wah, 2001.
Natsir, Mohammad [A.Moechlis]. "Persatuan Agama dengan Negara, II-III". *Pandji Islam* #27–36, 8 July–9 September 1940.
Natsir, Mohammad [Is]. "Koerang tegas jang meragoekan", *Pembela Islam* 35 (October 1931): 2–7.

———. "Kebangsaan Moeslimin, 1–5". *Pembela Islam* 41–45 (January–April 1932).

Natsir, Mohammad. "Islam dan Kebudajaan, June 1936". *Capita Selecta* [I]. Bandung, The Hague: Van Hoeve, [1954].

———. "Salah paham dan ragu2 tentang pembentukan Prop. Sumatera Utara tidak ada lagi". In *Suara Penerangan*, 20 January 1951.

———. "Sikap 'Islam' terhadap 'Kemerdekaan-Berfikir'". *Capita Selecta* [I]. Bandung, The Hague: Van Hoeve, 1954a.

———. *Some Observations Concerning the Role of Islam in National and International Affairs*. Ithaca, NY, Cornell Southeast Asia Program, 1954b.

———. "Kemampuan Mengendalikan diri sjarat mutlak bagi Kemerdekaan". *Capita Selecta* III, 7 November 1956.

———. "Reaksi pertama terhadap 'Konsepsi Presiden'". *Capita Selecta* III, 19 February 1957a.

———. "Itu bukan obat tetapi penjakit baru". *Capita Selecta* III, 28 February 1957b.

———. *Capita Selecta* III. Typescript dated 15 April 1960.

———. "Politik melalui Jalur Dakwah". *Tempo*, 2 December 1989.

Noer, Deliar. *The Modernist Muslim Movement in Indonesia 1900–1942*. Singapore: Oxford University Press, 1973.
Pembela Islam, nos. 35, 37, 39–47 (October 1931–June 1932).

———. no. 36 (October 1931), cited in "Persatuan Islam" (typescript, n.d.), p. 48.

Puar, Yusuf Abdullah, ed. *Muhammad Natsir: 70 tahun Kenang-kenangan Kehidupan dan Perjuangan*. Jakarta: Pustaka Antara, 1978.
Roem, Mohamad. *Bunga Rampai dari Sejarah 3*. Jakarta: Djaya Pirusa, 1983.
Rosidi, Ajip. *M. Natsir: Sebuah Biografi*. Jakarta: Girimukti Pasaka, 1990.
Soekarno. *Dibawah Bendera Revolusi*. Jakarta: Panitiya Penerbit Dibawah Bendera Revolusi, 1959.
———. *Nationalism, Islam and Marxism*. Trans. Karel H. Warouw and Peter D. Weldon, with an introduction by Ruth T. McVey. Ithaca, NY: Cornell University Modern Indonesia Project, 1969.
Yamin, Muhammad. *Naskah-Persiapan Undang-Undang Dasar 1945*. Jilid Pertama. Jakarta: Jajasan Prapantja, 1960.

9

RELIGIOUS FREEDOM IN CONTEMPORARY INDONESIA: THE CASE OF THE AHMADIYAH[1]

Bernhard Platzdasch

This chapter explains the controversy over the legal status of the Islamic Ahmadiyah sect, put into the larger context of the question over religious freedom and tolerance in today's Indonesia. It covers the disproportional influence of Islamist civil society groups on the Susilo Bambang Yudhoyono government and the government's intervention in religious and social affairs despite Indonesia supposedly being a secular state. It argues that in dealing with the Ahmadiyah issue, the government has been yielding to Islamist pressure because of concern with a backlash from the Muslim electorate. It also suggests that the deeper cause for the problems of the Ahmadis are the inconsistencies within Indonesian law, which is not clear-cut and absolute in its protection of religious freedom as is often erroneously claimed. It further highlights that most Muslim leaders from mainstream Muslim organizations tend to be firm in supporting those laws inimical to full religious freedom and legal recognition for Ahmadiyah.

Ahmadiyah (full name: Ahmadiyya Muslim Jama'at [Ahmadiyah Muslim Community], also known as Qadiyaniah) is a religious movement founded by Mirza Ghulam Ahmad (15 February 1835–26 May 1908) in Qadian in Punjab, India, in 1889. Like mainstream Islam, Ahmadiyah teachings are based on the Qur'an and the Hadith (account of the words and deeds of the Prophet Muhammad). Like mainstream Muslims, Ahmadis observe the five pillars of Islam: the belief in a single creator and Muhammad's prophethood, the five daily prayers, alms, fasting and — in theory — the pilgrimage (Ahmadis are banned from visiting Mecca in Saudi Arabia). Ahmadiyah has a central authority in Caliph Mirza Masroor Ahmad. He is based in London and the fifth successor of Mirza Ghulam Ahmad.

The main issue that separates Ahmadis from other Muslims is the question of whether there can be other prophets after Muhammad. Mirza Ghulam Ahmad claimed to have fulfilled the Qur'anic foretelling of the return of Jesus Christ and the world reformer at the end of times (known as the Mahdi, literally "The Guided One"). The Qur'an, verse 61:6, speaks of a successor to Muhammad, whose name is Ahmad.[2] The question of prophethood is the main reason that Islamist conservatives and many mainstream Muslims perceive Ahmadiyah as a distinctive faith outside Islam. A second charge is that the movement had its own holy book, named Tadzkirah, and, thirdly, that Ahmadiyah had its own holy sites in the Punjabi towns of Qadiyan and Rabwah (unlike mainstream Muslims' Mecca and Medina). Many Muslim organizations, therefore, believe that Ahmadis should be forbidden from referring to themselves as Muslims.

Doctrinally, Ahmadiyah stands in the line of other reformist Islamic movements promoting the adaptation of its teachings to the circumstances of a particular time and place in order for Islam to remain significant and progressive. In 1914, the movement split into two schools: the Ahmadiyah Muslim Community and, a much smaller wing, the Lahore Ahmadiyah Movement. The two streams differ in their interpretation of Ahmad's status. The Ahmadiyah Muslim Community is often thought to perceive Mirza Ghulam Ahmad to be a prophet but one who is subordinated to Muhammad. It further holds the Qur'an, as it was received by Muhammad, to be the final message of God for mankind. The Lahore Ahmadiyah Movement sees its founder more strictly as a religious reformer, thereby conforming to the mainstream Islamic view that there can be no prophet after Muhammad.

Other controversial Ahmadiyah beliefs are the denunciation of jihad (holy war) as physical struggle, except in the case of extreme persecution against Ahmadiyah members. Ahmadis perceive Islam as an inherently non-violent religion that has to be propagated through peaceful means only. Unlike other Islamic and religious movements, it does not have distinctively political ambitions and militant streams. Another contentious aspect of Ahmadiyah teachings is the belief that Jesus survived the crucifixion after which he emigrated to Kashmir in India. Ahmadis believe Jesus to be buried in Srinegar, Kashmir's capital, under the name of Yuz Asaf.

In Asia, there are sizeable Ahmadiyah populations in India, Bangladesh, Pakistan and Indonesia. In India, Ahmadis have legal status. The Pakistani government has identified Ahmadis as a non-Muslim religious minority, which means they are forbidden to refer to themselves as Muslims. But they are permitted to vote in elections. Ahmadiyah is banned in Saudi Arabia, where their followers are classified as heathen (*kafir*). Ahmadiyah is also banned in Brunei and Malaysia. In Indonesia, there has long been heated debate over Ahmadiyah's status.

The much more dominant Ahmadiyah stream is the "Muslim Ahmadiyah Community" or Jama'ah Ahmadiyah Indonesia in Indonesian (JAI, from here on "Ahmadiyah"). The Ahmadiyah Lahore is based in Yogyakarta with a small contingent in Jakarta. The records of Ahmadiyah's strength in Indonesia vary greatly. Ahmadiyah itself claims up to half a million members. Indonesia's Ministry of Religion gives a much smaller figure of 50,000 to 80,000 members. Ahmadiyah bases in Indonesia are the Sukabumi, Kuningan and Garut districts in West Java, and the North Sumatran city of Medan. Smaller Ahmadiyah communities exist in South Sulawesi, West Sumatra, Lombok and West Nusa Tenggara (International Crisis Group 2008, fn. 3).

Ahmadiyah's history in Indonesia goes back to 1925 when two preachers, Maulana Ahmad and Mirza Wali Ahmad, arrived in the Javanese city of Yogyakarta. They were welcomed by the local Muhammadiyah branch and permitted to speak at the organization's 13th National Congress.[3] A year later, another preacher arrived in the North Sumatran region of Aceh and began to promote Ahmadiyah's teachings. Soon, however, Indonesia's main Muslim organizations such as the traditionalist Nahdlatul Ulama (NU), the modernist Muhammadiyah, and the Masyumi political party, declared Ahmadiyah to be "deviant" [*sesat*]. In 1929, a Muhammadiyah National Congress for the first time stated this view officially. Similarly, NU's fifth National Congress in Pekalongan in 1930 proclaimed Ahmadiyah as being outside Islam (Purwanto 2008, p. 252). Such repudiation tended to differ from the official position of the Indonesian state. In 1953, the government declared Ahmadiyah as a lawful organization. Significantly, despite the repudiating stance of Indonesia's main Muslim organizations, Ahmadis faced little open hostility from mainstream Muslims and, for the most part, lived unperturbed amongst other religious communities.[4]

The year 1980 marked an important turn in the history of Ahmadiyah in Indonesia. It was the year when the Indonesian Ulama Council or Majelis Ulama Indonesia (MUI) issued a fatwa (legal ruling based on Islamic law) declaring Ahmadiyah as deviant [*sesat*] and outside Islam.[5] MUI was established with the endorsement of former President Soeharto. It comprises *ulama* (Islamic scholars) from a mixture of Muslim organizations, including NU and Muhammadiyah. This gives the erroneous impression that MUI's fatwas have greater influence on the Muslim community compared to those of individual organizations.

A summit of Indonesia's so-called "Coordinating Board for Monitoring Mystical Beliefs in Society" or Badan Koordinasi Pengawas Aliran Kepercayaan Masyarakat (usually abbreviated as Pakem or Bakorpakem) backed and re-emphasized MUI's ruling.[6] Importantly, Bakorpakem pointed out that the fatwa had a basis in the constitution as it was related to Law No. 1/PNPS/1965, which regulates the "Pencegahan Penyalahgunaan atau Penodaan Agama", or the "Prevention of the Misuse or Desecration of Religion". The first paragraph of this law reads:

> Every person is prohibited from deliberately speaking about, recommending, or lending support to interpretations of a religion that is adhered to in Indonesia [i.e., Indonesian religions], or participating in religious activities that are similar to those of a religion, interpretations and activities, which deviate from the central teachings of that religion.[7]

Bakorpakem then called on President Soeharto to act in accordance with MUI's fatwa by prohibiting Ahmadiyah as it was within his authority to dissolve a syncretist sect, known in Indonesia as *aliran kepercayaan*. The government, however, paid no heed to the call.

Next to MUI, the other organization leading the campaign against Ahmadiyah has been the Lembaga Penelitian dan Pengkajian Islam, or "Institute for the Study and Teaching of Islam" (LPPI). LPPI is a small Jakarta-based research institute funded with Saudi Arabian money. Particularly dedicated to the struggle against "deviant" sects has been the director of LPPI, Amin Djamaluddin. Djamaluddin, a respected conservative scholar of Islam, has also been active in MUI. He is also a member of the conservative-reformist "Islamic Association" (Persatuan Islam or Persis) and Dewan Dakwah Islamiyah Indonesia, or "Indonesian

Islamic Propagation Council" (DDII). Another pioneer in the anti-Ahmadiyah campaign was DDII's journal *Media Dakwah* and, in particular, DDII journalist Hartono Ahmad Jaiz. In 1990, Ahmadiyah filed and won a lawsuit against the *Media Dakwah* journal.[8] It had featured an illustration of Ahmadiyah's founder, Mirza Ghulam Ahmad, wearing a turban that was sporting a cobra motif. LPPI activists were among a large crowd of protesters who tried to attack the Ahmadiyah headquarters in the village of Parung in the district of Bogor, south of Jakarta, in 2002 (International Crisis Group 2008, p. 14).

In Djamaluddin's view, the book believed to be religious scripture for Ahmadis, the Tadzkirah, contained many Qur'anic verses that had been "marauded, distorted and extended" (Djamaluddin 1992, p. iii; Jaiz 2002, pp. 60–63). He likes to argue that if any book or piece of music was protected from being distorted and altered, the same must apply for the Qur'an, which unlike the other works, is believed by Muslims to be the word of God. In a meeting with Bakorpakem on 18 January 2005, Djamaluddin made the following analogy: "If someone distorted the anthem Indonesia Raya and then sang it on 17 August, that is, on Indonesia's National Day, what would you think of that?" (Djamaluddin 1992, p. 106). And further:

> Herein lies the problem: [if] people distort the National Anthem, surely the police will arrest them. But it is tolerated if people distort the holy Qur'an; the police doesn't arrest them. It is therefore appropriate that the Muslim community destroys the mosques and the houses of Ahmadiyah people, because the security forces don't act justly and don't pay attention to the demands of the Muslim community. (Ibid.)[9]

Ahmadis dispute this charge. They hold that the term "Tadzkirah" was Djamaluddin's own invention, first mentioned by him in a 1992 publication. What existed was a compilation of revelations and dreams Mirza Ghulam Ahmad had received during his lifetime, which, however, only existed in book form since 1935, that is years after his death in 1908 (Suryawan 2006, pp. 61–63).

Indonesian Muslim organizations' repudiation of Ahmadiyah must be seen in the context of Ahmadiyah's position in the wider Muslim world. The 1980 MUI ruling was basically a copy of a decree issued earlier in Saudi Arabia. Almost exactly a year after MUI issued its first fatwa, the Embassy of Saudi Arabia submitted a letter to Indonesia's Ministry of Religion, referring to what it called a "decision of the world's highest mosque committee [the World Mosque Council]" to ban Ahmadiyah. The Embassy pointed to the,

> opposition of the Muslim community against the destructive activities of the Ahmadiyah. [Ahmadiyah] is a destructive group that uses Islam as its vehicle to mask its putrid [*busuk*] objective which goes against Islam. The most obvious [of these violations] is the claim of its leader to be a Prophet and [thus the] rejection of Muhammad.... Qadiyaniah [that is, Ahmadiyah] collaborates with imperialists and Zionists and other parties which oppose Islam. These parties use Ahmadiyah as a tool to destroy ... the Islamic faith.[10]

The Embassy further declared:

> [T]he decisions and the recommendations of the World Mosque Council ... entirely confirm what had been established by [the] research bureau ... of the Saudi Arabian kingdom: this group [Ahmadiyah] is deviant and misleading [*sesat dan menyesatkan*]. And [the World Mosque Council] recommends issuing a fatwa which declares Qadiyaniah [Ahmadiyah] to be outside Islam ... It is, therefore, hoped that the [Indonesian] Ministry [of Religion] ... undertakes appropriate actions to ban the activities of the [Ahmadiyah] and explains its deviant and heathen nature to the religious people of Indonesia. (Ibid.)

A "recommendation" of the Organization of the Islamic Conference (OIC) dating back to 1976 gives a broader idea of the global, political, dimension of the Ahmadiyah question. The document refers to Ahmadiyah's origins in British India:

> Qadianiyah [Ahmadiyah] is a sect that is extremely destructive, that makes Islam its motto in order to veil its malicious aims. The most obvious [points] of its difference with Islam are a) its leader claims to be a prophet, b) the text of the Qur'an is altered, c) there is no jihad. Qadianiyah is the golden offspring of English imperialism and it did not emerge other than with the protection of this imperialism. Qadianiyah deceives the concerns of the Muslim community and it supports imperialism and Zionism. It works together with forces that oppose Islam, which struggle to destroy and distort the Islamic faith...[11]

The OIC, then, banned Ahmadiyah during a conference in Jeddah, Saudi Arabia, in December 1985.[12] Saudi Arabia has a big influence on OIC, and is believed to have played a vital role in this decision.

In 2000, Ahmadiyah caliph Mirza Thahir Ahmad visited Indonesia and met with NU leader and then President Abdurrahman Wahid. It was the first visit by the highest Ahmadiyah authority to Indonesia. Given Abdurrahman's wide network among non-Muslims and Islamist perceptions of him as a Zionist ally, the visit automatically fuelled suspicions of a plan to make Indonesia a hub for Ahmadiyah activities. Ahmadiyah's critics sometimes claim that the Ahmadiyah headquarters in England aimed to make Ahmadiyah Indonesia the largest Ahmadiyah community in the Muslim world.[13] The proof was the increase in the number of Ahmadiyah branches. In 1989, Ahmadiyah had 150 branches in Indonesia; in 1999 the number had risen to 228 and to 300 in 2008.[14]

The year 2005 came as another turning point in Ahmadiyah's history in Indonesia, as MUI issued a second ruling on the basis that "up to now Ahmadiyah still attempts to spread its beliefs in Indonesia even though a fatwa from MUI already exists and [despite] the prohibition of its [Ahmadiyah's] existence".[15] MUI again claimed that the "endeavors to spread Ahmadiyah beliefs have triggered uneasiness [*keresahan*] in the Muslim community". The fatwa then held that it was,

> Highlighting again the MUI ... 1980 fatwa which holds that Ahmadiyah stands outside Islam, [is] deviant and misleading, and that Muslims who follow it have abandoned Islam [*murtad*]. (Ibid.)

It further stated that,

> The government has the responsibility to prohibit the spreading of the Ahmadiyah faith everywhere in Indonesia, to dissolve the organization and to close down all the places of its activities. (Ibid.)

MUI's ruling explicitly referred to the OIC conference in December 1985 cited earlier, again highlighting the international dimension and political significance of the Ahmadiyah controversy. Underscoring the finality of Muhammad's prophethood remains the key issue in the quarrel with Ahmadiyah. The fatwa quotes the Qur'an, verse 33:40, which informs that Muhammad is the last of the prophets. It reads: "Muhammad is not the father of any of your men, but [he is] the messenger of Allah, and the seal of the Prophets" (Ibid.; Ali 1999, p. 1069).

Significantly, MUI has enjoyed much greater political clout in the Susilo Bambang Yudhoyono–led government than during the New Order.[16] Most of MUI executives in recent years have been conservative

Islamists, including its chairman Ma'ruf Amin.[17] The greater political clout of MUI in the Yudhoyono administration is to an important extent due to the President's open endorsement as he seems to perceive MUI as representative of the Muslim community. Between 2005 and 2007, Yudhoyono appeared in two major MUI summits in which he expressed his support for MUI's campaign against "deviant" Muslim sects. What is more, MUI chairman Ma'ruf Amin was appointed a member of the Dewan Pertimbangan Presiden or Presidential Advisory Council (DPP), which advised the President on the Ahmadiyah issue.[18] By allowing MUI to become more influential, the government appears to be responding to the current trend towards conservatism in Indonesian Islam; a trend it has opted to embrace and co-opt in the hope of better controlling it.[19] This policy has significantly added to the constant sense of threat under which many Ahmadis live today.

Several prominent Muslim leaders from the liberal Islamic camp rejected MUI's second fatwa. Among them were: NU leader Abdurrahman Wahid; the co-founder of the Jaringan Islam Liberal or "Liberal Islamic Network", Ulil Abshar Abdalla; the Director of the International Centre for Islam and Pluralism, Syafii Anwar; and Dawam Rahardjo, a noted economist and prominent Muhammadiyah member.[20] They, like others before, argued that the Indonesian Constitution promised freedom of religion.[21] Another argument was that actions against Ahmadiyah were in breach of regulations on Human Rights (Law No. 39/1999). Others pointed out that Ahmadiyah held legal status as it was registered by the Department of Religion on 2 March 1970 and by the Social Department on 15 May 1970.[22] It is also registered as a "mass organization" (*ormas*, Law No. 8/1985). Among all the registrations, however, the most significant is said to be the one with the Department of Home Affairs (Law No. 5/1985).[23]

Pressure on Ahmadiyah began to mount further from mid to late 2007 onwards.

Paramount in the campaign against Ahmadiyah leading to MUI's second fatwa and ever since has been what the International Crisis Group termed an "interlocking directorate of radical movements in the metropolitan Jakarta area and beyond" (International Crisis Group 2008, p. 15). Leading among these groups have been the aforementioned LPPI, the Front Pembela Islam (FPI) or Front of the Defenders of Islam, the Forum Umat Islam or Muslim Community Forum (FUI), DDII, the Forum Umat Ulama Islam (Islamic Scholars' Ulama Forum or FUUI) and

Hizbut Tahrir Indonesia (HTI).[24] Members of these organizations tend to be connected through holding more than one membership at the same time. The secretary general of Forum Umat Islam (FUI), for example, was HTI deputy-chairman Mohammad al-Khaththath. The chairman of FUI is Mashadi, a DDII member and a founding member and former MP of Partai Keadilan Sejahtera (Justice Prosperity Party, PKS, then Partai Keadilan, Justice Party or PK), now Indonesia's leading Islamist party. Many FUI leaders are, at the same time, active in MUI and Dewan Dakwah. FUI founding member Kholil Ridwan, another long-time campaigner against Ahmadiyah, is at the same time a member of DDII, a member of MUI's executive board, and head of the fatwa board of FUUI.[25]

The campaign against Ahmadiyah has turned both more intense and more hostile in recent years. Hizbut Tahrir has been proudly acting on a self-prescribed non-violent platform. It has, however, shown few qualms about building an enduring alliance with the more militant FPI, whose members have regularly carried out raids on nightlife spots, churches they declare to be constructed illegally, and Ahmadiyah-owned property. FPI activists, in turn, have provided the security personnel for FUI demonstrations (International Crisis Group 2008). FPI, FUI and Hizbut Tahrir leaders were present at a gathering that took place on 14 February 2008 in the city of Banjar in West Java, which had an anti-Ahmadiyah agenda.[26] The event was also attended by the Majelis Mujaheedin Indonesia, or "Indonesian Mujahidin Council" (MMI).[27] The speakers were Abu Bakar Bashir from the MMI, Mohammad al-Khaththath (FUI and Hizbut Tahrir) and Sobri Lubis, secretary general of the FPI. The most notorious part of the event was Lubis' sanctioning the killing of Ahmadiyah members. Lubis said:

> We say we urge the Muslim community to wage war against Ahmadiyah. Kill Ahmadiyah wherever they are, my brothers! God is great! Kill, kill, kill, kill!... This is self-defense. They destroy the faith, it is no longer sacred [the life of Ahmadis] ... it is already permissible [*holol*] ... already permissible! This is no joke [*bukan main*] ... it is permissible to shed the blood of Ahmadis. Later we will be said to have violated human rights. To hell with the Human Rights declaration; cat piss, the Human Rights declaration![28]

At the same time, Islamist groups such as FUI, LPPI and MUI (mostly through Amin Djamaluddin) intensified their lobbying efforts in parliament, with the Ministry of Religion, the Attorney General's office and other policymakers. Their efforts bore fruit when their call for a ban on Ahmadiyah got the specific attention of a parliamentary commission. Overall, Islamist conservatives have been more active and astute than pluralist Muslims in creating and cultivating networks among the bureaucracy in order to achieve their objectives.[29]

Under increasing pressure from its critics and the government, on 14 January 2008 the leadership of Ahmadiyah eventually issued a statement consisting of twelve clarifications that were to shed a more favourable light on the movement's beliefs. It was meant to lend evidence to the avowal that Ahmadiyah was part of Islam on the basis that its members believed in the Qur'an and the prophethood of Muhammad.[30] The statement declared that the Ahmadiyah community had "from the beginning believed in and voiced the *shahadah*", which consists of the vow that "I confess that there is no God other than Allah and Muhammad is His Prophet". More importantly, the second point of the statement held that: "From the beginning, we, the Ahmadiyah community, have believed in the final prophethood of Muhammad." The text further described Mirza Ghulam Ahmad as a "teacher … and mentor who inspired his disciples to strengthen Islamic proselytization (*dakwah*) and Islamic teachings, as conveyed by the Prophet Muhammad". It further highlighted that Ahmadis believed and followed solely the teachings of the Qur'an and the traditions of the prophet (Sunna). The Tadzkirah was "not Ahmadiyah's holy book but a series of notes about Mirza Ghulam Ahmad's spiritual experiences which were collected and made into a book titled Tadzkirah by his followers in 1935".[31]

The document was then handed over to the Bakorpakem, which in its assessment stopped short of calling for the dissolution of the Ahmadiyah whilst declaring that it would monitor the activities of Ahmadiyah on the basis of the twelve points. Around the same time, MUI and DDII declared Ahmadiyah's statement as null and void as it did not clearly refute that it perceived Ahmad as a prophet. DDII also argued that other points in the statement contradicted the teachings to be found in Ahmadiyah books (Purwanto 2008, pp. 256–57). The distinction between Muhammad as Islam's prophet and Mirza as "teacher" was futile as such an avowal ignored the fact that Mirza's prophethood was a deeply ingrained belief among Ahmadis. Facing ongoing protests from these organizations, the Ministry of Religion finally formed another team to reassess whether, and if so to what extent, the Ahmadiyah leadership and followers put into practice the assertions of its statement.

In mid-February 2008, the parliamentary commission assigned to the Ahmadiyah question issued its own report, calling on the government to ban Ahmadiyah. It argued that the government's toleration of Ahmadiyah had led to the proliferation of syncretist movements (*aliran kepercayaan*) which would go against Islamic teachings. The report further referred to MUI's first fatwa from 1980 and continued that:

> Ahmadiyah is deviant and misleading; it therefore must be immediately dissolved.... A presidential order is required instantly to dissolve Ahmadiyah and to declare it as being barred perpetually.... The case of Ahmadiyah has to be solved instantly together with the Minister for Religion...[32]

After three months of deliberation, Bakorpakem then issued a separate assessment. In this it described Ahmadiyah as "still deviant" and called on the Minister for Religion, the Minister for Home Affairs and the Attorney General to stop all activities of Ahmadiyah.

However, what brought the Ahmadiyah controversy really into the public eye was a march organized by the "National Alliance for Freedom of Religion and Faith" (Aliansi Kebangsaan untuk Kebebasan Beragama dan Berkeyakinan, AKKBB) at Jakarta's National Monument square to celebrate the commemoration of Pancasila (the date was 1 June 2008).[33] The procession aimed to draw attention to religious tolerance issues by proclaiming that Pancasila was the ideological basis for religious freedom and tolerance and that the actions of Islamist conservatives were endangering that freedom. Prior to the event, the organizers had issued a declaration which broadly addressed religious freedom but also made specific mention of Ahmadiyah. Ahmadiyah's opponents, however, distorted the event subsequently as having been a show of support solely for Ahmadiyah. AKKBB's handout addressed the vital question of what is often seen as the constitutional promise of religious freedom in Indonesia. It held that:

> Indonesia guarantees religious freedom to all its citizens. This is a human right guaranteed by the constitution. It is also the core of "Unity in Diversity" which is the fundament of our Indonesian-ness. However, lately there has been a group of people who wish to stamp out this human right and threaten [our] diversity ... They even use violence, as in their actions against followers of Ahmadiyah who have been living in Indonesia since

1925, and who have lived peacefully side by side with other Indonesians. Eventually they will insist on their plan to replace Pancasila, Indonesia's national doctrine, ignoring the constitution, and destroying that fundament of our togetherness. We call on the government [and] on [our] MPs not to fear the pressure that endangers this Indonesian-ness.[34]

On the day of the march, an Islamist umbrella group calling itself Laskar Komando Islam or "Defenders of Islam Command" under the leadership of Munarman and FPI Chairman Habib Rizieq Shabib appeared at the square and assaulted the marchers, beating up several prominent NGO Muslim leaders. Munarman subsequently said that the attack was related to AKKBB's media advertisement cited earlier.[35] He followed the particular logic that mainstream Muslims were threatened by Ahmadiyah.[36] This view is often shared by government officials. They argue that Ahmadiyah mosques should be closed in order to forestall "anarchic activities" by local Muslims, thereby taking pre-emptive actions against the victims rather than the aggressors.

Many Muslim organizations and individual leaders demanded the dissolution of FPI following the assault. Particularly vocal were individual branches of NU. On 3 June, fifty-eight Islamists, including FPI leader Habib Rizieq Shahib were arrested in a police operation involving 1,500 officers. Most FPI members were released shortly afterwards but Rizieq and seven others remained in police custody. Rizieq was sentenced to eighteen months in prison. Laskar Komando Islam leader Munarman went on the run.[37]

Ahmadiyah's reaction to the assault was noticeably muted. Some Ahmadis sought asylum at foreign embassies.[38] But they were unwilling to appear in the court trials against FPI members that followed. Their stance arguably reflected the pacifist, passive tradition and the obedience toward authorities which Ahmadiyah had shown in the past.[39] It was certainly related to the fact that Ahmadiyah has had few representatives and little lobby power with the higher echelons of the Indonesian bureaucracy. What is more, Ahmadiyah could expect little backing from the mainstream media which has been rather reluctant to discuss the topic. It certainly did not want to be seen as pro-Ahmadiyah.

THE GOVERNMENT'S ISLAMIC FAVOURITISM

On 9 June 2008, the government finally issued its verdict on Ahmadiyah. It contained five "considerations" and seven "decisions". Two "considerations" are of particular interest as they pay tribute to the claim of religious freedom in Indonesia. The first point declares that:

> The right to practise one's religion is a human right that must not be reduced in whichever situation; every man is free to adhere to his respective religion and worship in accordance with his religion and belief...[40]

The second paragraph, however, poses an important qualification to the first statement. It basically quotes the 1965 law on "blasphemy" mentioned earlier (p. 4):

> Every person is prohibited from ... speaking about, recommending, or lending support to interpretations of a religion that is adhered to in Indonesia [i.e., Indonesian religions], or participating in religious activities that are similar to those of a religion, [and] which deviate from the central teachings of that religion.

The "decisions" point in the same direction as the second "consideration". The second, third and fourth of these "decisions" are the most significant. The first point basically reiterates the second "consideration" cited above. The second point then,

> warns and orders followers, members, and/or board members of Ahmadiyah Indonesia, for as long as they refer to themselves as Muslims [*mengaku beragama Islam*], to stop spreading interpretations and activities that deviate from the central teachings of Islam, that is, the spreading of the view which acknowledges that there is a prophet fully versed in all teachings after the Prophet Muhammad.

The subsequent third section determines that breaching the above order will result in sanctions "in accordance with the set regulations of the legislation". Here, the government appears to say that Ahmadiyah members face five year jail terms on charges of "blasphemy" if found guilty of "participat[ing] in religious activities that are similar to those of a religion, [and] which deviate from the central teachings of that religion", and "spreading of the view which acknowledges that there is a prophet fully versed in all teachings after the Prophet Muhammad". But, while obviously referring to law No. 1/PNPS/1965, the decree makes no explicit mention of it. The final paragraph of the decree orders Muslims not to resort to any violent actions against Ahmadiyah members. It was issued on the same day another demonstration of Islamist groups against Ahmadiyah took place in front of the Presidential Palace.

Several conclusions can be made based on an analysis of the decree. It left the legal status of the Ahmadiyah unresolved. It banned Ahmadiyah from proselytization but not from internal activities, thus leaving its members in a legal limbo. Government officials have struggled to make sense of the decree's ambivalence, usually without much success. Attorney General Hendarman Supandji, one of the three signatories, for example, said it would "in essence order Ahmadiyah members to stop their activities [but] there is no banning of Ahmadiyah".[41] The decree is, the pro-pluralist Wahid Institute opined, "the safest path the government could take between those protecting and those demanding the disbanding of Ahmadiyah".[42] It contests Ahmadiyah's position as part of Islam but does not deny the right of Ahmadis to practise on the implied proviso that Ahmadiyah forms its own religion (i.e., denounces Islam). But this is an unworkable proposition as many aspects of Ahmadiyah's religious practice are the same as those of mainstream Muslims.

It remained at the same time unclear which activities the decree outlaws. Ahmadiyah leaders like to argue that the wording (of the second "decision" cited above) merely prohibits its members from teaching that Muhammad is not the final prophet. Other aspects of Ahmadiyah teachings were not mentioned specifically in the decree; hence, according to these Ahmadiyah leaders, they were not banned from being spread and taught.[43] In a press release following the issuance of the decree, the Ahmadiyah leadership went even further, arguing that "the [decree] does not prohibit, suspend, or dissolve Ahmadiyah Indonesia but [only serves] as a warning [*semata-mata peringatan*]".[44] It, however, did not elaborate what the warning referred to.

Others have argued similarly that the decree does allow Ahmadiyah members to continue carrying out their activities as long as they follow mainstream Islamic teachings. This would at the same time mean that Ahmadis are still permitted to pray in their mosques. Ahmadiyah can continue to exist in Indonesia and its followers are allowed to worship in their homes and mosques, but they must not preach or try to convert others, Vice President Jusuf Kalla said, seemingly confirming such an interpretation.[45] Not surprisingly, Ahmadiyah critics like MUI Chairman Ma'ruf Amin have rejected the provision that Ahmadis were still permitted to adopt Islamic attributes after forming their own religion (International Crisis Group 2008, fn. 31).

Rather than only raising concerns about its content, critics also expressed doubt regarding the legal validity of the decree. Significantly, it was not issued by the President's Office and was not signed by the President. Instead, it was released jointly by the Attorney General's office, the Ministry of Religion and the Ministry of Home Affairs, and signed by the respective ministers and the Attorney General.[46] It therefore only has the status of a Joint Resolution (Surat Keputusan Bersama, SKB). An SKB had earlier been recommended by the Bakorpakem, the body attached to the government and enforced with the task of monitoring mystic and syncretist religious movements and organizations. The parliamentary commission dealing with Ahmadiyah and Islamist conservatives, however, had both called for a "Presidential Resolution" known as Surat Keputusan Presiden or SKP to dissolve Ahmadiyah.

Ahmadiyah leaders have described the government's decision to issue the decree as a Joint Resolution [SKB] and not through the President's Office as an "exquisite manoeuver" [*permainan cantik*]. It was giving proof of the government's determination to please broader Muslim constituencies whilst trying to avoid a complete fallout with Ahmadis and other pro-Pancasila parties.[47] The government's stance is reflected in the result of surveys such as the Setara Institute and Indonesian Survey Institute (LSI). They show that a majority of people support its conservative approach toward religious matters, as it would avoid controversy.[48]

According to Law No. 8/1985, it is the Ministry of Home Affairs that has the authority to revoke the registration of a "mass organization" (*ormas*). However, during the constitutional amendments in 1999, this law was ratified by a new regulation (No. 29) which allocates the authority to dissolve or to suspend an organization to the President.[49] What is more, legal experts such as prominent lawyer Adnan Buyung Nasution and former State Secretary Yusril Ihza Mahendra have argued that, being issued as a "Joint Resolution" [SKB], the decree had no legal basis. They were referring to Law No. 10/2004 which regulates the formation and legal sources of laws and establishes their internal hierarchy (Pembentukan Peraturan Perundang-Undangan).[50] In its press release Ahmadiyah made a declaration in line with this view. It held that: "We very much deplore the SKB that has been issued, by bringing back to mind that a SKB does not exist in our legal system which has already been reformed."[51]

Responses to the government's SKB decree varied. In Cianjur (West Jakarta), Makassar (South Sulawesi) and Lombok, Ahmadiyah mosques were closed down by local authorities following threats from local Islamist groups.[52] Elsewhere local governors joined Muslim leaders in issuing their own "joint statements" calling for a ban of Ahmadiyah. These statements were then submitted to the local governments. In Bogor, twenty Islamic organizations submitted such a "statement" to the city's mayor. The local authorities rejected the plea, arguing that only the President was authorized to issue a ban.[53] South Sumatra was the first and remained the only region to issue a formal ban on Ahmadiyah, in September 2008.[54] This is despite the fact that local governments have the right to issue regulations to maintain public order, but have no authority to interfere in religious affairs directly.[55] The question then became whether local authorities can make a convincing case that Ahmadiyah activities were a potential threat to public order.

Critics of the government's SKB also argued that by ordering a stop to activities that went against central interpretations of Islam, the government had interfered in the personal lives of Indonesians. By deciding what a "proper" definition of Islam is, the government, they held, had thus abandoned what was supposed to be a neutral stand on religion.[56]

Ahmadiyah's predilection to avoid open conflict again was shown in the reaction to the decree. Its leaders held that Ahmadiyah "respects the decree but doesn't follow it", signalling a mixture of compliance and resistance. They held that while the decree had made missionary efforts more difficult, it would still continue, though in a more passive and cautious manner. Yet other Islamic organizations further reduced contacts with Ahmadiyah following the decree and its leaders were no longer invited to events held by these organizations.[57]

Police records to safeguard Ahmadiyah members from persecution following the decree remained mixed. The police have been facing a similar predicament as the mainstream Muslim organizations. While the police's task is protecting citizens regardless of their religious orientation, by giving the impression of protecting Ahmadiyah, they face the danger of being labelled as being pro-Ahmadiyah and thus anti-Islam.[58]

BETWEEN ANTI-AHMADIYAH SENTIMENT AND PRO-PLURALIST APPEARANCE

All of Indonesia's main Islamist parties — PKS, Partai Persaturan Pembangunan (Unity Development Party, PPP) and Partai Bulan Bintang (Crescent Star Party, PBB) — have, not surprisingly, joined the call for dissolving Ahmadiyah. This is in spite of the fact that PPP has a considerable number of Ahmadhis among its members.[59]

It is important to note that while the Islamist parties' stance reflected their opposition to Ahmadiyah teachings, they also believed that their vocal attacks on Ahmadiyah will get them sympathy not only from Islamists but also from many mainstream Muslims. This was particularly important ahead of the parliamentary elections in April 2009 during which Islamist parties had sought to foster their Islamic credentials. They were afraid of a voter backlash, if Muslims perceived them to be neutral or hesitant on the question of Ahmadiyah's status. However, when casting their vote at national ballots, Indonesian Muslims have been shown to consider bread and butter issues rather than religious concerns. As a result of PPP's call for a ban, many Ahmadiyah votes went to the victorious secular-nationalist Democrat Party.[60]

The official positions of the large Muslim mainstream organizations were naturally more vague and guarded than the blunt repudiation by the Islamists. The central NU leadership has tried to steer clear of the matter as far as possible. Internally, however, most leaders maintained their resolute stance that Ahmadiyah should be banned if it continues to claim the "Islam" label. In 2005, NU leaders had argued, similar to the conservatives in favour of a ban, that the Ahmadiyah question has to be assessed through faith [*akhidah*] and not on the basis of democracy and human rights.[61] In September 2005, following a forum, the central leadership of NU again issued a statement declaring Ahmadiyah as deviant on the basis that it did not acknowledge Muhammad as the final prophet (Purwanto 2008, pp. 254–55). Aside from theological reasons, NU also clearly had a self-interest in the Ahmadiyah case because it would like to control Ahmadiyah's valuable assets. But rather than confronting Ahmadiyah and calling for a ban of the group, many NU leaders have pledged to attempt to bring Ahmadis "back to the true Islam". Wary of issuing a fatwa on its own, NU has pointed to MUI's two rulings (1980 and 2005) as having already given clarification on the status of Ahmadiyah as outside Islam.[62] To some extent, NU's public dealing with the issue also seems to depend on who is holding the chairmanship. NU Chairman Hasyim Muzadi called on the government "to solve" the Ahmadiyah case without elaborating. On the one hand, he blamed the government's hesitant stance for the spread of syncretist beliefs; on the other hand, watchful not to put doubt on NU's pro-pluralist credentials, he stopped short of calling for a ban of Ahmadiyah.[63]

Other NU leaders did not agree with the leniency that some of its most prominent leaders displayed in public. When NU expressed support for the 1 June 2008 marchers in Jakarta, NU's East Java branch protested on the basis that Ahmadiyah was not Islam and should therefore not be defended.[64] In Cirebon, NU was one of five Islamic organizations declaring their support for a ban on Ahmadiyah. The others were Persis, Persatuan Umat Islam (PUI), Matlaul Anwar and Muhammadiyah.[65] Critics in NU held that objecting to a ban on Ahmadiyah would contradict previous NU resolutions that had declared Ahmadiyah to be "outside Islam".[66] Overall it appears that, being under greater public scrutiny, NU's central leadership has been more guarded in commenting forthrightly on the Ahmadiyah issue than local branches whose stance seemed to be more straightforwardly repudiating.

Muhammadiyah bore some similarities with NU. Like NU, Muhammadiyah leaders tend to favour a soft approach and dialogue instead of confrontation. A number of local Muhammadiyah leaders, however, rejected such a dialogue and flatly declared Ahmadiyah to be forbidden by Islam [haram]. An example was Muhammadiyah's branch in Bogor, the location of Ahmadiyah's headquarters.[67] At the same time, prominent Muslim leaders have appeared to adjust their statements in accordance with the organization they represent at a particular point in time. In 2005, Muhammadiyah chairman Professor Din Syamsuddin said Ahmadiyah should form its own religion, disaffiliated from Islam, if its followers continued to perceive Mirza Ghulam Ahmad as a prophet.[68] But when Din Syamsuddin held the position of a senior MUI executive, he was one of two signatories of MUI's 2005 fatwa on Ahmadiyah.[69] When he was chairman of MUI, NU's prominent leader Sahal Mahfudh signed a petition sent to the ministers of Home Affairs and Religion, the Attorney General and the head of the police, requesting them to "immediately take steps to ban [*melarangkan*] Ahmadiyah in Indonesia, to terminate the organization's legal status [*mencabut legalitas organisasinya*] and to take up decisive legal steps against the leadership and distributors of Ahmadiyah [teachings]".[70]

THE CLAIM OF RELIGIOUS FREEDOM REVISITED

As made clear in the previous discussion, human rights groups and pluralist Muslims have widely used the argument that banning Ahmadiyah would contravene the 1945 Constitution which is based on Pancasila on the basis that the constitution and Pancasila guaranteed freedom of religion. Following the attack on Ahmadiyah property at Parung, for example, they reiterated in a press release the common argument that "limiting and obstructing religious freedom breaches Indonesia's national foundation and the constitution".[71]

In fact, Indonesia's constitution and laws are deeply ambiguous and selective on the question of a religious freedom that is absolute.[72] There are two categories of laws and regulations: Those clearly in favour of religious freedom and others that put up restrictions on this freedom and which discriminate against particular religious interpretations. The constitution appears to guarantee religious freedom in various sections. One of these sections is the First and Second Article of Paragraph 28. The First Article reads: "Every citizen has the right to follow his/her religion and worship according to his/her beliefs". The Second Article reads: "Every citizen has the right to freedom to adhere to his/her beliefs,... according to his/her conviction (*hati nurani*)". Paragraph 28 I(1) reaffirms the previous points, reading: "The right to live, the right not to be maltreated, the right to free thought..., the right to practise religion,... is a human right that cannot be reduced under any circumstance". Hence, this section guarantees religious freedom, defined as a human right. Paragraph 28 I(4), then, defines the government's responsibility as: "The protection, progress, implementation, and fulfillment of human rights are the responsibility of the state, in particular the government".

Paragraph 28 J(2), however, makes an important qualification of the previous section. It holds: "In carrying out his or her right[s] and freedom, every citizen has the responsibility to abide by the restriction[s] set out by laws with the sole aim to guarantee the consideration and respect for the right[s] and freedom[s] of other citizens and to fulfill a just cause [*tuntutan yang adil*] in accordance with moral consideration, religious values, [public] security, and public order in a democratic society".

This last section thus establishes limitations to religious expression. As the Wahid Institute points out in its report: "In short, by means of this paragraph, religious beliefs can be desecrated if a group perceives its human right of practicing [its] religion and belief to be disturbed by the existence of the [other] religion and belief."[73]

Aside from the sections on human rights, there is the constitutional Paragraph 29 on "religion". The First Article holds: "The state is based on (the belief in) The One Almighty God." And the Second Article holds:

"The state guarantees the freedom of every citizen to follow his/her religion and to worship in accordance with his/her religion and belief." As argued before, in practice, this affirmation of religious freedom can be put under the qualification of Law No. 1/PNPS/1965 on the Prevention of Misuse or Desecration of Religion.

Interestingly, the wording used in the government's decree (SKB) against Ahmadiyah basically reiterates the wording of Law No. 1/PNPS/1965 (cited earlier in this chapter). This shows the enduring importance of Law No. 1/PNPS/1965 as it qualifies several pro-religious freedom paragraphs in the constitution. Together with Paragraph 28 J(2) cited above, Law No. 1 effectively renders authority to the state to determine what the proper key aspects of a religion are, and which ones are not.[74] Syncretist beliefs and unorthodox sects such as the Ahmadiyah can be charged with Paragraph 28 J(2) and Law No. 1/PNPS/1965 as disobeying central teachings of one of the recognized religions.[75] The initiative for a judicial review of the latter has been a long-time agenda of Ahmadiyah and its associates in AKKBB. In July 2009, a draft has been prepared but not submitted.[76]

Tellingly, the critics' argument on why Ahmadiyah should be banned by the government has given much consideration to the directives in the Indonesian Constitution rather than merely following doctrinal standpoints. In the doctrinal part of the argument, Djamaluddin referred to a section in the Qur'an that pro-pluralist Muslims and scholars sympathetic to them often used to back up Islam's supposed pro-pluralist disposition:

> Ahmadiyah is a matter of throwing Islamic teachings and its holy book into disorder. [It is] not merely a matter of religious freedom. This is also what is meant by the Qur'an, verse 2:256 which holds: "There is no coercion in religious matters". This verse does not mean that there is freedom of throwing into disorder [*mengacak-acak*] the Islamic faith. (Djamaluddin 2008, p. 107)

With regard to constitutional regulations, Djamaluddin wrote:

> What the 1945 constitution, Paragraph 29, First and Second Article and Paragraph 28 E, First Article guarantee is the freedom of religion and to … worship in accordance with this religion and belief. It does not give the freedom to throw into disorder [*mengacak-acak*] existing religions at one's own will and in accordance with one's own personal wishes…. If a group proclaims itself as belonging to a religion (Islam) whose existence in the

Indonesian state has already been declared as legal, and then produces teachings which are in conflict with that religion already declared as legal by that state, [it means that] it does not belong to the beliefs and convictions whose existence and activities are guaranteed by that state, as it is stated in Paragraph 29, First and Second Article and paragraph 28 E of the 1945 Constitution. (Djamaluddin 2008, pp. ii and iv)

POSTSCRIPT

Hostilities and attacks against Ahmadiyah mosques and properties resumed in mid to late 2010. In response, NU and Muhammadiyah officials repeated earlier calls on Ahmadiyah to "leave Islam" and dismissed a review of Law No. 1/PNPS/1965.[77] Minister of Religious Affairs Suryadharma Ali (NU) called in parliament for a ban of Ahmadiyah arguing that the incidents were consequences of the failure of the Ahmadiyah to adhere to the existing decree. While his government has maintained its resolute stance on Ahmadiyah, President Yudhoyono himself has continued to play it safe when it comes to addressing the issue, in line with the President's pattern of avoiding speaking out on controversial matters. At the time of writing, officials from a wide range of parties called on parliament to readdress the issue with a large majority appearing to back a formal ban on Ahmadiyah. This suggests that the June 2008 decree might not remain the final word on the matter.

CONCLUSION

From the case of the Ahmadiyah, it appears that the Yudhoyono government has been caving in to Islamist pressure when dealing with issues that it believes to have the support of a large number of Muslims. Due to the dominant position of Islam in Indonesia and a trend toward conservatism, the government has seen more at stake when it comes to issues involving Islam as compared to other religions. It has therefore impinged on religious freedom by issuing the June 2008 decree, effectively "half-banning" Ahmadiyah, and by its ongoing support for Law No. 1/PNPS/1965. However, while it cannot afford to offend the sensitivities of large sections of the Muslim community, the government also showed keenness to be seen as safeguarding the guarantee of religious freedom that many Indonesians associate with Pancasila. Echoing this predicament, the public positions of mainstream Muslim leaders on the status of Ahmadiyah have often been cautious despite a firm refusal to consider Ahmadiyah as being part of Islam. They also have sometimes displayed a hands-off attitude when speaking for a Muslim organization with pluralist credentials (NU and Muhammadiyah) whilst calling for a ban of Ahmadiyah when speaking on behalf of a conservative body (MUI).

With the SKB decree, the government issued a regulation it perceived to be a solution minimizing any harmful fallout but which was in fact an easy way out that did not tackle the actual problem and, as a result, failed to sustain Indonesia's claim to protect religious pluralism. It was another example of the President's frequently irresolute leadership style. The government basically allowed Bakorpakem to corner it on the Ahmadiyah issue, with little or no opposition from the President or Attorney-General Hendarman. Underlying the SKB's ambivalence and unclear legal status, conservative groups have continued to press the President to issue another decree through his office.[78]

The deeper problem is that the Indonesian Constitution is not absolute in its protection of religious freedom. It de facto reserves a special position for Islam. This is reflected in the first Pancasila principle of The One-All-Powerful God, reiterated in the First Article of Paragraph 29 on "religion". It is also reflected in Paragraph 28 J(2) and Law No. 1/PNPS/1965, which outlaw unorthodox interpretations of the religions acknowledged by Pancasila. In effect, this merely concerns Islam. As a result of this domination, the government has inadvertently assumed an active role in the religious lives of Indonesians.

At the same time, there tends to be a discrepancy between existing regulations and laws and the situation on the ground. The government's decree against Ahmadiyah is not merely of debatable legal validity, there has also often been little political will to implement it. However, a shaky legal platform remains, which can be exploited if the circumstances make it politically beneficial to certain factions.

Notes

1. I wish to express my gratitude to Mubarik Ahmad, the Wahid Institute, PT One Earth Media, the Yayasan Indonesia Damai, Maya Safira Muchtar, chairman of the Gerakan Integrasi Nasional or National Integration Movement, and Amin Djamaluddin from the Lembaga Penelitian dan Pengkajian Islam (LPPI) for their kind assistance in making material available to me. I also wish to thank Dr Greg Fealy for his comments on an earlier draft.

2. The verse reads: "And remember, Jesus, the son of Mary said: 'Oh Children of Israel! I am the messenger of Allah, sent to you, confirming the law (which came) before me, and giving glad tidings of a messenger, to come after me, whose name shall be Ahmad', but when he came to them, with clear signs, they said: 'this is evident sorcery!'" (Ali 1999, p. 1461).
3. Muhammadiyah, founded in 1912, is Indonesia's largest reformist Islamic organization.
4. For example, a visit of Mirza Mubarok Ahmad, the nephew of the Ahmadiyah founder, to Ahmadiyah communities in West Java in July 1981 went ahead without major disruptions. For the history of Ahmadiyah in Indonesia, see Zulkarnain (2005).
5. The verdict was made during a MUI summit held between 26 May and 1 June 1980.
6. Bakorpakem consists of representatives from the Attorney General's office, the National Intelligence Board (Badan Inteligens Negara, BIN), the police and the Department of Religion.
7. "Penetapan Presiden Republik Indonesia Nomor 1 Tahun 1965 Tentang Pencegahan Penyalahgunaan dan/atau Penodaan Agama" <http://hukum.unsrat.ac.id/uu/penpres_1_1965.htm>.
8. DDII is the main legatee of the Masyumi. Masyumi was Indonesia's largest Islamist party in the 1940s and 1950s.
9. Also, interview, Amin Djamaluddin and Dr Hoedaifah Koeddah, Jakarta, 2007. In the interview, Hoedaifah (LPPI) used Shakespeare's plays as an example.
10. The document is named "Kementerian Luar Negeri Kedutaan Besar Saudi Arabia Jakarta, Nomer 8/1/10/B374/1401, tanggal 6/5/1981", reprinted in Laporan Investigasi (Jakarta: LBH and Kontras, n.d.), pp. 153–54. In the text, Ahmadiyah is treated synonymously with Qadiyaniyah. Underscoring the importance of the letter, Amin Djamaluddin (2007, pp. 138–39) also quotes it.
11. "Penjelasan Rabitah Alam Islami Mengenai Keputusan dan Rekomendasi Konperensi Organisasi-Organisasi Islam di Dunia yang Diadakan di Makkah Al Mukarramah Tanggal 14 s/d 18 Rabiul Awwl 1394 H", reprinted in Djamaluddin (2007, pp. 128–29).
12. The OIC is an association of fifty-six Islamic states promoting Muslim solidarity in economic, social, and political affairs. Indonesia has been a member since 1969.
13. See the section "Rencana Jahat Ahmadiyah Pusat di Inggris Menjadikan Indonesia sebagai Pusat Ahmadiyah Dunia" [The malicious plan of the English Ahmadiyah Center to make Indonesia the center of Ahmadiyah in the world], in Djamaluddin (2007, pp. 15–26).
14. The first two figures are from Djamaluddin (2007, p. 106). The third figure is

from "HM Amin Djamalduddin [sic] 'Kita ditipu Mentah-Mentah'", *Tabloid Republika — Dialog Jumat*, 18 January 2008, p. 5.
15. Musyawarah Nasional VII Majelis Ulama Indonesia Tahun 2005: Keputusan Fatwa Majelis Ulama Indonesia Nomor: 11/Munas VII/MUI/15/2005 Tentang Aliran Ahmadiyah".
16. Soeharto endorsed MUI's formation in 1975 mainly in order to co-opt Muslim leaders.
17. Mah'ruf was in the 1970s head of NU's Religious (Syuro) Council.
18. The council also included pro-Ahmadiyah lawyer Adnan Buyung Nasution. It always remained deeply divided over the Ahmadiyah question.
19. Confidential remarks by a member of the Presidential Advisory Council. Interview, Jakarta, August 2008.
20. In 2002, the Forum Ulama Umat Indonesia (FUUI) issued a notorious death fatwa against Ulil Abshar Abdalla.
21. "Gus Dur tolak Fatwa MUI", *Radar Cirebon*, 30 July 2005.
22. "Serang Ahmadiyah Pelanggaran HAM", *Pikiran Rakyat*, 22 August 2005.
23. Email interview, Mubarik Ahmad, 7 July 2009. The interviewee is head of Ahmadiyah's Public Affairs Unit.
24. The Bandung-based FUUI comprises many DDII and Persis leaders. FUI was established in August 2005.
25. He has also been a founding member of KISDI, an influential Islamist group in the late New Order, and Partai Bulan Bintang (PBB, Crescent Star Party), Masyumi's main successor party in the post–New Order years.
26. Hizbut Tahrir's al-Khaththath was later forced out of the organization by the central leadership for his role in facilitating violent assaults against Ahmadis.
27. MMI is an umbrella group of several militant Islamist groups. It was established by Abu Bakar Bashir, once emir of Southeast Asia's largest jihadist Islamist group, Jemaah Islamiyah.
28. In the original Indonesian:
    [K]ami nyatakan kami ajak umat islam ayo mari kita perangi ahmadiyah, bunuh Ahmadiyah dimanapun mereka berada saudara! All Ahuaakbar! Bunuh, bunuh, bunuh, bunuh!… ini namanya bela paksa. Lu ngerusak akidah gw, udah bukan halal lagi udah… udah holol… udah holol. Bukan main… Ahmadiyah halal darahnya untuk ditumpahkan, nanti dibilang melanggar HAM, persetan kitab HAM, tai kucing kitab HAM!
    <http://www.youtube.com/watch?v=ikolHPCtFzc> features Sobri Lubis advocating the killing of Ahmadiyah members; the website <indonesiamatters.com> has the full speech. Bashyir resigned as Amir of MMI soon after.
29. Around the same time, Syamsi Ali, Imam of New York's biggest mosque, said that Ahmadiyah should establish its own religion and no longer call itself

Muslim. "Deklarasikan Ahmadiyah sebagai agama baru", *Terbit*, 12 January 2008.
30. "Ahmadiyah: Kami bagian dari Islam", *detikcom*, 15 January 2008.
31. "Penjelasan Pengurus Besar Jemaat Ahmadiyah Indonesia (PB JAI) Tentang Pokok-Pokok Keyakinan Dan Kemasyarakatan Warga Jemaat Ahmadiyah Indonesia", Jakarta, 14 January 2008.
32. "Catatan Audiensi Komisi VIII DPR-RI Dengan Lembaga Penelitian dan Pengkajian Islam", 18 February 2008. The document was signed by Hilman Rosyad Syihab, deputy chairman of the Commission VII and a member of PKS.
33. The AKKBB consists of forty NGOs.
34. Handout titled "Mari Pertahankan Indonesia Kita", Jakarta, 10 May 2008. The document contains the names of almost 300 community leaders, intellectuals and journalists, among them Professor Amien Rais, Anand Krishna, Professor Azyumardi Azra, Dr Djohan Effendi, Goenawan Mohamad, Mustofa Bisri and Abdurrahman Wahid (both NU), Professor Dawam Rahardjo, Mochtar Pabottingi, Professor Taufik Abdullah, Todung Mulya Lubis, Ulil Abshar Abdalla and Yenny Zannuba Wahid. Unity in Diversity or Bhinneka Tunggal Ika is the motto affiliated with the Pancasila.
35. The Wahid Institute, "Waiting for the Demise of the FPI", Monthly Report on Religious Issues, June 2008, p. 1.
36. Quoted in "Munarman: Jika tidak siap perang, jangan menantang", *Kompas*, 1 June 2008.
37. Ironically, Munarman was previously chairman of the secular Yayasan Bantuan Hukum Indonesia (Indonesia Legal Aid Foundation, YBHI). He later recorded a video declaring he would turn himself in on the condition that the government suspended Ahmadiyah. After the government issued its decree on Ahmadiyah, Munarman reported to a Jakarta police station and was subsequently jailed.
38. Both the Australian and German consulates in Bali rejected the pleas. The Wahid Institute, "Waiting for the Demise of the FPI", p. 8.
39. Interview, Maya Safira Muchtar, Jakarta, 13 April 2009. The interviewee is the chairman of the Gerakan Integrasi Nasional or National Integration Movement.
40. "Keputusan Bersama Menteri Agama, Jaksa Agung, dan Menteri Dalam Negeri Republik Indonesia Nomor: 3 Tahun 2008, Nomor: KEP-033/A/JA/6/2008, Nomor: 199 Tahun 2008 Tentang Peringatan dan Perintah Kepada Penganut, Anggota, Dan/Atau Anggota Pengurus Jemaat Ahmadiyah Indonesia (JAI) dan Warga Masyarakat".
41. The Wahid Institute, "The Government has Failed", Monthly Report on Religious Issues (n.d.), p. 12.
42. Quoted in the Wahid Institute, "The Government has Failed", p. 1.

43. Interview, Zafrullah Ahmad Pontoh, Jakarta, 13 April 2009. The interviewee is an Ahmadiyah leader and preacher (*mubaligh*) based in Jakarta.
44. "Siaran Pers", PB Jemaat Ahmadiyah, 10 June 2008. This is a press release.
45. "Ahmadiyah Can Worship, Kalla says", *Jakarta Post*, 11 June 2008.
46. These were Muhammad M. Basyumi as Minister of Religion, Hendarman Supandji as Attorney General and Mardiyanto as Minister of Home Affairs.
47. Interview, Zafrullah Ahmad Pontoh, Jakarta, 13 April 2009.
48. See, for example, the survey "Toleransi Sosial Masyarakat Perkotaan" by the Setara Institute, 29 November 2010. 60.9 per cent of respondents said they could "not accept" (*tidak menerima*) Ahmadiyah. On the question what the government should do about Ahmadiyah, 45.5 per cent said "disbanding", 20.7 per cent said "limit its expansion" (*dibatas perkembangannya*) and only 6.1 per cent opted for "protecting its existence" (*dijamin keberadaannya*). 52.1 per cent of respondents supported the "fight against deviating sects" <http://www.setara-institute.org/sites/setara-institute.org/files/reports/101129-setara-id-101129-toleransiurban-grafik.pdf>.
49. Email Interview, Mubarik Ahmad, 7 July 2009.
50. "State Cannot Meddle in Private Religious Beliefs", *Jakarta Post*, 28 April 2008.
51. "Siaran Pers", PB Jemaat Ahmadiyah, 10 June 2008.
52. The Wahid Institute listed eleven incidents between 9 June (issue of the decree) and 20 June 2008. "The Government Has Failed", pp. 10–11.
53. "Ditolak Muspida, Ormas Islam menyegel markas JAI", *Pikiran Rakyat*, 5 August 2005.
54. "Ahmadiyah Banned in S. Sumatra amid Pressure", *Jakarta Post*, 2 September 2008. There are at least 600 Ahmadiyah followers in the province, including 200 members in Palembang, with nine mosques in cities and regencies.
55. The Wahid Institute, "Pornography Bill Controversy", Monthly Report on Religious Issues, September 2008, p. 6.
56. The Wahid Institute, "The Government Has Failed", p. 12.
57. Interview, Mubarik Ahmad, Jakarta, 14 April 2009.
58. Interview, Maya Safira Muchtar, Jakarta, 13 April 2009.
59. Interview, Mubarik Ahmad, Jakarta, 14 April 2009.
60. Ibid.
61. "Sudah lama, Ahmadiyah bukan Islam", *Pikiran Rakyat*, 22 August 2005.
62. "PBNU: Ahmadiyah Aliran Sesat", *Republika*, 8 September 2005.
63. "Pemerintah Harus Serius Tangani Ahmadiyah", *Republika*, 6 March 2008 and "Pemerintah tak tegas, aliran sesat kian marak", *Terbit*, 28 December 2007. Ikatan Cendekiawan Muslim se-Indonesia or Indonesian Association of Muslim Intellectuals (ICMI) also expressed support for MUI's fatwa. "MUI akan pertahankan fatwa Ahmadiyah", *Mitra Dialog*, 2 August 2005.

64. The Wahid Institute, "Waiting for the Demise of the FPI", pp. 8–9.
65. "Lima Ormas Dukung Pelarangan Ahmadiyah, *Radar Cirebon*, 30 August 2005.
66. "Tolak Pelarangan Ahmadiyah, Wakil Rais Syuriyah NU Surabaya Diperingatkan", NU Online, 9 May 2008.
67. "Setelah Ahmadiyah, JIL Berikutnya", *Tabloid Jumat*, 29 July 2005.
68. "Ahmadiyah dipersilahkan bikin agama baru", *Radar Cirebon*, 22 July 2005.
69. "Musyawarah Nasional VII Majelis Ulama Indonesia Tahun 2005: Keputusan Fatwa Majelis Ulama Indonesia Nomor: 11/Munas VII/MUI/15/2005 Tentang Aliran Ahmadiyah".
70. Letter by MUI (headquarters), No. B-398/MUI/IX/2005, dated 10 September 2005, reprinted in Djamaluddin (2007, pp. 162–63).
71. "Press Release: Pernyataan Sikap atas Tindak Kekerasan Atas Nama Agama Terhadap Jemaat Ahmadiyyah Indonesia (JAI)", 18 July 2005. The group acted under the name Amanat Cirebon which stands for "Anti-violence in the name of Religion and God Societal Alliance". Among the signatories were local NU branches and the alumni organization of the HMI (Himpunan Mahasiswa Islam or Islamic Students' Association).
72. For a similar argument, see my "Religious Freedom isn't an Absolute", *Today*, 13 June 2008, and The Wahid Institute, "Laporan Tahunan The Wahid Institute Pluralisme Beragama/Berkeyakinan di Indonesia: Menapaki Bangsa yang Kian Retak", 2008.
73. The Wahid Institute, "Laporan Tahunan", p. 7.
74. Ibid., p. 10.
75. Interestingly, a press-related law reiterates this requirement. Law number 40 1999 (Second Chapter, Paragraph Five, Article 1) reads: The national press has the obligation to report and comment by respecting religious norms and societal ethics on the basis of benefit of the doubt". Quoted in "MUI protes Majalah Tempo", NU online, 2 June 2008.
76. Email interview, Mubarik Ahmad, 9 July 2009.
77. "Issue: 'NU Asks Ahmadiyah to leave Islam'", *Jakarta Post*, 26 October 2010, "NU Opposes Blasphemy Law Review", *Jakarta Post*, 1 February 2010.
78. In March 2009, various Islamist organizations again demonstrated in front of the Presidential Palace, demanding a Presidential Decree to dissolve Ahmadiyah. This time they threatened to boycott the 2009 general elections if not responded to.

References

Abdullah, Yusuf Ali. *The Meaning of the Holy Qur'an*. Beltsville, MD: Amana, 1999.

"Catatan Audiensi Komisi VIII DPR-RI Dengan Lembaga Penelitian dan Pengkajian Islam", 18 February 2008.

Djamaluddin, Amin. *Ahmadiyah dan Pembajakan Al Quran*. Jakarta: Lembaga Pengkajian dan Penelitian Islam, 1992.

———. *Ahmadiyah Menodai Islam (Kumpulan Fakta dan Data)*. Jakarta: Lembaga Penelitian dan Pengkajian Islam, 2007.

International Crisis Group. "Indonesia: Implications of the Ahmadiyah Decree", Asia Briefing No. 78. Jakarta/Brussels: 7 July 2008.

Jaiz, Hartono Ahmad. *Aliran and Paham Sesat di Indonesia*. Jakarta: Pustaka Al-Kautsar, 2002.

"Kementerian Luar Negeri Kedutaan Besar Saudi Arabia Jakarta, Nomer 8/1/10/ B374/1401, tanggal 6/5/1981". Reprinted in Laporan Investigasi. Jakarta: LBH and Kontras, n.d.

"Keputusan Bersama Menteri Agama, Jaksa Agung, dan Menteri Dalam Negeri Republik Indonesia Nomor: 3 Tahun 2008, Nomor: KEP-033/A/JA/6/2008, Nomor: 199 Tahun 2008 Tentang Peringatan dan Perintah Kepada Penganut, Anggota, Dan/Atau Anggota Pengurus Jemaat Ahmadiyah Indonesia (JAI) dan Warga Masyarakat".

"Laporan Tahunan The Wahid Institute Pluralisme Beragama/Berkeyakinan di Indonesia", 2008.

Letter by MUI (headquarters), No. B-398/MUI/IX/2005, dated 10 September 2005. Reprinted in Djamaluddin, Amin. *Ahmadiyah Menodai Islam (Kumpulan Fakta dan Data)*. Jakarta: Lembaga Penelitian dan Pengkajian Islam, 2007.

"Mari Pertahankan Indonesia Kita", Jakarta, 10 May 2008.

"Musyawarah Nasional VII Majelis Ulama Indonesia Tahun 2005: Keputusan Fatwa Majelis Ulama Indonesia Nomor: 11/Munas VII/MUI/15/2005 Tentang Aliran Ahmadiyah".

Penelitian dan Pengkajian Islam, 2007, pp. 128–29.

"Penetapan Presiden Republik Indonesia Nomor 1 Tahun 1965 Tentang Pencegahan Penyalahgunaan dan/atau Penodaan Agama" <http://hukum.unsrat.ac.id/ uu/penpres_1_1965.htm>.

"Penjelasan Rabitah Alam Islami Mengenai Keputusan dan Rekomendasi Konperensi Organisasi-Organisasi Islam di Dunia yang Diadakan di Makkah Al Mukarramah Tanggal 14 s/d 18 Rabiul Awwl 1394 H". Reprinted in Djamaluddin, Amin. *Ahmadiyah Menodai Islam (Kumpulan Fakta dan Data)*. Jakarta: Lembaga.

"Penjelesan Pengurus Besar Jemaat Ahmadiyah Indonesia (PB JAI) Tentang Pokok Pokok Keyakinan Dan Kemasyarakatan Warga Jemaat Ahmadiyah Indonesia", Jakarta, 14 January 2008.

Platzdasch, Bernhard. "Religious Freedom isn't an Absolute", *Today* (Singapore), 13 June 2008.

"Press Release: Pernyataan Sikap atas Tindak Kekerasan Atas Nama Agama Terhadap Jemaat Ahmadiyyah Indonesia (JAI)", 18 July 2005.

Purwanto, Wawan. H. *"Menusuk" Ahmadiyah*. Jakarta: CMB Press, 2008.

Setara Institute. "Toleransi Sosial Masyarakat Perkotaan", 29 November 2010 <http://www.setara-institute.org/sites/setara-institute.org/files/reports/101129-setara-id-101129-toleransiurban-grafik.pdf>.

"Siaran Pers", PB Jemaat Ahmadiyah, 10 June 2008.

Suryawan, M.A. *Bukan Sekedar Hitam Putih: Kontroversi Pemahaman Ahmadiyah*. Tangerang: Azzahara, 2006.

Wahid Institute. "Laporan Tahunan The Wahid Institute Pluralisme Beragama/Berkeyakinan di Indonesia: Menapaki Bangsa yang Kian Retak", 2008.

———. "Pornography Bill Controversy". Monthly Report on Religious Issues, September 2008.

———. "The Government Has Failed". Monthly Report on Religious Issues, n.d.

———. "Waiting for the Demise of the FPI". Monthly Report on Religious Issues, June 2008.

Zulkarnain, Iskandar. *Gerakan Ahmadiyah di Indonesia*. Yogyakarta: LKiS, 2005.

10

RELIGION AND THE POLITICS OF MORALITY: MUSLIM WOMEN ACTIVISTS AND THE PORNOGRAPHY DEBATE IN INDONESIA[1]

Rachel Rinaldo

In late 2008, Indonesia's parliament passed a law against pornography. The debate was short, because the bill had already been thoroughly discussed and revised in committees and a majority of legislators had agreed to support it. Prior to the vote, however, nearly a hundred legislators opposed to the bill stormed out of parliament in protest. The ratification of the legislation *Rancangan Undang-Undang Pornografi*, or *RUU Pornografi* as it is commonly known, marks the end of one of the many bitter public controversies that have preoccupied Indonesians since the collapse of the authoritarian Soeharto regime in 1998.

At a time when Indonesia is still in the process of political and social flux, the recent debates over issues such as pornography entail competing ideas about how Islam should be incorporated into the nation-state.

Arguments about the pornography bill, for example, revolved around whether the state should regulate the media to prevent it from disseminating images that offend Islamic norms of modesty. In this way, the debate over the role of the state in regulating images or behaviour was also a debate about the extent to which the state's actions should be guided by religious, in this case Islamic, ideologies. These controversies are moral debates, in that they involve arguments about individual or collective rights vis-à-vis the state, as well as struggles over what constitutes an ideal society, which are often informed by religion.

Gender ideologies are a profound, but often underappreciated aspect of moral debates. The Indonesian debates about pornography not only involve competing ideas about rights and freedoms, but also about how bodies, particularly those of women, should be seen in public. Feminist scholars have argued that moral debates such as the one over pornography reflect attempts to define collective identities and to shape the gender structure of society (Yuval-Davis 1997). And in the case of Indonesia, such debates are also part of a continuing process of struggle over the relationship between religion and public life (Brenner 2011; Rinaldo 2011).

Gender, then, has clear significance for moral debates. But women do not figure only as symbols in these debates. Increasingly in Indonesia, women activists from all sides of the political spectrum raise their voices in these controversies. The rapidly growing social science literature on Islam and gender has contributed to a more nuanced understanding of Muslim women's agency as culturally contingent and not necessarily oriented towards liberation (Deeb 2006; Mahmood 2005). Yet within this literature there is a tendency to treat Islam as monolithic. For example, Gole (2002) argues that pious Islam's gender practices and conceptions of the self pose a stark challenge to secular public spheres. This argument seems to suggest that pious Islam is a unitary subjectivity. One might therefore expect pious Indonesian Muslim women activists to take similar positions on the pornography legislation, but this did not happen.

In this article, I examine how women from two Muslim organizations, Fatayat Nahdlatul Ulama (hereafter Fatayat) and the Prosperous Justice Party (Partai Keadilan Sejahtera, PKS), took different sides in the pornography debate. These activists' political positions drew on different approaches to understanding Islam, and expressed markedly different visions for Indonesia's future. While Fatayat women opposed the bill as part of their struggle for a more egalitarian society, PKS women supported it as a first step towards what they hope will be a more pious Islamic society. Their political stances reflect Indonesia's varied heritage of Islamic thought, different conceptions of the relationship between the subject and the state, as well as the contemporary lack of consensus over the future of Indonesia. Investigating these women activists' public interventions reveals the ways in which the pornography debate was gendered, and also illuminates the intermingling of religion and politics in contemporary Indonesia.[2] While Indonesia is far from being an Islamic state, ideas about the nation's future are increasingly articulated within Islamic frameworks.

INDONESIAN CONTEXT AND RESEARCH METHODS

The pornography debate must be understood against the background of Indonesia's transition away from authoritarian rule and the emergence of a public sphere constituted by a free mass media, NGOs and civil society groups, students and academic intellectuals, and religious organizations. Indonesia was governed by a military regime, led by General Soeharto, from 1965 to 1998. The 1997 Asian economic crisis helped stimulate a popular democratic movement, and Soeharto stepped down from power in May 1998.

In the years after 1998, Indonesia was plagued by violence, including a number of bombings linked to Islamic jihadist groups. Yet there were also significant changes, including democratic elections, the ending of laws restricting the media, and the lifting of regulations that once criminalized demonstrations and other forms of collective action. In recent years, stability and economic growth have returned, but many Indonesians feel that reforms have not gone far enough. They cite the country's notorious corruption and cronyism records, as well as problems related to the political decentralization undertaken in the early 2000s. Under the rubric of regional autonomy, provincial legislatures have used their new authority to pass laws requiring women to wear Islamic headscarves, imposing nightly curfews on women or requiring Qur'anic study for students. Some scholars argue that such laws are mostly symbolic, but opponents claim that they are inspired by Islamic *shari'ah* law,[3] and that they impinge on the constitutional rights of women and religious minorities (Bush 2008). The central government has refused to review the laws.

Islamization is not new to Indonesia. Islam arrived in Indonesia in the 1400s and today nearly 90 per cent of Indonesians are Muslim. Historically, religion and politics in the Indonesian archipelago have often (but not always) been intertwined, and Islam has frequently been a source of opposition to authoritarian rule, especially during the colonial era (Ricklefs 2008). Islamic practice in the country has diverse local variants, with varying relationships to Middle Eastern Islam. Starting in the late 1970s, transnational flows of Islam helped to produce a resurgence of Islamic thought and a turn to more orthodox Islamic practices. This process was aided by growing numbers of Indonesians studying in the Middle East and returning to establish organizations and schools to disseminate new ways of thinking about Islam (Machmudi 2008). By the early 1990s, women of the expanding middle classes were adopting headscarves and new mosques were being built around the country. This revival has deepened in recent years, with increasing numbers of Indonesians studying Arabic and practicing Islam in a more visibly pious manner (Brenner 2005, 1996; Doorn-Harder 2005). In the 1990s, Indonesian Muslims became more politicized, as well as active in civil society (Hefner 2000). Muslim student organizations became a central part of the opposition to Soeharto. Yet the pornography debate reveals that a decade after Soeharto stepped down, there are profound divisions among Muslim activists.

Although this article is mainly an analysis of the pornography debate, I draw on my ethnographic research with women activists in Indonesia between 2002 and 2008, as well as analysis of secondary sources such as newspapers, magazines, and websites. I discuss the activism of women in the Jakarta headquarters of Fatayat and PKS.[4] At the national level, the women in these organizations are demographically similar.[5] I seek to understand the role of religion in their political differences.

Fatayat is part of one of Indonesia's largest Muslim organizations, Nahdlatul Ulama (NU), which was founded in 1926, and estimated to have 45 million members. Along with the mass organization Muhammadiyah, NU is often considered to represent the mainstream of Indonesian Islam. Both emerged in central Java, but have chapters across the country.

Fatayat is for women between the ages of 25 and 45. Most of the staff and volunteers I met were university educated and worked as teachers or lecturers.[6] Many grew up in urban areas and came from families affiliated with NU. Fatayat leaders take an interpretive and often historicized approach to Islamic texts, emphasizing what they view to be the substance of the religion — equality and justice. This distinctive approach is influenced both by NU, which long emphasized *fiqh*, the science of Islamic jurisprudence, as well as by both religious and secular discourses of gender equality (Rinaldo 2008; Doorn-Harder 2006). Coming from the NU milieu, many Fatayat members attended traditional Muslim boarding schools and, in many cases, Islamic state universities, where they were schooled in *fiqh*. Since the 1990s, revisionist interpretations of *fiqh* have become central to the work of Fatayat activists in disseminating understandings of Islam that emphasize women's equality. Some scholars have argued that the science of *fiqh* lends itself to feminist and other reformist Muslim projects. For example, Muslim feminist scholar Mir-Hosseini (2006) distinguishes between *shari'ah* as God's law, and *fiqh* as human law:

> It is essential, I maintain, to highlight this distinction and to draw attention to its epistemological and political ramifications. It underlies the emergence of various schools of Islamic law and within them a multiplicity of positions and opinions and also enables me — as a Muslim — to argue for gender justice within the framework of my faith. (Mir-Hosseini 2006, p. 633)

Indeed, Mir-Hosseini describes similar projects of reinterpretation of *fiqh* among Iranian Muslim feminists.

Although Fatayat was originally more of a service organization, its leaders have been directly influenced by global discourses of gender equality and Islamic feminism via their work with NGOs and international donors. This development was part of a more general liberalization of the NU that took place in the 1980s. As scholars have recounted, during this period, prominent NU figures began to argue for reconciling Islam with ideas of democracy, human rights, and pluralism (Hefner 2000). In the 1990s, translations of books and articles by Islamic reformist figures such as Fatima Mernissi and Ali Asghar Engineer became popular with NU activists. Fatayat leaders now see the promotion of women's rights and empowerment as a key part of their mission as pious Muslims.

The PKS was founded in 1998 as a Muslim political party as the political arena was liberalized following the resignation of Soeharto. In its initial incarnation as the Justice Party, it called for an Islamic state. In 2002, after poor electoral showings, it was reconstituted as the Prosperous Justice Party. While PKS does not call for an Islamic state, it does advocate making Islamic values the source of law and policy. PKS received approximately 7 per cent of the national vote in the 2004 elections and about 8 per cent of the vote in the 2009 elections. PKS boasts numerous women cadres, though it has just 3 female representatives out of 57 seats in the national legislature. The PKS women I met were also university-educated, married with children, and many also worked as teachers or lecturers. Like Fatayat women, most grew up in families of modest means in urban areas, with parents who also worked as civil servants or small business people. However, an important difference is that most PKS women I met were educated in secular schools and state universities and did not have strong connections to the NU milieu.

PKS represents a somewhat different and newer approach to Islam in Indonesia. It draws on the heritage of Muslim modernism, a movement that originated in Egypt in the late nineteenth century and which sought to integrate Islam with Western science. Modernism was critical of traditions such as *fiqh*, which required specialized education, and instead emphasized individuals being able to read the Qur'an (Moaddel 2005). Modernism was influential in Indonesia, inspiring the establishment of the mass organization Muhammadiyah in 1912. Many of the founders of PKS were influenced by the ideas of the Egyptian Muslim Brotherhood, through study abroad or as part of an Islamic study group while at university (Machmudi 2008). The Muslim Brotherhood was in many ways an outgrowth of the modernist movement. However, the Brotherhood diverged from the early modernists with its stronger rejection of traditional Islamic jurisprudence, its emphasis on a close reading of Islamic texts, its opposition to nationalism, communism, and democracy, and its insistence on strict separation of genders (Moaddel 2005). The Brotherhood has gone through many shifts, such as embracing electoral democracy in the 1990s, and remains an important ideological influence for PKS (Machmudi 2008). The party does not necessarily adopt a literalist approach, but it tends to foreclose interpretation, with members frequently arguing that the text of the Qur'an must be followed as it is written. PKS members are often labelled as conservatives or Islamists, but they see themselves as moderates, attempting to hold fast to the rules of Islam while also living in a modern society.

The women of Fatayat and PKS emerged from different Islamic backgrounds. Indonesians sometimes use the term *aliran* (streams) to describe religious networks that map on to class differences and political worldviews (Sidel 2006; Geertz 1963). According to this framework, Fatayat and PKS women simply represent the traditional and modernist *aliran* respectively, which account for their differences.[7] Yet in significant ways, the women in these organizations are quite similar. Their leaders are usually from the emerging urban middle class. As part of a generation that has been shaped by the global Islamic revival, they have in common a commitment to practising Islam in their own lives and society. But for these two groups of women, the notion of a more Islamic society holds different meanings and is associated with diverse political projects (see Rinaldo 2008 for a more thorough comparison of Fatayat and PKS). Women's political positions cannot simply be deduced from their *aliran*. After all, the NU contains deeply conservative tendencies, some of which are hostile to ideas of gender equality. Moreover, PKS has recruited people from many different kinds of backgrounds. Instead, I argue that Muslim women activists' political positions are shaped by their different religious interpretations, which are influenced but not determined by their relationships to various Islamic traditions. Religion has often been a key source of ideas about what constitutes an ideal society. The complex intersections between Islam and social movement activism demonstrate how deeply intertwined religion and politics are in the contemporary Indonesian context.

MORAL DEBATES, GENDER, AND THE NATION

Scholars of Indonesian politics first drew attention in the 1990s to increasing debates over gender and religion. Brenner (1999) and Sen (1998) argued that the media coverage of "career women" and discussions of veiling reflected tensions over economic changes that were drawing women into universities and the formal workforce. In these debates, women were often accused of neglecting their responsibilities and thereby risking the nation's future.

Rather than dying down after the regime transition in 1998, these kinds of debates became a prominent feature of Indonesia's newly open public sphere. Pornography, especially between 2005 and 2008, was one of the most contentious. The main participants in the controversy were, as might be expected, mostly members of the urban middle classes. Nevertheless, the issue of pornography attracted great popular interest, and women activists were especially vocal about expressing their opinions on the proposed legislation. The controversy about pornography in Indonesia is a debate with real consequences for how the state regulates media and creative production, and with implications for how the state governs its subjects. Moreover, the debate has been intimately connected with ideas about proper womanhood.

Debates like pornography are often viewed as a clash of "values", especially religious versus secular. For example, the *New York Times* reported that the trial of the editor of *Playboy Indonesia* on indecency charges, "highlighted growing divisions here between a rising conservative movement and the moderate Muslims who make up the majority of the population" (Gelling 2007). In a more scholarly vein, Allen (2007) pushes further to argue that the pornography debate is a struggle over the future of the Indonesian nation, between religious diversity and religious hegemony. While these framings are certainly accurate, I think they underestimate the centrality of discourses of gender to struggles over nationhood. Feminist scholars argue that gender ideologies are critical to nationalism and state-making. Not only do state policies constrain gender relations, but "ideas about the differences between men and women shape the ways in which states are imagined, constituted, and legitimated" (Gal and Kligman 2000, p. 4). Because of their reproductive capacities, women in many societies are seen as the embodiment of the community's traditions. Gender ideologies help to construct the symbolic boundaries of the community, whether that community is an ethnic group or a nation. In times of social change, as the boundaries of the community are threatened or identities are shifting, women's bodies and behaviour often become a focus of attention (Yuval-Davis 1997, Moghadam 1994). Communities in such times often seek to define themselves through regulation of women's behaviour or through ideologies of proper manhood and womanhood. I suggest this social phenomenon is at the heart of the current moral debates in Indonesia.

Brenner (1999) makes a similar argument in her article about media discourses on gender in 1990s Indonesia, noting that widespread social changes involving women have produced a strong counter-reaction. But what is different after 1998 is that the Indonesian nation-state has been engaged in a process of redefinition. In the last decade, Indonesia has gone through substantial social and economic change. Not only has the government changed, but control over state resources and power came up for grabs, new social actors like pious Muslims have entered the public sphere, processes like rural to urban migration have continued, and family life is shifting as the marriage age rises and more women enter higher education (Smith-Hefner 2007; Sidel 2006; Jones 2005; Hadiz and Robison 2004). In such a time of national shifts, many of the moral debates in Indonesia revolve around women's bodies and roles in the nation.

Gender, therefore, is often a crucial feature of moral debates because it is an arena for struggles over national identity. But what is also intriguing about gender in Indonesian public debates is how women activists are able to intervene in them. While the feminist scholars who study gender and the nation-state often see women as symbols or victims of these processes, I suggest here that it is this gendered nature of moral debates which can also help to sanction women's participation in those debates and in the public sphere more generally.

I now turn to a brief discussion of the pornography debate in Indonesia in order to examine how women activists from Fatayat and PKS intervened on different sides of this moral debate, and how their activism drew on different approaches to religious texts.

WOMEN ACTIVISTS AND MORAL DEBATES: THE CASE OF THE PORNOGRAPHY BILL

The recently passed pornography bill spurred angry demonstrations on both sides between 2005 and 2008, as well as myriad newspaper and magazine articles and op-eds, not to mention heated debates in parliament.

Concern about pornography emerged in Indonesia following the rise of a freewheeling popular media after 1998. Older laws providing censorship of sexual imagery remained on the books. But many Indonesians also became concerned about television shows and magazines that they felt were featuring increasingly racy subject matter. Pornographic images also became more accessible with the advent of the Internet, as well as with a flood of pirated VCDs and DVDs that were easy to buy on the street. The furore that erupted over the popular singer Inul Daratista's eroticized dance style in 2002 and 2003 was an early indication of a backlash from pious Muslims. Indeed, while some of my woman activist informants defended Inul, even attending a raucous demonstration in support of her in 2003, others saw Inul as heralding a more sexualized society. One young activist lamented the example Inul was setting for young women. Certainly, the perception that pornography was becoming mainstream seemed to be widespread. For example, in an article published in the popular newsweekly *Tempo*, Syamsul Muarif, the Minister for Communications and Information, said that 60 per cent of Indonesians were accessing porn on the Internet and beyond. "So, because that's what they like, the shows are also being allowed on television", he warned (*Tempo*, 14 May 2003).

Although a previous attempt to promulgate a new pornography law was shelved in the 1990s, according to Allen (2007), the momentum for new legislation on pornography in the post-Soeharto era came especially from PKS. During my fieldwork in Jakarta in 2003, I attended a seminar and demonstration against pornography which was held by the women's division of the party. The speakers included a representative from the Indonesian Council of Ulamas (Majelis Ulama Indonesia, MUI), a quasi-governmental body that rules on matters of Islamic law.

At the seminar, pornography was consistently depicted as a threat to the nation. The head of the party's women's division introduced the event with the statement: "We face the challenge of building an Indonesia which is moral." Later, a PKS legislator argued that Indonesia was under threat from "American cultural exports", including pornography. "We should not be afraid to express the desire of the majority", she said, "we have a responsibility to the next generation to make a better Indonesia."

Several of the speakers defined pornography very broadly, as showing a woman without covering her *aurat* (a term from Arabic meaning the parts of a woman's body that should be forbidden from public view — for many Indonesian Muslims, *aurat* stretches from a woman's upper chest to her ankles). At this time, although it was not discussed in the seminar, a bill to outlaw pornography was already being written.

In late 2005, representatives including PKS members introduced into parliament a draft legislation, written in collaboration with religious authorities such as the MUI. As originally written, the bill was extremely broad, and under the rubric of banning "porno action", which pertained to actions that exploited sex, obscenity, or erotica, would have outlawed kissing in public and bikinis on beaches (Harvey 2006). Public outcry forced its return to parliament for revision and it remained stalled there for over a year.

During this period, the hullabaloo over the launching of an Indonesian edition of *Playboy* magazine also energized the pornography debate. Premiering in April 2006, it was the first *Playboy* to be published in a Muslim country since a Turkish edition was discontinued in the 1990s (Perlez 2006). It had no nudity, featuring only fully clothed models, but provoked a strong reaction. NU's leader Hasyim Muzadi called for an anti-pornography movement as a reaction to its publication, and the MUI put out a fatwa demanding that the pornography bill be passed (Guerin 2006). Violent protests outside the magazine's offices by hard-line groups such as the Islamic Defenders Front (FPI) caused the building's owner to evict the media company. The magazine relocated its headquarters to Bali and continued to publish, but its editor-in-chief, Erwin Arnada went on trial for violating the indecency provisions of the criminal code. Arnada was acquitted of all charges in April 2007 (Gelling 2007), but by that time, the magazine was defunct due to the inability to attract advertisers.

Finally, in November 2008, a somewhat liberalized version of the *RUU Pornografi* was passed which made exceptions for "sexual materials" as part of traditional culture and fine arts.[8] This reflects the fact that the bill was strongly opposed by artists and by the Balinese, who argued that erotic and sensual expression is intrinsic to their traditional culture. The bill dropped references to "porno action" and defined pornography as coital acts, foreplay and sexual diversions pertaining to intercourse, sexual violence, masturbation or onanism, nudity or illusions/allusions to nudity, and genitalia. A further clarification in the bill's text defines nudity as appearance or reference to nude bodies. It exempts from the regulations clothing and behaviour associated with religious or spiritual rituals, as well as artistic productions or sports, if conducted in the proper arenas. Legislators who supported the bill also insisted that bikinis at the beach would not fall under its rubric.

Nevertheless, the bill expressly declares the aim of cultivating morality and ethics and of protecting the dignity of women and children from pornography. The goal of cultivating a moral community omits questions about how morality should be defined, assuming that it is universal. This objective also echoes the assessment of PKS made by Machmudi, that cultivating religious piety is as important as political reform:

> Since there is no separation of the religious and the political in the party, the activists of the PKS prefer to consider it merely an extension of the field of *dakwah* [religious call].... The effectiveness of the *dakwah* programme lies in its contribution to political, cultural and religious change in society as well as within the state. Such changes are needed to ensure that society and the state are always under the guidance of the teachings of Islam. (Machmudi 2008, pp. 178–79)

Finally, the bill's injunction to protect women and children by ensuring that their bodies are properly covered resonates with conventional Islamic discourses that position women's sexuality as disruptive, easily arousing men, whose gaze must therefore be circumscribed (Mahmood 2005; Mernissi 1987).

Women activists in Indonesia's public sphere found themselves on very different sides of the pornography debate. While those who saw themselves as part of the women's rights movement strongly opposed it, women in Muslim political parties like PKS supported it. Yet both thought that they had the broader interests of Indonesian women in mind. Interestingly, while pornography was a very divisive issue for the American and Australian feminist movements in the 1980s, this was not the case for women's rights proponents in Indonesia. Many religious and secular women's rights activists in Indonesia opposed the bill because of concerns about censorship and effects on gender equality. They felt that the bill criminalized women's bodies, while doing little to apply sanctions to men who control the sex industry. And after years of government censorship, they were profoundly concerned about freedom of speech. Concerns about preserving local cultures, many of which feature dances with erotic movements, also emerged as a significant aspect of the opposition. Allen (2007, p. 109) also notes that some opponents of the bill saw as degrading its apparent assumption that men cannot contain their sexuality. While few Indonesian women have advanced the kind of "pro-pornography" or "sex positive" positions that have emerged in the United States and other contexts, support for freedom of expression within women's rights organizations led even those who have expressed concern about pornography and public morality in the past to oppose the bill.

Demonstrations against the pornography bill were initiated by women's rights organizations, but it was at first unclear whether Muslim women's organizations would oppose or support the legislation. Indeed, some leaders of Nahdlatul Ulama and Muhammadiyah were strongly in favour of the bill. In March 2006, however, Fatayat leaders weighed in with a carefully worded statement opposing the bill because it failed to provide protection for women and children victimized by the sex industry, and arguing that pre-existing legislation could be more effectively implemented. This statement was reprinted in the national media and especially on the blogs that sprang up as part of the opposition to the bill. Former president and NU leader Abdurrahman Wahid and his wife also opposed the bill, earning them the ire of conservative groups. Wahid argued that the definition of pornography is highly subjective (Allen 2007, p. 105).

At demonstrations and other events, individual Fatayat leaders expressed more scathing views on the bill. One activist linked it to recent attempts to pass legislation inspired by Islamic law, noting:

> The phenomena of the anti-pornography bill started with the appearance of by-laws in some of the regions. Although not explicitly packaged

as anti-pornography, they have put in place of anti-prostitution laws, morality laws and even Islamic Shariah laws. All these laws attempt to force women back into their homes. (Koesoemawiria 2006)

For most of 2007, the bill was being revised in a parliamentary committee. Fatayat members who I spoke to about the bill in early 2008 wanted to make it clear to me that they supported laws against pornography in general, but they felt that the proposed law was harmful to women. One Fatayat activist argued:

> I think that the responsibility for pornography should be on the individual. If there is a problem related to the media or whatever, then there must be clearer laws for the media. But the pornography issue, as Fatayat sees it, the laws must be rational, and must not harm others.

She went on to question why pornography had become such a big issue and blamed PKS for trying to impose its thinking on others.

Fatayat women's criticisms of the bill reflect their broader concern for gender equality, which they felt was threatened by the legislation. But their opposition was also shaped by their approach to religious texts. Fatayat women understand Islamic *shari'ah* as a guide to life, one that is open to interpretation and discussion, but that should not be a source of national legislation (Rinaldo 2008; Doorn-Harder 2006). They are wary of the state becoming overly involved in setting moral standards, because they believe that this would privilege certain religious interpretations over others. One Fatayat leader told me, speaking in early 2008, that she viewed efforts such as the pornography bill and regional regulations inspired by *shari'ah*, as examples of "Wahhabism."[9] References to the eighteenth century Saudi purification movement are common among Indonesians who wish to distinguish a more flexible Islam from what they consider to be a strict Arabicized version. My informant argued:

> Fatayat itself is making an effort against Wahhabism. Since its birth, NU has been a counter to Wahhabism. The Shariah regulations are an effort toward Wahhabism or Arabicization of women. And because of this Arabicization, Fatayat is always trying to show that Islam must be contextualized within the society in which it exists, and Indonesia is not an Arab country, but a Pancasila state, which is actually also secular.[10]

Not all Fatayat activists would agree with her labelling of Indonesia as secular, as many seek a major role for Islam in civil society, partly as a counter to secular influences. But there seems to be consensus among many Fatayat women that the state itself should not be too involved in regulating moral and/or religious behaviour.

I also asked women from PKS about their support for the bill and why they thought it has proved so controversial. They did not think the bill was too extreme, but blamed the difficulties on the power of media interests as well as on supporters of the bill who had not explained it well enough so that people would understand it. A typical response came from a woman cadre who was confident that it would soon pass:

> I think it may be because of the communication factor, which isn't always easy. Sometimes there are obstacles, debates on various sides, which are not clearly communicated and so we don't understand each other ... are not open with each other. But the main thing is that we supported it because it protects society from the bad effects of pornography and porno activity.... In terms of our position, we have already been very clear that our support for it is related to how the next generation of children can be protected, so that our society will be morally better, because morality is very important for improving ourselves.

Here, the woman cadre feels that pornography is a threat to the future of the nation because of its deleterious effects on children. Many PKS women also brought up the theme of protecting future generations. They saw the bill as an easy choice between fostering immorality and safeguarding children. As another PKS woman explained:

> I look at it this way, we are an Eastern culture. Maybe we can absorb all kinds of knowledge and technology, but we should not leave behind the special characteristics of Indonesia, those things that are the unique image of Indonesia. We must think positively together about the pornography laws, which are meant to prevent bad things from happening.

Her answer is tinged with nationalist sentiment, in that she sees legislation as a way to protect not only Indonesia's children, but the nation itself. She differentiates Indonesia from the West, insisting that it is an Eastern culture. As Allen (2007, p. 103) suggests, and as I observed at the PKS pornography seminar, PKS support for the bill was often couched in terms of protecting Indonesia from immoral Western influences.

PKS women's support for the pornography bill was therefore linked to concerns about protecting women and children, as well as fears for the more general state of morality in Indonesia, which was seen as under threat from foreign influences. Yet it was also shaped by their party's distinctive approach to Islam. PKS promotes a reading of religious texts that leaves little room for interpretation. For example, my informants often argued that religious practices like polygamy or veiling had to be accepted by believers, because they are in the Qur'an, even though Islamic scholars have for centuries voiced quite varied interpretations of the verses in question.

Machmudi (2008) argues that the influence of the Muslim Brotherhood remains strong within PKS and that it is particularly visible in their conception of religion and politics as inseparable. PKS women argue that the state should have a role in regulating moral behaviour, and they see this as compatible with democracy. Indeed, many PKS women see the regional *shari'ah*-inspired regulations as a matter of the democratic rights of provinces to govern themselves. As one woman told me, speaking of regulations that impose night-time curfews for women:

> Maybe you have to look at the conditions. For example, maybe the conditions in that province are indeed unsafe for women, so maybe it's good they enacted that regulation.

Similarly, while PKS women often downplayed Islam when they spoke to me about the bill, it was clear that religious interpretations influenced their ideas about how bodies should be displayed. For example, while they maintain that women should not be forced to wear the headscarf, they also view the full covering of a woman's body as obligatory under Islamic law. For PKS women, moral behaviour is a very public issue. They see their party as a vehicle for instilling Islamic values in society, especially through influencing families to become better Muslims. As a woman legislator told me:

> PKS is a *dakwah* (religious call) party, and the family should be the first to be called before anyone else. It's meaningless to persuade others to righteousness if our own family is not doing it…. We cannot deny the fact that the future generation lies in the hands of our children, and if we fail to bear this in mind, there will not be much to expect from Indonesia's future development.

Thus, during the course of the pornography debate, virtue became linked to concerns for national progress. Women in PKS maintained that images they consider risqué harm women and children, and thereby threaten the future of the nation. They saw the bill as a way to build national morality. Interestingly, men were rarely mentioned in the discourse about morality and nationalism. While this partly reflects the fact that I was asking PKS women questions about women, it also is indicative of how discourses on family and morality are often tied to ideologies of gender that position women as primarily responsible for children, and as requiring moral protection and/or guidance. It suggests that women are more likely to be the focus of public moral regulation. Meanwhile opponents of the bill argued that the bill went too far in restricting creative expression and that it would contravene progress towards women's empowerment. In particular, women in Fatayat wielded discourses of individual freedom and women's rights to contend that greater state regulation of expression and behaviour is not the way to achieve gender equality.

What is remarkable here is that not only did women activists intervene on very different sides of the pornography debate, but that their engagement in this debate helped thrust them into the national spotlight. While activists worried that the legislation would set back progress towards gender equality, the controversy propelled increasing numbers of women into the public sphere to participate in a controversy that was at the centre of national attention, and also brought differences in ideologies of gender and Islam to the fore. Muslim women activists' different political positions reflected important differences in their approaches to Islam and their relationship with the state as gendered subjects. Fatayat women's opposition was shaped by their emphasis on equality and rights, which draws on an interpretive and contextualized approach to Islam and also positions morality as independent of the state. PKS women's support was based on their concern for national morality, which draws on a less interpretive approach to Islam and emphasizes public regulation of morality. The debate may eventually be seen as a defining event in the ongoing process of reworking the relationship between religion, the state, and public life in Indonesia.

RELIGION, GENDER, AND MORALITY IN THE PUBLIC SPHERE

This chapter has sought to investigate how gender is central to the moral debates that have become such a deep-rooted feature of the Indonesian public sphere in recent years. The controversy over pornography involves a struggle between different conceptions of Islam, gender, and rights, and also hints at significant differences among Indonesians in conceptualizing the relationship between the subject and the state. Supporters of the pornography bill argue that it is necessary to combat national moral degradation and promote more appropriately Islamic values, while opponents claim that it is detrimental to freedom of expression and erodes women's rights by criminalizing women's appearances and behaviours.

The gendered aspect of the controversy was inescapable, though often overlooked in the popular media's framing of it as a debate over free expression versus protection. The pornography bill allows the state to regulate not only the ways bodies are depicted in media, but also how they appear in public spaces. The concept of modesty inherent to this legislation is not gender neutral, for it is nearly always the female body that is considered disruptive and must be covered. And while many religions urge modesty for women, I suggest that the bill institutionalizes an Islamic ethic of modesty in its injunctions against nudity, or the allusion to nudity, and its stated purpose of cultivating a moral and ethical community as well as protecting women and children.

Why are women's behaviours and rights such a subject of debate in contemporary Indonesia? Feminist scholarship on gender and the nation-state provides an important framework for understanding this. The events of 1998 and the decade since have been a period of tremendous social and political change in Indonesia. Islam has become a major force in politics and public life, the state no longer provides many important social programmes, the ranks of the middle class continue to expand, and the country continues to urbanize (Sidel 2006). Many of these shifts have direct consequences for gender relations. The rising age of marriage and growing numbers of women attending higher education and joining the formal workforce have certainly produced anxieties around family and reproduction, as well as resulted in some women seeking more egalitarian marriages (Jones 2005). And because women often symbolize the maintenance of tradition and community identity, gender easily becomes the focus of moral debates in the public sphere (Yuval-Davis 1997).

The global Islamic revival since the late 1970s has called into question norms of citizenship and the relationship between religion and state (Mahmood 2005; Roy 2004). In Indonesia, as we have seen, women have been key participants in the Indonesian pornography debate. In the course of the controversy, women activists from Fatayat and PKS drew on different approaches to understanding Islam, as well as different ideas about women's rights and moral behaviour, and in so doing they expressed their own visions for Indonesia's future. While Fatayat women seek what they see as a more egalitarian society in which women are empowered, rather than dominated by a patriarchal state or society, PKS women are working towards what they understand to be a more pious Islamic society. Their activism is also linked to rather different conceptions of the relationship between the subject and the state. For Fatayat, morality is not tied to the state, but is an individual obligation. While PKS women would not disagree that morality is an individual obligation, they see a greater role for state regulation of morality. Ultimately, in their view, all citizens, but especially women, are moral subjects of the public sphere. Yet both groups of women consider their goal to be a more moral society, and Islam is an essential source for their ideals. These differences among pious Muslims indicate that the global Islamic revival is multifaceted and its consequences for politics are complex. In any case, the rival ideals of morality, subjecthood, and the nation-state that have emerged in many parts of the world should be understood as part of modernity rather than a holdover from the past (Roy 2004). Indeed, such competition and lack of consensus over what constitutes an ideal society is characteristic of modernity, according to classical sociologists like Weber, as well as for recent theorists who argue that modernity is multiple (Eisenstadt 2003).

We should also remember that the women activists in the leadership of Fatayat and PKS are a relatively empowered group, if not necessarily the ruling elite. Despite their different political ideologies, they share middle-class lifestyles. While the expansion of education and communications technologies have facilitated the participation of middle-class women in vital national debates, women of the lower classes face much greater barriers to having their voices heard in mainstream politics, let alone achieving legitimacy in the public sphere. Nevertheless, the Indonesian controversy over pornography reveals the complex and unexpected ways in which gender is implicated in contemporary moral debates. Moreover, examining these moral debates more closely demonstrates how gender ideologies play into competing visions of religion and the nation-state. Indeed, in the current era, gender remains one of the most significant arenas for struggles over broader social and political change.

Notes

1. The original draft of this article was written while the author was a Kiriyama Postdoctoral Fellow at the Center for the Pacific Rim, University of San Francisco. The author also wishes to thank the Asia Research Institute,

National University of Singapore, for funding follow-up research in Indonesia during a postdoctoral fellowship in 2008–09. This article also benefited from comments by participants at the Institute of Southeast Asian Studies conference on "Religion in Southeast Asian Politics: Resistance, Negotiation and Transcendence" (2008), and from feedback during the University of San Francisco's conference on Religion and Globalization in Asia (2009).
2. I use a broad definition of women's activism to refer to women organizing other women for purposes thought to benefit women more generally. This includes activism by women oriented towards equality or rights (which I call women's rights activism), as well as activism by women oriented towards the goal of building an Islamic society.
3. *Shari'ah* law is the body of law in the Islamic tradition, which is based on the Qur'an and the Sunnah. There are different schools of interpretation of *shari'ah* law. *Shari'ah* law encompasses both religious practices as well as matters addressed by secular law, including crime and economics.
4. Some of the data and quotes in this article are also used in a longer work-in-progress which examines the debates about pornography and polygamy and their relationship to globalization.
5. This article is based on an ethnographic study of women in four organizations, including PKS and Fatayat, which I undertook between 2002 and 2008. The research was centred in Jakarta at the headquarters of the organizations. However, I also spent time with women from smaller Jakarta branch offices of PKS and Fatayat, and visited their offices in a smaller city in East Java. The organizations in this study have encouraged me to use their real names. All individual names have been changed.
6. Fatayat has chapters in nearly every town and city in the country. While the leaders of urban branches of Fatayat often are university graduates, the majority of women in the organization are lower class and are not university educated. My research is thus most generalizable to leaders of Fatayat in other Indonesian cities.
7. Geertz (1963) delineated four *aliran*: traditionalist (NU), modernist, nationalist, communist. Most Indonesians would categorize PKS as part of the modernist camp. There is an ongoing debate among scholars of Indonesia about the relevance of *aliran* in contemporary Indonesia. I find the concept to be overly deterministic. Moreover, not only does PKS attract members who are from the broader NU milieu, but for a variety of reasons the category of traditionalist no longer seems appropriate for many NU members. What I wish to emphasize is the demographic similarity of the women leaders of PKS and Fatayat — I see their middle class *habitus* as a major force in shaping their subjectivities, while their educational and activist trajectories help to account for their

ideological differences. See also Machmudi (2008) for an argument that the traditionalist/modern divide in Indonesian Islam has lessened in importance in recent years.
8. See <http://www.library.ohiou.edu/sea/blog/wp-content/uploads/2008/10/ruu-pornografi-4-september-2008.pdf> for the text of the bill. An English translation is available at <http://www.indonesiamatters.com/2474/porn-laws/> (accessed 19 May 2010).
9. Wahhabism is the name for an eighteenth century movement for the purification of Islam in what is now Saudi Arabia. The sect advocated a return to the practices of early Islam, rejecting innovations. The term is often used to describe a puritanical or extremely conservative form of Islam.
10. Pancasila is the official philosophy of the Indonesian state, which stipulates belief in one God, as well as democracy and social justice as the foundations of the nation. Following this philosophy, Indonesia recognizes six official religions: Islam, Protestantism, Catholicism, Buddhism, Hinduism, and Confucianism. As such, by referring to the notion of "Pancasila State", my informant is invoking inclusiveness and tolerance with regard to religion.

References

Allen, Pam. "Challenging Diversity: Indonesia's Anti-Pornography Bill". *Asian Studies Review*, vol. 31 (2007): 101–15.

Asad, Talal. *The Idea of an Anthropology of Islam*, Occasional Papers. Washington, DC,: Center for Contemporary Arab Studies, Georgetown, 1986.

Brenner, Suzanne. "Reconstructing Self and Society: Javanese Muslim Women and the Veil". *American Ethnologist* 23, no. 4 (1996): 673–97.

———. "On the Public Intimacy of the New Order: Images of Women in the Popular Indonesian Print Media". *Indonesia* 67 (1999): 13–37.

———. "Islam and Gender Politics in Late New Order Indonesia". In *Spirited Politics: Religion and Public Life in Contemporary Southeast Asia*. Ithaca, NY: Cornell University Southeast Asia Program, 2005.

———. "Private Moralities in the Public Sphere: Demoratization, Islam, and Gender in Indonesia". *American Anthropologist* 113, no. 3 (2011): 478–90.

Bush, Robin. "Regional 'Sharia' Regulations in Indonesia: Anomaly or Symptom?" In *Expressing Islam: Religious Life and Politics in Indonesia*, edited by Greg Fealy and Sally White. Singapore: Institute of Southeast Asian Studies, 2008.

Deeb, Lara. *An Enchanted Modern: Gender and Public Piety in Shi'I Lebanon*. Princeton: Princeton University Press, 2006.

Geertz, Clifford. *Peddlers and Princes: Social Development and Economic Change in Two Indonesian Towns*. Chicago: University of Chicago Press, 1963.

Gelling, Peter. "Editor of Playboy Indonesia is Acquitted". *New York Times*, 5 April 2007.
Gole, Nilufer. "Islam in Public: New Visibilities and New Imaginaries". *Public Culture* 14, no. 1 (2002): 173–90.
Guerin, Bill. "No Playmates for Indonesian Playboys". Asia Times Online, 10 February 2006 <http://www.atimes.com/atimes/Southeast_Asia/HB10Ae01.html> (accessed 19 May 2010).
Hadiz, Veddie R. and Richard Robison. *Reorganizing Power in Indonesia: The Politics of Oligarchy in an Age of Markets*. London: Routledge, 2004.
Harvey, Rachel. "Playboy Sparks Indonesia Porn Row". BBC Online, 2006 <http://news.bbc.co.uk/2/hi/asia-pacific/4689054.stm> (accessed 19 May 2010).
Hefner, Robert. *Civil Islam: Muslims and Democratization in Indonesia*. Princeton: Princeton University Press, 2000.
Jones, Gavin. "The Flight from Marriage in Southeast and East Asia". *Journal of Comparative Family Studies* 36, no. 1 (2005): 93–119.
Kligman, Gail and Susan Gal. *The Politics of Gender after Socialism: A Comparative-Historical Essay*. New Jersey: Princeton University Press, 2000.
Kosoemawiria, Edith. "March for Diversity". Qantara.de, 2006 <http://en.qantara.de/webcom/show_article.php/_c-478/_nr-442/i.html> (accessed 19 May 2010).
Machmudi, Yon. *Islamizing Indonesia: The Rise of Jemaah Tarbiyah and the Prosperous Justice Party*. Australian National University E-Press, Islam in Southeast Asia Series, 2008.
Mahmood, Saba. *The Politics of Piety: The Islamic Revival and the Feminist Subject*. Princeton, NJ: Princeton University Press, 2005.
Mernissi, Fatima. *Beyond the Veil: Male-Female Dynamics in Modern Muslim Society*. Indiana University Press, 1987.
Mir-Hosseini, Ziba. "Muslim Women's Quest for Equality: Between Islamic Law and Feminism". *Critical Inquiry* 32, no. 4 (2006): 629–45.
Moaddel, Mansour. *Islamic Modernism, Nationalism, and Fundamentalism: Episode and Discourse*. Chicago: University of Chicago Press, 2005.
Moghadam, Valentine. *Identity Politics and Women: Cultural Reassertions and Feminisms in International Perspective*. Boulder, CO: Westview, 2004.
Perlez, Jane. "Playboy Tests Tolerance in Indonesia". *New York Times*, 24 July 2006.
Rancangan Undang Undang Republik Indonesia Tentang Pornografi. <http://www.library.ohiou.edu/sea/blog/wp-content/uploads/2008/10/ruu-pornografi-4-september-2008.pdf> (accessed 19 May 2010).
Ricklefs, Merle. *A History of Modern Indonesia since c.1200*, rev. ed. Stanford, CA: Stanford University Press, 2008.

Rinaldo, Rachel. "Envisioning the Nation: Women Activists, Religion, and the Public Sphere in Indonesia". *Social Forces* 86, no. 4 (2008): 1781–804.

———. "Muslim Women, Moral Visions: Globalization and Gender Controversies in Indonesia". *Qualitative Sociology* 34, no. 1 (2011): 539–60.

Roy, Olivier. *Globalized Islam: The Search for a New Ummah*. New York: Columbia University Press, 2004.

Sidel, John. *Riots, Pogroms, Jihad: Religious Violence in Indonesia*. New York: Cornell University Press, 2006.

Smith-Hefner, Nancy. "Javanese Women and the Veil in Post-Suharto Indonesia". *Journal of Asian Studies* 66 (2007): 389–420.

Tempo Interactive. "Tayangan Mistik di Televisi Tidak Ada Nilai Positifnya". 14 May 2003 <http://www.tempo.co.id/hg/nasional/2003/05/14/brk,20030514-15,id.html> (accessed 19 May 2010).

Van Doorn-Harder, Pieternella. *Women Shaping Islam: Reading the Qur'an in Indonesia*. Chicago: University of Illinois Press, 2006.

Yuval-Davis, Nira. *Gender and Nation*. London: University of East London Press, 1997.

PART V
Muslim Minorities

11

MALAY MUSLIMS AND THE THAI-BUDDHIST STATE: CONFRONTATION, ACCOMMODATION AND DISENGAGEMENT[1]

Ernesto H. Braam

The Malay Muslims in the deep south of Thailand have a long history of asserting their identity against the assimilating force of a dominant Buddhist worldview. Buddhist Siam and its successor, Thailand, have had significant success in assimilating the wide variety of ethnic groups within its borders, including the Chinese, Lao, Khmer and others, into a form of national Thai identity. The only group that has successfully withstood the assimilation policies is the Malay community in the country's southernmost provinces of Pattani, Yala and Narathiwat.[2] The greater the pressure that was put on to this community to surrender its explicit Malay identity, the more it has searched for — and found — ways to preserve its identity.

Historically, relations between the old Kingdom of Patani[3] (the past incarnation of the three provinces, parts of Songkhla province and northern Malaysia) and Ayutthaya — later Bangkok[4] — regularly led to conflict. Whenever the Burmese attacked the Siamese capital Ayutthaya, Patani would take advantage of its distraction and wrestle itself free of Siam's yoke. When the Ayutthaya kings (and sometimes queens) finally managed to push back the invading Burmese armies, they would send punitive expeditions to the South to bring the Malay vassal state back under their control. The Anglo-Siamese agreement of 1909 codified this conflict and left the Malay Muslims in Siam, as it were, on the wrong side of the border, separating them from the Malay community in what is now Malaysia, with which they share language, religion and family ties.

For many decades, Malay-Muslims in South Thailand have been discriminated against, and were considered to be *khaek* (guests or visitors) in Thailand. The height of the application of assimilationist policies towards Malay Muslims is generally agreed to have been during the governments of Prime Minister Phibunsongkhram (1938–44 and 1948–57). This nationalist leader glorified the Thai race, changed the name of the country from Siam to Thailand and left no space for minority identities like the Malay Muslims (and the Chinese).[5] A host of forceful measures were put into effect. Speaking Malay was forbidden and there was strong pressure to change family names into Thai-sounding names (Gilquin 2005, p. 73). Sarongs were forbidden and Western-style dress, such as long trousers and hats, were compulsory (Forbes 1982, p. 1059). The popular habit of chewing betel and areca nut was banned. A measure that infuriated the Malay Muslims was the abolition of *shari'a* law regarding marriage, divorce and inheritance, as well as the function of the Islamic judge. The Thai Buddhist legal system replaced the existing Islamic laws. Thanet Aphornsuvan differs from most other scholars in that he dates the intensification of the assimilation policies to right after the founding of the constitutional monarchy in 1932, before Phibunsongkhram came to power (Apornsuvan 2008, pp. 92–93). He states that the new regime consolidated and unified the Thai nation state "based upon the Central Thai imagination". This regime "turned to a policy of cultural assimilation to stabilize its power and control over the politically active and culturally self-conscious north-eastern and southern regions of the country" (ibid., p. 93). The provincial administration was reorganized and Thai officials took over the positions of local Malay rulers in the South. By not attributing the harsher periods of assimilation solely to Phibunsongkhram, Thanet creates a sense of historical continuity.

Many of the more insensitive measures aimed at assimilating the Malay Muslims have been abandoned over the years, as the Thai Government realized that they were counterproductive. However, in everyday life there are still instances in which there is no recognition of the Malay Muslim identity. This is, for example, the case when civil servants and locally elected officials who are Malay Muslim have to participate in state rituals. Official Thai ceremonies have strong Buddhist overtones and this puts Muslims who have to interact with or are part of official Thai institutions in a position of conflicting loyalties. Those who object to explicit Buddhist elements of such ceremonies are easily portrayed as disloyal to the Thai state or even to the King. In many official ceremonies, like the Queen's birthday, attendants have to stand in front of a picture of the King and pay respect to it by clasping their hands together in a *wai*.[6] According to interviewed Malay dignitaries, Islam does not allow this form of paying respect to a picture. In their view, it is a clearly Buddhist aspect of the ceremony. A Malay Muslim politician at the national level added that to even talk about this matter is dangerous as it might be interpreted as disrespect for the King. He also said: "Formally, you are free to express any religion, but in practice not."[7] The law on *lese majesté* and its enforcement are notoriously severe. For a Malay Muslim, prosecution for such an offence might be aggravated by the charge of separatism, which could form a lethal combination.

Today, the Malay Muslim community continues to maintain an identity distinct from the rest of the Thai population. At the local level this identity is expressed in education, language and religion. When pressure from the Thai state becomes too great and threatens to quash the cherished Malay-Muslim identity, national aspirations sometimes find a voice through violent resistance. Another, at times successful, way to resist this pressure, and even to enhance the socio-economic position of the community, has been through the electoral process and party politics. There are different approaches to analysing the outcomes of such friction between Malay Muslims and the Thai-Buddhist state. Imtiyaz Yusuf identified six types of politico-religious influences on Thai Muslims, focusing on their integrationist or separatist attitudes towards the Thai state.[8] My analysis concentrates on how such friction, experienced not only in the formal political sphere, but also at the level of everyday life, leads to different forms of outcomes. In this chapter I examine three main outcomes, namely, violent confrontations, accommodation and disengagement. In reality, people do not sit in neatly defined categories. I will not analyse each and every political or religious group, but use the ones I consider to be most prominent to illustrate the different forms of outcomes. As a general remark I would like to echo the words of Snow and Marshall, who emphasized "the extent to which religious and political factors are frequently intertwined and should therefore be considered together" (1984, p. 146), an observation which I consider very much applicable to the Malay Muslims of the Deep South.

The methodology of my research is mainly qualitative. I have conducted in-depth interviews, attended meetings (sometimes confidential) and made observations during numerous long and short visits to South Thailand since 2004. I have also made use of secondary sources where events lie in the remote past, or to back up my empirical findings from a factual or conceptual angle.

VIOLENT CONFRONTATIONS

The feature of Thai state/Malay minority contention that receives most attention in journalistic and academic circles is the violent expression of this confrontation. Acts of violence attributed to separatist groups or to government-affiliated actors make headlines in newspapers and monopolize public attention. I admit that my own interest in South Thailand started when violence escalated in 2004, while working in Bangkok.[9] Therefore, it is expedient to start my analysis with an empirically based interpretation of some of the most prominent acts of violence that have been committed in the Deep South since the escalation of violence in 2004. On that day, there were coordinated and simultaneous attacks against an army base, police posts and twenty schools which were burned. The action that shocked the Thaksin government most was the theft of more than 400 guns from the army base in Narathiwat province. Thaksin responded with harsh measures, sending more troops to the South and imposing martial law. This marked the beginning of an ongoing spate of disappearances and extrajudicial killings of persons suspected of belonging to separatist groups. The South had long been an area plagued by violence in a variety of forms, but January 2004 marked a significant escalation of this violence. In August 2011 the death toll stood at 4,846 and the number of injured people at 7,995.[10] About 60 per cent of the dead were Muslim and 40 per cent Buddhist. For the injured it was the other way around. Half of the victims were ordinary citizens, in declining order followed by so-called insurgents, military personnel, heads of sub-districts and villages, police officers, village defence volunteers, civil servants, teachers, and others.

The Thai public, political players and the media have oversimplified the background of the violence and have tended to frame it in terms of a Malay-Muslim struggle for independence and counter-violence by the Thai state security apparatus. After 9/11, some security experts have applied the models they developed for interpreting violent jihadi movements in other parts of the world to the conflict in South Thailand. In this effort to make sense of the violence, subtle and less subtle differences in motivation, character and scope have been overlooked, whether deliberately or out of ignorance. Within the scope of this chapter violent confrontation is framed as one of the outcomes of the friction between Malay Muslims in South Thailand and the Thai-Buddhist state. The aim here is not to give a comprehensive analysis of each and every incident in which armed force was used in the South. Rather, this is an attempt to interpret a limited number of high-profile violent incidents. At first sight, the many incidents since 2004 may look like a string of beads connected by a single narrative. This is a tempting concoction, served up by many analysts and gladly imbibed by an unwitting audience. Upon closer inspection, the beads do not look so similar, and may not even fit the same string. I will focus on three unique incidents of violence, which, in my view, have entirely different characters. All three, namely Krue Se, Tak Bai and Al Furqan, have added new dimensions to the discourse. While my interpretations may not be conclusive, I do hope to draw attention to the diversity of the violent incidents.

Krue Se

An event that defies reason most clearly, is the widely publicized and debated Krue Se incident on 28 April 2004.[11] At dawn hundreds of men conducted synchronized attacks against eleven police and army posts across the provinces of Pattani, Yala and Songkhla. On that day, 105 militants died, thirty-two of them inside the historical Krue Se mosque. A further five security personnel and one civilian were also killed. The character of this incident is very different from other violent events before and after. Strangely, the insurgents, organized in small groups of young men with a middle-aged leader,[12] attacked well-armed policemen and soldiers with nothing more than machetes and the occasional gun. In Pattani, thirty-two of the assailants retreated into the Krue Se mosque. There, they used a loudspeaker to incite the local population, which was gathering at some distance, to take up arms against the Thai Government. Thai security forces laid a siege around the mosque and attacked it at the end of the day, killing all inside, possibly after some had already surrendered. The

Krue Se Mosque, South Thailand. Photograph courtesy of the author.

guardian of the mosque, Hajji Niseng, gave an eyewitness account when I met him six weeks later.[13] This underlined the extraordinary mindset of these insurgents. The group of men that arrived at the mosque after sunset on 27 April told him they wanted to meditate in the mosque and die there. The next morning, after killing two policemen nearby and retreating to the mosque, these men repeated their wish to die for jihad[14] against the security forces. They died indeed. Afterwards there was speculation as to why these militants seemed so fearless, and what possessed them to attack well-armed security forces with machetes. Growing evidence indicates that (at least some of) the militants believed they were protected by supernatural powers. Before the attacks they had consumed "sacred water" and received magic spells which were supposed to protect them against bullets. This conviction of invincibility and the mysticism of the rituals that had been performed before the insurgents attacked, pointed in the direction of a cult or sect. The rituals are reminiscent of Sufi practices. There are similarities with the mysticism of armed sects like the former God's Army in Burma or the more brutal Lord's Resistance Army in northern Uganda. Similarly, followers of the Karen twin brothers Johnny and Luther Htoo, only ten years old when the sect was established, believed they were invulnerable to bullets and landmines.[15]

Another element of the Krue Se incident that caught the attention of observers was the thirty-four-page pamphlet "Berjihad Di Patani",[16] which was reportedly found on the bodies of some of the insurgents. It contains a long and detailed call, full of Qur'anic references, to jihad in order to push the Thai authorities out of the Malay Muslim provinces and (re)establish the (Islamic) Kingdom of Patani.[17] As such, the Krue Se clash can be seen as an extremely violent expression of the desire of insurgents to expulse Thai rule from the South. Some security experts interpret this further as being part of global jihad. But this assertion of a global link is not supported by any evidence.[18] The motives, goals and methods are very local. The violent and, most notably, suicidal character of the incident, remains largely unexplained. In the Thai context such a suicidal mission may be unique, but there are striking parallels with for example the Acehnese wars of the nineteenth and early twentieth century. During the resistance struggle of the Acehnese against Dutch colonial rule, local *ulama* used an epic of the war, the "Hikajat Prang Sabi" (Story of the Holy War), in order to rouse the community to fight a jihad against the Dutch.[19] Like the "Berjihad Di Patani", this work is brimming with Qur'anic references and it too calls on the population to sacrifice their lives and become martyrs. In both Aceh and Patani those fighting the jihad and dying for it presumably go to paradise. The Acehnese were obviously fighting Dutch colonialists, but the "Berjihad Di Patani" also refers to the Thai authorities as "colonialists", who oppress the local Muslims, plunder their wealth, curb their rights and freedom, and sully their religion and culture (Gunaratna, Acharya and Chua 2005, p. 120). In the first four decades of the twentieth century there was a spate of suicide attacks in Aceh (Siegel 2000, pp. 82–83). In order to go to paradise, an individual Acehnese would go to a place where he knew he would find a European and then slay him with a knife. Usually he was captured or killed himself. These individual suicide attacks and also the larger scale fights with the Dutch colonial army share with the Krue Se clash similarities in motives and methods applied. However, the case of Krue Se is not so clear cut, because the claim of invincibility does not concur with the desire to die in a jihad. You cannot have it both ways.

Nidhi Aeusrivongse (2004) offered a new sociological perspective on the Krue Se clash when he described it as a Millenarian revolt. In

Thai, the uprisings of what he calls "small people", are referred to as "kabot chaonaa", literally "peasant revolts". Nidhi draws a parallel with other millenarian uprisings by "small people" (peasants, rubber tapping labourers, fishermen, indigenous people, etc.) and states that they revolt against changes coming from the outside which affect their lives and which they do not understand. They attack the enemy's symbols (like police officers) and lack a sophisticated ideology, holding on to "religious beliefs that are not those of the learned religious scholar" (ibid.). Nidhi speaks of a large-scale social movement, and points to the fact that the clash took place on the same day as the Dusun Nyior revolt exactly fifty-six years before, which he considers a millenarian revolt.[20] However, since the Krue Se clash, no similar attacks have taken place. As such, except for the rural background of most attackers, nothing else indicates that this was indeed a revolt by "small people".

Tak Bai

Altogether very different from the Krue Se incident is the incident in Tak Bai in Narathiwat province during Ramadan,[21] on 25 October 2004. On that day, a large crowd gathered to protest against the arrest of six village volunteers who were accused of selling their guns to separatists. The crowd grew in size to hundreds of people and at some point shots were fired, which killed at least six protesters. About 1,370 demonstrators were detained, piled up on top of each other in three or four layers, and transported to an army base, in a five-hour drive. Upon arrival, seventy-eight persons turned out to have died from suffocation or inflicted injuries. The National Reconciliation Commission concluded that senior military officers were responsible for this tragedy. This report stated that the protest was organized and that some of its leaders provoked violence from the security forces.

The Tak Bai incident, more than Krue Se, infuriated the Malay-Muslim community, especially after pictures and videos of the brutal treatment of the detainees were distributed and appeared on the Internet. Also, the victims of this incident were viewed as innocent demonstrators and bystanders. Following this tragedy, a series of revenge killings took place, starting a new phase that escalated the level of the conflict. Prior to Tak Bai, it was mainly the police that had a bad reputation among the security forces. The Thai police had an image among the Malay Muslims of being corrupt, rude and dangerous. Mothers used the police as bogeymen to get their children to be obedient. On the other hand, soldiers were seen as disciplined and not so corrupted. The image of the army drastically deteriorated after the Tak Bai massacre. Prime Minister Thaksin lost any support he still had among Malay Muslims, not least because of his praise for the way the army handled the demonstration. His remarks, that many people had lost their lives due to fasting during Ramadan, added insult to injury. Muslim politicians who supported Thaksin or were part of his government lost all credibility among the Malay Muslim community and were seen as traitors by many.

Al Furqan

Yet another type of incident took place on 8 June 2009, in a small village in Chok Airong district in Narathiwat province. During evening prayer at Al-Furqan mosque, an estimated number of ten gunmen shot at Malay Muslims, killing eleven instantly, including the Imam, and wounding more than ten others. One more victim died later. Deputy Prime Minister Suthep Taungsuban and Army Chief General Anupong Paojinda were quick to state, even before an investigation was conducted, that the government was not involved in the attack. Academic and Senator Worawit Bahru, a Malay Muslim, responded to the press, saying that no conclusions could be drawn before an investigation was concluded. Another academic said anonymously that the army was not pleased with such criticism.[22] Generally, the Malay Muslims thought these killings had been committed by the army or by a Buddhist militia. Not long before this incident, a Buddhist was killed in the same area, and the shooting in Al Furqan mosque could have been an act of revenge. In the ensuing climate of fear and suspicion, speculation was rife. One theory, which was supported by some military officers, claimed that separatists were the perpetrators, wanting to create more antagonism towards the Thai Government.[23] Another theory pointed to the presence in the mosque of a group of seven followers of the Islamic missionary movement Tablighi Jama'at. The separatists were supposedly angry at this movement because of its apolitical stance. In August, warrants were issued for the arrest of a number of Thai Buddhists who belonged to a village militia, which was trained and armed by the Thai security forces, in order to defend Buddhist villages. This incident has further deepened the wedge between Thai Buddhists and Malay Muslims in the South.

Apart from the three above-mentioned incidents, there are numerous others, involving bomb attacks, shootings and even a number of beheadings.

In several instances, simple pamphlets and drawings portraying the Thai Government, particularly Prime Minister Thaksin at the time, as an oppressor of the Malay Muslims have been found at the scene of such violent incidents. However, in the vast majority of cases no written motivation or list of demands has been left behind nor were these attacks claimed by any particular group. The media and some researchers ascribe these violent incidents to separatist insurgents (McCargo 2008, p. 7). The Thai security services, too, blame these attacks on separatists, and during an interview a senior police officer voiced this conviction, stating that the separatists want to establish the republic of Patani Darussalam based on Islam, and exclusively for Malays.[24] The territory of such a state would include the Thai provinces of Pattani, Yala, Narathiwat, as well as Satun and (parts of) Songkhla. The main militant organization is identified as Barisan Revolusi Nasional-Coordinate (BRN-C). The International Crisis Group surmises that this organization "spearheaded the resurgence of separatism in the early 1990s" (International Crisis Group 2007, p. 6). Two other militant organizations are the Patani United Liberation Organization (PULO), which has the longest history, and Gerakan Mujahidin Islam Patani (GMIP). There are several other militant groups, of which McCargo (2008, pp. 168–75) provides an excellent overview. Some explanations of the violence focus on the economic situation in the South, applying the Relative Deprivation Theory.[25] Yet another explanation, often expressed by local Malay Muslims, states that some violent incidents are committed by the security forces themselves. Among others, these theories mention police-army rivalry, competition for government budgets, and turf wars over the spoils of illegal trade in the border areas. While these explanations may have some validity in a number of cases, I agree with McCargo that in many cases the most plausible reason for the violence can be found in "separatist aspirations" (McCargo 2008, p. 7). Those Malay Muslims who support or condone such violence, do so on the basis of experiences and the perception that their identity as a distinct group cannot be safeguarded within the current administrative and constitutional set-up of Thailand. Violence is the most extreme manifestation of the friction between Malay Muslims and the Thai Buddhist state.

The almost daily violence in the southern provinces has created a situation whereby Malay Muslims, particularly those with a public profile, are forced to choose sides. Some locally elected Malay Muslim officials sympathize with the militant groups, and others have chosen the side of the Thai Government. From interviews with local people it appears that these groups have a strong presence in the countryside of the southern provinces, particularly in Narathiwat.[26] The continuous attacks against anyone who is perceived to have some relationship with the authorities and the harsh measures taken by the security forces have created a climate of fear and suspicion. Many people who have the means are leaving the South in response to the violence, especially Thai Buddhists. The biggest fear of the Thai and Western governments is that foreign jihadi groups would get involved in the struggle in South Thailand. So far, there are no indications that this has actually happened, although Jemaah Islamiyah (JI) has made some overtures, which were turned down by Malay-Muslim separatists.[27] They conduct a Malay nationalist struggle — in their eyes — to "liberate" their lands from "foreign oppression". They do not want international terrorists, with a different agenda, to get involved.[28]

POLITICAL PARTICIPATION AND ACCOMMODATION

The media and most researchers focus on the explicit and violent rejection of Thai-Buddhist dominance over Malay-Muslim lands. Non-violent political action is less visible to outsiders. There is a long history of political participation of Malay Muslims within the Thai political system, aimed at improving the position of their community. This section analyses the main attempts in recent history to organize Malay-Muslim influence in representative politics, and the extent to which the Thai polity has been able and willing to allow space for such a venture. It is important to assess what benefit this process of mutual accommodation has yielded to the Malay-Muslim community.[29]

Participation in Electoral Politics

In modern Thai politics, the most successful Malay-Muslim political grouping or faction was Wahdah, which means "unity" in Arabic. The Wahdah faction was formed in 1986 by Malay-Muslim politicians and religious leaders from the South.[30] Wahdah wanted the concerns of Muslims, especially Malay Muslims, to be taken seriously by the vestiges of power in Bangkok. At the top of its agenda were the improvement of education for Muslims, the promotion of economic development and protection, and the preservation of the "Islamic way of life" (Yusuf 1998). Malay Muslims had, for many years, supported the Democrat Party. For a long time, this party had been the "natural home" for Muslims, claiming it wanted to reform Thailand into a modern society where minority groups would have equal rights. However, it seemed to have taken the "Muslim vote" for granted, rather similar to complaints in the United States against the pre-Obama Democratic Party concerning the "African American vote". In the 1988 parliamentary elections, Wahdah members won six seats in the provinces of Pattani, Yala and Narathiwat, but none of their MPs were appointed to ministerial posts by the Democrat Party–led government. Wahdah politicians felt disenfranchised and left the Democrat Party. In an interview, a school director and local politician in Yala province articulated the general sentiment that Malay Muslims felt cheated by the Democrat Party, which promised them positions (in government) but ultimately did not deliver.[31] Wahdah saw itself as an independent grouping (Yusuf 2007, p. 16) trying to win as many votes as possible in the predominantly Malay-Muslim provinces in the South, and then claiming cabinet seats (Bajunid 1999, p. 290). In its view, this strategy offered the best opportunity for achieving its goals. But this was only possible by allying itself with a strong Thai political party. When the alliance with the democrats yielded no results, they started casting about for a new partner. From the early 1990s Wahdah joined forces with the New Aspiration Party (NAP) led by former army chief, General Chavalit Yongchaiyudh, which was a coalition partner in several governments, among them the cabinet of Democrat Chuan Leekpai.[32] It yielded the sought-after dividends, and in the following years Wahdah members were appointed to several cabinet posts.[33]

Thai politics is highly personalized and the name and fame of individual politicians are often more important than the party they represent. In the cradle of Wahdah stood a number of influential Muslim politicians (Bajunid 1999, p. 226), among whom Den Tohmeena was the most prominent. His family history is closely connected with post–World War II events in South Thailand, and, indeed, the Tohmeena family helped shape modern Malay-Muslim history. Den's father was the famous Haji Sulong bin Abdul Kadir, president of the Islamic Council of Pattani, who on 24 August 1947 presented a list of seven demands to the government of then Siam. The demands included a locally elected governor, proportionate representation of Malay Muslims in the local government, and other measures aimed at preserving Malay-Muslim identity and countering the official policy of Siamization (Syukri 2005, pp. 93–94). The demands were not very different from what can be heard from Malay Muslims today, more than sixty years later. Haji Sulong was extremely adept at understanding and articulating the aspirations of the Malay Muslims in South Thailand. This capacity and his (religious) authority within local society — centred in that typically Malay network of *pondoks* and Islamic councils — made him the ideal representative of his people to challenge Thai authority. It was exactly this powerful combination of characteristics which sent a chill down the spine of local Thai officials and soon caught the attention of Bangkok. In the morning of 16 January 1948, Siamese police arrested Haji Sulong, and he along with several other local leaders were sentenced, for the offence of sedition, to three years and then four years and eight months in Bang Kwang prison in Bangkok.[34] A period of oppression of the Malay Muslim voice had started, escalating in the Dusun Nyior clash on 28 April of the same year. Released in 1952, Haji Sulong and his eldest son Ahmad were summoned by the police in Songkhla two years later. They reported to the police station on 13 August 1954 and were never seen again, rumoured to have been murdered under still-unexplained circumstances. Haji Sulong's disappearance contributed to his myth and he continues to live on in the minds of Malay Muslims as a martyr and source of inspiration.

Den Tohmeena rode in part on the prestige of his father, which greatly contributed to his own political success (McCargo 2008, p. 63). He went on to become an MP in the Thai parliament, Deputy Minister of Public Health and Deputy Interior Minister, and since 2000, a senator. The security forces have accused him of supporting the separatist cause. Besides Den, there was another Muslim politician who left a big imprint on the Thai political landscape. It can be argued that Wan Muhammad Nor Matta, or Wan Nor for short, from Yala province, was the most powerful person within Wahdah and benefitted most from its rise. In fact, the emergence of Wahdah could not have taken place without Wan Nor, and he could not have made such an extraordinary political career without Wahdah. Wan Nor took over the leadership of Wahdah in 1995 when Den Tohmeena (temporarily) lost his seat in parliament. He held several cabinet posts, including the powerful portfolio of the Interior Ministry.[35]

Wahdah's decline started when it stayed on after NAP joined the first cabinet under Prime Minister Thaksin Shinawatra in 2001 and merged with Thaksin's Thai Rak Thai (TRT) a year later. Initially, Thaksin's special assistance to Thailand's poor was well received by a large portion of the predominantly rural population in the Deep South. The 30 baht health scheme (about USD 0.90) — providing universal healthcare for only 30 baht per medical treatment — and the one million baht village fund (about US$30,000), which enabled each village to disburse cheap loans to its residents, for the first time gave the vast underprivileged masses in Thai society the sense that they mattered, and empowered them. A farmer in Pattani province told me in 2005: "Chuan Leekpai (former Democrat leader and Prime Minister) understands Muslims, but concerning the economy and drugs, I like Thaksin".[36] In February 2003, Thaksin unleashed his war on drugs, which was particularly vicious in the South and took hundreds of lives through extrajudicial killings of "drug suspects" and anyone else who had the misfortune to be put on a blacklist. The iron fist which Thaksin applied in South Thailand (after the escalation of violence in 2004) to any action ascribed to militant Malay Muslims, also turned public opinion in the South against his government. The event that all locals mentioned in private conversations as the point of no return for Thaksin's credibility is the Tak Bai massacre on 25 October 2004. In the parliamentary elections of 2005, Wahdah lost all its seats. The then mother party Thai Rak Thai did not win a single seat in the Deep South, though nationwide it captured 377 of the 500 parliamentary seats in a landslide victory (Ockey 2008, p. 153). Wahdah politicians who had stayed on in Thaksin's cabinet, such as Wan Nor, were branded as traitors to the Malay-Muslim cause. They were in fact caught between a rock and a hard place as several Wahdah politicians were also being accused of supporting separatism. In a time span of seventeen years, Malay-Muslim politics saw the rise and demise of an influential faction in national politics. Though this had benefitted a number of politicians, the record of achievement for the Malay-Muslim community was not unequivocally positive. On the one hand, the participation of Wahdah in the government resulted in several developmental projects being focused on Malay-Muslim areas,[37] and under the Thaksin administration, subsidies to South Thailand, as to other parts of the country, had increased. On the other hand, participation in government did not increase the influence of the local Malay-Muslim community concerning its own destiny; nor did this community receive any safeguards for the preservation of Malay-Muslim identity. Perhaps Ibrahim Syukri (2005, p. 100) had a point when he said that "democracy made in Siam is not fit for the Malay people" and that "Siamese democracy apparently reaches only the area of Bangkok and the territory surrounding it". But as Thanet Aphornsuvan (2008, p. 103) argues, elections gave Malay

Muslims another public space to express themselves. This, in his view, reduced violent resistance to the Thai state.

A major event in recent Thai history which drastically changed the Thai political landscape was the 2006 *coup d'état* that ousted Thaksin Shinawatra. On the surface, the coup of 19 September offered hope for a peaceful turn of the Malay-Muslim saga. Along with Thaksin, it seemed the hard-line approach had been discarded, and the coup leader, General Sonthi Boonyaratkalin, being a Muslim himself (but not Malay), would surely show more sensitivity towards the Malay-Muslim community. Moreover, the new Prime Minister of the interim government and privy councillor, General Surayud Chulanont, issued an apology for the Tak Bai massacre committed under the Thaksin regime. Unfortunately, these positive signs were not followed up with any structural measures by the government. The rhetoric turned out to have no more meaning than the millions of origami cranes that Thaksin had dropped out of aeroplanes over the South as a goodwill gesture.[38] In fact, the higher expectations of the new government made the disappointment all the more poignant. Soon after, violence increased significantly.

The polarization which took place within Thai society after TRT, with its far-reaching reform agenda, was elected into power in 2001, also affected Wahdah. As a counterweight to Wahdah, some Democrat MPs formed a faction called "glum Darussalam".[39] This faction became obsolete because it lost its direct opponent when Wahdah left TRT following the anti-Thaksin coup of 2006. TRT's executives, including Wan Nor, were banned from politics for five years. More recently, attempts were made to emulate the (initial) success of Wahdah in unifying the Malay Muslims and giving them a voice at the national level. A new and somewhat promising initiative was the establishment in November 2008 of a faction called Matuphum, which means motherland in Thai.[40] The Election Commission of Thailand approved the name six months later, on 23 May 2009. Three former Wahdah members, MPs Arifin Utarasin and Najmuddin Umar from Narathiwat, and MP Farida Sulaiman[41] from the northeastern province of Surin, were founding members of Matuphum. In fact, they were looking for a new political home after the successor to TRT, the Thaksin-backed People's Power Party (Phak Palang Prachachon, PPP), was disbanded by the Constitutional Court. Former PPP MPs were repositioning themselves and either reviving old parties, joining existing ones, or establishing new parties. The bulk of them joined the new Peua Thai ("For Thai") party.

However, these three Muslim MPs wanted to dissociate themselves from Thaksin's political legacy, which was perceived negatively in the South. They knocked on the door of Peua Paendin (literally "For the Land/Soil"[42]), established in 2007 by former TRT members and former TRT opponents, but they were turned away.[43] Their journey through political "no-man's land" ended when they joined the revived Rasadorn (People) party. This party was revived by two dissidents from Peua Paendin who did not, like the rest of the party, support Democrat Party leader Abhisit Vejjajiva's bid to become Prime Minister. The three Muslim politicians later also left this party because one of its leaders, Vatana Asavahame, was on the run from the law, after being sentenced to ten years' jail for corruption. Attempts were made to get former Wahdah leader Wan Nor to participate in Matuphum, but he was not yet ready to support it, as his brother, Sukarno Mata, was still active in Peua Paendin.

Several politicians I interviewed encouraged former coup leader, General Sonthi Boonyaratkalin, to lead the new Muslim faction. In fact, a number of politicians from other parties indicated that they would join Matuphum if Sonthi became its leader. Initially, he became the party's advisor and said he was focusing his attention on trying to obtain a PhD in Political Science from Ramkhamhaeng University in Bangkok.[44] Peua Paendin leader Pracha Phromnok made some overtures in the direction of Matuphum, stating that his eight MPs might join the party if his own party was disbanded by the Constitutional Court for electoral fraud.[45] At the same time, Mathuphum was aiming to win twenty parliamentary seats at the next election.[46]

When General Sonthi finally accepted the leadership of Matuphum on 18 November 2009, this immediately gave the party credibility and publicity beyond the Malay-Muslim community. Several of his former classmates from the army academy even said that they would join Matuphum. Sonthi denied that he staged the coup in 2006 in order to pursue a political career. He wanted to be "a politician who has integrity and morality".[47]

But given General Sonthi's record so far, he and Malay-Muslim politicians seem to make for strange bedfellows. As army chief, he had ordered more troops to the South and took a hard-line stance regarding insurgents. As a coup leader, he discarded the constitution and was very reluctant to lift martial law and restore parliamentary democracy. Whether Sonthi will manage to find a solution to the unrest in the South remains to be seen. In the July 2011 general elections, Matuphum only won two seats.

Those who believe change in the South has to be achieved through the electoral system are divided on the choice between a Malay-Muslim faction that will partner with the highest bidder, or joining different mainstream parties and slowly changing their policies from the inside. Considering the small size of the Malay-Muslim community in Thailand, neither option is likely to specifically benefit this community. However, government policies aimed at supporting all underprivileged communities in Thailand, enforcement of laws protecting human rights, including rights of minorities, would also benefit Malay Muslims and might be less difficult to achieve. It remains to be seen what role Matuphum, or any other Muslim faction,[48] can play in Thai politics.

The Puritan Islamic Reformist Movement

Besides this active participation in the political system there is the strategy of accommodating the Thai state and its institutions and rules in order to be able to create one's own religious space. The clearest example of this approach is the way the puritan Islamic reformist movement in South Thailand operates. This puritan movement is a relative newcomer to the religious landscape of South Thailand, and only started having a significant following from the second half of the 1980s. It receives support from Saudi Arabia and the Gulf States and propagates a scripturalistic approach towards the sources of Islam. In a sense it has built on earlier reformist movements from the beginning of the 1900s when Ahmad Wahab, a political refugee from the Minangkabau community in the then Dutch East Indies (Scupin 1980, p. 2), was exiled to Thailand and started spreading reformist ideas from the Middle East. The new puritan movement, however, has a stricter doctrine and approach. The worldview of this movement is very different from the traditional heterodox form of Islam among the Malay Muslims, which is a syncretic mixture of Islamic and pre-Islamic traditions, such as Malay supernaturalism, phii worship,[49] and Hindu and Buddhist practices and beliefs. Obviously there are no monolithic categories and it is all a matter of shades, but the widely shared view (among researchers), one to which I subscribe, is that the Malay-Muslim population of South Thailand is still predominantly traditionalist, albeit to varying degrees. It is estimated that about 80 per cent of the community has a traditionalist world view.[50] The mainly rural character of the South offers some explanation as to why people stick to traditions and rituals. The perceived pressure from Buddhist authorities to assimilate, criticism from puritan reformists, the challenges of modernity and daily violence and uncertainty all reinforce this attitude. Many of the old traditions and practices are very much alive in the twenty-first century. For example, during fieldwork in 2008 I found that practically every village in the countryside had one or more *bomoh* (shaman) who act as intermediaries between the human and the spiritual worlds. Villagers, but also some educated people I spoke to, visit a *bomoh* when they are ill, or when someone or a place is believed to be possessed by a spirit. In the case of illness, people either first consult their village *bomoh* and then a modern doctor, if it is necessary and if they can afford it, or the other way around. On one occasion, I attended a session where a *bomoh*, Hajji Ishok,[51] attempted to cure a woman who had a badly infected eye by invoking spirits and reciting Qur'an verses, while continuously blowing into a small bag of rice. The required fee was three leaves, some betel nut and 12 baht (about 35 U.S. cents). If the treatment turned out to be successful, she had to come back with a goat for slaughter.[52]

Puritan reformists are horrified by such practices and want to purge religion of all rituals they consider to be "un-Islamic". This includes communal feasts known as *kenduri*,[53] which are held on the occasion of life-cycle events, and the widely celebrated *Maulid an-Nabi* (birthday of the Prophet), which according to the puritans find no basis in the Qur'an and Hadith and are therefore "un-Islamic". This has led to heated debates and division within communities and even within families. There are also several doctrinal differences.[54] The leader of the contemporary puritan movement is Dr Ismail Lutfi Japakiya, a charismatic personality with great religious authority, who has managed to establish a university which is expanding year by year. Dr Lutfi was actually born in Mecca in 1950 of Malay parents from South Thailand, and had spent his early childhood in Saudi Arabia. He returned to Thailand when he was six years old and studied Islam and the Arabic language under the tutelage of his father, who owned a *pondok*[55] in Baraho village in Pattani province. Then he managed to secure a scholarship to travel to Saudi Arabia, where he studied for fourteen years at well-known "Wahhabi" universities, obtaining a BA in *Usuluddin* (theology and religious studies) from Madinah University, and a MA and a PhD (First Class), both in Comparative *Fiqh* (Islamic jurisprudence), at the Islamic University of

Al-Imam Mohammad Ibn Saud in Riyadh. After returning to Thailand, Dr Lutfi established the Yala Islamic College in 1998 with substantial financial support from private and government donors in Saudi Arabia and the Gulf States. Dr Lutfi's large network in that region, combined with his accommodating attitude towards the Thai authorities, resulted in the consolidation of puritan reformism in Thailand. In 2007, Yala Islamic College received the status of university from the Thai Ministry of Education. Dr Lutfi's stamina, as well as his religious and social skills, had paid off. The immediate goal of this educational institution is to upgrade Islamic education in the South, but the longer-term goal is to give puritan reformist Islam a firm foothold in the southern Thai provinces. The Islamic university's position as both a manifestation of reformist trends and an agent for reinforcing such trends among the Malay-Muslim population of South Thailand supersedes its function as an academic institution. The puritan reformist movement had to create parallel educational and religious structures because the existing ones were dominated by the traditionalist Islamic worldview. The *pondok* system and the important Islamic Councils[56] in the three provinces offer no opportunity to the puritans to disseminate their ideas. A limited number of the many *rohngrian ekkachon sonsassana Islam*[57] (Thai name for Islamic private schools, *madrasah* in Arabic), are influenced by puritan reformist thinking.[58] In the competition between traditionalist and puritan worldviews, Dr Lutfi's movement is often labelled as "Wahhabi", and Yala Islamic University (YIU) "the centre of Wahhabi in Yala, Pattani and Narathiwat".[59] I share the opinion of Dr Joseph Liow that Dr Lutfi is not Wahhabi, but that he does have some Salafi characteristics.[60] A well-known reformist scholar, in response to my question of why no school or institution in the South calls itself "Salafi", said that people would then label the institution as "Wahhabi". He added: "Everyone is happy to be called Salafi, because that's the real Muslim.... People just don't like to be called Wahhabi."[61] Aware of the suspicions some people hold against YIU, one of its staff made it a point to state in an interview: "Don't think we'll bring the context of Saudi Arabia here."[62]

The question is why and how the puritan reformist movement managed to create so much religious and educational space for itself that it could establish its own university and continue to propagate its brand of Islam. The answer to this question, which will be elaborated upon below, is basically twofold:

Yala Islamic University. Photograph courtesy of the author.

1. Puritan reformists are inclined to work with the Thai system;
2. Thai authorities are suspicious towards traditionalist Malay Muslims and prefer to cooperate with reformists.

1. Reformist Cooperation with the Thai Government

The dynamics affecting the attitude of Islamic reformists in Thailand towards the state are different from Muslim-majority states. With the Malay-Muslim community in South Thailand being predominantly traditionalist in outlook, it was not easy for the puritan reformist movement to carve out its own niche. A good relationship with the Thai authorities both locally and in Bangkok was instrumental to creating such a space in spite of local constraints. It should also be noted that this puritan movement has goals which supersede the confines of the Malay-Muslim provinces. In fact the puritan Muslims do not attach much significance to the preservation of Malay-Muslim culture. Theirs is a mission without boundaries, motivated and financed by their puritan brethren in the wider Muslim world. Imtiyaz

Yusuf positioned "the rise of a local Salafi-Wahhabi movement with the aim of establishing a pure Islamic society" within the global religious revival of Islam (Yusuf 2007, p. 12). The whole *umma* (Muslim world) is their target group, although as far as Thailand is concerned, the vast majority of Muslims live in the Deep South. The movement's leader, Dr Lutfi, has a deliberate strategy of accommodating and interacting with the Thai authorities, especially at the national level. He has held several positions as advisor to the Thai Government on religious matters. A clear sign of his entry into the highest echelons of the Thai state came right after the 2006 coup when Dr Lutfi was asked to be a member of the newly formed National Legislative Assembly, tasked with drafting the new constitution. He has also been advisor to the *Chularatmontri* or *Sheykh ul-Islam*, a dignitary appointed by the Thai King as nominal head of the Muslim community in the country. In 2007 and again in 2009, Dr Lutfi was appointed as *Amir al-Haj*[63] by the Thai Government. This position is normally held by the *Chularatmontri* himself, but the then office bearer, Sawat Sumalayasak, had been ill for some time and could not take up the responsibility. Lutfi was appointed *Amir al-Haj* because of his excellent contacts in Saudi Arabia, including with the royal family.[64] A reformist scholar joked with me that in 2008 when Phichet Sathirachawan, a former vice-minister under Prime Minister Thaksin and a convert, was *Amir al-Haj*, everyone in Saudi Arabia asked: "Where is Lutfi?" The appointment as *Amir al-Haj* afforded Dr Lutfi great prestige within the Muslim community in Thailand, but also led to misgivings among traditionalist Malay Muslims. They felt that Dr Lutfi was not representing the majority of Muslims in Thailand and privately some traditionalists complained of favouritism.[65] Dr Lutfi's appointment can be viewed as an implicit seal of government, or even royal, approval. In fact, the puritan reformist movement advertises its relations with the Thai royal family. For example, in the visitor's room at Yala Islamic University there is a large photographic display of a visit by the Thai Crown Prince to the university. The international prestige of Dr Lutfi in the Gulf region was demonstrated in October 2009, when the Kuwaiti Deputy Prime Minister flew in on his private jet to attend the inauguration of a large Kuwaiti sponsored mosque[66] on the main YIU campus. The Thai Government was taken by surprise when it heard of the high-level foreign visitor to the South, particularly because he had not planned to visit Bangkok.

The puritan Muslims see cooperation with the Thai Government not as a threat but as an opportunity. Close relations with the Thai authorities, for example, helped the then Yala Islamic College with its petition to the

Ministry of Education for the status of university. YIU has become the pre-eminent institution in Thailand for academic education based on an Islamic foundation. Indeed, Muslim students from all over Thailand, and even from Cambodia and China, enrol at the university. There is no equivalent among the educational institutions run by the traditionalist Muslims. It is important to note here that reformists attach great value to education as a means of achieving their goal of Islamization of society. Deliar Noer (1973, p. 42) has said:

> The reformists recognized the importance of education for the training and upbuilding of the younger generation. Any change in ideas and thoughts would certainly be considered of lasting value if they could get a grip on the younger generation.

James Peacock — applying Weberian theories[67] regarding reformist Christians and society to Islamic reformists — concluded concerning his research in Indonesia, Singapore and Malaysia that "all educational types (also) gravitate toward reformist theology" (1978, p. 37).

2. Thai Preference for the Puritan Reformist Movement

The Thai Government's perception of puritan reformists, though far from uniform, has undergone somewhat of a change over the years. Following 9/11, the Bali bombings of October 2002, and even more so after the escalation of violence in South Thailand from 2004, Thai security services became highly suspicious of Dr Lutfi's intentions and his international contacts. News stories and self-proclaimed terrorism experts linked Dr Lutfi with Jemaah Islamiyah (JI). However, there was never any proof presented of his involvement in terrorist acts.[68] Diplomatic circles in Bangkok surmised that a deal had been made between the Thai security services and Dr Lutfi, according to which Lutfi would not grant JI a foothold in the South in exchange for freedom for his movement to proselytize.[69] Security services, aware of the antagonism between puritan and traditionalist Muslims, have come to view puritans as a useful partner in what, with a sense of overstatement, might be called a "marriage of convenience". The main threat to security, in the eyes of the Thai Government and the security apparatus, are the separatists. They are Malay nationalists fighting for an independent state of Patani.[70] The separatist organizations are generally traditionalist in their religious and cultural outlook. The traditional *pondoks* are seen by Thai officials as the recruiting centres for the separatists, although this is vehemently denied by traditionalist leaders. In contrast, the puritan reformist movement is no longer perceived as a threat to security. During an interview in 2008, a high ranking military officer confided that the puritans, whom he called Wahhabi, were tactical allies in the fight against the separatists. He stated:

> The first priority of the Thai government is to deal with the grasae Yihad (separatist movement) because they want to separate from Thailand. Only when this group diminishes, will the Thai government turn to the Wahhabis and deal with them. The Wahhabis are no threat to the Thai state.[71]

It was also clear that the army had contacts and meetings with Dr Lutfi and sometimes cooperated with him. Regardless of which group will prove to be the biggest challenge to the Thai state in the long term, the current government policy seems to allow the puritan reformist movement the space to assert itself and expand its following in South Thailand. In that sense Dr Lutfi's strategy of accommodating the Thai state is expedient at this stage of the movement's development. Nevertheless, his opponents in the South managed to get another arrow in their bow with the appointment of a new *Chularatmontri* on 16 May 2010, namely the traditionalist chairman of the Islamic Council of Songkhla province (bordering on Pattani and Yala), Aziz Pitakkumpon.[72] He is the first *Chularatmontri* from the South in its almost four-century-long history. Aziz Pitakkumpon, who was educated at a *pondok* in Pattani, beat eight other candidates during the election, which was held after the previous *Chularatmontri* passed away on 24 March of the same year. It is yet unclear what effect this appointment will have on the traditionalist-reformist discourse, but it reinforces Dr Lutfi's conviction that the existing religious structures are dominated by traditionalists, and that he has to continue with his strategy of carving out his own religious space.

DISENGAGEMENT WITH A PURPOSE — THE TABLIGHI JAMA'AT

In South Thailand there is a movement that has turned its back on politics, but is at the same time far from apathetic. That movement is the Tablighi Jama'at (TJ), which is also known as *Da'wa*[73] in the South. The TJ is an

Islamic missionary movement originating from the Indian subcontinent. The chief aims of the TJ are to renew the faith of its followers, and to persuade other Muslims to go to the mosque more often and follow in the footsteps of the Prophet. Tablighis are required to practice the Sunna as shown by the Prophet in a very literal and formalistic sense. The main means of achieving these aims is the *khuruj*, the obligatory travels of each follower. Tablighis must go on *khuruj* three days every month or forty days a year, in groups of six to seventeen persons. The goal is to spend four months in a lifetime on *khuruj*, all at ones' own expense. When travelling, Tablighis are very visible in their white Saudi style *thawb* (loose long-sleeved ankle-length shirt) and *taqiya* (skull cap). Some followers wear the traditional Malay *sarong* and *songkok* (cap).

During the *khuruj* an instruction manual, the "Guide for Tableegh Journey and Six Points", is used. This publication contains stories from the *Faza'il A'maal*,[74] which are told during inspirational speeches (*bayan*) and explained afterwards in smaller groups, sitting on the floor of the mosque. It also contains rules on what to do and what not to do, as well

Tablighis out on *khuruj*. Photograph courtesy of the author.

as precise instructions on, for example, how to eat, how to sleep, and even how to go to the toilet. The *khuruj* I was allowed to join in 2005 to a mosque in the small town of Prigi in Pattani province was undertaken by a group of seventeen very motivated men, including a *jama'ah* (group) of seven Saudis (Braam 2006). Most rules were strictly observed, except for some of the instructions, such as sleeping on the right side, that would have made sleeping very uncomfortable. At every prayer session there were between fifty and eighty Malay men from the kampongs (villages) in the vicinity present. Women sat behind a curtain. In the late afternoon the whole congregation split up into groups of five to ten men and visited nearby villages by car, scooter, or on foot. In my group a local Malay who knew this area walked at the head to show the way through paddy fields and bushes to preselected houses. The group leader, in this case one of the Saudis, would say a loud "as salamu alaykum" to urge the inhabitants of the house in question to step outside and then try to persuade them to come to the mosque that same night. Teenage boys playing football outside and random passers-by were also addressed. Most listened to the appeal with a mixture of shyness and guilt about not having attended the mosque more often. Most also nodded an agreement to come to the mosque, but did not show up that night.

The sight of white-clad Tablighis in the back of pick-up trucks travelling the roads of South Thailand has become very common, especially in the rural areas. From the first *ijtimas* (major gatherings) in Thailand in the early 1980's, the Tablighi movement has experienced tremendous growth and its followers have visited almost every village in the countryside. During fieldwork, even in the remotest areas of rural Narathiwat province, I was told by local Malays that groups of TJ followers visited their villages regularly. Imam Soray of Kampong Dahong (about 1,000 villagers) in Narathiwat province gave a typical response when he said in Malay: "They [TJ] sometimes visit the village a few times in one month."[75] He was very happy with these visits, as "people are improving their attitudes." In his view the TJ had given the villagers a fresh impulse to live as good Muslims. An Imam in another village, Kampong Che-Hok, also in Narathiwat, said there was a lot of TJ influence and that "Da'wa [TJ] visits sometimes five times in a month and sometimes not at all."[76] Even TJ followers from Pakistan and China had visited this small village. This traditionalist Imam regularly goes on *khuruj* himself. This picture of the TJ quietly penetrating the villages of South Thailand and gaining a wide following is intriguing and needs to be addressed here.

The question that begs an answer is how the expansion of the TJ in South Thailand can be explained and interpreted. Within the scope of this chapter we have to specifically look at relations and approaches of the TJ towards Thai Government institutions and vice versa. The perceived apolitical attitude of the TJ is an important dimension of this relationship. Non-involvement in politics is one of the tenets from the early days of the TJ. Muhammad Khalid Masud (2000, pp. 97–99) places this in the context of the debate between Muslims of twentieth century (British) India on whether Muslims should be politically active at all. Traditionalist *ulama* at the time felt Muslims should not participate in politics. Mawlana Muhammad Ilyas, who founded the TJ in the 1920's, held the opinion that the *ulama* were not equipped to engage in politics. Rather, Muslims should concentrate on *Da'wa* and try to live as good Muslims. Another reason Masud gives for the early apolitical stance of the TJ was the desire to avoid confrontation with the (then British colonial) government, who might otherwise have suppressed the movement. There is a fundamental choice here and in other challenging environments, of whether Muslims should engage or disengage the government. Mawlana Ilyas had observed the attempts of the Ikhwan al-Muslimun (Muslim Brotherhood) under the Egyptian Hassan al-Banna to change society through political means and warned him that the government would suppress the Ikhwan. Ilyas' son and successor as TJ leader, Mawlana Muhammad Yusuf, concluded that the TJ was more successful in reviving Islam than the Ikhwan, which indeed ended up being suppressed by the government. Behind the political versus apolitical dilemma stood the argument of whether personal renewal of the (inner) faith or societal and political activism was the proper way. Masud (ibid., p. 99) argues that the TJ, in a broad sense, is in fact political, because it makes Muslims "conscious of their separate identity and aware of their social obligations from a religious perspective". He concludes that, therefore, the TJ has a political vision and agenda.

One of the reasons why so many Malay Muslims become temporary (during *khuruj* only) or more permanent (lifelong) followers of TJ, is also the social and political environment in which it can be dangerous to engage in political activities with religious motivation. In the South Thailand environment of almost daily violence, the TJ is considered to be outside of the battlefield. This movement is not seen as a threat to stability or to the rule of the Thai authorities in the South. A high ranking officer at the Police Security Center in Yala city explained to me that the TJ does not do anything wrong. Because the TJ is not seen as a threat by the Thai Government, it gets all the space it needs to expand its missionary work in Thailand. According to TJ leaders I met at the *markaz* (TJ centre) in Yala, many Thai army soldiers who are Muslim go on *khuruj*. The TJ leadership wants to show the Thai authorities that it has nothing to hide and invites them to go on *khuruj*. On the other hand, the TJ is sometimes accused of being too passive and indifferent to the Malay Muslims' quest to improve their political fate through some form of self rule. Even in the early days of the TJ in India, it was criticized by, among others, the Islamist Jama'at Islami for its apolitical stance (ibid., pp. 90–91).[77] At several points in history, Islamists have tried to take advantage of TJ gatherings to rally support for their political causes, but each attempt thus far has been rebuked by the TJ leadership (ibid., p. 19). Such gatherings, large and small, would have been the perfect recruitment places for other Islamic organizations and movements. As a consequence of the apolitical stance of the TJ, the gap with political activists and Islamists remains wide today. Besides the Tablighi principle of non-interference in politics and the Thai Government's favourable reaction to it, there are a number of other equally important reasons why the TJ has expanded so rapidly. These reasons, though not exhaustive, are the appeal of the Tabligh's message and its methods, the feeling of belonging to a brotherhood (locally and worldwide), the sense of a common purpose, and the organizational structure of the movement. The appeal of the message of renewing one's own faith and retreating from daily worries into little sanctuaries is especially strong in South Thailand where day-to-day life is marked by the constant threat of violence. Going on *khuruj* provides a reprieve from such tensions, as well as from the more mundane pressures of making a living. It also provides an escape from the routine at home and at work. Joining the TJ provides a break with a purpose. The Tabligh method, with its precise instructions on what to do and how to do it, and telling stories or listening to them during the *bayan*, does not require a great deal of textual exegesis or intellectual exercise. That is one of the reasons why it appeals to less-educated people, especially in the rural areas of South Thailand, although it does command some educated following too. Unlike the puritan reformist movement, the TJ does not directly challenge traditionalist beliefs and practices. While Tablighis leave their family behind when they go on *khuruj*, they find a new "family" in fellow travellers who share the same purpose. This creates strong and often lasting bonds between people from different places. The transnational aspect lends the feeling of belonging to a wider brotherhood and a purpose that supersedes one's own geographical, cultural and ethnic background.

The organizational structure of the TJ ensures the continuity of the movement and facilitates its dynamic expansion. While the practical and operational aspects are decentralized, the main decisions are taken in a hierarchical manner. At the top of the pyramid sits the *shura* in the historical headquarters in Nizamuddin in Delhi, India (Gaborieau 2000, p. 130). From there, decisions are taken on strategy and doctrine, but also on the appointment of the members of *shuras* abroad. For example, the decision on who is appointed to the *shura* of Thailand, is decided in Nizamuddin. During an interview with a member of the Tabligh *shura* of Thailand, the local organizational structure of the TJ was explained to me in detail.[78] The *shura* of Thailand, residing in the *markaz* in Minburi (an outlying district of Bangkok) is in direct contact with the world headquarters in Nizamuddin and officially has fifteen members, though three have passed away. Currently, four members are from South Thailand. Thailand is divided in two regions, Bangkok and the North, and South Thailand with its *markaz* in Yala. This *markaz* is responsible for fourteen provinces in South Thailand, not only for the three predominantly Muslim provinces. These three provinces are divided into twenty-one big *halaqa* (rings or areas), which are subdivided into 147 small *halaqa*. Each small *halaqa* covers between ten and fifteen mosques. This structure safeguards the administration of the TJ in South Thailand, and ensures the fanning out, in a coordinated way, of all the different local and foreign *jama'at* who visit the towns and villages. Often when I visit the *markaz* in Yala, groups of men are sitting on the floor with maps and money, planning the many trips they take each year. No other movement in South Thailand has such a well-coordinated system. The success of the TJ in South Thailand can to a great degree be attributed to its structure. According to the Tablighi leadership in South Thailand, an estimated 20,000 people go on *khuruj* every year.

TJ's ambitions sometimes get in the way of sound financial planning. The establishment of a new *markaz* for the ASEAN region in Pattani province,[79] ordered by Nizamuddin, faltered due to a lack of funding. The owners of the land that was earmarked to be purchased raised the price when they heard of TJ's plans. However, TJ's leadership turned out to be resilient and went back to the drawing board. A new plan was designed and at another location, the small village of Tase in Yala province, a plot of land measuring 1,850 rai (2,960 km^2) was bought. The cost was covered by an amount of 277 million baht (about US$8.5 million) collected from local TJ followers, and about 600 rai (960 km²) was resold to individual Tablighis for proportionally higher prices. The plan was to build an entirely new town, partly owned by the TJ as an organization and partly by individual Tablighis. The new Tablighi town should include a mosque (capacity of 100,000 people), dormitories and a hospital. In a few years time, the world Ijtima of the TJ should be held there.[80]

In South Thailand the TJ operates in an environment of competing worldviews. The puritan reformist movement, in particular, sees the TJ as a deviation from Islam and TJ followers are not welcome in mosques dominated by puritans. Generally, there is resistance among traditional Malay Muslims against outside influence that challenges the legitimacy of traditionalist institutions, or is perceived to have the potential of changing the way of life of the community. Some traditionalist Malay Muslims hold negative views of this movement, saying it is alien to South Thailand. Such an opinion can be found among some of the older traditionalist Imams who feel that their authority is threatened by the TJ. However, most traditionalist Malay Muslims appreciate the capacity of the TJ to blend in with the local community, and not to sternly instruct them how to practice their faith, which is quite different from the puritan reformist approach. The quietist appeal of the TJ is less confrontational then the head-on methods of the puritans. Joining the TJ on *khuruj* satisfies a person's need to perform pious acts, to compensate for his daily failings. Such a public expression of piety greatly contributes to his prestige, particularly in the rural areas.

CONCLUSION

In this chapter, I have analysed the main outcomes of the friction between the Malay-Muslim community in Thailand and the Thai-Buddhist state. The most visible outcome, militant violence, has caused great loss of life and disrupted society without leading to any significant gains for the perpetrators. Indeed it can be argued that such violence has in fact been counterproductive and caused deterioration in the daily lives of the same people in whose interest it was intended to be used. The only positive side effect has been that the acts of violence have drawn the attention of the central government and the Thai people to the plight of the Malay-Muslim community. This has led to substantial budget allocations to the South, albeit at the high price of almost daily loss of life. On the other side of the coin, militant violence has also had the effect of legitimizing, in the eyes of many Thai Buddhists, violence and human rights abuses by the Thai security forces. I suspect some separatist leaders are hoping that a stimulated *"Verelendung"*[81] will rouse the people to rise up against the Thai state. The initiator of the Krue Se clashes may just have had this in mind when sending dozens of young people to certain death. Separatist violence has not brought its main goal, self-determination of the Malay-Muslim people, any closer to being realized. Those with a long-term view might argue that the Kosovar Albanians, the people of Timor-Leste, or the Flemish in Belgium did not get their form of self-determination overnight. It is extremely unlikely that the unitary, centralized, Thai state will ever agree to any form of secession, when many Thai still believe they have been robbed of territory in the East.[82] Even the idea of autonomy for the predominantly Malay-Muslim provinces is anathema to the Thai-Buddhist majority.

The main peaceful way to further the Malay cause has been participation in the Thai political system. In the early years of the Muslim political faction Wahdah, everything looked promising. Several Malay Muslims joined the Thai ruling elite and held influential ministerial posts. At some point Wahdah was corrupted, and its leaders started to behave like "normal" Thai politicians, such that "Idealpolitik" gave way to "Realpolitik". The corridors of power were too intoxicating. Continued collaboration with Thaksin, even after the Tak Bai massacre, discredited Wahdah in the eyes of the Malay Muslims and spelled its electoral doom. It has to be said that several developmental policies for the South were initiated by Wahdah, but it did not succeed in giving the Malay Muslims a substantial say in their own provinces nor was their advancement in Thai society realized in any structural way. The participation of a Malay-Muslim politician like Wan Nor at the highest strata of Thai politics did not fundamentally change Thai perceptions of Malay Muslims, nor did it create lasting positive results for the people who had voted him into power. On balance, Wahdah had not achieved its goals. Whether the new Muslim faction Mathuphum will succeed where Wahdah has failed remains doubtful. Politics in Bangkok will remain focused on the deep societal rift between the haves and have-nots, to the detriment of the conflict in the South.[83] Judging by their participation in elections, the majority of people in the South still have not given up on achieving their goals through non-violent democratic means. The question is: Can Malay-Muslim participation in the Thai political system ever be more than a safety valve taking some pressure off the South Thailand pressure cooker?

The strategy of the puritan reformist movement, that is, cooperation with the Thai Government and its institutions, turned out to be more effective. It has allowed the puritans to create their own politico-religious space and its leader, Dr Lutfi, has entered the highest echelons of the Thai state. Such cooperation with state authorities is remarkable for a movement that wants to Islamize society in accordance with its own puritan, or Salafi, worldview. This is possible because Dr Lutfi does not challenge the canon of Thai self-identity: "Nation, Religion, and King".[84] Both the Thai Government and Dr Lutfi have pragmatic reasons for cooperating with the other in a "marriage of convenience". Thai security forces view puritan reformists as (ideological) allies against the separatists, who are Malay nationalists and have a predominantly traditionalist worldview. In this setting Dr Lutfi's movement will continue to grow, mainly among the better educated or those who desire a higher education. This movement is likely to show steady growth, especially with an Islamic university to disseminate its ideas. Rapid growth, however, will be difficult in the still mainly rural South, where *bomohs* and mysticism are deeply embedded in the lives of Muslim villagers.

Behind the scenes of the clashes between militant organizations and government forces, the apolitical Tablighi Jama'at is quietly expanding. Its stated policy of non-involvement in politics is proving to be very effective in warding off any unwanted interference from the state. The organizational structure of this missionary movement and the appeal of going on *khuruj* have facilitated its penetration into even the smallest kampongs in the South. The TJ seems to be well accepted by most traditionalist Malay Muslims, especially the less educated. They feel they can maintain their Malay identity when participating in TJ activities. The *khuruj* also serves as an alternative hajj, giving its participants a sense of piety. The expansion is expressed in plans for a brand new TJ town in the countryside of Yala province.

At this point in time, it is not likely that the militant groups will drastically change their tactics, nor will the deeply divided Thai political establishment allow Malay Muslims to be better represented in local administration and express their own identity more freely. If Malay-Muslim politicians are able to team up with a major Thai political party and find a balance between common and personal interests, they could negotiate improvement of the social and economic position of their community. With the political aspirations of Malay Muslims effectively blocked, the most profound changes in this society are taking place in the religious and cultural spheres. Real changes in the fabric of society are actually being woven together daily by different religious movements, with the Tablighi Jama'at and the puritan Islamic reformists as the main actors. What is clear is that the outcome of the competition between different worldviews will have deep and lasting effects on Malay-Muslim society in the Deep South and on its place in Thailand.

Notes

1. I would like to thank Dr Hui Yew-Foong for the opportunity to contribute to this publication, as well as for his skilful editing and patience. Of course, this does not absolve me of the responsibility for errors, omissions or other shortcomings which the reader may find in this chapter. Without the advice, hospitality and practical help from many people in South Thailand my research and the drafting of this chapter would not have been possible. I would like to warmly thank my indispensible local assistants, two Faisals and Mukhtar, for organizing transportation, making appointments, and for many other practical affairs. I also express my gratitude to the board and staff of the Prince of Songkhla University in Pattani, particularly to Dr Ibrahem Narongraksaket for his illuminating insights and to Dr Srisompob Jitpiromsri. A special thanks goes to Dr Chidchanok Rahimula for arranging my long stay on campus in 2008. Furthermore, I am very grateful to the late Dr Hasan Madmarn and to Abdullah Hajiyama for answering my many questions on local events, customs and religion. My understanding of South Thailand has greatly improved (albeit still rather modest) through communication with international scholars who are much more experienced, such as Dr Raymond Scupin, Dr Michael Montesano, and Dr Joseph Liow. In the wider context of my PhD research I express my gratitude for the guidance and patience of my supervisor Dr Martin van Bruinessen. I also respectfully thank Dr Ismail Lutfi Japakiya and his staff, particularly Dr Suntorn Piyawason and Dr Sukree Langputeh, for the many informative meetings within and outside Yala Islamic University. The Islamic Councils in Pattani, Yala and Narathiwat, as well as the office of the Sheikh ul-Islam, were always ready to receive me, for which I sincerely thank them. The local leadership of the Tablighi Jama'at and many of its members deserve my utmost appreciation for their hospitality. Dr Perayot Rahimula, whom I met on my first trip to the South, has been instrumental in the snowballing of my network, for which I owe him my deepest gratitude.

I feel heavily indebted to many others, ranging from local authorities at all levels to imams, *tok gurus*, farmers and rubber tappers. The list of people who provided invaluable information and insights is too long to mention, and I also respect the request of many to remain anonymous due to security concerns. My heartfelt wishes for a lasting peace go out to all who live in the Southern provinces.

2. Skinner (1957, p. 237) describes assimilation as a social process, the progress of which "is defined by increasing social intercourse with members of Thai society, first public and then private and intimate; and by self-identification in an ever larger proportion of social situations as Thai rather than Chinese". However, Chan and Tong (1993) criticize Skinner for overemphasizing "the powers of the forces of assimilation". They sketch a nuanced picture of the Chinese in Thailand, who have adapted to Thai society and culture in some areas, but have maintained their own distinct Chinese identity in other areas. Assimilation is not a lineal process, but a two-way process.

3. The sultanate of Patani is here spelled the Malay way with one "t". For the current province of Pattani I use the Thai spelling ปัตตาน with double "t" (ต).

4. After the sacking of Ayutthaya in 1767 by the Burmese, Bangkok became the capital.

5. The ultra-nationalist Phibun regime issued a series of edicts on national culture (*ratthaniyom* in Thai), which included the name change of the country. This regime also discouraged the use of terms denoting the cultural (and ethnic) diversity of Thailand's citizens. The term "Thais" was favoured over terms such as "north easterners" (*khon Isaan*), Thai Muslims, etcetera. People who had names that did not sound "Thai" had to change them. This regime was particularly suspicious of the Chinese and they were excluded from certain trades. After Phibun's reign, many of the measures were no longer in force. However, until today the term "Thainess" (*kwaampenthai*) is a yardstick for expressions of Thai culture. See also Reynolds 2002, pp. 4–5; and Sivaraksa 2002, pp. 38–40.

6. Thai greeting with folded hands.

7. Interview with Malay-Muslim politician (name withheld) on 4 August 2008.

8. Imtiyaz Yusuf mentions the following types of politico-religious influences that impact the attitude of Thai Muslims regarding the state and society: (1) the integrationist attitudes of Thai-speaking Muslims of the upper South, Central and northern Thailand; (2) the integrationist and separatist attitude among traditionalist Malay Muslims in South Thailand; (3) the pro-integration attitude of "moderate Wahhabis" led by Dr Ismail Lutfi and Dr Ismael Alee representing Kaum Muda reformists in the South; (4) the "radicalized Islamist" perspective among the Malay militant youth (the Krue Se incident is mentioned);

(5) the non-integrationist Islamist militant perspective of the "neo-Wahhabists inspired by al-Qa'ida and the Taleban"; and (6) "the non-integrationist view of the secular Malay nationalists separatists". See Yusuf 2007, p. 18.
9. From August 2001 till July 2005, I was political counsellor at the Royal Netherlands Embassy in Bangkok.
10. Figures are provided by Deep South Watch, an institute operating from the Prince of Songkhla University in Pattani, which tries to register and analyze all violent incidents related to the unrest. See also <http://www.deepsouthwatch.org/node/2343 and www.deepsouthwatch.org/english>.
11. For a detailed account and analysis, see McCargo 2008, pp. 135–46.
12. According to the International Crisis Group, the attackers belonged to the Hikmat Allah Abadan (Brotherhood of the Eternal Judgement of God) or simply Abadan or Abadae, and coordinated as of 2000 by a Yalaborn, Indonesian educated *ustadz* (religious teacher) named Ismael Yusof Rayalong (alias Ustadz Soh alias Ustadz Ishma-ae). See <http://www.crisisgroup.org/~/media/Files/asia/south-east-asia/thailand/098_southern_thailand_insurgency_not_jihad.ashx>.
13. In June 2004, I headed an EU fact-finding mission to the South. An erroneous article in the *Bangkok Post* claiming that the mission planned to draft a public human rights report, almost started a diplomatic row. The Thai Government wanted to block the visit, invoking Article 26 of the Vienna Convention on Diplomatic Relations. The mission, initially planned for May 2004, was postponed till June, but went ahead anyway.
14. Jihad means struggle or religious war. There is a lesser jihad (against the *Dar al-Kufr*/abode of unbelief) and a greater jihad (*Jihad an-Nafs*), which is for self improvement. In the international discourse normally jihad refers to the religious war against unbelievers. See also Meijer 2009.
15. When I spoke in 2006 to the father of Johnny and Luther Htoo in a Burmese refugee camp on the Thai border, he said the boys wanted to lead a normal life now.
16. Malay for "Making Jihad in Patani".
17. For a full translation into English, see Gunaratna, Acharya and Chua 2005, pp. 118–45.
18. Islam expert Dr Imtiyaz Yusuf sees some possible influence by jihadist texts from the Middle East. See Yusuf 2006, p. 181.
19. I am grateful to Hui Yew-Foong for alerting me to Siegel 2000, pp. 74–77.
20. In Kampung Dusun Nyior in the province of Narathiwat, "close to 400 Malays" were killed, according to the person writing under the pseudonym of Ibrahim Syukri (2005, p. 97). According to Davisakd Puaksom (2008, pp. 79–87) this work was first published in 1949 and partly based on the influential *Hikayat Patani*, the story of the founding of Patani, written between the end of the seventeenth century and the beginning of the eighteenth century.

21. Ramadan is the Islamic month of fasting. Muslims are obliged to refrain from eating and drinking, with some exceptions, from dawn until sunset. It is the ninth month on the Islamic calendar.
22. Talk with academic on 20 June 2009. For his safety, his identity is withheld.
23. Interview with an officer on an army base in the South on 5 October 2009.
24. Interview on 8 August 2008 with a senior police officer. Name withheld for security reasons.
25. This theory describes a situation in which people feel they are deprived of something which another group possesses, and this can potentially lead to action in the form of political violence. See also Gur (1970).
26. Interviews with Malay Muslims in several villages in Narathiwat province in August 2008.
27. Information from interviews with local Malay Muslims and diplomatic circles. These sources are kept confidential. See also *Majalah jihadmagz* 1, no. 3 (2008), which reports on four international jihadis who travelled to Pattani in 2004. They were members of the Majlis al-Shura al-Mujahidin.
28. The army subscribes to this assessment, which was confirmed during an interview on 5 October 2009 with an army officer in the South. Name withheld.
29. In the context of Dutch politics, Lijphart (1975, p. 103) uses the term accommodation "in the sense of settlement of divisive issues and conflicts where only a minimal consensus exists. Pragmatic solutions are forged for all problems, even those with clear religious-ideological overtones ... and which therefore may seem insoluble and likely to split the country apart."
30. In the literature, different dates are mentioned for the establishment of Wahdah. Researchers like Bajunid (2005, p. 13) and McCargo (2008, p. 65) consider 1986 as the year of Wahdah's inception. However, Imtiyaz Yusuf (2007, p. 16, n. 66) presents 1988 as the year in which Wahdah was formed. He refers to the Master's thesis of Suria Saniwa bin Wan Mahmood (1998). Strangely, the same Suria Saniwa bin Wan Mahmood mentions 1986 in his PhD dissertation (2007). In chapter 4.2.1, he refers to *Al-Wahdah News* 1994:128 as the source. Ockey (2008, p. 146) may have the answer when he writes that Tohmeena began to organize a group of MPs from the South in 1986, which later developed into the Wahdah faction.
31. Interview with director of a private Islamic school and member of the provincial parliament of Yala province, on 9 June 2009.
32. The fully integrated Malay-Muslim academic-turned-politician, Dr Surin Pitsuwan, held the post of Foreign Minister in the second Chuan Leekpai cabinet (1997–2001). However, he was a democrat and not a Wahdah member, and he was not from the deep South. Dr Surin was appointed Secretary-General of ASEAN in 2008. During a conference in August 2008 at Prince of Songkhla University in Pattani, Dr Surin spoke and several traditional Malay Muslims

privately commented to me that he was not one of them and had become too cosmopolitan.

33. This reflects the Thai political custom of allocating cabinet seats proportionate to the number of MPs which a particular faction contributes to the ruling coalition. It is not unusual for the leader of a faction who is disappointed with the allotted cabinet seats to switch sides and withdraw "his" MPs from the ruling coalition to join the opposition benches.
34. The person writing under the pseudonym Syukri describes in detail the oppressive and humiliating actions by the Siamese government and the "reawakening" of the Malay people, though it is a mixture between an account of history and a political pamphlet. See Syukri (2005, pp. 83–101).
35. During an interview with Den Tohmeena on 5 October 2009 at the office of his bus company in Pattani city, he repeated his earlier accusation that Wan Nor broke his promise to step down as minister after two years and rotate with him. Another widely supported allegation was that Wan Nor was only concerned with his personal interests and enriched himself as Transportation Minister, one of the most lucrative portfolios in the Thai cabinet.
36. Interview with farmer couple in Pattani province on 16 March 2005.
37. In his PhD dissertation, Suria Saniwa bin Wan Mahmood (2007) points out that Wan Nor, as Minister of Communications, built facilities for *hajj* travellers at several airports, organized direct flights from Thailand to Jeddah (Saudi Arabia), and started the construction of four-lane super highway routes from Sungai Golok in Narathiwat through Pattani and Songkhla up to Northern Thailand.
38. An estimated hundred million paper birds with peace messages from ordinary Thai citizens were dropped over the three provinces on the King's birthday, 5 December 2004. One contained a message from Thaksin, worth a scholarship for the finder.
39. A combination of Thai and Arabic. *Glum* means group and *Darussalaam* means abode of peace, a Qur'anic name for paradise.
40. The deliberate choice of a Thai name could indicate an attempt not to alienate Thai Buddhists. On the other hand, the word "motherland" could also hint at more ambitious political goals.
41. Wife of former Wahdah MP Muk Sulaiman. See also McCargo (2008, pp. 73–74).
42. The Peua Paendin party is sometimes in English translated as "Motherland Party", which is confusing as Matuphum means literally "motherland".
43. *The Nation*, 25 June 2009.
44. *The Nation*, 16 June 2009.
45. *The Nation*, 17 June 2009.
46. Interview with Den Tohmeena. With reference to the usual money politics in

Thailand, he said 500 million baht (about US$15.4 million) was needed to get 20 MPs elected.
47. *The Nation*, 19 November 2009.
48. A new political party that was established about the same time in South Thailand is Prachatham. Its members are younger Malay Muslims from student associations and from the foundation Hilal Ahmad, which runs ambulances and provides other services. Its aim is to reform the political system and eradicate money politics. It did not win any seats during the 2011 general elections.
49. The belief in spirits inhabiting trees, caves, waterfalls and other natural places, which have to be appeased by offerings.
50. Members of provincial Islamic councils, imams and academics have consistently mentioned this percentage during interviews.
51. Hajji Ishok has a wide reputation for exorcising spirits (Malay: *hantu*), curing snakebites and a variety of ailments, including cancer. Besides local Malay Muslims, also Thai Buddhists, local Chinese, Pakistani businessmen and Arabs visit him.
52. Interviews and participant observation in Muubaan Lemah, Tambon Krong Pinang in Yala province on 26 August 2008. This was part of extensive fieldwork, in Pattani, Yala and Narathiwat provinces from July to September 2008, and in June 2009.
53. *Kenduri* are considered to be part of the heritage of pre-Islamic Southeast Asia. In Indonesia they are known as *slametan*.
54. One of the most important doctrinal differences concerns the role of the *ulama*. Reformists claim that individual Muslims must interpret the Qur'an and the Sunna independently (*Ijtihād*) from the prevailing opinions of the lawyers of the four *madhahib* (juridical schools within Islam), as opposed to the method of relying on the word of the *ulama* (*taqlid*). This is not to say that reformists do not accept interpretation by scholars from the early days of Islam, but they want to access the sources of Islam themselves without the monopolizing mediation of religious teachers.
55. A *pondok* is a traditional Islamic school at the head of which stands the *tok guru*, a respected religious teacher, who does not teach according to a standard list of topics at fixed times. Rather, he relies on his expertise in a particular area of Islamic knowledge, and shares this with his students. A *pondok* attracts students on the reputation of its *tok guru*. For a thorough explanation of the *pondok* system, see Madmarn (1999).
56. These provincial Islamic Councils have jurisdiction in many religious matters concerning the Muslim community, such as performing Islamic marriages, dividing inheritances, supervising the mosques and Islamic schools in that particular province, appointment of all imams, approval of the *khatib* (person

who delivers the sermon) and muezzin (person who calls other Muslims to prayer), and advising the governor on religious affairs.
57. These schools offer dual education. Students are expected to study the academic subjects of the official Thai educational system in the Thai language, and study Islamic topics in the Arabic language. They are government subsidized, more modern and much larger than the traditional *pondok*.
58. Liow (2009, pp. 93–94) mentions an estimated number of twenty Islamic private schools which are substantially influenced by puritan reformism.
59. Interview on 17 march 2005 with the deputy director of an Islamic private school in Narathiwat province.
60. In an innovative analysis of the reformist leader's texts and speeches, Liow (2009, pp. 90–92) finds that, in some respects, Dr Lutfi distances himself from Wahhabi doctrine. Dr Liow stresses that the Salafi and the Wahhabi doctrines or worldviews can not be equated, though they share similar points of departure. He finds that Dr Lutfi is less scripturalistic than he is normally viewed because, for example, in his dissertation he emphasizes that time, space and context have to be considered when applying Islamic law. Furthermore Dr Lutfi's writings show distinct Salafi beliefs when he cautions against exaggerating the wisdom and authority of *ulama* and to be aware that as human beings these *ulama* are fallible. Dr Imtiyaz Yusuf (2007, p. 12) does identify Dr Lutfi as "Wahhabi". He finds much similarity between the way Saudi Arabs profess and shape Islam and the way the Malay-Muslim reformists in South Thailand do this. In his view, both groups have "parochialist and ethnocentric worldviews", which "betray(s) the universality of the Islamic message". In my view, the ethnocentric worldview of Saudi Arabian Wahhabism just as well turns the argument around and supports the notion that Wahhabism is a strictly Arab peninsular belief. Worldviews resembling Wahhabism, but adhered to by non-Arab Muslims are then by definition not Wahhabi. They may be Salafi, which has a more universal outlook and is more diversified in terms of practices.
61. Talk with a respected religious authority and scholar, while driving through Narathiwat province on 1 August 2008.
62. Interview on 15 December 2006 with a lecturer at Yala Islamic College.
63. Leader of the pilgrims from Thailand to the Holy Places in Saudi Arabia.
64. Dr Lutfi managed to secure a larger quota of pilgrims to Mecca because of his excellent connections with Saudi Arabia. He met with the King of Saudi Arabia and got the Thai quota increased by 2,000 to a total of 16,000 pilgrims.
65. They said that Dr Lutfi allotted the hundred so-called "Royal places" within Thailand's hajj quota — for whom the Saudi government paid aeroplane tickets and accommodation — to his own followers. This is denied by Dr Lutfi's close associates, who claim that the Saudi embassy is responsible for the allotment.

66. Kuwait paid 16 million baht (about US$493,000) for the construction of the new mosque.
67. See also Weber (1904/1905).
68. Dr Joseph Chinyong Liow (2006, fn. 16) has stated that "no evidence has surfaced linking Ismail Lutfi to the violence".
69. This information was obtained from talks with diplomats.
70. Often, the name *Patani Darussalam* is used for the Islamic state of Patani.
71. Interview on 30 July 2008 with a military commander in Pattani.
72. *Naewna* (Thai language newspaper) on 17 May 2010 and *Bangkok Post* on 16 May 2010.
73. *Da'wa* can be translated as "call to God".
74. The *Faza'il A'maal* contains stories of companions of the Prophet, virtues of the Holy Qur'an, virtues of *salaat* (prayer), virtues of zikr (remembrance), virtues of *tabligh*, virtues of Ramadan and "Muslim degeneration and its only remedy". It is prescribed literature for Tablighis and for each sermon a story is selected and applied to a current day situation.
75. Interview with villagers of Kampong Dahong, Amphoe Si Sakhon, Narathiwat province, 27 August 2008.
76. Interview with imam in Kampong Che-Hok, Amphoe Tak Bai, Narathiwat province, on 6 August 2008.
77. The Jama'at Islami (also written as Jama'at-i-Islami) is an Islamic revivalist party founded in 1941 in Lahore by Mawlana Sayyid Abul A'la Mawdudi. Its goal is the establishment of a pure Islamic state.
78. Interview on 10 June 2009 with Ustaz Nawawi in his house close to the Tabligh *markaz* in Yala.
79. Interview on 11 June 2009 with Abdel Wahid Piyaa, village head of Piyaa Muumang in the countryside of Pattani province.
80. Visit to the site with the son of a TJ leader on 26 February 2010. Currently, the land consists of grass fields and rubber plantations, cut in half by a railway track.
81. In Marxist theory the German word "Verelendung" means the continuing impoverishment of the proletariat. This creates the conditions for an uprising or revolution. I use it here in the sense of a drastic deterioration of the security and living conditions of the Malay-Muslim community.
82. During the second half of the nineteenth century, colonial powers, in particular France and Britain, increased pressure on Siam. This escalated in the "Paknam crisis" of 1893, when French warships sailed up the Chao Praya River. As a result of this confrontation Siam was forced to cede its northeastern territories (i.e., Laos and parts of Cambodia) to France. The Anglo-French declaration of 1896 made Siam a buffer between French Indochina and British India (particularly Burma). See Davisakd Puaksom (2008, p. 77) and Thanet Aphornsuvan (2008, p. 91).

83. There is a divide in Thai society between on the one hand the rural poor, particularly in North and Northeast (Isaan) Thailand, as well as their brethren in the cities, and on the other hand the urban middle class and traditional Thai elites. This divide is epitomized by the conflict between the "Yellow Shirts" (urban middle class, elites, royalists) and the "Red Shirts" (rural and urban poor, provincial "bosses", pro-Thaksin businessmen). Thaksin and his political allies and business associates managed to mobilize class and provincial sentiments for the benefit of his political and business interests. The "Red Shirts" felt disenfranchised by the 2006 army coup against PM Thaksin. The conflict erupted during bloody clashes on the streets of Bangkok between "Red shirts" and the Thai army in May 2010. This conflict is hardly relevant in the Deep South.
84. According to Kobkua Suwannathat-Pian (2008, p. 163), King Watchirawut (1910–1925) introduced this slogan. Interestingly, she argues that globalization in the 1990s transformed the nationalist version of Thai identity into a more pluralist form.

References

Aeusrivongse, Nidhi. "Morng sathannakarn phaktai phan wæn kabot chaona" (in English:"Understanding the Situation in the South as a "Millenarian Revolt"). *Sinlapa Watthanatham* 25, no. 8 (2004): 110–24.

Apornsuvan, Thanet. "Origins of Malay Muslim 'Separatism' in Southern Thailand". In *Thai South and Malay North: Ethnic Interactions on a Plural Peninsula*, edited by Michael J. Montesano and Patrick Jory. Singapore: National University of Singapore Press, 2008.

Bajunid, Omar Farouk. "The Muslims of Thailand: A Review". *Southeast Asian Studies* 37, no. 2 (1999): 210–34.

———. "Islam, Nationalism, and the Thai State". In *Dynamic Diversity in Southern Thailand*, edited by Wattana Sugunnasil. Chiang Mai: Silkworm Books, 2005.

Braam, Ernesto H. "Travelling with the Tablighi Jama'at in South Thailand". *ISIM Review* 17 (2006): 42–43.

Chan, Kwok Bun and Chee Kiong Tong. "Rethinking Assimilation and Ethnicity: The Chinese in Thailand". *International Migration Review* 27, no. 1 (1993): 140–68.

Forbes, Andrew D.W. "Thailand's Muslim Minorities: Assimilation, Secession, or Coexistence?" *Asian Survey* 22, no. 11 (1982): 1056–73.

Gaborieau, Marc. "The Transformation of the Tablighi Jama'at into a Transnational Movement". In *Travellers in Faith: Studies of the Tablighi Jama'at as a Transnational Islamic Movement for Faith Renewal*, edited by Muhammad Khalid Masud. Leiden: Brill, 2000.

Gilquin, Michel. *The Muslims of Thailand*. Chiang Mai: IRASEC and Silkworm Books, 2005.

Gunaratna, Rohan, Arabinda Acharya and Sabrina Chua, *Conflict and Terrorism in Southern Thailand*. Singapore: Marshall Cavendish International, 2005.
Gur, Ted Robert. *Why Men Rebel*. New Jersey: Princeton University Press, 1970.
International Crisis Group. *Southern Thailand: The Impact of the Coup*. Asia Report No. 129 (15 March 2007) accessed at <http://www.crisisgroup.org/~/media/files/asia/south-east-asia/thailand/129_southern_thailand___the_impact_of_the_coup_web.ashx>.
Lijphart, Arend. *The Politics of Accommodation: Pluralism and Democracy in the Netherlands*. California: University of California Press, 1975 (second edition).
Liow, Joseph Chinyong. "International Jihad and Muslim Radicalism in Thailand? Toward an Alternative Interpretation". *Asia Policy* no. 2 (2006): 89–108.
———. *Islam, Education and Reform in Southern Thailand: Tradition & Transformation*. Singapore: Institute of Southeast Asian Studies, 2009.
Masud, Muhammad Khalid. "The Growth and Development of the Tablighi Jama'at in India" and "Ideology and Legitimacy". In *Travellers in Faith: Studies of the Tablighi Jama'at as a Transnational Islamic Movement for Faith Renewal*, edited by Masud. Leiden: Brill, 2000.
McCargo, Duncan. *Tearing Apart the Land: Islam and Legitimacy in Southern Thailand*. Ithaca and London: Cornell University Press, 2008.
Meijer, Roel (ed). *Global Salafism: Islam's New Religious Movement*. London: Hurst & Company, 2009.
Noer, Deliar. *The Modernist Muslim Movement in Indonesia 1900–1942*. Oxford: Oxford University Press, 1973.
Ockey, James. "Elections and Political Integration in the Lower South of Thailand". In *Thai South and Malay North: Ethnic Interactions on a Plural Peninsula*, edited by Michael J. Montesano and Patrick Jory. Singapore: National University of Singapore Press, 2008.
Peacock, James L. *Muslim Puritans: Reformist psychology in Southeast Asian Islam*. California: University of California Press, 1978.
Puaksom, Davisakd. "Of Lesser Brilliance: Patani Historiography in Contention". In *Thai South and Malay North: Ethnic Interactions on a Plural Peninsula*, edited by Michael J. Montesano and Patrick Jory. Singapore: National University of Singapore Press, 2008.
Reynolds, Craig J. "Introduction: National Identity and its Defenders". In *National Identity and its Defenders: Thailand Today*, edited by Craig J. Reynolds. Chiang Mai: Silkworm Books, 2002 (Revised edition).
Scupin, Raymond. "Islamic Reformism in Thailand". *Journal of the Siam Society*, Vol. 68.2 (July 1980): 1–10.
———. "Muslim Intellectuals in Thailand: Exercises in Reform and Moderation." Unpublished manuscript, n.d.
Siegel, James T. *The Rope of God*. Michigan: University of Michigan Press, 2000.

Sivaraksa, Sulak. "The Crisis of Siamese Identity". In *National Identity and its Defenders: Thailand Today*, edited by Craig J. Reynolds. Chiang Mai: Silkworm Books, 2002 (Revised edition).

Skinner, G. William. "Chinese Assimilation and Thai Politics". *Journal of Asian Studies* 16, no. 2 (1957): 237–50.

Snow, David A., and Susan E. Marshall. "Cultural Imperialism, Social Movements, and the Islamic Revival". *Research in Social Movements, Conflicts, and Change* 7 (1989): 131–52.

Suria Saniwa Bin Wan Mahmood. "De-Radicalization of Minority Dissent — A Case Study of the Malay-Muslim Movement in Southern Thailand". Master's Thesis, Universiti Sains Malaysia, Penang, Malaysia, 1998.

———. "The Politics of Ethnic Representation: Malay-Muslims in Southern Thailand and Thai Buddhists in Northern Malaysia". Ph.D. dissertation. Faculty of Social Sciences and Humanities. Universiti Kebangsaan Malaysia Bangi, 2007.

Suwannathat-Pian, Kobkua. "National Identity, the 'Sam-Sams' of Satun, and the Thai Malay Muslims". In *Thai South and Malay North: Ethnic Interactions on a Plural Peninsula*, edited by Michael J. Montesano and Patrick Jory. Singapore: National University of Singapore Press, 2008.

Syukri, Ibrahim. *History of the Malay Kingdom of Patani*. Translated by Conner Bailey and John N. Miksic. Chiang Mai: Silkworm Books, 2005.

Weber, Max. *Die protestantische Ethik und der Geist des Kapitalismus*. Archiv für Sozialwissenschaften und Sozialpolitik, Bd. XX und XXI, 1904/1905. English translation: *The Protestant Ethic and the Spirit of Capitalism*. Talcott Parsons (trans). New York: Scribner, 1958.

Yusuf, Imtiyaz. "Islam and Democracy in Thailand: Reforming the Office of Chularajmontri/Shaikh Al-Islam". *Journal of Islamic Studies* 9, no. 2 (1998): 277–98.

———. "The Ethno-Religious Dimension of the Conflict in Southern Thailand". In *Understanding Conflict and Approaching Peace in Southern Thailand*, edited by Yusuf and Lars Peter Schmidt. Bangkok: Konrad Adenauer Stiftung, 2006.

———. *Faces of Islam in Southern Thailand*. East-West Center Washington Working Papers, No. 7. Washington, D.C.: East-West Center Washington, 2007.

12

IDENTIFYING WITH FICTION: THE ART AND POLITICS OF SHORT STORY WRITING BY MUSLIMS IN THE PHILIPPINES

Coeli Barry

The short story in the Philippines has proven to be an exceptionally popular genre. Awards offered by magazines and other literary outlets are sought after and in traditional media, literary magazines, college publications as well as on Internet sites the prospect of publishing a short story continues to hold great appeal for writers and aspiring authors. Although introduced in English in the early part of the twentieth century during the American colonial period, the short story took root on fertile soil: established vernacular narrative traditions in the Philippines and publishing outlets in languages including Spanish, Tagalog and Cebuano paved the way for the short story's acceptance as a new genre in Filipino literature. In 1940, the Filipino literary critic and writer Jose Garcia Villa wrote that the short story was the Philippines' "most developed art".[1] By the 1950s and 1960s, the most popular short stories were being written in English: the short story was regarded as indisputably Filipino, a genre in which Filipino artistic expression could flourish.

Muslim Filipinos have their own as yet under-explored relationship to the short story in English. Muslim Filipinos participated in this national literary culture by mastering the same literary rules their Christian counterparts adhered to and by telling stories that resonated with the English-language reading audiences. The writing styles of the Muslim authors are, at times, indistinguishable from other short story writers. But the stories by Muslim writers also conjure the differences they experienced moving within and across different social worlds. Short story writing was a way for Muslim Filipinos to move inside the artistic and literary life of the nation. They represented themselves and their home communities as well as the dominant culture within which they studied, worked, and lived. This chapter looks at Muslim Filipino short story writing in thematic and historical perspectives and argues that their writing and publishing can be read as acts of self-representation and negotiation of individual and collective identities. It considers works written between the 1940s and the early 2000s by men and women, most of whom were born in the Muslim south.

The idea that writing stories constitutes identity making builds on the insights expressed by Anthony Appiah. "For those of us", Appiah writes, "raised largely with texts that barely acknowledged the specificity of our existence, each work that simply places before us the world we know — and this is a point that has been made eloquently by feminism — can provide a moment of self-validation" (Appiah 1992, p. 67). The self-validation Appiah refers to is linked in important ways with power and empowerment. Even if only experienced fleetingly, there is meaning in the moment of recognition when a text describes a familiar world for people who are otherwise absent from the stories they are given to read in school, for example, or are allowed to see themselves represented only in negative terms in those official texts. The "us" in Appiah's quote includes the great majority of people who have lived under colonialism or in its shadow. In the case of Muslims in the Philippines, their position both under American colonial rule (1898–1946) and in the independent Philippine nation-state was that of people marginalized and stereotyped in texts other than those of their own making.[2]

For English-language educated Muslim Filipinos, the texts available to them when they entered the path of formal education, especially at secondary and university level, included little that either placed their world before them or reflected back to them the cumulative experiences, dreams and imaginings of their childhood landscapes. Other narrative forms served that purpose: in the languages of the different Muslim groups in the Philippines and in oral rather than written form, myth, poetry, song, drama and prayer could serve as vehicles for telling stories (Rixon 2000; Madale 1986). But the further Muslims went into the modern educational system the more the world they knew expanded: the specificity of their lives became constituted by other worlds and they found other vehicles for expressing themselves, such as writing fiction in English.

Throughout the American colonial era and even after World War II when the Philippines became independent, English was also the *only* language Muslim Filipinos could publish in, as no sustainable vernacular-language press was available to them. Publishing thrived in the languages of the more dominant groups, such as Tagalog or Cebuano speakers where there was a large enough market to support magazines and newspapers. But publishing in the languages of the more marginalized Muslim groups was not an option — either commercially or politically. In the minds of most American colonial officials, Muslim cultural life was worth preserving only insofar as it served the political goal of ethnicizing the Muslims into a group who could (eventually) be integrated into the political system. With the determination that English would be the most effective means of achieving these objectives, Muslim languages were dismissed as not deserving of support in the schools.

Muslims who wrote fiction in English lived at the boundary between the lives they knew as children and the adult world within which they lived as young adults and into maturity — the period in which they became writers, in other words. Muslims from smaller towns and cities moved towards larger ones in Mindanao, in Cebu or to the capital city of Manila in pursuit of education within the English-language school system built by American colonial officials as well as Catholic Filipinos. The short story in English was the vehicle through which they could express themselves — though only to other English-educated readers.

This chapter anchors itself within Muslim-authored short stories written and published from the 1940s to the present, many of which were compiled in a first-ever anthology of Muslim short stories by this author (Barry 2008). In turning to literature written by Muslim Filipinos, we have the chance to explore fictional representations and narratives of a story still being written and rewritten today: namely how this minority navigates the socio-political terrain of the modern Philippines, across differences from one Muslim group to another, within Muslim families and clans, and between Muslims and Catholics.

THE FORMATION OF SHORT STORY WRITERS: SCHOOLING, LANGUAGE AND THE NEGOTIATIONS OF CULTURE UNDER COLONIAL RULE AND BEYOND

American colonialism fostered the emergence of a pan-Muslim identity across diverse linguistic groups among Muslim Filipinos. Educational policies enacted throughout the first half of the twentieth century — particularly the decision to use only English in schools and in public life — were decisive in establishing the parameters within which the intellectual and literary life of this minority could conceivably take shape. In the American colonial era, English became the language of education, governance and mainstream culture and it was the language through which American imperialists attempted to make subjects out of Muslims. American colonialism was pivotal in the development of a self-conscious Muslim identity among a generation of educated Muslim elites who were otherwise divided by significant linguistic, geographical, and, to some extent, cultural barriers. American rule was thus instrumental in creating a pan-Muslim identity (McKenna 2000, p. 17) but this Muslim identity was not homogenous: divides persisted between and within Muslim communities, as the stories discussed below reflect.

In the southern Philippines, before the spread of English, there was no single language by which all Muslims from different areas of Mindanao or the Sulu islands could communicate. According to the scholar Abdullah T. Madale, certain linguistic groups were similar enough to others such that communication was possible (Tausug and Sama or Maranao with Maguindanaon, for example). However, across these groups and among these groups differences persisted well into the twentieth century. In Madale's assessment "except for religion and, probably a common history which is largely contemporary, Muslim Filipinos are distinct and different by themselves as they are with Christian Filipinos" (Madale 1998, p. 495). (It should be noted that Madale's view that the common history does not stretch far into the past is not one shared by other Muslim intellectuals, including the preeminent historian Cesar Majul, whose more explicitly nationalist readings of Muslim history suggest a longer shared past for Muslims across language and geographic divides.)

The intent of the colonial administrators was to prepare the Muslim elite for participation in the Philippine democracy-in-the-making, but as a singular ethnicized minority. Most American colonial administrators believed that to achieve this vision there could be no compromise where language was concerned — only English would be used. One key colonial administrator in the Muslim South, Leonard Wood, wrote: "local languages are crude, devoid of literature, and limited in range.... we can hope ... to make English the main language and the medium of transacting all official and most business affairs in the comparatively near future" (Wood 1904, pp. 14–15, quoted in Milligan 2005, p. 62). American colonial rule placed the highest priority on the political integration of Muslims into the emergent democratic regime. Colonial officials minimized the importance of Muslim intellectual life and cultural practices deemed incompatible with Christian American notions of civilized life were stigmatized or outlawed.

After a brutal military campaign in the early 1900s, political leaders among the Muslim communities adapted to the new political order, notwithstanding the fact that resistance to American rule persisted in some places up to the 1920s. Many factors were at work in determining how groups responded to the presence of the American military and civilian officials after the military campaigns ended. Depending on one's location, both in the geography of Mindanao and the Sulu islands and within the hierarchies of Muslim society, the experience of American colonialism might be very direct or more mediated. Certain parts of the southern islands had long-established contact with neighbouring sultanates and with traders from other parts of the world, and exposure to outsiders was much more established. Americans relied on the Muslim political elites as they established their presence, but poorer Muslims were in less-direct contact with colonial officials and colonialism shaped their lives differently as a result. Hierarchy, stratification and uneven concentrations of power within Muslim groups remained compelling topics for writers from the 1940s on, as did themes that highlighted the tensions and uncertainties experienced by poorer Muslims when confronting representatives of the state either in bureaucratic or educational guise.

The first story in English published by a Muslim Filipino, *Blue Blood of the Big Astana*[3] (published in 1941), was written by Ibrahim Jubaira. It depicts a world where people are enmeshed in a community but also made to feel the presence of a more formidable authority beyond the community's boundaries (Barry 2004). In this story an orphaned boy is placed in the home of the *datu*[4] because his elderly aunt cannot care for him. It is the dynamics and politics of life in the home of the *datu* (the *Astana* of the story's title) which shape the boy's early years. As a young man returning to the *Astana* it is clear that the Christian state — faceless, nameless — has been challenged and the community has suffered defeat for having confronted the government. The state is virtually absent from the childhood idyll of the narrator and it is the politics of that home — the *Astana* — that affect his early years far more deeply than any political force beyond his grasp. But the child experiences first-hand the politics of poverty: he is relegated to a position which shifts between servant and childhood playmate of the *datu*'s daughter.

In using the term "Christian state", Jubaira leaves unspecified whether this state was comprised of American officials or Filipinos who replaced Americans when the bureaucracy was Filipinized beginning in 1916. (To put this change in the civil service in perspective, in 1913 there had been 2,623 American and 6,363 Filipino officials; in 1921 there were 13,240 Filipino and 614 American administrators.) That the terms Christian or Northerner and not American or Filipino are used suggests the possibility that either counted as an outsider. It was in the schools where the most-sustained contact with the alien teachers took place and conflicts that draw attention to the contrast between existing cultural beliefs and the values which informed the new officially secular schools appear with some frequency in Muslim short stories.

Direct contact with Americans was likely infrequent for most Muslims (and for non-Muslims as well) but the new regime made its presence felt with the expansion of a school system. These schools occasioned different responses from the local populations. In the first decades of colonial rule, schools tended to serve only a small percentage of Muslim children: it is estimated that in the 1920s only one in five school-aged children were enrolled in government-recognized schools (Milligan 2005, p. 78). Milligan persuasively argues that the low numbers of Muslim children attending school could be explained by the location of the schools, namely in urban areas where Christian settlements had tended to develop, and the fact that Christians taught in the schools. American-style schools were officially secular, but American Protestant values informed the outlook of the teachers and impressed on the students the hierarchy of knowledge that located local, religious learning well below that of the modern school.

Consequently the school was regarded as a place where one's culture or religious education would be compromised.

Conflict over schooling in the short stories did not only single out Americans as the threats to Muslim life. Nor was religious knowledge necessarily pitted against secular learning; rather a number of stories reveal how strong the pull between traditional beliefs and self-consciously modernizing schooling might be. This conflict anchors one story of the writer, Calbi Asain. Asain is himself from a very poor family and went on to receive a PhD from the University of the Philippines.

In one of Calbi Asain's best known stories "The Rebel" (published in 1985), the protagonist/narrator is leaving childhood and is becoming more and more aware of the divide between the knowledge he learns at home and "school knowledge". The story pits the science of the school against the superstitious ways of the boy's grandmother and the risks entailed in forgoing the superstitions of a strong-willed grandmother become very clear to the boy. If he chooses to follow his teacher and believe in what he is learning about health and science in school, not only will his grandmother be angry, he will risk bringing bad luck to his family by disrespecting the spirits who determine the family's well-being.

Although the story was written and published in the height of some of the worst violence between Muslim separatists and the Philippine Government, the rebel of the title is an adolescent boy fighting against his grandmother's worldview from which he struggles to escape. While other stories written in the 1970s, 1980s and 1990s foreground the violence of Muslim separatists fighting with the Philippines Government, Asain's rebel fights a battle common to children in countless settings in the Philippines and elsewhere in the world: embracing the modern knowledge offered in school can be interpreted as a "rebellion" against what is familiar and legitimate in the home.

Mastery of English remained a stark reminder of the divides that separated Muslims from one another, as can be seen in a story written in the late 1960s by the first woman author of short stories, Noralyn Mustafa, called "A Day in the Life of Dr Karim" (published in 1971). In this story Karim has returned to his hometown to practise as a doctor in a hospital desperately lacking in supplies. A young man is brought in with a gunshot wound and he will need the hospital's only available oxygen machine to survive. Shortly after tending to the man, Karim is faced with an awful decision: the governor of the province is also brought in for emergency care and Karim is forced to take the oxygen tank from the man and give it to the governor. If the governor dies, Karim is warned by a senior physician in the hospital, there will be chaos, "you know how it is", the elderly doctor tells Karim. (The chaos here could refer to political violence that would likely ensue after the governor's death.)

Karim knows that he is revered by the poor relatives who trust him to save the man and this makes his situation the more wrenching. When Karim makes the fateful decision to give the functioning tank to the governor, he must do so in front of the family. The victim's family cannot understand English so Karim uses English to communicate with the nurse about what he is going to do. This excerpt describes Karim talking to the nurse in one language and the relatives of the victim in another:

> The other relatives came nearer at his sign of something unusual. Why, what's wrong? Why is the machine being removed?
> "We are going to change it," he told them in the *dialect*.
> The nurse gave him an abrupt glance. "Change it?" she asked in English.
> "Have the other one brought here, the one by the door of the operating room."
> "But it is empty, doctor," the nurse said.

In his position as an English-speaking doctor, Karim has authority that comes from his mastery of medical knowledge and his status as a doctor, though the limits of this authority within the hospital are evident when Karim must yield to the senior staff who will care for the governor first — regardless of the consequences for the young Muslim man. Mustafa conveys the sense of powerlessness the young doctor feels, aware as he is of how little he can do in the face of the conditions within which he works. Karim is reminded throughout the story of what opportunities he has given up by returning to serve in his home province. He also knows that he lives at great distance from those same people who look to him as one of their own: "he was of them, yet separated from them ... from the first day he learned to write the English alphabet".

The pattern of travelling both geographic and social distances in order to receive higher education continued throughout much of the twentieth century. Though American colonialism discouraged or thwarted the possibilities for developing writing in languages used by Muslims in the Philippines, through their educational and language policies, Muslims who were able to pursue schooling could make the short story in English their own. These Muslim writers carried stories of those less-English-literate as they moved into other educational and professional worlds. One important outlet for their writings, as well as those of other Filipinos from around the country, was the magazines established during the American colonial era.

MAGAZINES AND MUSLIM PARTICIPATION IN AN EMERGENT NATIONAL CULTURAL FORM

The history of the short story in the Philippines is intertwined with that of the modern magazine. English-language magazines established in the American colonial period were vital to the short story's popularity and they nurtured and showcased a literary style that was modern, secular and national. In the days before television and the Internet, a magazine with national distribution provided an author exposure impossible to come by otherwise. The potential reach of a magazine made it an important part of the cultural life of the growing middle classes whose members comprised the most earnest readership. For Muslim Filipinos to publish in a major magazine in the Philippines was to be a part of the emergent, national culture being created and represented therein. In this next section, I look in particular at the role of one magazine, the *Philippines Free Press*, a publication which set the standard for modern English-language writing in the Philippines.

The *Philippines Free Press* was founded in the 1910s and published continuously until its closure by President Marcos in the early 1970s when Martial Law was declared. The *Free Press* resumed publication after the end of the Marcos regime, though it never regained its previous stature. The *Free Press* outlived most of its rival publications and, over time, it developed a style that won loyal subscribers throughout the Philippines. Though the readership was concentrated heavily in the largest cities of Manila and Cebu, it also extended to other urban areas throughout the Philippines and included provincial and rural-based school teachers and civil servants as well. In the estimation of a cultural historian of the Philippines, Resil Mojares, the *Free Press* was the "bible of the middle-class homes" throughout the 1940s, 1950s and into the 1960s (Mojares 2007). With its mixture of politics, commentary and literature, the magazine focused heavily on news of national (Manila-centred) politics and also featured shorter news articles, letters and commentary from around the country.

The Muslim writers who published there before its closure in 1972 were as comfortable writing about the milieu of small towns and cities of the Philippines as they were conjuring what might be construed as Muslim settings. Their focus within their imaginary landscapes and how they conveyed the ordinariness of those settings revealed their position as insider or outsider, depending upon their authorial voice.

In the story "Obituary for Today" (published in 1968) by Noralyn Mustafa, for example, about the funeral for a mentally disabled son of a prominent small-town family, there is nothing that marks the author as a non-Christian. However, in the way she draws attention to the smallest details of a landscape dominated by Catholic symbols, Mustafa achieves a critical perspective on the routine rituals — and cruelties — of the dominant culture that is hard to find in other Filipino short stories.

> There was an almost unbearably heady profusion of flower scents coming out of the church, and even the atmosphere outside could not diffuse the intense perfume. There were flowers leading all the way to the altar, flowers by the doorway, flowers scattered on the ground, where some blossoms had fallen from the bouquets and wreaths that had been continuously brought to the church since yesterday, when the body was taken to lie in rest.
>
> Today Pilo was to be buried.
>
> ...[T]he people who had attended the funeral rites slowly began to come out of the church followed by the coffin, a beautifully wrought box that shone golden in the sun, decorated with elaborate carvings of angels, roses and fern leaves — a thing of such masterful commercial artistry.
>
> The funeral procession, to be sure, had more than the requisites that would rate plenty of superlatives the next day in the society column of the local weekly. It was good coincidence that the funeral was held on a Friday afternoon because the paper came out Saturday morning, and therefore, every detail would still be alive and fresh in the society editor's mind. She was known to give more treatment to more recent affairs regardless of its degree of importance.
>
> It seemed that all cars in town were lined up in the procession, which meant that almost all who owned cars were in attendance. In fact Mrs De los Reyes, the outgoing president of the women's auxiliary of the church organization, who was known to suffer from a mysterious allergy to funerals, precisely insisted on attending, much to the dismay of her husband. He was very sensitive about her health, but the De los Reyeses had just acquired their new car three days earlier.

The bite in Mustafa's tone, when combined with her detailed rendering of the scene at the church, conveys the view of an outsider with a critical eye. Its criticism, however, does not pertain to the religious symbols per se, but to the ways they are deployed by the small-town elite whose main preoccupation is using the funeral as an occasion to show-off their finery and impress the town. The narrator's position is that of an outsider, but one all too familiar with the rules and habits of the insiders.

Mustafa's "Termites" (published in 1970), by contrast, sidesteps the issue of religion altogether and is set squarely inside a small city radio station where the younger employees watch as their middle-aged manager descends into despair. Here, and in her other stories, she writes with total ease, and sensitivity, on the changing times of the 1960s in which the allure of the modern (in this story conveyed by the musical tastes of the young disc jockeys at the radio station) is contrasted with the stolid ways of the older generations.

The *Free Press* actively sought contributions from writers outside Manila and helped to shape a literary style that was to have national and cross-regional appeal. Though minimal biographical information of the author might be included along with the story, local accents and the provincial base of writers were muted in the short stories published during the heyday of these magazines. The magazine showcased and nurtured writing that could be read nationally, at least by the English-educated middle classes. But in cultivating this type of "un-accented" literary voice that was so definitive in the making of Filipino short stories from the 1940s through the 1970s at least, the *Free Press* was a platform for Muslim writers to sharpen their skills and gain a readership, but not as Muslims per se. Rather they were simply good writers of the Philippines. The facility a writer like Noralyn Mustafa demonstrated in her stories published in the 1960s and early 1970s has meant that she escaped notice as a "Muslim writer". This simultaneous exposure/blending in that the magazine made possible had the effect of keeping the contributions of some Muslim Filipinos from being recognized in this genre that came to be regarded as quintessentially national.

The fate of another writer, Ibrahim Jubaira, born some twenty years before Mustafa, was quite different. Ibrahim Jubaira is the best known and most prolific Muslim Filipino writer. Like many other writers in his generation (Jubaira was born in 1920), he owed his reputation to the *Free Press*: he published close to fifty stories in the *Free Press*, beginning with his first on the eve of World War II. These stories were set in varied contexts, some of which would clearly have been very foreign to readers in the 1950s and 1960s, but many of his stories were set inside of cities, suburban neighbourhoods, somewhat non-descript towns that could be any number of places. Jubaira developed an authorial voice that the literary editors of the *Free Press* thought its readers would find appetizing as well, to judge by the number published there. But interestingly, he was singled out for his "Muslim-ness", an attribute that was laden with colonialist overtones even when used by Filipino intellectuals writing in the first decades of Philippine independence.

Nick Joaquim, one of the Philippines' best-known intellectuals and a writer of fiction himself, wrote in 1964 about Muslims contributing an "exotic branch of our writing", by which he did *not* mean the epics, myths, and folklore of Muslims, but the short stories of Ibrahim Jubaira (Joaquim 1964). In spite of the fact that Jubaira's stories take place in settings distinctly outside of any place that might be described as Muslim and that his writing style was similar to non-Muslims, he was not seen in this way by his fellow writers.

How can we account for such a reading of Jubaira by a writer of Joaquim's standing? At the time that this observation was made, the foundations were also being laid for categorizing many aspects of Muslim cultural life as traditional, by which was often meant isolated from and impervious to change. The still-young Philippine nation was at that time in the beginning stages of developing folklore studies and the seeds were being sown for official, nationalist readings of the cultural history and landscape of the emergent nation. Though short-story writing was no more new to Muslims than it was to lowland, Christian Filipinos, the forces of nationalism were well under way and hierarchies and boundaries drawn that marked Muslim cultural life as distinct. Muslim intellectuals wrote in English in the 1950s and 1960s on topics of urgency: the increasingly entrenched nature of Muslims' disadvantaged position was becoming clearer, as were the political consequences of neglecting the socio-economic betterment of Muslims. In these writings, which appeared in the same magazines as the short stories, the authors were very self-consciously claiming to speak as Muslims and for Muslims. (The politics behind their claiming authority to write for Muslims is an important issue but not one that can be addressed in this essay.) But creative writers remained few and, thanks ironically to their success in magazines like the *Free Press*, writers such as Mustafa blended into the magazine's literary landscape as very able writers of the short story in English (with the exception of Jubaira, who was always recognized as Muslim).

But there is little question that the reading of Jubaira through the lens of the "Muslim as exotic" was also a consequence of the political divide that was growing throughout the 1950s as the southern islands of Mindanao and the Sulu archipelago (but mostly the former) were receiving tens of thousands of migrants from other parts of the Philippines. Conflict was growing apace and the violence that conflict generated only served to make it possible to conceive of Muslim Filipinos as living by different codes from that of their majority Catholic fellow citizens. (This, in spite of the fact that violence in post-war democratic elections in the Philippines was rampant.)

Carol Hau's path-breaking study on literature and nationalism in the Philippines observes that culture in general, and literature in particular, is yoked to nation-state building. And that in modern Philippine history, culture was invoked to heal rifts that are part and parcel of that very building process (Hau 2000, p. 14). By the 1960s, when Muslim disenfranchisement and violent conflict in Mindanao became difficult for Muslims and non-Muslims alike to ignore, there were efforts on the part of scholars and academics to make Muslim culture more widely known among non-Muslims. One example of this can be found in a much-cited study on Muslim Filipino literature by the scholar Alfredo T. Tiamson. Published in the early 1970s, Tiamson's monograph chastised the reigning literary historians of the day for glaring errors and too brief treatment of Muslim literature in writings to date. He argued that there was an urgent need for the majority Christians to become more knowledgeable about Muslim literary traditions. But significantly these traditions did not include English-language writings being published in the magazines people like Tiamson read regularly:

> [I]n light of the so-called Muslim-Christian conflicts raging in predominantly Muslim areas ... we are forced to take a more serious view of our relations with our Muslim brothers. Perhaps a knowledge of their oral literary traditions will help in an initial understanding of this people. (Tiamson 1976, p. 2)

Convinced though Tiamson was that a greater awareness of Muslim literary achievements on the part of non-Muslims could help to bridge the increasingly rancorous divide between these groups, the idea that

Muslims' written output in English was also worth investigating did not figure into Tiamson's thinking.

In Tiamson's writing the logic of nation building reveals itself: culture and literature can serve their healing function only if the majority population is willing to become more knowledgeable in the history of this largely alienated minority and, importantly, if that minority's separateness from the majority remained in place. Others, though, sounded less sanguine in their assessment of the odds of having integration, let alone reconciliation. The best-known Muslim intellectual of the twentieth century, Cesar Majul, is quoted in the close of Tiamson's piece. Majul states that no solution to the problems of Muslims can be permanent or even possible "without taking into consideration ... the principle that the Muslims in the Philippines have an older history than that of other Filipinos or even that of the Filipino nation and that they are aware of this" (Majul 1971, p. 21).

CONFLICT AND VIOLENCE IN MUSLIM STORIES AND MUSLIM LIVES

In the 1950s and 1960s, there was large-scale migration from the overcrowded and politically restive northern and central islands of the county into the large (and then much less populous) island of Mindanao. Government policies and everyday political practices combined to privilege the Catholic Filipino population. This migration changed the demographic character of the island and generated tension between Muslims and Catholics. Violent confrontations (isolated and small-scale at this stage) between Muslims and Christians ensued throughout the 1950s and 1960s and by the early 1970s the government of Ferdinand Marcos ordered tens of thousands of soldiers into the Southern Philippines to quash a growing separatist movement. The stories produced at the height of some of the worst violence between the Philippines Government and separatist groups that took place from the 1960s through the 1980s reveal feelings of being overpowered, confused and ultimately weary from the conflict.

Said Sadain's story, "Spirits in the Box" (published in 1978), takes one phase of the violent conflict of the 1970s as its frame. Set against the backdrop of the destruction of the city of Jolo in 1974, Sadain's young narrator, the twelve-year-old Ghafur, has been forced to leave his home with his mother for shelter in a camp while the city below burns. He has lost his father to the war and now his teenaged brother has taken up the gun. Ghafur is confused about what is going on and why he has been forced to leave his home. Said himself gives his readers only small pieces of information that might clarify what is going on and why, and he uses the child narrator to highlight the lack of clarity about who is responsible for breaking his family up and leaving them homeless. Though the audience's knowledge is presumed to be greater than that of the narrator, Said is very subtle in identifying the deeper causes of the violence. As a result the audience is only slightly less confused than the child narrator by the situation.

> It had just been barely two weeks ago when his mother and his Kah Abing had shouted at each other in their mountain hut. The argument was over a matter which Ghafur's twelve-year-old sense could not understand. It was not completely settled, for Kah Abing, his solidly built body bespeaking the firmness of his heart, disappeared the next day, presumably with the memory of his slain father driving him. Shortly thereafter, Ghafur and his mother moved out to Jolo, hurrying through the mountain trails in the manner of hunted boars.
>
> It was at the Center that he met Layla, a hometown friend, she with the dimples in her cheeks. Together, they attended barrio school, and used to laugh at a teacher who stuttered in speaking a foreign language and never quite got the lessons across to the pupils. They used to talk about the airplanes that hovered above the barrio once in a while, about the wheels that rolled under the ratting machines, and exchanged vague ideas of the cities beyond the sea. And always, together or apart, they would understand none of these things they talked about. Then the war came: strange happenings in a familiar place and people had to move away in search of the familiar things in strange places.

Said wrote this story when he was a teenager himself (seventeen years old), and, not long before writing the story, he had witnessed the burning of his hometown, Jolo, as separatists and the Philippine Navy battled, house by house, leaving the town destroyed in their wake.

In the 1990s and coming closer to the present, political violence is either absent or backgrounded. In its place, struggles within Muslim families and communities are the focus of the stories. In a story set much closer to the present, Pearlsha Abubakar's "Maghrib" (written in 2004), one can see how the long years of violence from the 1970s on have left deep divides between the military and local Muslim leaders. In the story, the father's life in Southern Philippines politics leads him to seek financial support from sources in the Middle East, and when the father takes to wearing Arab dress he comes under suspicion in the eyes of the local police and military.

Close to forty years after the worst of the violence began in Mindanao and in the Sulu Islands, Muslim nationalism transmuted into Muslim pride, and this sentiment and worldview is in evidence in the most recent generation of writers. Many of the younger female writers are simultaneously proud of their Muslim identity, their "dialect" and their community. But they are not uncritical of what is being asked of them as Muslim women, nor do they shy away from depicting conflict. However, these writers seem more likely to take up conflict *within* Muslim communities rather than against the Philippine state. One notable trend in the writings that were produced over the past decade or so is the use of languages besides English for the dialog in English-language short stories. The writers used languages such as Maguindanao or Tausug or even Tagalog more frequently, though only in the dialog, suggesting changes in their view of what constitutes an "English"-language short story as well as the authors' ideas about readership. If the stories are not being written for a national audience, the presence of languages incomprehensible to groups other than members of the "speech community" of the writer is not an issue.

Tensions within families, especially those between generations, are taken up in the stories of the last two decades and there are few outsiders, either Americans or Christian Filipinos, as was the case in the stories profiled above. Rather the characters are surrounded by fellow Muslims and concerned about maintaining practices that are meaningful only to other Muslims. In Loren Lao's "Trip to a Forbidden Land" (unpublished), a mother is enraged that her daughter went to her husband's hometown without having waited for the formal rituals of introduction and welcoming. The mother will hear nothing of the daughter's protest that those rituals are costly and impractical. The world inhabited by mother and daughter, though clearly in the process of changing, is one separate from non-Muslims.

In Arifah Jamil's "Aesthetics" (published in 2005), a mother teaches her daughter how to choose what veil to wear with what clothes. The selection of the right colour is much more than fashion — on the basis of the daughter's appearance the family will be judged. In Jamil's "Mukna" (published in 2005), a teenaged-girl rebels against the forms of Muslim life she must master and abide by if she is to live within her family.

She forgets the prayer she should say before her morning bath and is restless at the community's prayer session throughout which she must sit properly alongside her mother. Her father's strictures on her dress and conduct at a party force her to choose between the claustrophobic atmosphere at home and escape.

Here is the final section of the story:

> The girl decides to take the last trip of the town's public transport. She thinks she should leave the house. She thinks she has to go away from rules. She tells herself the conventions of the family are as tight as the mukna she wore on the Idl Fit'r. The girl has to breathe. As the girl steps out of the bus, a man her Father's age blocks her. "Bapa, can't you see I was about to step out?" the girl looses control of her temper. "All of us want to get out," he says. The girl waits for a ride. She realizes no other means of transportation is used there except for private cars and the bus, which just left. She is close to crying as she sits on the bench at the terminal. She wonders why the schedule for the next trip is taking longer than usual. Three hours — that won't be long. That is how far their town is from the next town. But the girl looks at the bus with the name of a town farther away.

Making certain she will put enough distance between herself and her father, the girl waits for the bus that will take her as far as possible. Depicting the girl's break from the family, the open rebellion implied by that act, a story like this would have been hard to write in the decades before social norms in Muslim communities underwent so many changes.

Young women in many of these stories are conscious but not necessarily accepting of the expectations that are placed on them by their families and communities. What is striking is the degree to which they feel comfortable revealing those reservations. This confidence indicates the extent to which Muslim Filipinos have claimed the genre of the short story and use it so effectively to depict and reflect upon their identities. The stories reflect the changes in consciousness taking place in which definitions of "us" are contested and negotiated without invoking an "us/them" referent in the construction of Muslim identities.

CONCLUSION

In this chapter, I have argued that the analysis of fiction can shed light on the study of Muslim identity politics and that their writing is an important part of their identity making in the modern Philippines. Muslim

Filipinos writing short stories over the past seventy years contributed to the genre embraced and celebrated as Filipino, though their participation was generally overlooked, obscured or misrepresented. The story told and retold in textbooks, in English-language histories and in the media was that of conflict in the form of feuds and infighting between political clans, between separatists and the national government, which resulted in large-scale militarization, and the often violent and uneven process of the political integration of Muslims. The unhappy ending of this story is "marginality, dissatisfaction and ultimately, rejection [by Muslim Filipinos] of the Philippine nation-state" (Amoroso 2003, p. 143).

Looking at works of fiction written by men and women across a time span of nearly seventy years, it is possible to see the experiences of Muslims in the development of the modern Philippines throughout the twentieth century being reconstructed and reimagined in ways that bring nuance or another dimension to the political histories. Fiction written in the 1950s, 1960s and even into the 1970s, for example, dealt with the theme of the rupture that resulted from the coming of American rule in the first decades of the twentieth century. The violence that shook Mindanao and the Sulu islands in the 1970s and 1980s was taken up in short stories, but the writings by Muslim Filipinos were also set squarely in landscapes far from the areas where the conflicts took place. Muslims could narrate their specificity or they could slip in quietly beside their non-Muslim classmates, officemates, colleagues and write without any reference at all to their identities. Though the integration of the majority of Muslims into the predominantly Catholic Philippines has been uneven, inadequate and unsatisfactory, many Muslims have succeeded in carving out ways of being both conscious of their minority status and able to navigate comfortably within non-Muslim settings. Particularly over the past ten to twenty years, a generation of Muslim Filipinos has entered adulthood embracing their Muslim identity — whether they see that as deriving primarily from religious practice or in terms of language and cultural practice — but they do not feel any less Filipino as a result (Horvatich 2002).

English has been, and remains, the language by which Muslims from different language groups and different parts of Mindanao, Sulu and elsewhere in the Philippines communicate. In addition to being the language through which Muslims are educated in the national schools, colleges and universities, and which they use if they find work outside the Philippines, English is also the language which the nationalist and separatist movement leaders used as well when they pursued more radical visions of self-identity within or apart from the nation-state. The scope of those visions change and there is more diversity within and across Muslim communities in how to define and give meaning to their identities within the Philippines as Muslims. As is evident in this chapter, there are recognizable shifts in how being Muslim can be conveyed through fiction.

The short story's popularity and vitality in the Philippines and perhaps more widely within Southeast Asia indicates that this genre is one that resonates with readers from different backgrounds and interpretative techniques that draw on a mixture of disciplinary fields. It is a literary form which is open to experimentation and, while short fiction is clearly undergoing many changes, especially with Internet technologies, short story writing has secured its place as a vehicle for giving meaning to changing cultures and social worlds. Muslim Filipino writers have claimed this genre as their own and they will likely continue to narrate their specificity through it in the years to come.

Notes

1. Jose Garcia Villa, "The Rise of the Short Story in the Philippines", first published in the *Philippine American News Digest*, August 1940. Cited in *The Critical Villa: Essays in Literary Criticism by Jose Garcia Villa*, compiled and edited by Jonathan Chua (Quezon City: Ateneo de Manila University Press, 2002), p. 280.
2. A prominent Muslim author and career civil servant, Ibrahim A. Jubaira made an impassioned plea in the first decade of postcolonial independence to confront these stereotypes head on. Focusing on one trope in particular, the "Muslim as pirate", Jubaira called for Muslim Filipinos to reject the "Christian history" of the Philippines that depicted Muslims who resisted Spanish colonial rule as "Moro pirates", while Christian Filipinos were called heroes. "Revise that history", Jubaira wrote "or throw it away". "So You are a Moslem Now", *Philippines Free Press* (October 1, 1955), p. 47.
3. *Astana* refers to the home of the *datu*, a person of high social or political status. It is sometimes spelled as *Istana*.
4. This is a title traditionally used for royalty, and subsequently used for a person of high social or political status.

References

Abinales, Patricio N. *Making Mindanao: Cotabato and Davao in the Formation of the Philippine Nation-state*. Quezon City: Ateneo De Manila University Press, 2000.

Abubakar, Pearlsha. "Ayesha's Pretty Hate Machine". In *Necessary Fictions: Philippine Literature and the Nation, 1946–1980*, by Caroline S. Hau. Quezon City: Ateneo de Manila University Press, 2000.

———. "Maghrib". In *The Many Ways of Being Muslim: Fiction by Muslim Filipinos*, edited by Coeli Barry. Ithaca, NY: Cornell Southeast Asia Publications; Manila: Anvil, 2008.

Amoroso, Donna. "Inheriting the 'Moro Problem': Muslim Authority and Colonial Rule in British Malaya and the Philippines". In *The American Colonial State in the Philippines: Global Perspectives*, edited by Julian Go and Anne L. Foster. Durham, NC: Duke University Press, 2003.

Appiah, Anthony Kwame. *In My father's House: Africa in the Philosophy of Culture*. New York: Oxford University Press, 1992.

Asain, Calbi. "Pannuggud (The Rebel)". In *The Many Ways of Being Muslim: Fiction by Muslim Filipinos*, edited by Coeli Barry. Ithaca, NY: Cornell Southeast Asia Publications; Manila: Anvil, 2008.

Barry, Coeli, ed. "Polyglot Catholicism: Genealogies and Reinterpretations of the Philippine Catholic Church". *Pilipinas*, no. 32, Special Issue: Philippine Post-War Nationalism, 1999.

———. *The Many Ways of Being Muslim: Fiction by Muslim Filipinos*. Ithaca, NY: Cornell Southeast Asia Publications; Manila: Anvil, 2008.

Chua, Jonathan, ed., *The Critical Villa: Essays in Literary Criticism by Jose Garcia Villa*. Quezon City: Ateneo de Manila University Press, 2002.

Guro, Elin Anisha. "The Homecoming". In *The Many Ways of Being Muslim: Fiction by Muslim Filipinos*, edited by Coeli Barry. Ithaca, NY: Cornell Southeast Asia Publications; Manila: Anvil, 2008.

Hau, Caroline S. *Necessary Fictions: Philippine Literature and the Nation, 1946–1980*. Quezon City: Ateneo de Manila University Press, 2000.

Horvatich, Patricia. "The Martyr and the Mayor: On the Politics of Identity in the Southern Philippines". In *Cultural Citizenship in Island Southeast Asia: Nation and Belonging in the Hinterland*, edited by Renaldo Rosato. 2002.

Jamil, Arifah Macacua.. "Initiation". In *Necessary Fictions: Philippine Literature and the Nation, 1946–1980*, edited by Caroline Hau. Quezon City: Ateneo de Manila University Press, 2000.

———. "Mukna". In *Necessary Fictions: Philippine Literature and the Nation, 1946–1980*, edited by Caroline Hau. Quezon City: Ateneo de Manila University Press, 2000.

———. "Aesthetics". In *The Many Ways of Being Muslim: Fiction by Muslim Filipinos*, edited by Coeli Barry. Ithaca, NY: Cornell Southeast Asia Publications; Manila: Anvil, 2008.

Joaquin, Nick. "The Young Writers". In *Literature and Society: A Symposium*. Manila: Florentino, 1964.

Jubaira, Ibrahim.. "Bird in a Cage". In *The Many Ways of Being Muslim: Fiction by Muslim Filipinos*, edited by Coeli Barry. Ithaca, NY: Cornell Southeast Asia Publications; Manila: Anvil, 2008.

———. "Blue Blood of the Big Astana". In *The Many Ways of Being Muslim: Fiction by Muslim Filipinos*, edited by Coeli Barry. Ithaca, NY: Cornell Southeast Asia Publications; Manila: Anvil, 2008.

———. "The Tall Big Man". In *The Many Ways of Being Muslim: Fiction by Muslim Filipinos*, edited by Coeli Barry. Ithaca, NY: Cornell Southeast Asia Publications; Manila: Anvil, 2008.

Lao, Loren Hallilah I.. "Good Old Bapa". In *Necessary Fictions: Philippine Literature and the Nation, 1946–1980*, edited by Caroline Hau. Quezon City: Ateneo de Manila University Press, 2000.

———. "The Trip to a Forbidden Land". In *The Many Ways of Being Muslim: Fiction by Muslim Filipinos*, edited by Coeli Barry. Ithaca, NY: Cornell Southeast Asia Publications; Manila: Anvil, 2008.

Madale, Nagasura T. *A Preliminary Classification of Muslim Literature in the Philippines*. Marawi City: Mindanao State University, 1974.

Majul, Cesar Adib. "The Muslims in the Philippines: A Historical Perspective". *Graphic*, 9 June 1971.

McKenna, Thomas M. *Muslim Rulers and Rebels: Everyday Politics and Armed Separatism in the Southern Philippines*. Berkeley: University of California Press, 1998.

Milligan, Jeffrey Ayala. *Islamic Identity, Postcoloniality, and Educational Policy: Schooling and Ethno-Religious Conflict in the Southern Philippines*. New York: Palgrave Macmillan, 2005.

Mustafa, Noralyn. "A Day in the Life of Dr Karim". In *The Many Ways of Being Muslim: Fiction by Muslim Filipinos*, edited by Coeli Barry. Ithaca, NY: Cornell Southeast Asia Publications; Manila: Anvil, 2008.

———. "Obituary for Today". In *The Many Ways of Being Muslim: Fiction by Muslim Filipinos*, edited by Coeli Barry. Ithaca, NY: Cornell Southeast Asia Publications; Manila: Anvil, 2008.

———. "Termites". In *The Many Ways of Being Muslim: Fiction by Muslim Filipinos*, edited by Coeli Barry. Ithaca, NY: Cornell Southeast Asia Publications; Manila: Anvil, 2008.

Rixon, Gerard. "Muslim Voices: An Introduction to Islam's Oral Dimension". In *Asian Cooperation: Problems and Challenges in the New Century*. Quezon City: Ateneo Center for Asian Studies, Ateneo de Manila University, 2005.

Sadain, Mehol K. "Ocean". In *The Many Ways of Being Muslim: Fiction by Muslim Filipinos*, edited by Coeli Barry. Ithaca, NY: Cornell Southeast Asia Publications; Manila: Anvil, 2008.

———. "Old Father". In *The Many Ways of Being Muslim: Fiction by Muslim Filipinos*, edited by Coeli Barry. Ithaca, NY: Cornell Southeast Asia Publications; Manila: Anvil, 2008.

———. "The River Below". In *The Many Ways of Being Muslim: Fiction by Muslim Filipinos*, edited by Coeli Barry. Ithaca, NY: Cornell Southeast Asia Publications; Manila: Anvil, 2008.

Sadain, Said, Jr. "Babel Rising". In *The Many Ways of Being Muslim: Fiction by Muslim Filipinos*, edited by Coeli Barry. Ithaca, NY: Cornell Southeast Asia Publications; Manila: Anvil, 2008.

———. "Pages". In *The Many Ways of Being Muslim: Fiction by Muslim Filipinos*, edited by Coeli Barry. Ithaca, NY: Cornell Southeast Asia Publications; Manila: Anvil, 2008.

———. "Spirits in a Box". In *The Many Ways of Being Muslim: Fiction by Muslim Filipinos*, edited by Coeli Barry. Ithaca, NY: Cornell Southeast Asia Publications; Manila: Anvil, 2008.

Tiamson, Alfredo T. *Essays in Muslim Filipino Literature*. Manila: Office of the Special Assistant on Cultural Communities, Department of Public Information, 1976.

Wood, Leonard. *First Annual Report of Major General Leonard Wood, Governor of the Moro Province*. Zamboanga City: Mindanao Herald Publishing, 1904.

13

ISSUES ON ISLAM AND THE MUSLIMS IN SINGAPORE POST-9/11: AN ANALYSIS OF THE DOMINANT PERSPECTIVE

Noor Aisha Abdul Rahman

The 11 September attack, the Bali bombings, and arrest of Jemaah Islamiyah (JI) operatives in Singapore reveal once again the centrality of ethnicity in Singapore's ideology of survival. Political discourse on these issues resurfaced concerns for the fragility of Singapore's ethnic relations and its vulnerability as a cohesive nation in which the Chinese comprise the majority (74.1 per cent), while the Malays (13.4 per cent), Indians (9.2 per cent) and a diverse array of other ethnic groups officially categorized as "Others" (3.3 per cent) constitute the minorities (Department of Statistics 2010, p. 3). While historical factors in the management of race relations have contributed to persistent concerns over the issue, Singapore's position as a small nation in the midst of two predominantly Malay/Muslim neighbours with entrenched communal politics vis-à-vis their more economically dominant Chinese populations has exacerbated it.[1] The 9/11 attack and its aftermath may have also compounded the problem. Being the only country in the region that supported the U.S. invasion of Iraq, fear of terrorists' reprisals could have induced the need to balance its foreign policy with ethnic relations management. Hence, while the discourse centring on the nation's vulnerability and the overriding emphasis on national cohesion is directed at all Singaporeans, it is the Malay community, 98.7 per cent of whom are Muslims (Department of Statistics 2011, p. 14), that has generally been the focus of attention.

The Malays' cultural, linguistic and particularly religious affinity with Singapore's neighbours has had implications on the way they are perceived and managed politically. Islam's transnational character and its impact on Malay identity and culture have given rise to the presumption of deep spiritual bond between Muslims in the region and globally. It has conditioned speculation of their potentially divided loyalty to the nation in the face of aggression by its neighbours. The global Muslim resurgence that has emerged in the last four decades or so, bringing along with it greater demands for Islamization of state and society by specific interest groups within the Muslim world and in the region, has heightened this concern. These could have also been compounded by the more recent intense focus on conflicts, violence and terrorism involving Muslims perpetuated in the name of Islam both within and beyond the region.

This chapter contends that the tendency to perceive these political events in ethnic terms is conditioned by the dominance of the culturalist approach. While not confined to the understanding of Islam and Muslims per se, in the context of 11 September, the approach thrusts the Malay/Muslim community into the national spotlight. It is maintained that while 9/11 is not the defining event that marked a shift towards the strong influence of the culturalist approach in understanding Muslims, its occurrence and the events that subsequently unfolded, including the discovery of home-grown terrorists, have intensified it. Not only has the approach influenced the conceptualization of the problems of radicalism and terrorism, it has also impacted the type of strategies and measures employed in countering them. The chapter further contends that the dominance of the approach has also conditioned reactions and initiatives undertaken by the elite within the Muslim community itself. Muslims' response to the problems so far mirrors the culturalist approach in as much as they are conditioned by it. The chapter's overriding interest is to examine the implications of the dominance of this perspective on the problem of social cohesion and the extent to which it serves to alleviate the problem.

TRAITS OF THE CULTURALIST APPROACH

The 9/11 attack and the ensuing events that emerged thereafter revived national attention on the fragility of Singapore's ethnic cohesion. As Goh Chok Tong, then Prime Minister, declared,

> Our greatest worry is the threat to our security, and to our racial and religious harmony following the discovery of terrorist activities in our country.... Should a terrorist threat in Singapore by some extreme group ever succeed, it would do untold harm. Not only would it cause the loss of life and property, but far worse, it would result in profound misunderstanding and distrust between the different communities.[2]

While forging social cohesion is a major challenge in the interest of the nation, affecting all, it is the Malay/Muslims' religious life and identity that has been thrust under the national spotlight. This focus is largely conditioned by the dominance of the culturalist approach in the understanding of Islam and the Muslims. The approach is characterized by a style of thought in which perspectives and methodology from the social sciences utilized in understanding culture and society are largely neglected. Although culturalists are not anti-culture and do not ignore it in defining a community, the problem lies in their tendency to shore up an essentialist culture, one perceived as a static, homogenous set of common identifiers that defines a community, such as language, race or religion, wrapped into a sense of common identity. This identity is deemed more or less stable, permanent and fixed at any given point in time in terms of its meanings and forms. Within this perspective, societies become multicultural in the sense that they are made up of a collection of various distinct "cultures" in which a dominant, even hegemonic culture coexists with a cluster of minority groups each having its distinct cultural traits and forms which constitute the basis of social classification.

Although they do not completely ignore the transformations that history and social changes bring to a community, culturalists, nevertheless, tend to assume communities as static and isolated, divorced from the myriad of influences that continuously affect them. They also overlook the basic sociological fact that any given community is generally plural in the sense that it comprises competing and conflicting interest groups, distinguished by class and orientations, vested interests and ideologies that shape the way people within a community think and define their identities. The approach facilitates the tendency to over rely on specific interest groups, either self declared or politically appointed, as guardians of the community and interpreters of its "culture". This poses a problem when the views expressed by such a group form the basis for understanding the "community's" problems and policies affecting them. Not only is heterogeneity within ethnic groups overlooked or downplayed, commonalities between groups also tend to be obscured.

Although not confined to the understanding of Muslims, the prevalence of the approach is evident in matters concerning them partly because Islam offers a set of rituals, practices and, more importantly, a stable set of principles, the observance of which could define a "community". The problem however is that culturalists ignore the variety of meanings and extent of significance given to these principles and values by the social actors within the community. Their understanding misses the significant influence of this sociological dimension which conditions how the religion is understood and experienced. Within the approach, Islam is essentialized as a "discrete entity, a coherent and closed set of beliefs, values and anthropological patterns embodied in a common society, history and territory" (Roy 2004, p. 9). Furthermore, it is generally perceived as the major, single force that shapes Muslims' sentiments, attitudes, values and orientations, relationships with Muslims and non-Muslims and perceptions on a myriad of issues quite isolated from the larger socio-political influences and environment in which Muslims exist and interact with. It is believed to condition not only how individuals and groups think, feel and act, but also their relations and sentiments for members within and outside the community. In short, Islam is reductively presumed as the main motive that conditions Muslims' thought and action in ways that are common and predictable. It is the factor accorded overriding significance in explaining their problems and drawbacks. (Roy 2004, pp. 9–17).[3]

Such a conception neglects the fact that while Islam is perhaps the major cultural identifier of the Muslim community, how it is understood and experienced and the extent of its influence on individuals and groups within the community, like any other, is extremely varied and complex. The tendency to attribute to Islam the main motive for anything to do with Muslims is also problematic for its presumption that Muslim communities observe Islam from top to bottom or are bound by its set of fixed norms and precepts at all times in all domains of their lives. Because of these limitations, the culturalist perspective in attributing to Islam the cause of Muslims' problems, drawbacks, reactions, responses is problematic in understanding a host of issues affecting the community.

The dominance of the culturalist approach in influencing the understanding of Islam and the Muslims may be conditioned by several factors. Not the least important is the impact of orientalism as a discourse and style of thought pertaining to the Muslims. Orientalism was developed in the context of the colonial hegemonic power of the West over the "Orient", a large part of which was inhabited by Muslims. As a style of thought, it penetrates perspectives and understanding of the Muslims and Islam such that what emerges is a consistency of ideas, opinions, representations and judgment about them. As knowledge of the "Other" is predominantly attained through continuous reliance and repetition of a lineage of ideas, orientalism is limited by its alienation from the very peoples it seeks to portray. Its non-sociological streak is also manifested by the tendency to neglect the contributions of methodologies, perspectives, theories and concepts developed in the social sciences, generally employed in understanding culture and society. Hence it is disposed to reductive reasoning, overgeneralizations, essentialism and misleading deductions. Despite these limitations, however, it remains powerfully entrenched since it is buttressed by a strong and extensive network of interests and institutions. Its gripping influence is reinforced over time through continuous transmission, outside the context of colonialism, such that it even penetrates perspectives of the "Other" about themselves (Said 1976).

These salient traits of orientalism as a style of thought in understanding Muslims and Islam survive in the postcolonial context in the form of the culturalist approach. It is reinforced by the recent spate of violence and terror involving Muslims, exacerbated by the compelling need for instant analysis by laymen, politicians, academics and observers alike. The problem is compounded by the strong influence of ideology that has shaped recent discourse on terrorism characterized by Mamdani as "culture talk" (2004, pp. 17–22). Unlike culture studied by anthropologists (face-to-face, local and intimate), this rhetoric, which makes the religion/religion-based culture the issue, comes in ready-made geopolitical packages and is used as the basis to explain those in favour of a peaceful, civic existence and those inclined to terror. This global discourse, accompanied by the massive inundation of publications on terrorism, extremism and violence that focus on Islam as the issue as well as apologetic denials of them, reinforces the prevalence of this approach in official discourse in Singapore.[4] The limitations of the approach and its dominance impede a more comprehensive understanding of the problem. They also bear implications on the overriding aim of the government at strengthening social cohesion.

9/11 AND THE CULTURALIST APPROACH

The culturalist mode in understanding Muslims and Islam precedes 11 September but was reinforced by the occurrence of the tragic event and its aftermath. It has, for instance, conditioned the basis for the policy underlying restrictions of appointments of Muslims to strategic positions in defence and security. At the Singapore 21 forum in 1999, Lee Kuan Yew, then Senior Minister, in responding to a question by a student who asked whether certain instinctive emotional bonds among the ethnic groups could be overcome so that Singapore could truly become a nation, had declared that the Muslim's religious belief can put him in a position of conflict with the interests of the nation (*Straits Times*, 19 September 1999). He reiterated this view at a dialogue with Malay/Muslim community leaders when he explicated that "it is a difficult matter to put a Malay Muslim of deeply religious family background in charge of a machine gun as he may face a conflict of loyalties which should never have to be asked of anyone".[5] Such a perception, which strongly implies that should Singapore be attacked by a Muslim aggressor, Malays' loyalty may not be vouched for, reveals the strong presumption that bonds forged by Islam have the potential of overriding loyalty to the nation. That Muslims would presumably face a dilemma because the aggressor is another Muslim, irrespective of any other consideration, including even diversity of thought and understanding of religious principles itself reveals the essentialist streak of the approach.

This looming apprehension with Malay/Muslim bonds perceived as having the potential to override loyalty to the nation was compounded by the global resurgence of Islam which impacted Muslims in the region. Amidst the backdrop of the resurgence, political discourse reiterated concerns over the lack of integration of the Malay/Muslim community into the "mainstream". This was conditioned by changes to traditional norms and practice of Islam amongst some Muslims as depicted in forms of attire, diet, lifestyles, and other aspects of religiosity, including, in some cases, although not in the local context, highly politicized rhetoric that challenged existing institutions and demanded alternative systems supposedly based on Islam. Given these changing expressions of religiosity amongst those affected, the Muslim community as a whole was alleged to be subscribing to isolating tendencies that segregated them from the "mainstream". Such discourse exacerbated apprehension for the compatibility of Muslims' religious belief and practices and their involvement and interaction with the multicultural society they live in. It also reinforced the dichotomy between being Muslim and being Singaporean. Debates concerning Malay loyalty were further fuelled by the protest by some Malay/Muslims against the former Israeli President, Chaim Herzog's visit in November 1986. Shortly thereafter, the Prime Minister in his National Day Speech in 1987, reasserted that Malays were "not yet in the mainstream" of Singapore society and expressed doubts over their degree of loyalty (*Straits Times*, 11 August 1987).

The 11 September attacks and particularly the arrest of JI operatives reinforced and intensified the culturalist approach as underscored in official discourse. The approach resurfaced the perception that the common bond of Muslims forged by Islam could potentially undermine Singaporean Muslims' backing for the state's support for the war on terror spearheaded by the United States, with repercussions on the well-being of the social fabric. It conditioned a sense of anxiety for Muslims' sympathy for fellow radical Muslims who would manipulate and exploit them using the common religion. Thus, though acknowledging the support of the majority of Muslims for the government's stand on the invasion, speeches reiterated the problem of the *umma* (community of believers) on social cohesion and warned of its growing strength with global communications and Saudi Arabia's oil wealth. For instance, Goh Chok Tong, then Prime Minister, had constantly advised Muslims not to be taken in by terrorists that portray the United States as being against Islam.[6] The same perspective is evident in his statement to the effect that Osama's message strikes a chord amongst many Muslims, even moderate ones, because of deep-seated historic reasons and the strength of Muslim brotherhood, making it understandable why Singaporean Muslims feel strong sympathy for the fate of the Afghan civilians who are at risk of a humanitarian disaster.[7]

That Muslims may have sympathy or concern for other Muslims affected by the perils of war is not the issue, as such sentiments are inevitable and not confined to them. The major problem of the culturalists' mode of thinking lies in the presumption that this religious bond can have the effect of giving rise to dilemmas and conflicts for Singaporean Muslims in matters involving their own religious kind, which can potentially undermine integration irrespective of any other principles or factors. The presumption reveals the tendency to perceive Muslims as a homogenous community, negating differences of opinions, ideologies, worldviews, politics, vested interests and principles which affect them in much the same ways as any other community. It overlooks internal dynamics and the plurality within the community and misses the fact that like any other, the Malay/Muslim community is characterized by a variety of social groups, including contesting and conflicting ones, influenced by diverse considerations and motives. The perspective also reduces the Muslim community to an isolated entity devoid of the influence and exchanges of ideas. While Muslims may well feel for their fellow Muslims threatened by war, their sentiments are also shaped by a myriad of considerations and principles that are not exclusive to them as Muslims, of which the cost to innocent human lives is not the least significant. The significance accorded to the *umma* clouds the possibility of conceiving that Singaporean Muslims' thinking and sentiments on this issue are not necessarily determined by ties of common faith in isolated, static, exclusive conditions. On the contrary, like others, their sentiments may well be shaped by interaction with ideas produced and circulating in this shrinking global world in which dissenting views on the war on terror, even within the American public itself, cannot be overlooked. By locating the dilemma as one confronting the Muslim community per se, the culturalist approach also conveys the presumption that Muslims react differently from other Singaporeans to Singapore's policy on the invasion due to their common religion. This may affect a more accurate understanding of the sentiments of Singaporeans generally, as well as diversity within the Muslim community itself. Focusing on Muslims as potential opponents of the war also strongly suggests that non-Muslims do not have an issue with it.

The pervasiveness of the culturalist approach is also manifested in inconsistencies in political speeches made shortly after the attack. On the one hand, stern warnings were levelled at those who tried to exploit the situation to inflame racial and religious relations. This was vital to defuse the rising contempt for Muslims by a section of non-Muslims as the backlash of inter-communal hatred could cause serious disruption to national cohesion as Singapore prepared to support the United States' initiatives against Iraq, Afghanistan and the al-Qaeda terrorist network. However, the pervasiveness of the culturalist approach which tends to condition perceiving the issue as a religious one, also makes it difficult to ensure that the conflict is seen for what Goh himself succinctly stated it should be, "a war against a common enemy, terrorism and not one against Islam".[8]

The attack and events that unfolded thereafter intensified the culturalist approach by deeming the problem of terrorism as one inextricably linked to a particular theological interpretation of Islam that is maladjusted to modernity. Hence, discussion on radicalism is generally reduced to the issue of how Islam is conceived and interpreted. Goh's National Day Rally Speech the year following 9/11 illustrates the point. The speech focused on the problems of theological differences and conflicts in interpretations of Islam against the backdrop of the attack and the looming threat of terrorism. Goh noted that while the moderates were disposed to modernity, worldly knowledge and openness, extremists succumbed to narrow and rigid interpretations of Islam. They are reluctant to practise *ijtihad* (independent reasoning) which allows Muslims to find new solutions to problems that will help make Islam relevant to the changing times and circumstances (*Straits Times*, 20 August 2002, p. 10).

Such reiterations tend to associate the problem of radicalism with the religious orientation and theological construction of Islam by Muslims. While now and then some reference is made to the socio-political underpinnings of its emergence, consistent reflection of this perspective is not sustained. Hence, though political leaders have declared that the war on terror is not a war against Islam nor is the Muslim community in Singapore in any way associated with the perpetrators of the tragedy who have called for a global holy war, the notion that terrorism and radicalism are inextricably intertwined with the way Islam is understood, makes Islam or interpretations of the religion, the crux of the issue. Lee Kuan Yew's declaration illustrates the reasoning: "We have as neighbours over 200 million Muslims in Indonesia and some 15 million in Malaysia. At first sight, this is a struggle between extremist radicals in the Muslim world on one side and America, Israel and their western allies on the other. But look deeper and you will see that at its heart, it is a struggle about what Islam means between the extremist Muslims and the rationalist Muslims, between fundamentalist Muslims and modernist Muslims (*Straits Times*, 20 February 2003, p. 17). That the crux of the problem is religion is also reflected in Foreign Minister George Yeo's statement to the effect that 11 September has complicated the troubled and difficult interaction between Islam and Christianity in which "memories of the crusade still run deep". The tragic event, he maintained, has "forced religious leaders to look hard at each other's positions wondering whether any reconciliation is possible" (*Straits Times*, 18 March 2008, p. 20).

Echoes of "civilizational conflict" that has found its way into public discourse post 9/11 is a further manifestation of the intensification of the culturalist paradigm which perceives the problem as one rooted in religion. While hitherto the concern has been with Muslims' integration into the "mainstream", the culturalist approach has extended it to the level of "civilizational conflict" involving Muslims and others. Goh's reference to the "clash of civilization", which draws on Huntington's thesis (1996), reflects this influence. Being a symptom of the approach, the thesis is premised on an imagined confrontational binary between two opposing camps, Islam and the Western Other, characterized by conflicts and clashes. It has been vehemently criticized for its non-sociological and non-historical basis. Not only has it overlooked internal dynamics and the plurality of civilizations, it also reduces societies to isolated entities devoid of the influence of human history that has not only contained wars but facilitated exchanges, cross-fertilization and sharing (Said 2001).

This overemphasis on the theological dimension of the phenomenon clouds the significance of the political and ideological dimensions of the problem debated in social scientific scholarship. They reveal the problems of ideology, group dynamics, and socio-historical, as well as political factors that influence specific radical groups and shifts in their ideology and orientation over time. Such works caution against the overriding significance accorded to Islam or its theological variants as the crux of the problem. They systematically demonstrate that political Islam, especially radical political Islam, and more specifically, the terrorist wing in radical political Islam, did not emerge from conservative religious currents but, on the contrary, from a secular intelligentsia, although it employs religious language as part of its strategy in addressing specific audiences. Such contributions dispel the "ummist" perspective that makes Islam the issue.[9]

IMPACT ON REMEDIES

"Moderates" versus "Extremists"

The culturalist mode bears direct implications on the selection of measures deemed relevant to counter the problem of radicalism. It conditions prescriptions that treat the Malay/Muslim community as a kind of "interest association" bound to fight its own misguided kind. As Islam is the issue, the onus falls on the Muslims themselves to battle the extremists. Though this approach is not unique to the governing elite's management of race relations (Brown 1993, pp. 26–31), it is reinforced by the pervasive wider discourse that frames the issue as intertwined with Islamic leanings and interpretations.[10] Thus, official discourse revealed the tendency to overlook the complexity of the Muslim community and Islam by dividing the community into two clear cut dichotomous entities — the moderates and the extremists — terms which are largely undefined and malleable in the sense that they are not based on clear principles. Such divisions do little to portray accurately Muslims' thoughts and opinions on concrete issues that confront them. Like any other community, the Muslim community comprise groups who may adopt an extreme stance on one issue while assimilating normative Islam on others. Groups are also dynamic in terms of their changing ideologies and orientations over time, which cannot be clearly understood by subscribing to static overarching dichotomies. Nonetheless, the construction is used as the basis for direction as the "moderates" within the community were told to battle their own erroneous and misguided fellows. As Lee Kuan Yew declared: "Governments can beef up their intelligence services, ferret out and destroy terrorist networks … but only the Muslims themselves, those with moderate, more modern approach to life — can fight the fundamentalists for control of the Muslim soul. Muslims must counter the terrorist ideology that is based on a perverted interpretation of Islam" (*Straits Times*, 7 October 2003, p. 18). Goh's following statements also reveal a similar line of argument: "This ideological struggle is far more complex than the struggle against communism because it engages not just reason but religious faith. You and I as non Muslims have no locus standi to engage in this struggle for the soul of Islam. It is a matter for Muslims to settle among themselves."[11] These statements reflect the view that both the problem of radicalism and the onus for its remedy are isolated and confined to the Muslim community, quite apart from whatever conditions prevail outside of the community.

That the moderates must fight the extremists or suffer the negative consequence of remaining silent persistently featured in official discourse. Stern warnings of a backlash to them not only by extremist Muslims but non-Muslims if they chose to remain silent resurfaced time and again, despite numerous condemnations of extremism by the community elites and Muslim civil society. The same perspective provided the basis for the apparent silence of the moderates underlying Goh's argument:

When we ask why it is that moderates in such a spectrum do not raise their voices to challenge extremists, we must acknowledge that one reason is that on so many issues they share much in common even when they disagree on particulars.... we know we should work with the moderates and isolate the extremists. But as we seek to separate the wheat from the chaff, we need to recognise that both come from the same plant. How we seek to engage and encourage the Muslim world to fight the ideological battle against the extremists must reflect this sensitivity and awareness. This is complicated but not impossible.[12]

MUSLIMS' RELIGIOSITY

The culturalist approach in the understanding of extremism has reinforced the apprehension for Muslims' religiosity which extends back to the 1980s with the global Islamic resurgence that affected the region. The phenomenon propelled leaders to express concern over what they perceived as the increasing religiosity of Singaporean Muslims. Thrust into the national spotlight, the community was targeted with allegations of not being part of the "mainstream". They were alleged to be spending more time in mosques and other religion-based institutions at the expense of involvement in grass roots and other national multi-ethnic platforms. It has also been reiterated that Muslims have become stricter in their observance of food restrictions and other taboos, dress and lifestyle, all of which are believed to segregate them from greater social interaction with non-Muslim Singaporeans.

The events of 11 September intensified and extended the culturalist perspective by attributing radicalism to religious teachings and practices. While hitherto, the major concern of the governing elite centred on Muslims' religious practice and their implications on integration into the mainstream, the attacks provided justification for seeing in Muslim religious belief and practices the seeds of radicalism. Perceived increased Muslim religiosity with separateness and susceptibility towards terrorism was evident in the 2003 parliamentary debate on the "Jemaah Islamiyah Arrests and the Threat of Terrorism" White Paper. Similarly at the 2002 National Day Rally Speech, Goh had raised the problem of Muslim religiosity amidst the global Islamic resurgence and its implications for the community. He noted that while most Muslims in Singapore are moderate, open-minded and inclusive, there are some who have become rigid in the practice of their religion, such as those who insisted on headscarves in schools for girls and who preferred to eat separately from non-Muslims. This concern with the stifling impact of a narrow and rigid interpretation of the religion on critical thinking was incited by the fear that it could expose Muslims to exploitation by radical clerics, as was believed to be the case with the JI members who were indoctrinated into believing that taking part in a jihad could alone atone for their sins.[13]

Focussing on Muslim religiosity as the potential fodder for ineffective integration and radicalism thwarts the development of systematic and comprehensive understanding of the problems of extremist ideologies and terror. It also does not explain how religiosity can give rise to terror. Admittedly there are within the Muslim community segments who attempt to construct a pristine Islamic identity and lifestyle that differs from how Muslims have experienced and practised the religion all this while.[14] However, seeing in changing religiosity the seeds of radicalism cannot comprehensively explain how Islamic resurgence facilitated the emergence of violence and terrorism nor throw sufficient light on the largely non-violent characteristic of many resurgent groups in this region in the last three decades or more. It also does not explicate how and why resurgent movements or groups, hitherto non–violent in its orientation, could subsequently resort to violence.

The *Tudung* Issue

Controversy surrounding the *tudung* (Islamic headscarf) issue highlighted by Goh and how it is perceived and managed is another manifestation of the intensification of the culturalist approach in understanding Muslims since the 9/11 attack. The issue was triggered in January 2002 when four six-year-old schoolgirls were sent by their parents on the first day of school wearing a *tudung* in clear defiance of school rules.[15] The parents justified their decision on the ground that wearing the headscarf is an Islamic obligation to protect a girl's modesty. Although official discourse refrained from explicitly maintaining that the demand for *tudung* in schools by some parents is a reflection of radicalization of Muslims, the saga which erupted shortly after the attack conjured this association. This problem may also have been compounded by the ongoing controversy and anguished debates over the issue of headscarves for Muslim girls in schools and the public service sector in the West, such as in France even before 9/11. Arguments by some quarters to the effect that the headscarf is a visible symbol of rising militancy and radicalism among Muslims that violate principles of gender equality and opposed Western values could have provoked the perception that the demand for it in schools here is conditioned by similar forces (*Straits Times*, 10 February 2004).[16]

In fact, views to the effect that the confrontational means adopted by the four parents could have been influenced by "precepts found in the religion itself" did feature in the local press. Citing the Islamic jurisprudential principle that "every harm or hindrance must be removed", a senior journalist for instance had asserted that this probably fuelled political action in furtherance of religious rights (*Straits Times*, 20 February 2002). Such reductive reasoning manifests the salient trait of the culturalist approach which reduces the parents' defiant strategy to Islamic teachings. It connotes that the source of radicalism may well lie in the very teachings of Islam itself. It is, however, pertinent to note that even the Religious Teachers' Association (PERGAS), which had first cited the principle in local discourse on the *tudung*, did not advocate confrontation as a means of changing the official policy. On the contrary, they have consistently called for change by way of dialogue (PERGAS 2003, pp. 343–47). A similar approach has also been undertaken by other community leaders generally, which differs from the adversarial stance adopted by groups such as Fateha.com and the Malay-based opposition party, the Singapore Malay National Organisation (PKMS) (*Straits Times*, 21, 22, 28 January 2002). The failure to account for the reasons why the majority of Singaporean Muslims, even those who believe that the *tudung* is a religious obligation, did not defy school rules all this while, further reveals the limitation of the argument. Consistent with the traits of the culturalist approach, such variations are overlooked or missed. While politically motivated groups may use religion to promote their cause, one cannot simplistically conclude that the religious precepts sanction its politicization.

The tendency to associate Islamic religious belief and practice with radicalism within the culturalist approach that developed after 9/11 facilitated a more hard-line stance on the issue. It has been reported that all along, attempts by Muslim parents to modify school rules were not generally met with any hue and cry. The Malay/Muslim leadership had also apparently negotiated for the use of the *tudung* behind closed doors. Some Singaporeans have said that in the past a handful of Muslim children were allowed to modify their uniforms on the basis of religious consideration. For instance girls who requested to use pants instead of shorts during physical exercise and longer skirts have had their requests granted (*Straits Times*, 30 January 2002).

These developments were arrested in the aftermath of 9/11. Government leaders articulated the *tudung* issue as one that centred on the potential threat it posed to the vulnerability and fragility of Singapore's multi-ethnic nation and its cohesion. The Ministry, for instance, explicated that school uniforms serve to remind every student of the common ties that bind them as Singaporeans and that school is where they interact with other Singaporeans regardless of race, religion or social status, even if diversity abounds in Singapore. If schools rules were allowed to be modified according to religious or customary practices, over time they will lose their values as key places where the young learn about unity and togetherness (*Straits Times*, 2 February 2002). Government leaders opined that the demand for *tudung* in schools reduces and segmented the common spaces schools provide and is a step back for racial integration because it heightens differences. While acknowledging that the policy was not cast in stone, it was declared that the priority is to establish a successful multi-racial society. The government reiterated that it cannot be certain whether diversity in uniforms will lead to a greater sense of understanding, harmony and unity as each community may well attempt to assert its own distinct identity. Goh reinforced this fear in reaction to critiques, issuing a stern warning of the potential of a backlash to the community by insisting on the *tudung*. He declared that the government was concerned with social division and that it was not the right time for people to be advocating for wearing the *tudung* in schools. He further added that "to try and push the wearing of the *tudung* in schools will only cause greater concern among non-Muslims", and added that Muslims who were trying to assert their identities strongly might suffer backlashes in the long term. They might be abandoned by Chinese companies since they wanted to be on their own. This would mean that jobs could be more difficult to come by for Muslims (*Straits Times*, 18 February 2002).

Such statements reveal the lack of confidence that the *tudung* will not impair cohesion. They underscore the weakness of the cohesiveness of society and connote concern that allowing the change may bring about unwarranted repercussions on social cohesion that may not be remedied easily (*Straits Times*, 3 February 2002). The potential threat posed by *tudung* in school in the long battle of forging common bonds among Singaporeans is exacerbated by the strong tendency to deal with the issue as a communal one. This tendency is an extension of the dominance of the culturalist approach in understanding issues involving Muslims. Although the case involved a very small group of Muslims, it received national limelight as a community issue in official and public discourse. As the issue developed, the focus of attention became the issue of Muslims' religious belief and preference for *tudung* in school, while the circumstances of the initial confrontational means adopted by the parents who rebelled against the official policy that sparked the entire saga in the first place was somehow forgotten. This had the effect of magnifying the issue as the focus shifted to the concerns of Muslim parents who preferred to have their daughters don the headscarf in school. Needless to say this would invite substantial responses given the dominant religious opinion widely circulated and influential here.

It is not surprising then that Fateha.com, the group whose leader was at the centre of the controversy for supporting the four parents, igniting the support of Malaysian opposition groups and lashing at the governments' policy in foreign media as well as expressing the intent to test the constitutionality of the policy in court, was able to mobilize 3,300 Singaporeans to endorse a petition opposing the government's "no-*tudung*" policy. Although the endorsement did not mean that these respondents would resort to radical means as the parents of the four students had done, this crucial factor was missed. Overlooking this factor is yet another manifestation of the culturalist approach in understanding the Muslims. It illustrates the tendency to gloss over vital difference in their thought and sentiments even amongst those who deem the *tudung* a religious obligation. It also fails to consider the possibility that the strategy employed reflects an attempt to politicize the issue, a motive which is not shared by the vast majority of Muslims here. Hence, despite holding a similar theological opinion on the issue, the majority would not agree with the strategy of defiance adopted by the parents. Such vital difference is downplayed or overlooked given the culturalist framework.

It is also the influence of this approach that conditioned framing the issue as a community one rather than a matter involving a few defiant or politically-motivated Muslims. This is illustrated in the following statement by a Member of Parliament (MP) reiterating the government's justification: "Our national project in multi-racialism and national integration is an experiment, often a high risk one. It is a precious one, and something all of us want to put above *our own community's interests*. We must not forget we share a common destiny as Singaporeans. Wise compromises are required all around, from the different races, to achieve our ideal of a cohesive, multi-racial society" (*Straits Times*, 3 March 2002). Similarly Goh's assertion that conceding to this demand will open the floodgates to further demands by the Muslim community as well as from other religious groups, which will threaten the common space and ethnic harmonization and integration, further attests to the tendency to treat the issue as a community's problem.

Such thinking is yet another manifestation of the culturalist approach which essentializes Islam and the Muslim community. Although the theological view on the *tudung* can be said to be dominant here, treating the *tudung* in school controversy as a community issue based on a religious obligation in Islam, overgeneralizes the matter. It fails to consider the fact that such demands are alien to many Muslims who see in them the influence of resurgent ideas that oppose or depart from the belief and practice of many Muslims.[17] The overgeneralization fuelled by the culturalist approach is to some extent illustrated by responses to a survey poll obtained in the midst of the *tudung* controversy involving 823 Singaporeans. The survey revealed that not only were the majority of Muslims surveyed (72 per cent) against the *tudung* in schools, the figure did not differ much from the non-Muslims (80 per cent) (*Straits Times*, 20 February 2002). Although it is not conclusive of the general attitude of Muslims, nor does it portray attitudes over time as some critiques allege (*Straits Times*, 3 March 2002), it does provide a starting point that cautions unquestioned assumptions about the Muslim community's beliefs and attitudes (*Straits Times*, 23 February 2002). It can be said that the results certainly depicted divergence of opinion within the Muslim community which the culturalist approach tends to overlook or downplay.

The perception of the issue as a community problem is to some extent fuelled by the reactions of the community's elites themselves. All without exception declared that donning the *tudung* is a religious obligation for girls. In affirming this standpoint in absolute terms they ignored the wide spectrum of theological opinions on the *tudung* within Muslim tradition. In this respect they reveal the mirror version of the culturalist approach. Amongst the major spokesmen are the Singapore Religious Teachers Association (PERGAS) and the Religious Council of Singapore. PERGAS's theological view does not differ from the fatwa passed by the Muslim Religious Council of Singapore (MUIS), wherein donning the *tudung* is deemed essential for girls. However, acknowledging the crucial fact that they differed on the question of whether the *tudung* should be donned in school should have checked the tendency to treat the issue as reflecting the concern and preference of the community as a whole (*Straits Times*, 6 February 2002).[18] MUIS was explicit in its standpoint that the importance of education overrides the obligation of the *tudung*. Malay political leaders also did not provide an alternative direction in the discourse that could have checked the overriding tendency towards perceiving the matter as a community issue. The same limitation is reflected in the articulation of the issue expounded by Fateha.com to the absolute effect that "the hijab is a matter of Islamic belief" (*Straits Times*, 21 January 2002). Fateha's position does not depart from the culturalist approach in so far as it assumes that all Muslims share this view. The organization did not address the issue coherently and consistently as one of violation of the rights of a certain group of Muslim citizens to practise their religious faith without causing harm to others instead of as a matter of religious belief affecting the entire community. Its argument obscured diversity of theological views within the community itself.

Reactions from leaders of political groups across the causeway further reinforced the dominant perception of homogeneity of views pertaining to the *tudung*. Their intervention on this specific issue published in the local media reinforced the culturalist notion of the transnational *umma*, which speaks out concerning Muslims' plights and oppression. These political interest groups articulated the policy as one that violated religious freedom and discriminated against Muslims without distinction. A letter from Parti Islam SeMalaysia's (PAS) spiritual leader Nik Aziz to Senior Minister Lee Kuan Yew which sought to pressure the government to rescind the policy merely reinforced the issue as reflecting the interests of the community as a whole as he alluded to the *tudung* requirement as a universal one. He also maintained that by forbidding the *tudung*, the Singapore Government will be considered to have eroded the freedom of religion in the republic and this will in turn lead to other negative perceptions especially among Muslims in both countries (*Straits Times*, 6 February 2002). Similarly, the Muslim Youth Movement's (ABIM) President alleged that following 9/11, the Singapore government has adopted a policy that oppresses the rights of Muslims (*Straits Times*, 1 February 2002).

Numerous journalistic and academic publications further fuelled the perception that the issue is a community-based one. It is not uncommon to find opinion pieces in the mainstream media that discuss the *tudung* within the problematic of accommodating a community's wish to be different from the rest in multi-ethnic societies. This frequent use of the term community as synonymous with a segment of the Muslims in Singapore who wanted the wearing of *tudung* in school, merely reinforced and reflected the notion that the desire for the "Islamic" dress in schools represents the religious value of the community as a whole. The tendency to think in these terms exacerbated the notion of homogeneity of Muslims' understanding of this issue (*Straits Times*, 9 March 2002). There is no doubt that for many Muslims, the *tudung* "symbolises the Muslim women's commitment to Islamic principles and her conscious quest for identity and dignity, one guided by modesty and righteous self-esteem."[19] However, while such views are dominant, culturalists tend to overgeneralize matters pertaining to Muslims that fall outside their mental framework, a tendency exacerbated by the use of religious language by those whom they are attempting to analyse.

Academic discourses that analyses the problem from a multicultural perspective also fail to depart from the dominant assumption. Some, while acknowledging the need for the government to recognize and acknowledge differences on the basis of rights that do not undermine the interests of others, tend to overlook diversities within the particular cultural Malay community. In this sense they are not free from the fetters of the culturalist perspective inasmuch as they too address the *tudung* issue as if it concerned the entire Muslim community.[20] The same manifestation of the perspective is reflected in the thinking of those who use the issue to point out inconsistencies in government policies for its alleged preference for the majority. The comparison often made with the ban on the *tudung* in schools is the government-supported Special Assistance Plan (SAP) schools that seek to promote and maintain Chinese culture (Lily 2009, p. 357). Yet, the *tudung* has nothing to do with education which would have provided a common basis for comparison. The reasoning also implies that if the government allowed Muslim girls to don the *tudung*, then the SAP will not be an issue. However, justification and support for the SAP national schools raises its own issues and questions which are quite independent of allowing *tudung* in schools. More significantly, the viewpoint has the effect of framing the *tudung* issue within a majority-versus-minority polarity while missing the significance of plurality within the Muslim community itself.

Deeming the issue as a prescription of Islam without qualification misses the crux of the matter, which is not one of Islamic teachings and values, but dominant thought and orientation of specific groups of Muslims within the community. In presuming that the issue is a religious one that is absolute, discussions driven by the culturalist approach fail to capture the diversity of religious opinions that have been manifested in the thought and practice not only of the multitudes of generations of Muslims generally but within the community specifically.

The impact of the culturalist approach that framed the demand for *tudung* in school as a community issue has reinforced the fear that it might undermine Singapore's fragile ethnic relations, but has left many questions raised by Singaporeans unanswered. It does not deal with the argument to the effect that acceptance and tolerance for diversity in dress, looks and culture best begins in schools. It deflects the question of how the clothes one wears impinges negatively on common space. It also does not address convincingly inconsistencies that permit *tudung* at tertiary levels and teachers who are allowed to use it in schools. The speculation that allowing for it will open the floodgates to further demands that will undermine integration does not effectively address the counterargument that the problem warrants review based on the principle of whether that demand infringes on the rights of others and the common good. Furthermore, it does not deal with some Muslim's self-perception as illustrated in the assertion by the Minister in charge of Muslim affairs to the effect that the *tudung* does not impair integration as Muslim parents' aspirations for their children are the same as parents of other races, including wanting their children to be enrolled in good national schools (*Straits Times*, 8 December 2002). While the "*tudung* in school" controversy has exposed unwarranted presumptions of Muslims who put it on, these have yet to be critically examined. For instance, an MP, in articulating her reasons against it, had maintained that at her constituency functions, she noticed that children who put on the *tudung* do not mix with others. Without a basis for comparison with the extent of social interaction and attitude of other children both from within the Muslim community who do not wear the *tudung* and others outside it, such claims do not provide strong justification that the *tudung* undermines integration (*Straits Times*, 3 March 2002).

A more dangerous consequence of the culturalist influence is that it can easily create the tendency to view problems in ethnic terms and reinforce communalist streaks that exist in society. These will undermine not only objectivity in understanding issues but, worse still, positive values that ensure the well-being of plural society. For instance, some Muslims, in objecting to the "no *tudung*" policy in schools, have reacted by lashing out at the policy of SAP schools funded by the government and which cater almost exclusively to the Chinese population. The existence of these schools, geared towards maintaining culture, is seen as inconsistent with not giving in to demands of parents for daughters to wear the *tudung*. In response some Chinese are reported to "see red that pot-shots were being taken against one of their dearly-held icons", prompting a senior journalist to warn that the ease of observing Islamic values and practices depends on how far their demands impinge upon the majority race and whether the latter is comfortable with and can accept those changes (*Straits Times*, 9 March 2002). The problem with such an attack as well as the response it generates, reveal clearly ethnic tensions that will only be exacerbated with the influence of the culturalist approach, which clouds examining issues in relation to the specific interests of their social bearers even if religion or ethnic terms are utilized in justifying the claims or demands. This threatens social cohesion, the very value sought as a safeguard against conflicts and misunderstanding in multi-ethnic societies.

Focus on Mosques

An extension of the culturalist approach in understanding radicalism is also manifested in the spotlight on mosques and other religious institutions. Lee Kuan Yew, for instance, had maintained that though his original concern was over the growing separateness of the Muslim community, which centred their social activities in mosques instead of in multiracial community clubs, what came as a shock was that this heightened religiosity facilitated Muslim terror groups linked to al-Qaeda to recruit Singaporean Muslims from mosques into their network (*Straits Times*, 30 December 2002, p. 30).

Concern for the impact of mosques on integration had been in the national spotlight pre 9/11, but was reinforced thereafter. In March 2001, at a dialogue with Malay community leaders, Lee had expressed some regret at his initiative in establishing the Mosque Building Fund as he did not intend for the institution to have expanded in terms of the activities it provides (*Straits Times*, 11 March 2001). The Fund, which facilitates the construction and maintenance of new satellite mosques, is believed to reinforce tendencies of Muslims to isolate themselves from the mainstream. This may be compounded by the numerous activities and services conducted within mosque premises, including preschool education, premarital counselling, computer classes and many others which may have given rise to the view that Muslims' interaction with others are curbed.

The persistence of the focus on mosques may have been fuelled by the spotlight on certain mosques in London and Indonesia which were hijacked by radical preachers to obtain recruits. These may have exacerbated the overgeneralized image of these institutions as conveyors of radicalism for young people. However, such perceptions have been subject to scrutiny and qualification by studies revealing the fact that not only were these mosques few in number, their connection with violence are tempered by a collusion of factors that have received scant systematic investigation (Sageman 2004). Targeting mosques has also incited reactions levelled at other places of worship that facilitate numerous services and social activities for members across age and gender groups. It has also given rise to anecdotal claims that such presumptions fail to effectively consider whether those who partake in grass roots organizations are in fact effectively integrated.

IMPACT ON SOCIAL COHESION

The prevalence of the culturalist perspective in understanding the phenomenon of terrorism impedes positive efforts at forging social cohesion. It has given rise to a siege mentality amongst some Muslims.[21] It also compounds the problem of negative traits that threaten the well-being of plural society as already evident in the reactions of some Singaporeans towards Muslims after the 11 September attacks. Media reports reveal that some Singaporeans have declared that if a bomb went off in Singapore and if radicalized Muslim Singaporeans were found to be responsible, distrust and hate crimes between races will result. Government speeches revealing that after 9/11 some non-Muslims feared entering the same lift with Muslims and that Muslims may be refused employment by Chinese companies provided further evidence of the deep distrust harboured against Muslims that could only be understood in view of the impact of the culturalist perspective, in which the understanding of the issue is associated strongly with Islam (*Straits Times*, 17 December 2005: H7). The fact that innocent Muslims will be victimized by the actions of a handful of deranged Muslims reveals the existence of irrationalism and extremist tendencies that exist in our midst which the prevalence of the culturalist perspective will not alleviate. In fact, it can be readily abused as justification by those who succumb to bigotry, malice, tribalism and other negative orientations that undermine the well-being of plural societies that must necessarily rest on consciousness of fundamental values of vital importance to our common humanity.[22]

The government has since 2005 more pronouncedly adopted a more holistic strategy in dealing with the challenge of cohesion by continuing to engage and embrace civil society, in particular the Muslim civil society (Tan 2007, pp. 443–62). Influence in the development of Islam in Singapore through civil society involvement did not begin with the 11 September attacks or events thereafter. Since the 1970s, it has developed efforts to exclude the impact of political Islam ushered in by the global resurgence on Singaporean Muslims. Apart from MUIS and the Minister-in-Charge of Muslim Affairs, Muslim civil society has also created other channels through which issues pertaining to cultural policies and ethnic interests can be responded to or defused.[23] Through these forums, an alternative vision of Islam that emphasizes the resilience of Muslim families and integration into the wider Singapore society has been articulated. The events of 9/11 resulted in an increasing intensity of this focus accompanied by an expansion of discourse on the role of Islam and Muslims in combating the threat of terrorism. To this end, partnering with various stakeholders in the religious sector has been carried out. This has developed alongside the urge for non-Muslims to take on collective responsibility in enhancing social cohesion, which was conveyed by the Prime Minister in 2005:

> This is not a Malay-Muslim problem. This is a national problem and non-Muslims also have to play your part, for example, by preserving the space for minorities in the majority Chinese society, by upholding the principles of meritocracy and equal opportunity and treatment, regardless of race, language and religion and by clearly distinguishing the small number of extremists who are a threat to us from the majority of moderate, rational, loyal Muslim Singaporeans with whom we work together to tackle a shared problem. And this way, we can build confidence and trust between the different communities and the best time to do that is now when we don't have a crisis. This is because building trust takes time and it requires frequent interaction between leaders and members of the public and between leaders of different groups and it underlines the importance of our integrating our housing estates, our schools, National Service and everyday life.[24]

Various strategies aimed at developing social and psychological defences against terrorism have been introduced, including the Inter-Racial Confidence circles (IRCC), the Code of Religious Values and the

Community Engagement Program (CEP). These involve support from leadership across ethnic groups in various domains and levels aimed at "widening networks and deepening linkages" that transcend existing community-based self-help groups in the hope of strengthening interracial understanding and trust.

IMPACT ON THE MUSLIM COMMUNITY

The Promotion of Moderate Islam

While the urge for "moderation" in the practice of Islam within Singapore's multiracial context has been intensified, the impact of the culturalist perspective in conditioning the conception of radicalism and extremism remains unquestioned. The framing of the problem within the culturalist paradigm has strongly impacted the Muslim community's elite's understanding of the issues affecting them, with implications on the direction and course of action they have thus far undertaken. It has also conditioned the level of abstraction of the problem of extremism and terror, reducing it to one that does not transcend beyond the communal and theological dimension. Although the Minister-in-charge of Muslim Affairs in his address to Parliament did attempt to draw attention to the problems of fundamentalism across ethnic groups that can threaten social cohesion, this angle was never pursued. The Malay community elite's predominant responses through various initiatives reveal the persistent attempt to convince Muslims and others of the compatibility of their Islamic and Singaporean identities and to forge a Malay-Muslim community that sees itself as an integral part of Singapore. Programmes introduced by community leaders and organizations have inculcated the need for moderation, aligned with the state's approach within the culturalist mode. This mirror image of the approach makes the challenge to thwart its prevalence an uphill one as it reinforces the understanding or perspective of the non-Muslim leadership.

Members of the Muslim elite for instance have responded by urging moderate Muslims to "stand up and speak up". They have declared that Muslims have a duty to put Islam "in the right perspective" so as to prevent the religion from being misunderstood. Muslims are also told that they need to adjust their approach by taking into account the changing environment and circumstances. The importance for Muslims to achieve peace and harmony, not animosity with all mankind, especially with their fellow citizens, has also been emphasized. Furthermore, Muslims have also been urged to heed substance rather than forms in their religious practice (*Business Times*, 3 August 2002, p. 1).[25] Constant reiterations on the need for Muslims to be "moderate in outlook, conscious of the situation around them and respond accordingly" are no less emphasized (*Straits Times*, 17 December 2001). The overriding concern constantly repeated is that Muslims must articulate an Islam relevant for Singapore, one that is not inconsistent with being a loyal Singaporean citizen (*Berita Harian*, 8 August 2002).

These statements reinforce the dominant presumptions of the problem of radicalism and extremism. They are characteristically rhetorical for the lack of concrete examples of problems raised. For instance, they do not enlighten one's understanding of how Muslims are not integrated or are unconscious of the context and surroundings in the practice of their religion. They also do not contribute in explicating the aspects whereby religious emphasis is given to forms rather than substance and how these have impacted on Muslims' adjustment to life in Singapore. The statements also overlook the need to identify which segments within the community are responsible for these manifestations and the extent of the problem. Consequently, overgeneralizations and unsubstantiated claims that do not effectively clarify the problems of Muslims nor provide coherent diagnosis of the problems of the religious life of the community are not uncommon. Such declarations cannot be effectively utilized to promote genuine reform to the religious life of the Muslim community.

Indeed reform ideas have been contributed by Malay/Muslim thinkers who have long battled against backward religious ideologies within the community. Propelled by the deep consciousness of the underdevelopment of Muslims and their vital need to adjust to the demands of the modern world, these reformers emphasized the significance of religion for the emergence of the new Malay who embraces modernization and is well adjusted to social change. They not only explicated the importance of basic religious values such as rationality, dignity of man, individual moral accountability and humanity as bases for progress, they also examined impediments that undermine their materialization.[26] Although not directly related to the problem of terrorism and radicalism, these contributions are highly significant in understanding the fundamental problems of development lag which can have serious ramifications on the state of Muslims' well-being in the modern world. Continuous efforts at developing and giving effect to these reform ideas that can strengthen key Muslim religious institutions in Singapore must be undertaken as they bear repercussions on the overall progress of the community. This will ensure not only a more cohesive society but one that is based on fundamental universal and humanitarian values.

Focus on Religious Elite

Being an institution which officially administers the affairs of the Singapore Muslim community, MUIS is perhaps the major institution that has undertaken a more significant role in the issues at stake. Its responses, however, also reveal acceptance of the defined problem through its emphasis on the promotion of "moderate" Islam as a counter to radical religious beliefs. MUIS has galvanized the various organizations and institutions under its purview towards achieving this objective. Various schemes it has initiated reveal an alignment with the approach stemming from the dominant perspective. One of these is the Asatizah Recognition Scheme, which aims to control the teaching of religion that will arrest the propagation of deviant teachings and the promotion of radical religious ideas. By virtue of this initiative, a board comprising religious officials vets an applicant's knowledge of Islam before accrediting him as an Islamic religious teacher. The qualifications and expertise of religious teachers are made accessible to the public. The scheme also rewards accredited *asatizah* with professional development opportunities offered by MUIS. In addition, MUIS has also introduced a system requiring foreign religious teachers and preachers to have the institution's approval before they can preach locally (*Straits Times*, 10 June 2007, pp. 2–3). In effect this scheme reinforces the dominant perspective which closely associates the problem of radicalism and terrorism with theological interpretations of Islam. By focusing on Islamic teachings in the battle for the hearts and minds of Muslims against extremism and terror, MUIS reinforces the notion that the problem at issue lies in the erroneous interpretation of Islam. The scheme is also problematic for it deems that formal accreditation of religious teachers on the basis of their qualification and background can prevent radical theological interpretation of the religion. Yet this is a complex and difficult task to achieve in the absence of close and consistent monitoring of religious teaching, not only in mosques but through numerous other channels, platforms and media.

Furthermore, accreditation for religious teachers cannot address fundamental problems that have long pervaded the religious life of the Malays. Such problems undermine the development of a progressive religious orientation based on a philosophy of life imbued with universalistic values and principles, free from irrational dogmas, pertinent for the well-being of a plural society. A scholar highlighted some of these problems as follows: "the disproportionate emphasis on rituals as opposed to ethical aspects of religion, individual and personal salvation to the point of neglecting social problems, a focus on other worldly concerns at the expense of concrete historical problems of life, a lack of emphasis on the importance of universal values in religious teachings, and the attention to dogmas and practices which are the products of past historical epochs (Shaharuddin 1992, p. 262). Neglect of these fundamental problems may well facilitate acceptance of ideologies that promote irrationalism, exclusiveness, parochialism and other negative traits which are inimical to society, including Muslims themselves. Other features that warrant serious consideration is the pervasive influence of myths, magic, superstitions, collective representation and other irrational beliefs woven into religious thought.[27] While the struggle to raise consciousness of the negative traits of Muslim religious orientations and the need to eradicate them have been the overriding concern of Muslim reformers and scholars all this while, the danger of these negative traits to the well-being of plural society has been largely overlooked. It is also pertinent to note that such traits, inimical to the well-being of society, are not confined to Muslims. The existence of these fundamental problems and the need to effectively deal with them cannot be tackled by schemes, such as the one introduced by the council above, since many involved in the promotion of such teaching are themselves graduates from accredited traditional religious institutions of learning which are generally regarded as prestigious here.[28]

Equally pertinent, the culturalist paradigm prevalent in official discourse has given rise to groups of theologians who have positioned themselves as guardians of moderate Islam. One of the most popular in terms of media coverage and attention is the Religious Rehabilitation Group (RRG). Self-initiated in 2003, the group, which consists of about thirty members today, functions as religious counsellors for JI detainees and their families with the aim of rehabilitating them. Its significance and role has been considerably enhanced by the government's support for their efforts. The RRG has expanded its role by taking on the task of educating the public on the dangers of the JI ideology. Constrained by their theological training, the group resorts to the language of theology in the battle against terrorism by focusing on correcting what it deems as erroneous interpretations of the religion. Hence it embarks upon counselling detainees on the accurate meanings of concepts and terms such as jihad, Darul Islamiyah (Islamic state), *baiath* (oath of loyalty), *istimata* (seeking death through suicide), and *Al Wala Wal Bara* (love and hatred), among others (*Straits Times*, 18 October 2005: H3; 19 February 2006, p. 7). The thrust of the RRG reinforces the culturalist diagnosis of the problem of terror as conditioned by misinterpretations of Islam. Hence its overriding aim is to convince the detainees that Islam does not tolerate unjustified killing and violence.

The mirror image of the culturalist approach is also evident in the reaction of yet another segment of the Muslim religious elite which has also ideologically positioned themselves as guardians and spokesmen for Islam within the community in reaction to the call for moderates to speak up. In their book, *Moderation in Islam* (PERGAS 2002), their reasoning reveals the underlying attempt to counter extremism by focusing on a construction of Islamic teachings that promotes moderation. Yet, some of their views on specific issues are extreme. For instance they insist on the necessity of a collective voice on any issue pertaining to Islam, a standpoint that reflects their sense of intolerance for diversity or individual opinion and judgment which are part of the essential values of the religion. Furthermore, while they assert that Islam is a comprehensive religion which Muslims generally uphold, the meaning they ascribe to this slogan departs from normative understanding of the concept. In their construction, Islam prescribes complete, fixed and absolute systems, including legal and political ones which differ fundamentally from what exists. In this sense they accentuate dichotomies and polarities between Islamic and existing institutions which they deem as secular. They also subscribe to the belief that in principle, Muslims must reject the secular state and its institutions. However, by virtue of the theological principle of minority *fikh*, they are exempted from their Islamic obligations given their politically emasculated status. Thus, while they uphold *hudud* and its implementation as a religious obligation and hence compulsory as a matter of principle, they contend that their minority status excludes them from implementing it.

This group does not promote political activism that seeks fanatically to transform existing institutions and replace these allegedly secular institutions with Islamic ones. On the contrary, they do accept that existing institutions are compatible with Islam. Nevertheless their essentialist leanings and rhetoric create ambivalence towards these institutions that can impede effective integration. Delving into tenth century theological discourse on the legitimacy of the territory of existence (*darul harb* as opposed to *darul Islam*) and the rights and obligations of minority Muslims in these contexts, while acknowledging at the end of the day that it is not incompatible with Islam for Muslims to work and live in Singapore, accentuates the binary opposition between what is deemed Islamic and secular.

In many ways such styles of thought reveal traits of the utopian mentality as discussed by Karl Mannheim, that characterize the thinking of oppressed groups bent on transforming a given social order. Starkly incongruent with existing conditions, their ideas are not at all concerned with what really exists but reveal overriding preoccupations with imagined ideal systems based on their construction of an Islamic state, society and history (Mannheim 1976, p. 36). Such thinking cannot correctly or objectively diagnose existing conditions of society, for they are critical of the existing social order without being clear as to what they are objecting to or disapprove of. While not historically grounded, views promoted reflect striking resemblance in terms of perceptions, issues raised and methodology employed (such as "minority *fiqh*") to those taking place amongst more recent migrants to the West, grappling with issues of identity as minorities in the context of largely Western, non-Muslim majority states.[29] Undiscerning import of such discourse unnecessarily brings along with it concerns irrelevant to the Muslim community in Singapore. Furthermore, though not seeking to demolish existing institutions, such perceptions can also impair Muslims from making real contributions to the larger society in which they live. Should such an orientation dominate, it would impede contributions of Muslims as active citizens working for the betterment of the larger society.

Mosques and Interfaith Dialogue

Apprehension for mosques, which again focuses on the issue of religion, has also conditioned efforts at remodelling the institution with the overriding aim of ensuring that Muslims are integrated with the multiracial society in which they exist. Community leaders represented by MUIS which oversees the administration and management of the majority of mosques in Singapore are hence made to ensure that the institution is not only more accessible to younger groups of Malay/Muslims so as to curb their susceptibility to extremist ideology, but non-Muslims as well. Programmes, such as aL.I.V.E. for teenagers and children, have been developed with the aim of teaching young Muslims to better understand, appreciate and practise Islam within the context of a multi-ethnic society. To this end, some mosques are providing part-time religious classes in English using a revamped religious curriculum that is deemed to be in sync with the concerns and needs of the young and their modes of learning. To facilitate these changes, MUIS has committed financial support and resources for the training and retraining of the *asatizah*.[30] Furthermore MUIS has also embarked on a programme aimed at promoting *asatizah*'s understanding of the different religions as well as national issues. It is not the extent of the effectiveness of these changes in imparting religious values to the community that is the issue. Of pertinence is the fact that review and changes in religious instruction via part-time madrasa offered by MUIS is a reaction to the defining problems that have dominated the discourse on radicalism which makes religious institutions such as the mosques an object of focus.

Collaboration with grass-roots organizations in organizing mosque visits for non-Muslims with the aim of explaining the Muslim faith further reveals the mirror image of the culturalist approach that pervades community leaders' acceptance of problems. This is further manifested by the establishment of the Harmony Centre within one of the mosques that seeks to promote interfaith understanding. This function is administered by a team of youths and religious and community leaders who have received special training in the domain of interfaith relations to handle the programmes of the centre. The centre also undertakes the task of coordinating interfaith and community engagement programs carried out by the Muslim community in Singapore. While interfaith dialogues have been an established feature of religious organizations' agenda in Singapore, MUIS' central role in its promotion, concretized through the establishment of the Harmony Centre under its wing, can be seen as a response to the culturalist approach intensified by 9/11.

FOCUS ON VALUES AND IDENTITY

Yet another manifestation of the influence of the culturalist approach is MUIS' Singapore Muslim identity project that aims to develop a model progressive Singaporean Muslim minority community. Culminating in the publication of a charter entitled "Risalah for Building a Singapore Muslim Community of Excellence" (2006), the project is a response to the challenge to promote moderate Islam. The *Risalah* (treatise) exhorts the Muslim community to strive for religious excellence by having "the ability to perform rituals of Islam while appreciating their significance and internalizing the values embedded within them". It also calls upon Muslims "to fully partake in nation-building" and to position themselves as "full members of the Singaporean society". Ten attributes are delineated which MUIS deems necessary for the creation of a community of excellence. These include holding on strongly to Islamic principles while adapting to the changing context, appreciating Islamic civilization and history, having a good understanding of contemporary issues, appreciating other civilizations, being morally and spiritually strong, practising Islam beyond rituals and riding on the modernization wave, being well-adjusted and contributing to Singapore's multi-religious society and secular state, being inclusive without contradicting Islam and believing that good Muslims are also good citizens.

This identification and promotion of good values based on Islam is certainly not the issue. The task has long been undertaken in the propagation of religious teaching by the various Islamic religious institutions. However, given the context, the focus on values in the *Risalah* reinforces the spotlight on Islam, consistent with the culturalist mode. Furthermore, the fact that some of these values reiterate the issue of compatibility between being Muslim and Singaporean, strongly suggest that Muslims have a problem with their identity. Although none of these presumptions are substantiated in concrete terms, they reinforce the widely held view that Muslims' identity can potentially undermine loyalty to the nation. It is also pertinent to note that the *Risalah*'s reassertions of values and attributes of Islam are largely formulated in the abstract or, at best, as they were manifested centuries ago. This does little to enhance deeper understanding of these values in relation to modern problems and challenges. Statements within the *Risalah*, such as "Islam places great importance on knowledge, creativity and critical thinking", that it "benefits mankind and the environment", "embraces other civilizations and cultures", that "the *shariah* is dynamic", or that "the holy Koran discusses interfaith and inter-communal relations and dialogue", are not unknown to most Muslims. What would have been more helpful would have been an analysis of how these values can be institutionalized and impediments that thwart their realization.

Such an effort goes beyond identification of values per se. The *Risalah* also raises other problems pertaining to personalities upheld as imbibing the values delineated. For instance, it highlights Sheikh Yusof Qardhawi as a contemporary Muslim intellectual on Islamic economics and law. However, not only does it not explain how the modern economic system is un-Islamic such that it warrants an alternative one based on Islam, it also does not help explain how the Sheikh, who is unfamiliar with modern economics, can be upheld as providing an alternative to the modern economic system. Similarly, while upholding Qardhawi as a legal scholar, the *Risalah* does not deal with controversies relating to concepts such as minority *fikh* and *fikh* of priorities that he is closely associated with. These concepts are known to invite negative implications on the integration of Muslims in America and Europe into the larger societies in which they exist. Though the implications of his thought and fatwa need to be addressed, these issues did not receive any attention in the *Risalah*.

Religious Schools

Responses to the development of madrasa education in the context of post 9/11 further depict the prevalence of the culturalist approach. The madrasa itself has not been perceived as the hotbed for radicalism by the dominant elite as is the case with some other states such as Pakistan and Indonesia. However, long before 9/11, concern has been raised over the quality of madrasa education in equipping students with the relevant skills needed for their effective integration into the knowledge-based economy and the larger Singapore society. Existing apart from mainstream national education, the madrasa is perceived as being isolated from broad currents of educational thinking and reform that put a high premium on knowledge, skills and talent. Its ability to foster national integration and social cohesion has also been highlighted. Although the discourse on integration is lodged outside the domain of schooling, the madrasa had been to some extent implicated. Amidst the backdrop of the government's reiteration for the Malay community to participate more fully in the mainstream, perceptions arising from its separate existence were woven into the issue of national integration. These problems were compounded by the rising rates of enrolment of students into the six full time madrasa in the eighties and nineties amidst the global Islamic resurgence. In view of the madrasa's dismal passing rate as well as its high attrition rate, serious doubts have been cast on its ability to achieve its dual goal of providing both religious and secular education. Fear that these problems would create a marginalized underclass that would exacerbate tension was evident.[31] The debate on the madrasa and compulsory education has given rise to certain compromises acceptable to the Malay/Muslim community. It was agreed that compulsory education introduced in 2003 would be extended to the madrasa, subject to their fulfilment of the benchmark based on the average aggregate score for Malay students in the six lowest-performing national schools who sat for the Primary School Leaving Examinations in the same year. This means that students attending madrasa are exempted from the compulsory education law. In addition, the overriding concern of the government over the growing numbers of those who enrolled into the madrasa and the ability of the institution to ensure their academic success is checked by the imposition of a cap on enrolment at the primary level at 400 in total for all the six full-time madrasa each year. It was also reported shortly after the debate that the government will raise two million dollars over five years to help one full-time madrasa groom Islamic scholars and teachers who are well versed in English, Science and Mathematics. This benevolent gesture could have been intended to remove the allegation by certain madrasa stakeholders of the government's "sinister motive" in attempting to close down the madrasa with the introduction of compulsory education.

The influence of the culturalist perspective woven into the understanding of events relating to radicalism and terrorism after 9/11 could have induced a more hard-line stance of the government towards the madrasa. Although the madrasa are not perceived as the hotbed for the teaching or propagation of militant ideas, apprehension for Muslims' religiosity in facilitating extremism and terror may have contributed to the non-materialization of funding for the one madrasa as earlier promised. This means that all the six full-time madrasas continue to be funded solely by the community and students' fees. If this is the motive for the change of mind, it can be argued that it blocks consideration of the crux of the madrasa's problem. It is contended that the major limitation of the madrasa is not the lack of integration or common experience of students. On the contrary there have been consistent attempts on its part to integrate into the Singapore society and the national education system long before 9/11. This is evident in the various programmes and strategies it has devised, including providing for the national curriculum as well as a religious one.

Efforts at integration have long taken place, although recent coverage tends to portray the direction and goals of the madrasa as if they were a recent post 9/11 development.[32] In fact the major shortcoming of the madrasa lies in its attempt to achieve its dual objective of producing both religious scholars and Muslim professionals. This takes a heavy toll on the institution, resulting in a host of problems, including high drop-out rate, low passing rate and standards that are generally low in both academic and religious education (Noor Aisha and Lai 2006, pp. 58–92). Yet, this problem has not been raised or addressed.

The mirror image of the culturalist perspective is reflected in the various steps and directions taken by the elites within the community since 9/11. While none have found it necessary to review the madrasa's dual roles, much effort has been undertaken to intensify the image of the institution as one that is well integrated and well adapted to the demands of the modern world by its ability to balance both objectives. The institution continues to pride itself with success measured by students who have gone on to junior colleges and the state universities although, in fact, only a mere handful have been able to do so. The recent revamp of the madrasa under the Joint Madrasah Scheme facilitated by MUIS is yet another effort that reveals this overriding concern. The scheme, which is supported by three of the six full-time madrasas, would mean that each can only provide either primary or secondary education so that limited resources can be better utilized and academic standards raised (*Straits Times*, 27 October 2007). Madrasas that are part of the scheme will receive funding from part of the accumulated monies from the Mosque Building Fund, which will be used for teacher training and recruitment, systems and facilities enhancement, curriculum and content development as well as student enrichment programmes. While there has been some discussion over how the community's resources are to used, the crux of the problem of the madrasa's dual objective of attempting to produce both religious teachers and professionals within each school while ensuring the attainment of academic standards in both domains is not discussed.[33] The problem is compounded by the tendency to see the madrasa as yet another identity marker of the Muslims threatened by closure if they do not produce graduates for the market as well as religious scholars. Such views to the effect that the madrasa can provide the best Islamic education to the majority of students while at the same time equip them with sufficient skills and knowledge for employment continue to be upheld, although they fail to address the reality of the limitations of the institution (Yang Razali Kassim 2008).

CONCLUDING REMARKS

This chapter has attempted to analyse major issues confronting the Muslims in Singapore that have emerged since 9/11. It reveals the impact of the culturalist approach in the selection and perception of these issues in dominant discourse. Though the approach in understanding Malay/Muslims did not begin with the attack, it is reinforced and intensified by its occurrence, fuelled by factors both internal as well as external to Singapore. It has impacted perceptions of radicalism and terrorism as conditioned by religious theology, thereby extending and reinforcing concerns pertaining to the community and the problem of integration that have hitherto prevailed. The mirror image of the approach is manifested in the reactions of the Muslim community's elites to the problem and the type of strategies and measures they have adopted in dealing with it. While a more holistic effort has been initiated with the overriding aim of strengthening social cohesion, greater awareness of the limitations of the culturalist approach is vital to its realization.

Notes

1. Some of these historical factors include the impact of racial division of labour and racial stereotyping during British colonial rule in Singapore as well as the link, during the 1950s, between Chinese "chauvinism" and pro-communist agitation, which predisposed the People's Action Party moderates towards the view that ethnic loyalties are potentially disruptive (Brown 1993, p. 20). Singapore's position within the region had prompted the PAP to liken the state to an "independent Israel in Southeast Asia" in its rationale for merger and had influenced the strong alliance with the United States, based on the Israeli experience (Chan 1971, p. 11).
2. Goh Chok Tong, "Prime Minister's New Year Message 2002" <http://stars.nhb.gov.sg/stars/public/> (accessed 6 May 2009).
3. For a good discussion on the problems of the traits and problems of the culturalist approach, see Clammer (1998, pp. 164–74), Roy (1999, pp. 56–65; 2002, pp. 8–17), and also Said (1997, pp. xv–xlviii).
4. See, for instance, Lewis (1990), Desker (2003), Tan (2002) and Ramakrishna (2002).
5. Lee Kuan Yew, "Loyalty and the SAF", Speech at Dialogue Session with the Association of Muslim Professionals and Majlis Pusat, Parliament House Auditorium, Singapore, 3 March 2001 <http://stars.nhb.gov.sg/stars/public/> (accessed 5 May 2009).
6. As Goh asserted, "we are a multiracial and multi-religious society and

Singaporeans may not all react in the same way to the same events. It is important ... that we get across the message that we support the US because it is fighting terrorism ... we must expect Osama, the Taliban and their followers to portray the US as being against Islam and attacking a Muslim country. They have called all Muslims to start a jihad against the US. I am comforted that our Muslims understand the issues and are not confused by the call." Goh Chok Tong, Speech at the Dialogue Session with Union Leaders/Members and Employees, Nanyang Polytechnic, Singapore, 14 October 2001 <http://stars.nhb.gov.sg/stars/public/> (accessed 6 May 2009).
7. Goh Chok Tong, "Beyond Madrid: Winning against Terrorism", Speech to Council on Foreign Relations, Washington DC, 6 May 2004 <http://stars.nhb.gov.sg/stars/public/> (accessed 5 May 2009).
8. Goh Chok Tong, Speech at the Dialogue Session with Union Leaders/Members and Employees.
9. Some instances of contributions informed by the social science perspective have been discussed in Noor Aisha Abdul Rahman (2009). These include the works of Mariam Abou Zahab and Oliver Roy (2004), Mahmood Mamdani (2004), Marc Sageman (2004), Edward W. Said (2001), Oliver Roy (2004), Azra Azyumardi (2005) and John Sidel (2008).
10. Mamdani (2004, pp. 22–23) traces the framing of the issue, which places the onus on moderates to resolve to Bernard Lewis. Lewis believed that there are other groups (apart from the fundamentalists) and had warned of a hard struggle between them which the West can do little or nothing about. The West, he maintains, must remain a bystander while Muslims fight their internal war, pitting "good" against "bad" Muslims.
11. Goh, "Beyond Madrid: Winning against Terrorism".
12. Ibid.
13. Goh Chok Tong, "National Day Rally Address", University Cultural Center, National University of Singapore, Singapore, 18 August 2002 <http://stars.nhb.gov.sg/stars/public/> (accessed 6 May 2009).
14. On the problems in orientation of resurgence ideas, see Chandra Muzaffar (1987). Refer also to Shaharuddin Maaruf (2001).
15. In Singapore, uniforms are compulsory for students enrolled in elementary and secondary schools as well as junior colleges. The *tudung* is, however, permissible in private schools that are established and managed independently, the polytechnics and tertiary institutions.
16. For a good account of the debate in France, refer to Bowen (2007).
17. As Siddique explicated, the *tudung*, like any fashion item, has a history. Tracing the trend to female university students in campuses under the influence of Islamic resurgence in the 1970s, she maintained that donning the *tudung* then was as much a political as it was a religious statement. It was conditioned by an affirmation of the sense of being a good and pious Muslim, rejecting

Western fashion and reinforcing universal solidarity by rejecting culture-bound, ethnic-based, traditional Muslim women's fashion (*Straits Times*, 20 February 2002). The socio-historical context underscores the problem of deeming the *tudung* as synonymous with religious obligation per se. While Muslims have always been generally conscious of the principle of modesty in dressing, the notion that the headscarf is a compulsory aspect of Islamic dress did not emerge as an issue in religious discourse till the nineties. Hence although the *tudung* had long been used as part of the women's garment within the Malay community underlined by the principle of modesty, it has never had the kind of religious significance and manifestation as it does in recent times. Even for girls attending religious schools until the late seventies, the *tudung* was not deemed an essential part of the school uniform. In the madrasa, not all school girls then donned the *tudung*, strongly suggesting that the trend must be understood in its socio-historical context. In some madrasa, it was not uncommon to see school teachers and even principals merely wearing a short and transparent scarf. The *tudung* was also never raised as an issue by parents whose daughters attended national schools. The school uniform did not pose an obstacle to Muslim religious beliefs and values. One can go so far as to assert that even in the heyday of Muslim resurgence, conformity with school uniforms for daughters was not an issue even if more young parents began to don the headscarf.

18. The mufti asserted that "education is a general requirement for all Muslims which will benefit them, their communities and their countries, whereas wearing the scarf is a specific requirement for Muslim girls and women to dress modestly" (PERGAS 2004, p. 343). Since there is a conflict, parents should choose education over the dress code. Although the *tudung* is compulsory, given the context, prominent religious teachers within the community concur that girls should attend schools.

19. These are expressions of sentiments of Muslim women in *Tudung: Beyond Face Value* (2002).

20. See, for instance, Law (2003). Law maintains that "by not allowing Muslim schoolgirls to wear the *tudung* at school, the government has violated Malay Muslim's right to religious freedom, a right that does not infringe on the rights of others." The author, however, did not examine the problem of plurality of views within the community and the implications of this cultural diversity within the multi-culturalist perspective adopted.

21. Excerpt from a speech delivered by the Minister in charge of Muslim Affairs illustrates this siege mentality: "Practices of the Malay community which have evolved naturally became the subject of scrutiny. There were even some questioning as to whether these practices were desirable or otherwise. A community, which had hitherto lived peacefully with other communities found itself the subject of discussion by all — with some participants taking

their reference points from outside the Singapore context. The local context did not matter as we were swathed with exciting stories of terrorism and extremism prefaced by the word 'Islamic' supplied by overnight experts. There were increased concerns and questions about the implications of overt symbols and signs of Muslim identity and beliefs. Some wondered why Muslims needed to consume food that was halal (or permitted) as though it was a radical behavioral departure. Observing religious practices became a sort of shorthand for hovering at the edge of terrorism." Yaacob Ibrahim, Speech by the Minister for Community Development and Sports and Minister in-charge of Muslim Affairs at the Wee Kim Wee Seminar on Cross-Cultural Understanding, Singapore Management University, 2 August 2003.

22. Shaharuddin's (1980) discussion on the traits of the backward mind in religious experience and its impact on the well-being of plural society is highly useful to the problem at issue. Though his critique focuses on traits of negative orientation shaped by religion, its underlying thrust on the need for humanitarian philosophy vital for the well-being of plural society is of wider relevance.
23. These included MENDAKI (Council for Malay Education) formed in 1981 and the specially designated Malay MPs in the Group Representation Constituencies introduced in the 1988 elections.
24. Speech by Prime Minister Lee Hsien Loong at the Community Engagement Programme Dialogue, 9 February 2006.
25. This declaration is found in the speech of Guntor Sadali, the chief editor of *Berita Harian*, the only Malay daily in Singapore, at a community award presentation ceremony.
26. See, for instance, the works of Alatas (1972; 1977; 1979; 1996; 2000). See also Chandra Muzaffar (2002).
27. For an explication of the concept of collective representation, please refer to Alatas (1977, pp. 53–64). Some examples on collective representation woven into religious beliefs which are circulated in Singapore can be found in "Sesi Soal Jawab Mengenai Makhluk Halus", *Siri Kursus Perubatan*, Masjid Assyakirin, 2005 <http://www.ceramahislam.com>; Ismail Kamus (1999).
28. For a good account of some of the problems of religious education in traditional Islamic centres of learning, see Azhar Ibrahim (2006).
29. See for instance the issues raised by Tariq Ramadan (2004). See also Al-Awani (2003) and Skovgaard-Petersen, Jakob and Bettina Graf (2009).
30. <http://app.mcys.gov.sg/web/corp_speech_story.asp?> (accessed 15 October 2009).
31. The concern is conveyed by Yeong Yoon Ying, the Press Secretary of Lee Kuan Yew, then Senior Minister, in response to a letter to the press from a Malay voicing dissent against the Special Assistance Schools and its objective of

creating a Chinese cultural elite instead of a national one. Yeong replied to the effect that madrasa education kept a part of the Malay-Muslim community distinctive and separate. Following a different curriculum which did not teach critical skills nor prepare students to fit into the emerging knowledge-based economy, madrasas can give rise to problems much like the Chinese clan-funded schools in Singapore in the past which produced many students who became dissatisfied and rebellious (*Straits Times*, 8 April 1999; 24 April 1999).

32. See, for instance, Norimitsu Onishi, "Balancing Secular and Religious, Singapore School is Viewed as Model of Future", *New York Times*, 23 April 2009.

33. Speech by Dr Yaacob Ibrahim, Minister-in-Charge of Muslim Affairs, at the Ministry of Community, Youth and Sports Committee of Supply Sitting 2008, 5 March.

References

Abou Zahab, Mariam and Olivier Roy. *Islamist Networks: The Afghan-Pakistan Connection*. New York: Columbia University Press, 2004.

Alatas, Syed Hussein. *Modernisation and Social Change*. London: Angus and Robertson, 1972.

———. *Intellectuals in Developing Societies*. London: Cass, 1977.

———. *Kita Dengan Islam: Tumbuh Tiada Berbuah*. Singapura: Pustaka Nasional, 1979.

———. *The New Malay: His Role and Future*. Singapore: Association of Muslim Professionals, 1996.

———. *Cita Sempurna Warisan Sejarah*. Bangi: UKM, 2000.

Al-Alwani, Taha Jabir. 2003. *Towards a Fiqh for Minorities: Some Basic Reflections*. London: International Institute of Islamic Thought, 2003.

Azhar Ibrahim. "An Evaluation of Madrasah Education: Perspectives and Lessons from the Experiences of Some Muslim Societies". In *Secularism and Spirituality: Seeking Integrated Knowledge and Success in Madrasah Education in Singapore*, edited by Noor Aisha Abdul Rahman and Lai Ah Eng. Singapore: Marshall Cavendish Academic, 2006.

Azyumardi Azra. *Islam in Southeast Asia: Tolerance and Radicalism*. Paper presented at Miegunyah Public Lecture, University of Melbourne, 6 April 2005.

Bowen, John R. *Why the French Don't Like Headscarves: Islam, the State, and Public Space*. Princeton: Princeton University Press, 2007.

Brown, David. "The Corporatist Management of Ethnicity in Contemporary Singapore". In *Singapore Changes Guards: Social, Political and Economic Directions in the 1990s*, edited by Garry Rodan. New York: St. Martin's Press, 1993.

Chan, Heng Chee. Singapore: *The Politics of Survival, 1965–1967*. London: Oxford University Press, 1971.
Chandra Muzaffar. *Islamic Resurgence in Malaysia*. Kuala Lumpur: Fajar Bakti, 1987.
———. *Rights, Religion and Reform: Enhancing Human Dignity through Spiritual and Moral Transformation*. London: Routledge, 2002.
Clammer, J.R. *Race and State in Independent Singapore 1965–1990: The Cultural Politics of Pluralism in a Multiethnic Society*. Aldershot: Ashgate, 1998.
Desker, Barry. "The Jemaah Islamiyah (JI) Phenomenon in Singapore". *Contemporary Southeast Asia* 25, no. 3 (2003): 489–507.
Ismail Kamus. *"Jin": Rasukan dan Pengubatannya*. Kuala Lumpur: Al-Marzuk, 1999.
Law Kam-Yee. "The Myth of Multiracialism in Post-9/11 Singapore: The Tudong Incident". *New Zealand Journal of Asian Studies* 5, no. 1 (June 2003): 51–71.
Lewis, Bernard. "The Roots of Muslim Rage". *The Atlantic*, September 1990, pp. 1–6.
Lily Zubaidah Rahim. "A New Dawn in PAP-Malay Relations". In *Impressions of the Goh Chok Tong Years in Singapore*, edited by Bridget Welsh. Singapore: NUS Press, 2009.
Mamdani, Mahmood. *Good Muslims, Bad Muslims: America, the Cold War and the Roots of Terror*. New York: Three Leaves, 2004.
Mannheim, Karl. *Ideology and Utopia*. London: Routledge, 1976.
Noor Aisha Abdul Rahman. "The Dominant Perspective on Terrorism and its Implications for Social Cohesion: The Case of Singapore". *Copenhagen Journal of Asian Studies* 27, no. 2 (2009): 109–28.
Noor Aisha Abdul Rahman and Lai Ah Eng, eds. *Secularism and Spirituality: Seeking Integrated Knowledge and Success in Madrasah Education in Singapore*. Singapore: Institute of Policy Studies/Marshall Cavendish, 2006.
PERGAS. *Moderation in Islam: In the Context of Muslim Community in Singapore*. Singapore: PERGAS, 2004.
Risalah for Building a Singapore Muslim Community of Excellence. Singapore: MUIS, 2006.
Roy, Oliver. "The Elusive Cultural Community". In *People, Nation and State: The Meaning of Ethnicity and Nationalism*, edited by Edward Mortimer and Robert Fine. London: IB Tauris, 1999.
———. *Globalised Islam*. London: Hurst, 2004.
Sageman, Marc. *Understanding Terror Networks*. Philadelphia: University of Pennsylvania Press, 2004.
———. "The Next Generation of Terror". *Foreign Policy* (March/April 2008): 165.
Said, Edward W. *Covering Islam: How the Media and the Experts Determine How We See the Rest of the World*. New York: Vintage Books, 1997.

———. "The Clash of Ignorance". *The Nation*, 22 October 2001, pp. 1–3.
Shaharuddin Maaruf. "Some Theoretical Problems Concerning Tradition and Modernization among the Malays of Southeast Asia". In *Asian Traditions and Modernisation: Perspectives from Singapore*, edited by Yong Mun Cheong. Singapore: Times, 1992.
———. *Religion and Utopian Thinking among the Muslims of Southeast Asia*. Singapore: NUS, 2001.
Sidel, John. "The Islamist Threat in Southeast Asia: Much Ado About Nothing?" *Asian Affairs* 39, no. 3 (November 2008): 339–51.
Skovgaard-Petersen, Jakob and Graf, Bettina, eds. *Global Mufti: The Phenomenon of Yusuf al-Qardawi*. London: Hurst, 2009.
Tan, Andrew. "Terrorism in Singapore: Threat and Implications". *Contemporary Security Politics* 23 (2002): 1–18.
Tan, Eugene K.B. "Norming Moderation in an 'Iconic Target': Public Policy and the Regulation of Religious Anxieties in Singapore". *Terrorism and Political Violence* 19, no. 4 (2007): 443–62.
Tariq Ramadan. "What are European Muslims' Concerns and Aspirations".*Tariq Ramadan*, 26 September 2004 <http//www.tariqramadan.com/spip.php?article 42/> (accessed 26 September 2004).
Yang Razali Kassim. "Remodelling the Madrasah in Singapore: Past, Present and Future". *Karyawan* 9, no. 1 (July 2008): 27–29.

Index

A
"A Day in the Life of Dr Karim" story (Mustafa), 319
Abdullah administration, 160, 173, 179
Abdullah, Munshi, 50
Abdullah, Taufik, 195
Abdul Majid, Haji, 51
ABIM. *See* Angkatan Belia Islam Malaysia (ABIM)
accommodation, 305n29
   political participation and. *See* electoral politics participation, Thailand
Acehnese wars, 277
Aceh, suicide attacks in, 277
Administration of Muslim Law Enactment 1952, 114
"Aesthetics" story (Jamil), 328
Aeusrivongse, Nidhi, 278–79
Afghanistan terrorist network, 342
AGC. *See* Al-Arqam Group of Companies (AGC)
Ahmadiyah
   ban of, 223, 227, 233–35, 238–39
   beliefs, 219
   campaign against, 225–26
   community, 227
   critics' argument on, 237
   government's toleration of, 228
   history in Indonesia, 220–21, 224
   mosques, 232, 238
   origins in British India, 223
   populations, 220
   protecting, 233
   religious freedom for, 218, 235–38
Ahmadiyah Muslim Community, 218, 219
Ahmadiyya Muslim Jama'at. *See* Ahmadiyah
AKKBB. *See* Aliansi Kebangsaan untuk Kebebasan Beragama dan Berkeyakinan (AKKBB)
Al-Arqam Group of Companies (AGC), 79
Al Fata At Tamimi, 83
Al-Furqan incident, 11, 279–80
Al-Helmy, Burhanuddin, 69, 70, 88n7
Aliansi Kebangsaan untuk Kebebasan Beragama dan Berkeyakinan (AKKBB), 228–29, 237, 242n33
alim, 27, 35
aliran (streams), 252
   in contemporary Indonesia, 265n7
aliran kepercayaan, 221, 228
Al-Ittihad, 74
Al-Ittihadiyyah, 74
aL.I.V.E. programmes, 364
Allah, 89n18
   and Muhammad, 224, 227

al-Qaeda, 342, 355
Amangkurat I, 22, 25
Amangkurat II, 39
American colonialism in the Philippines, 314, 316–17, 320
American feminist movements, 258
American imperialists, 316
Amin, Ma'ruf, 225, 231
amir, 27
Anderson, Benedict, 56
Angkatan Belia Islam Malaysia (ABIM), 103, 108, 352
Anglo-Siamese agreement, 272
Annabel Gallop of British Library, 50
anti-Ahmadiyah agenda, 226
anti-Ahmadiyah sentiment, 233–35
anti-pornography bill, 10, 258
anti-prostitution laws, 258–59
anti-religion stance, 207
Anwar sodomy trial, 127
Appiah, Anthony, 314
Arabicization of women, 259
archipelago pilgrims, 50–51
Arjomand, Said Amir, 32–33
Arnada, Erwin, 256–57
Asain, Calbi, 319
asatizah, 364
Asatizah Recognition Scheme, 360
Ashaari Muhammad, Ustaz, 76–79, 86
Asian economic crisis, 249
assimilation of Muslim immigrants, 9
assimilation policies, Thailand, 271–72, 303n2
Astana, 318, 331n3
Aurad Muhammadiah congregation, 72, 85
  in Malaysia, 77–84
  in Singapore, 74–77
aurat, 256
Australian feminist movements, 258
authoritarianism, 206–7

Ayat Lima, 73
Ayutthaya kings, 272
Aziz, Nik, 352

B

Babad ing Sangkala, 22
Badan Koordinasi Pengawas Aliran Kepercayaan Masyarakat. *See* Bakorpakem
Badan Penyelidik Usaha Persiapan Kemerdekaan Indonesia (BPUPKI), 201
Badawi, Abdullah, 141, 162–63, 165, 181n7
Badie, Betrand, 28
Bakorpakem, 221–22, 227, 240n6
Bali bombings, 292
Barisan Nasional (BN), 171
Barisan Revolusi Nasional-Coordinate (BRN-C), 280
Bashir, Abu Bakar, 226
Basyumi, Muhammad M., 243n46
Batak account, 56
Batavia, 19, 24, 38
Batu Caves temple, 142–43
bay bithaman ajil, 117
Berjaya administration, 169–70, 172–74
"Berjihad Di Patani", 277
Beyer, Peter, 40
Bijapur, 31
blasphemy, 230
Blue Blood of the Big Astana (Jubaira), 317
BNBC. *See* British North Borneo Company (BNBC)
bomohs, 301
Boonyaratkalin, Sonthi, 285–86
Borneonization of Sabah civil service, 176
Brahmins, 28–29, 38

British colonial rulers, 31
British India, Ahmadiyah's origins in, 223
British North Borneo Company (BNBC), 166
BRN-C. *See* Barisan Revolusi Nasional-Coordinate (BRN-C)
Buddhism, 38, 125
  in South Asia, 29
bumiputra, 70, 140, 159, 165–66, 173–75, 177
bumiputraism, 150
bureaucratization of Islam, 105

C

Carita Sultan Iskandar, 21, 23
Catholic Filipinos, 315
Central Java, 19
Chakri dynasty, 30
chauvinism, 369n1
chauvinists, ethnic, 141
children, Indonesia, 260
  dignity of, 257
  immorality and safeguarding, 260
  Islamic discourses, 257
  moral protection, 262
  protection, 258, 262–63
Chinese communities, demographics of, 134
Chinese populations, 335, 355
Chinese War, Islamizing trend in, 24
Christian Filipinos, 316, 324, 331n2
Christianity, Islam and, 343
Chularatmontri, 291, 293
citizenship, Islamization and, 160–65
civilizational conflict, 344
civil laws, 119, 125
  civil definition of Malay-Muslim, 125
  harmonization of, 117–18
  syariah and, 119

civil rights of Muslim citizen, 105
civil society
  Muslim, 345, 357
  organizations, 35
clash of civilization, 344
Cobbold Commission, 168
Colonialism, American. *See* American colonialism
colonial rule in the Philippines, 316–21
common penal code in Malaysia, 114
Community Engagement Program (CEP), 358
community, Indonesia, 254, 257, 263
Confederation of Muslim Graduates of the Peninsula, 108
conflict in Muslim stories/lives, 326–29
confrontations. *See* violent confrontations
constitutional rights in Indonesia, 249
contemporary Indonesia, 19, 34–38, 44n10
  aliran in, 265n7
  religion and politics in, 249, 253
Contract Act 1950, 118
conversion law, 135
Coordinating Board for Monitoring Mystical Beliefs in Society, 221
Crescent Star Party, 233
cultural identity in Java, 22, 25
culturalist approach in Muslims
  9/11 and, 340–44
  impact of, 354
  mirror image of, 362
  pervasiveness of, 342
  traits of, 337–40
culture talk, 339

D

Dahlan, Kyai Haji Ahmad, 212n7

Dahm, Bernhard, 194
dakwah, 27, 73, 78, 182n22, 227
Daratista, Inul, 255
Darul Arqam, 76–79, 82, 92n41, 110
Darul Islam movement, 25
Da'wa. *See* Tablighi Jama'at (TJ)
DDII. *See* Dewan Dakwah Islamiyah Indonesia (DDII)
Defenders of Islam Command, 229
de-Indianization of Malay culture, 139
democracy, 286
　criticisms of, 206
　definition, 206
　guided, 198, 205–6
　Islam and, 197–98, 211, 251
　Islamic, 206, 207
　of Malaysia, 115
　and Natsir, 206, 211
　religion and, 206
　Siamese, 284
　and social justice, 266n10
　and Sukarno, 211
　Western characteristics, 199
　wild or unfettered, 207
　without an opposition, 210
Democrat Party, 234, 281–82
Department for the Development of Syariah Judiciary in Malaysia, 111
Department of Home Affairs, 225
Dewan Dakwah Islamiyah Indonesia (DDII), 25, 221–22, 225, 227, 240n8
Dewan Pertimbangan Presiden (DPP), 225
divine justice, 146–47
Djamaluddin, Amin, 221–22, 226, 237, 240n10
dual-jurisdiction system, 118
Dusun Nyior clash, 283

Dutch colonial army, suicide attacks, 277
Dutch colonialism, 202
　PNI's condemnation of, 193
Dutch colonialists, 277
Dutch colonial rule, 277
Dutch East India Company (VOC), 19–20
　alliance, 22
　attacking garrison, 24
Dutch-Indonesian relationship, challenges in, 204

E
Eastern democracy, 206. *See also* Western democracy
egalitarian marriages, 263
Egyptian Muslim Brotherhood, 252
Election Commission of Thailand, 285
electoral politics participation, Thailand
　Constitutional Court for electoral fraud, 286
　Malay-Muslim community, 284–86
　Malay-Muslim politicians, 281–82
　New Aspiration Party (NAP), 282
　People's Power Party, 285
　Tak Bai massacre, 284
　Thaksin's Thai Rak Thai (TRT), 283–85
　Wahdah members, 282
Embassy of Saudi Arabia, 222
"endangered identity", 159
Engineer, Ali Asghar, 251
English common law, 116–17
ethnic chauvinists, 141
ethnic consciousness in Malaysia, 135
ethnic factor, 168
ethnic groups, 335

Index

ethno-nationalistic urgency, 133
extrajudicial killings in South Thailand, 284
extremism, 339, 359
extremist Muslims
  moderates *vs.*, 344–46
  struggle with rationalist Muslims, 343

F

"fantasized homogeneity", 119
Fatayat, 265n5
  demonstrations, 258
  gender equality and Islamic feminism, 251
  pornography debate in Indonesia, 255
  understandings of Islam, 251
  Wahhabism, 259
  for women, 250
Fatayat Nahdlatul Ulama, 248
fatwa, 27, 81, 85, 119, 128n1, 221, 224, 228
fatwa councils, ban of religious practices of Muslims, 120–22
fatwas, 221–22, 224
Faza'il A'maal, 294, 309n74
Federal Constitution, 126
  Article 11 of, 180n1
  Article 11(1) of, 123
  Article 121(1A) of, 113, 129n4
federal law, 181n10
Federal Reserve Units (FRU), 142–43, 148
feminism, 314
Feminist scholars, 248, 254, 256
fiqh, 250–52
"First Reaction to the President's Concept", 206
fitrah, 197
force of law, 153

Forum Ulama Umat Indonesia (FUUI), 241n20
Forum Umat Islam (FUI), 225–26
Forum Umat Ulama Islam (FUUI), 225
FPI. *See* Front Pembela Islam (FPI); Islamic Defenders Front (FPI)
Franssen, Pieter, 20
freedom of speech, 258
Front of the Defenders of Islam, 225
Front Pembela Islam (FPI), 35, 45n13, 225, 229
FRU. *See* Federal Reserve Units (FRU)
FUI. *See* Forum Umat Islam (FUI)
fundamentalist Muslims and modernist Muslims, 343
FUUI. *See* Forum Umat Ulama Islam (FUUI)

G

gangsterism, 142
Garcia Villa, Jose, 313
Gasche, Rodolphe, 147
gender, 262–64
  equality and Islamic feminism, 254
  global discourses of, 251
  in Indonesian public debates, 254–55
  media discourses on, 254
  and religion, 253
  religious and secular discourses of, 248–49
  separation of, 252
  structure of society, 248
gender ideologies, 248, 262, 264
  nationalism and statemaking, 254
  symbolic boundaries of community, 254
Gerakan Mujahidin Islam Patani (GMIP), 280

Ghulam Ahmad, Mirza, 219, 222, 227, 235
Global Ikhwan, 83, 93n62
globalization, 67, 265n4
"glum Darussalam", 285
GMIP. *See* Gerakan Mujahidin Islam Patani (GMIP)
Goh Chok Tong, 337, 341, 369n6, 370n7, 370n8, 370n13
Gonda, Jan, 28
Guided Democracy, 198, 205–7
"Guide for Tableegh Journey and Six Points", 294

H
Hadith, 219
hajj
 accounts of, 47, 50
 housewives on, 57
 journey, 7
 occupation, 56–57
 pilgrims, 48, 52–59
 sacred sites, 51–55
 and the self, 55–60
Hajji Ishok, 307n51
hajj memoirs, 47–48
 from pre-independence period, 48–51
Hang Tuah, 61
"haram zone", 52
Harmonization of Civil Laws and Syariah in 2007, 117, 129n5
harmonization of civil legal and syariah systems, 110, 116–18
Hassan, Ahmad, 193
 beliefs of, 213n11
Hasyim, Wahid, 27, 36
Hatta, Mohammad, 202, 203
headscarves. *See tudung*
Hejaz
 archipelago pilgrims, 50

holy sites of, 61
 Southeast Asian pilgrims in, 48
"heroines of Islam", 58
Herzog, Chaim, 341
Hijaz, Wahhabi conquests of, 70
"Hikajat Prang Sabi", 277
Hikayat Hang Tua, 49
Hikayat Patani, 304n20
Hikmat Allah Abadan, 304n12
Hindraf. *See* Hindu Rights Action Force (Hindraf)
Hinduism, 38
 in India, 28
 Tamil, 151, 154
Hindu lunisolar era, 20
Hindu Rights Action Force (HINDRAF), 8, 10, 135, 138–40, 151–52, 154n7
 Ramaji, spiritual advisor to, 143–47
 Regu, leader and co-founder of, 140–43
Hindus, marginalization of, 128n2
Hizbut Tahrir Indonesia, 34–35
Hizbut Tahrir Indonesia (HTI), 226
Holy War, 18, 24, 219
homogenization of Islam, 118–19
 and ring-fencing, 105
HTI. *See* Hizbut Tahrir Indonesia (HTI)
Hujjatul Islam, 89n15
Human Rights
 breach of regulations on, 225
 declaration, 226
human societies, religion functioning in, 39

I
Ibrahim, Khalid, 136
Ida Leman, 58
Identity, Malay. *See* Malay identity
ideologization of *kebangsaan*, 195

ihram, 53
ijazah, 69
ijtihad, 76, 343
ijtimas in Thailand, 295
Ilyas, Mawlana Muhammad, 296
imam, 71
IMM13 document, 175, 183n32
Imtiyaz Yusuf, 303n8, 304n18
India
   Ahmadiyah populations in, 220
   Hinduism in, 28
   Tablighi Jama'at (TJ) in, 297–98
Indian Ocean, 49–50
"Indian origin" theory, 87n5
Indians, marginalization of, 142
Indo-European kingship, 28
Indonesia
   Ahmadiyah's history in, 220–21, 224
   claim of religious freedom, 235–38
   communities in, 84
   constitution and laws, 236
   constitution of, 236
   contemporary, 19, 34–38, 44n10
   debates on public sphere, 253
   freedom of speech, 258
   future of, 254
   gender and religion, 253
   histories of, 19–26
   Islamic groups, 5–6
   Islamic organization in, 81
   Islam in, 5, 7–8, 191–92, 252
   Islamist parties in, 233
   Islamization in, 249
   marriage age in, 254, 263
   media, 253, 263
   moral debates in, 253–55
   mosques in, 356
   Muslim modernism, 252
   Muslims in, 195, 343
   nationalism, 201
   nationalist and Islamic movements in, 199
   political and religious elites in, 26–34
   political decentralization, 249
   political party in, 44n4
   politics, 7–8, 10
   pornography debate in. *See* pornography debate in Indonesia
   process of redefinition, 254
   religion and politics in, 249–50
   religions in, 266n10
   religious freedom in, 228–29
   social and economic change in, 254
   social and political change in, 263
   stability and economic growth, 249
   traditional culture and fine arts, 257
   violence in, 249
   women's rights proponents in, 258
Indonesian children, 260
Indonesian Constitution, 225, 237, 239
Indonesian Council of Ulamas, 256
Indonesian Independence Preparatory Committee, 202
Indonesian Islamic Propagation Council, 221–22
Indonesian Mujahidin Council, 226
Indonesian Muslim women activists, 248
Indonesian National Party, 26, 192–93
Indonesian Survey Institute, 232
Indonesian Ulama Council, 36, 221
Institute for the Study and Teaching of Islam, 221
Internal Security Act (ISA), 69, 127, 140
International Crisis Group, 225, 280, 304n12

International Islamic University, 112, 129n5
Inter-Racial Confidence circles (IRCC), 357
interregional mobility, 67
Iranian Muslim feminists, 254
Iranian revolution, 32
Iraq terrorist network, 342
IRCC. *See* Inter-Racial Confidence circles (IRCC)
ISA. *See* Internal Security Act (ISA)
Islam, 3, 212n3, 336
  bureaucracy and legal institutions in, 8
  bureaucratization of, 105
  and Christianity, 343
  in civil society, 259–60
  concept of Islamic statehood, 107
  culturalist approach in, 337, 339, 340
  custodians of, 124
  and democracy, 197–98, 211
  global resurgence of, 340, 346
  homogenization of, 105, 118–19
  ideologies of, 5, 262
  Indonesia, 5
  institutionalization of, 160
  legal-bureaucratic, Malaysia. *See* legal-bureaucratic Islam in Malaysia
  legal system in, 162
  Malaysia, 5
  moderate, promotion of, 358–60
  and nationalism, 195, 200–201
  and Natsir, 196, 198–201
  in Netherlands East Indies, 192
  pillars of, 219
  political commitment to, 163
  political dimension of, 6
  public role of, 160–61, 166, 173, 177, 179–80
  purification of, 266n9
  and racism, 195
  radical political, 344
  religious belief, 348
  religious pluralism and tolerance in, 10
  role in politics, 12
  Salafi-Wahhabi movement, 291
  Saudi Arabia and, 287
  and social movement activism, 253
  in Southeast Asia, 6
  Sufi variety of, 126
  and Sukarno, 193–94, 199, 211
  Syariah Court, 124
  Tablighi Jama'at (TJ), 296, 299
  teachings of, 348, 360
  theological interpretation of, 343
  traditional heterodox form of, 287
  UMNO, 104
  and United States, 341
"Islam Hadhari", 163, 165, 180n7
Islamic Advancement Department of Malaysia, 73
Islamic affirmation, 123
Islamic and Martial Arts Association of Singapore, 76
Islamic Banking Act of 1983, 117–18
Islamic bureaucracy, 128
Islamic Centre, 111
Islamic civilization, 165
Islamic civil society, 109
Islamic community, 27, 135
Islamic conversion, 169
Islamic Council(s), 307n56
  of Pattani, 282
  of Songkhla province, 289
Islamic criminal code, 114
Islamic Deep South of Thailand, 11
Islamic Defenders Front (FPI), 256
Islamic democracy, 206–7
Islamic Development Bank (IDB), 90n21
Islamic dress in schools, 353

Islamic economy, 117
Islamic education, 74, 88n13, 289
Islamic eschatology, 90n26
Islamic family laws, 114–15
Islamic favouritism, 229–33
Islamic feminism, gender equality and, 254
Islamic hardliners, 141
Islamic headscarf. *See tudung*
Islamic institutions, 106
  centralization of, 108, 111
  federal-level, 110–12
  proliferation and multiplication of, 110, 112–13
Islamic jihadist groups, 249
Islamic jurisprudence, 250, 252
Islamic kingship, 18
Islamic law, 8, 124, 126, 251, 254–56, 258, 261, 272
  Administration of Muslim Law Enactment 1952, 114
  syariah institutions, 112
Islamic leadership, 173
Islamic legal-bureaucracy, 105, 110
  civil legal system with Syariah system, 116–18
  federal-level Islamic institutions, 110–12
  homogenizing Islam, 118–19
  laws under Syariah statutes, 113–16
  proliferation and multiplication of Islamic institutions, 112–13
  ring-fencing the Muslim subject, 119–26
Islamic missionary movement, 293–94
Islamic moderation, 104
  UMNO, 104
Islamic modernism, 134
Islamic modern, Michael Peletz's concept of, 104
Islamic morality, 9–10

Islamic norms of modesty, 248
Islamic orthodoxy, 10, 119
Islamic principles, 163
Islamic rebellion, 25
Islamic reformers, 135
Islamic Religious Council of Singapore, 73
Islamic religious laws, 105
Islamic revivalism, 179, 182n22
Islamic sects, 9, 119, 120–22
  marginalization of, 12
Islamic *shari'ah* laws, 249, 258–59
Islamic society, 248–49, 253, 265n2
Islamic state, 209
Islamic teachings, 119, 120–22
Islamic women's groups, 10
Islamic youth movement, 103
Islamist civil society groups, 218
Islamist groups, 226
Islamist Jama'at Islami, 297
Islamist parties, Indonesia, 233
Islamist political parties, 34
Islamist politicians, 26
Islamists' zakat agenda, 38
Islamization, 66–67, 110, 117, 125, 138, 176, 179
  of bureaucracy, 112
  and citizenship, 160–65
  conditions of, 166–68
  in Indonesia, 249
  of laws, 112
  legislative phase of, 125
  local leadership of, 168–72
  in Malaysia, 126, 139
  politics of, 159
  process of, 159
  of society, 292
  syariah Islamists, 109
  syariah legal system, 110
  UMNO's legitimacy, 104
"Islam's attitude toward Freethinking", 194

J

Jabatan Kemajuan Islam Malaysia (JAKIM), 111, 119, 129n7
Jabatan Pembangunan Persekutuan Sabah (JPPS), 171, 183n26
Jakarta Charter, 26, 44n4
   seven words of, 202, 207
JAKIM. *See* Jabatan Kemajuan Islam Malaysia (JAKIM)
Jama'ah Ahmadiyah Indonesia, 220
Jama'at Islami, 309n77
Jamilm, Arifah, 328
Japakiya, Ismail Lutfi, 288–89
   Amir al-Haj, 291
   contemporary puritan movement, 288, 301
   Jemaah Islamiyah (JI), 292
   Kaum Muda reformists, 303
   puritan reformism in Thailand, 289
Japanese Occupation, 202
   in Malaya, 166, 176
Java
   cultural identity in, 22, 25
   monarchs, 18
Javanese calendrical system, change in, 20
Javanese historical traditions, 22
Javanese kingship, 18, 21
Javanism, 201
Jawatankuasa Kemajuan dan Keselamatan Kampung (JKKK), 171
Jawi community, 69
Jeddah, 48, 51
   airport in, 52, 59
   communication in, 52
Jemaah Islah Malaysia (JIM), 108
Jemaah Islamiyah (JI), 241n27, 281, 292, 335, 341
   dangers of ideology, 361
   parliamentary debate on arrests, 346
   terrorists, 35
jihad, 304n14
   denunciation of, 219
   against Dutch, 277
   in South Thailand, 275, 281
JIM. *See* Jemaah Islah Malaysia (JIM)
JKKK. *See* Jawatankuasa Kemajuan dan Keselamatan Kampung (JKKK)
Joaquim, Nick, 324
Joint Madrasah Scheme, 368
Joint Resolution, 232
"joint statements", 233
JPPS. *See* Jabatan Pembangunan Persekutuan Sabah (JPPS)
Jubaira, Ibrahim, 323–24, 331n2
judicial partiality in Malaysia, 135–36
Justice Prosperity Party, 248, 251

K

kadi (Islamic judges), 112–13
kafirs, 22
Kahn, Joel, 134
Kalla, Jusuf, 231
Kampung Dusun Nyior, 304n20
Kampung Medan attacks of 2001, 138
kaoem Muslimin, 212n8
karamah, 71
kebangsaan. *See* nationalism
Kelantan, 114
   syariah laws in, 115
Kemal, Mustafa, 196–98
kenduri, 288, 307n53
kerajaan, 50
khalifah, 69, 73, 77
Khamanei, Ali, 32
khanqahs, 69
Khomeini, Ayatollah, 32, 39
khuruj, 294–95, 301

Tablighis, 297
Thai army soldiers, 297
Kingdom of Patani, 271–72, 277
King Mongkut, 30
King Rama I, 30
Kitab Usulbiyah, 21, 23
konsepsi, 206, 210
Korean War, 25
Krue Se incident
   sociological perspective on, 277–78
   violent events, 275
Ksatriyas, 28–29, 38
KTHCF. *See* Kudat Thean Hou Charitable Foundation (KTHCF)
Kudat Thean Hou Charitable Foundation (KTHCF), 184n41
kwaampenthai, 303n5
kyai, 21–22, 35

L

labour migration, 160, 163
Lahore Ahmadiyah Movement, 219
Laskar Komando Islam, 229
Lee Kuan Yew, 340, 343, 345, 352, 355, 369n5
legal-bureaucratic Islam in Malaysia
   expansion, elevation and empowerment of, 110–18
   homogenization, 105, 118–19
   political islam and state-society relations, 105–10
   ring-fencing Muslim subject, 119–26
legal recognition for Ahmadiyah, 218
Legge, John, 210
Lembaga Dakwah Islam Indonesia, 35
Lembaga Penelitian dan Pengkajian Islam (LPPI), 221–22, 225
Lewis, Bernard, 370n10
Liberation Tigers of Tamil Eelam, 144

lifestyle, Islamic identity and, 347
Lord's Resistance Army in northern Uganda, 276–77
Lubis, Sobri, 269
Lutfi Japakiya, Ismail, 301, 308n60, 308n64, 308n65
Lutfi's movement, 289

M

Madale, Abdullah T., 316
madhahib, 307n54
madrasa
   and 9/11, 366
   and compulsory education, 367
   development of, 366–68
   part-time, 364
Madrasah Al-Ma'arif, 75–76, 90n22
Mahathir, Mohamad, 162, 163, 170
Mahdi, 219
Mahendra, Yusril Ihza, 232
Mahfudh, Sahal, 235
Majelis Mujaheedin Indonesia (MMI), 34, 226, 241n27
Majelis Ulama Indonesia (MUI), 36–37, 221, 226–27, 240n5, 256
   campaign, 225
   executives, 224
   fatwa, 235, 256
Majlis Ugama Islam Sabah (MUIS), 169
Majlis Ugama Islam Singapura (MUIS), 73, 81, 351–52, 357, 360
Majul, Cesar, 316, 326
Malacca, Islam in, 68
Malaya
   Japanese Occupation in, 166, 176
   non-Muslim communities in, 160
   traditional customs in, 160
Malayanization of Sabah civil service, 176
Malay-based opposition party, 348

Malay community, 135, 271, 336, 340, 344
  characterizing, 342
  elite, 358
Malay culture
  aspects of, 135
  de-Indianization of, 139
Malay identity, 133–34, 150, 178
  aspects of, 135
  and culture, Islam's impact on, 336
  intractable hold of, 137
Malay-Islamic nationalism, 151
Malay leadership, 348
Malay loyalty, 340
  debates concerning, 341
Malay Muslim, 340
Malay-Muslim community, 278–79, 281, 286
  electoral politics participation, Thailand, 284–85
  madrasa education, 373n31
Malay-Muslim constituency, 104
Malay-Muslim culture, 290
Malay-Muslim politicians in South Thailand, 281, 286
Malay-Muslim separatists, 281
Malay Muslims in South Thailand
  abolition of *shari'a* law, 272
  Al-Furqan mosque, 279
  aspirations of, 283
  assimilationist policies, 272
  identity of, 272–73
  political participation and accommodation, 281–92
  population of, 287, 289
  puritan Islamic reformist movement. *See* puritan Islamic reformist movement
  in Siam, 272
  struggle for independence, 274–75
  Tablighi Jama'at, 293–99
  Thai-Buddhist dominance, 281
TRT, 283
violent confrontations, 274–81
Malay protesters, 136
Malay schism, 107
Malaysia
  Aurad Muhammadiah congregation in, 77–84
  citizens in, 163
  common penal code in, 114
  constitutional monarchs of, 111
  Darul Arqam controversy in, 76
  democracy, 108
  demolition of temple in, 142
  2008 election campaign, 127
  ethnic consciousness in, 135
  ethnic group in, 161
  fatwa councils of, 120–22
  Hindu tamils in, 8
  Hindu temples in, 135, 137
  Islam, 5
  Islamic bands in, 86
  Islamic bureaucracy, 128
  Islamic groups, 5–6, 108
  as Islamic state, 163
  Islamization, 126, 139, 159
  judicial partiality in, 135–36
  lawmaking institutions in, 111
  legal-bureaucratic Islam in. *See* legal-bureaucratic Islam in Malaysia
  Muslims in, 182n22, 343
  non-Muslims in, 135, 160
  political equality in, 180
  political struggles, 106
  politics development in, 134
  politics in, 160
  public caning in, 115
  racialism in, 150
  racialized thinking and identification in, 153
  religio-cultural identity, 109
  religious conversion in, 125

religious group in, 161
revenues of, 168
secular state in, 161–62, 178
self-rationalization in, 134
socio-economic reality in, 153
state governments in, 85
syariah system in, 116
Tamils in. *See* Tamils in Malaysia
transformation of land usage in, 133
urban development in, 134
Malaysian common law, 117
Malaysian Constitution, 160, 165
Malaysian developmentalism, goal of, 133–34
Malaysian Federation, 164, 166–67, 173, 179
Malaysian Indian Congress (MIC), 138, 148–49
Malaysian National Fatwa Council, 129
Malaysian society
Muslim citizens in, 162
non-Muslim citizens in, 162
Malaysian *syariah* laws, 115
Malay supernaturalism, 287
Malay Tamil, demographics of, 134
Malay University Leader, 147–52
Mannheim, Karl, 363
Marcos, Ferdinand, 326
marginalization
Hinduism, 148
of Indians, 142
political Islam, 106
ma'rifah, 87n3
"Mari Pertahankan Indonesia Kita", 242n34
marriage of convenience, 301
martial law, 286, 321
in Thailand, 272
Marxist theory, 309n81
Masroor Ahmad, Mirza, 219
Masyumi party, 25, 27, 35, 220, 240n8

Mathuphum, 300, 306n42
Maududi, Abul A'la, 25, 67
Maulid, 89n19
Maulid an-Nabi, 288
Mawdudi, Abul A'la, 25
"May 1969 racial riots", 107
Mecca, 7, 48, 52
ban for visiting, 219
Hang Tuah pilgrimage to, 49
Jawi community in, 88n10
pilgrims, 53, 69
religious studies in, 71
Media Dakwah journal, 222
media in Indonesia, 253–54
Medina, 7, 48, 54
Prophet's mosque in, 89n19
MENDAKI, 372n23
mengacak-acak, 237
"men of prayer", 17–18, 25
Mernissi, Fatima, 251
MIC. *See* Malaysian Indian Congress (MIC)
Michael Peletz's concept of "Islamic modern", 104
militant groups, 301
militant violence, 299–300
Mina, 48
stone pillars in, 54
Mindanao, violence in, 328
Minister-in Charge of Muslim Affairs, 357–58
Ministry of Home Affairs, 232
Ministry of Religion, 227, 232
Ministry of Religious Affairs, 36
minority *fikh*, 362, 366
minority Muslims, 363
moderate Islam, promotion of, 358–60
moderates *vs.* extremists, 344–46
modernism, Islamic, 134
modernist Muslims and fundamentalist Muslims, 343

modernity, 51
modernization, benefits of, 85
modesty
 concept of, 263
 Islamic ethic of, 263
Mohamad, Mahathir, 133–34
Mojares, Resil, 321
monarchs of Java, 18
morality in Indonesia, 253–55, 260, 262–64
 pornography debate in Indonesia. *See* pornography debate in Indonesia
 public regulation of, 262
 state regulation of, 264
morality laws, 258–59
Mosque Building Fund, 355, 368
mosques
 Ahmadiyah, 232
 impact of, 355–56
 and interfaith dialogue, 363–64
Mubarok Ahmad, Mirza, 240n4
mufti, 105, 112
Muhammadan Marriage Ordinance 1946, 114
Muhammadiyah, 34, 196, 201, 220, 235, 238, 240n3, 250, 252
Muhammadiyah National Congress, 220
MUI. *See* Majelis Ulama Indonesia (MUI)
MUIS. *See* Majlis Ugama Islam Singapura (MUIS)
mujaddid, 83
multiracial principles, 169
musharakah, 117
Muslim Ahmadiyah Community, 220
Muslim citizen, civil rights of, 105
Muslim civil society, 357
Muslim community, 11, 224, 238, 336, 344
 characterizing, 342

cultural identifier of, 338
impact on, 358–64
impact on remedies, 344–46
leaders, 340
tudung issue in, 347–55
Muslim conversion, 123
Muslim Court (Criminal Jurisdiction) Act 1965, 113
Muslim Courts (Criminal Jurisdiction) Act 1984, 113
Muslim elite, members of, 358
Muslim Filipinos, 314, 316–17, 329–30, 331n2
 English-language educated, 314–15
 to publish magazine in Philippines, 321
Muslim girls, issue of headscarves, 347
Muslim identity, self-conscious, development of, 316
Muslim immigrants, 9
Muslim Lawyer's Association, 108
Muslim leaders, 168–69
Muslim lives, conflict and violence in, 326–29
Muslim minorities, 10–11
 Singapore, 11–12
Muslim modernism, 252
Muslim movement, 201
Muslim nation, 209
Muslim organizations, 196, 218–19
 Indonesia's, 220, 222
 with pluralist credentials, 239
 ulama from, 221
Muslim population in Southeast Asia, 5
Muslim Professional Forum, 108
Muslim Religious Council of Singapore (MUIS), 351, 363
 Singapore Muslim identity project, 364–66
Muslims, 9

mainstream, 219, 229
pro-pluralist, 237
proportion of, 177
religious practices of, 120–22
social behaviour of, 12
Syariah Court, 109
Muslim separatists and the
    Philippines Government, 319
Muslims in the Philippines, 11
    American colonialism, 316–17, 320
    brutal military campaign, 317
    conflict and violence in Muslim
        stories/lives, 326–29
    emergent national cultural form,
        321–26
    languages of, 314–15
    political integration of, 317
    schooling, language and
        negotiations of culture, 316–21
    short story writers, formation of,
        316–21
Muslims in Singapore, 336
    culturalist approach in, 337, 339
    leadership, 348
    and non-Muslims, 338
    religious belief of, 340–41
    restrictions, 346
    terrorist ideology, 345
Muslims' religiosity, 346–47
    impact of mosques, 355–56
    tudung issue, 347–55
Muslims' sympathy, 341
Muslim stories, conflict and violence
    in, 326–29
Muslim traders, 68
Muslim women activists, 247–64
    and pornography debate in
        Indonesia. *See* pornography
        debate in Indonesia
Muslim writers, 314, 321–22
Muslim Youth Movement, 352
Mustafa, Noralyn, 319, 322–23

Muzadi, Hasyim, 234
    anti-pornography movement, 256
mysticism, 301

N
Nahdlatul Ulama (NU), 10, 81, 238,
    250, 265n7
    anti-pornography movement, 256
    central leadership of, 234–35
    East Java branch of, 235
    fifth National Congress in
        Pekalongan, 220
    gender equality, 252
    general liberalization of, 251
    kyai of, 34, 36
    religious elite of, 27
    Wahhabism, 259
NAP. *See* New Aspiration Party
    (NAP)
nasionalisme, 195
National Day Rally Speech, 343, 346
National Economic Policy (NEP), 79
National Fatwa Council (NFC), 73
nationalism
    Islam and, 195, 200–201
    Malay-Islamic, 151
    Natsir and, 193, 195
    and religion, 200
    of Sukarno, 193
Nationalist Party, 26
National Land Code 1965, 118
National Reconciliation Commission,
    278
National Registration Identity Card
    (NRIC), 125
national schools, *tudung* issue in, 353
Natsir, 9, 10, 25, 35. *See also* Sukarno
    arguments with Kemal, 198
    beliefs of, 213n11
    and characteristics of Western
        democracy, 199
    and democracy, 206, 211

ideologization of *kebangsaan*, 195
imprisonment, 210
and Islam, 196, 198–201, 211
kaoem Muslimin, 212n8
oemmat, 212n8
opposing Western democracy, 199
and Pancasila, 207–8
recognizing and criticizing Sukarno, 199
speech to Constituent Assembly, 207–8
and Sukarno, 192, 197–99, 203–5, 209–11
Western classical education, 199–200
NEP. *See* New Economic Policy (NEP)
New Aspiration Party (NAP), 282
New Economic Policy (NEP), 107, 164
Ninth Buddhist Council, 30
non-Malays, 134
non-Muslim leaders, 183n24
non-Muslims, 35, 37
in enhancing social cohesion, 357
in Malaysia, 135
Muslims and, 338
non-Muslim vote bank, 127
non-state Islamism, 86n1
Nor Matta, Wan Muhammad, 283
"no-*tudung*" policy, 350
in schools, 354
NRIC. *See* National Registration Identity Card (NRIC)
NU. *See* Nahdlatul Ulama (NU)
Nusantara, 67

O
Obama, Barack, 43
"Obituary for Today" story (Mustafa), 322
objet petit a, 137
oemmat, 212n8

OIC. *See* Organization of the Islamic Conference (OIC)
Orang Asli, 154n3
Orang Asli communities, 137
Organisations in Defence of Islam, 128n3
Organization of the Islamic Conference (OIC), 223–24, 240n12
orientalism, salient traits of, 339
ormas, 232
orthodoxy, 42
orthopraxy, 42
Ottoman Turkey, 49

P
Padang Jawa
demolition of temple in, 142, 145
temple, reconstitution of, 152
Pakistan, Ahmadiyah populations in, 220
Paknam crisis, 309n82
Pakubuwana II, 18, 22–24, 38
Pakubuwana, Ratu, 18, 22–23
Pancasila, 201–2, 207–8, 235–36, 238
Pandji Islam (Natsir), 194, 196–97
Panitia Persiapan Kemerdekaan Indonesia (PPKI). *See* Indonesian Independence Preparatory Committee
Pan-Malaysian Islamic Party. *See* Parti Islam SeMalaysia (PAS)
pan-Muslim identity, 316
Partai Bulan Bintang (PBB), 233
Partai Demokrat, 34
Partai Keadilan (PK), 226
Partai Keadilan Sejahtera (PKS), 34–35, 226, 233, 248, 265n5
aliran, 253
democratic rights of provinces, 261
electoral democracy, 252

Index

moral behaviour, 261
national votes in elections, 251
politics, 261
pornography, 255–56
religion, 253, 261
women's support for pornography, 259–60
Partai Kebangkitan Bangsa (PKB), 36
Partai Kebangkitan Nasional Ulama, 36
Partai Nasional Indonesia (PNI). *See* Indonesian National Party
Partai Persatuan Pembangunan (PPP), 34
Partai Persaturan Pembangunan (PPP), 233–34
Partai Sarekat Islam Indonesia, 201
Parti Bersatu Sabah (PBS), 170
Parti Bulan Bintang (PBB), 34
Parti Islam SeMalaysia (PAS), 103, 130n
   Islamic bureaucracy, 128
   Islamization of Malaysia, 127–28
   Malay nationalism, 106
Parti Islam SeMalaysia's (PAS), 352
Parti Keadilan Rakyat (PKR), 136
PAS. *See* Parti Islam SeMalaysia (PAS)
Pasundan movement, 201
Patani Darussalam, 309n70
Patani Kingdom, 271–72
Patani United Liberation Organization (PULO), 280
PBB. *See* Parti Bulan Bintang (PBB)
PBS. *See* Parti Bersatu Sabah (PBS)
Pembela Islam (Natsir), 195
Penang Syariah Appeals Court, 125
Pencak Sunda, 73, 76–77
Pencegahan Penyalahgunaan atau Penodaan Agama, 221
People's Consultative Assembly (MPR), 35

peranakan, 139
PERGAS, 348, 351
PERIPENSIS. *See* Persatuan Islam dan Pencak Silat Singapura (PERIPENSIS)
Permi party, 200
Persatuan Islam, 192, 195
Persatuan Islam dan Pencak Silat Singapura (PERIPENSIS), 76, 81, 84
Persatuan Islam organization, 25
Persatuan Umat Islam (PUI), 235
pesantrens, 69
Phak Palang Prachachon (PPP), 285
Phibun regime, 303n5
Phibunsongkhram, Plaek, 272
Philippines
   American colonialism in, 316–17, 320
   English-language magazines established in, 321
   Muslims in. *See* Muslims in the Philippines
   vernacular narrative traditions in, 313
Philippines Free Press, 321, 323–24
pilgrimage
   to Medina, 54
   memoirs of, 50
   notion of place *(topos)* in, 48
   occupation of, 56
   Southeast Asian memoirs of, 55
pilgrims, hajj, 48, 52–59
Pitsuwan, Surin, 305n32
PKB. *See* Partai Kebangkitan Bangsa (PKB)
PKR. *See* Parti Keadilan Rakyat (PKR)
PKS. *See* Partai Keadilan Sejahtera (PKS)
plain of Arafat, 48, 53
Playboy magazine, 256

pluralism, 251
political authority, 39
  in precolonial Java, 24
  primacy of, 31
political elite, 18, 26, 38, 40
  comparative primacy of, 41
  conflict or challenge, 42
  problem with religious agendas, 43
"political game", 80
political integration of Muslims, 317
political Islam, 105–6
  centralization, 108–9
  contestation, 106–8
  expansion, 109–10
  impact of, 357
  marginalization, 106
  radical, 344
politics
  of Indonesia, 263
  religion and, 6
  role of Islam in, 9
pondok, 69, 71, 88n13, 307n55
pornography debate in Indonesia, 247
  context and research methods, 249–53
  moral debates, gender and nation, 253–55
  religion, gender and morality, 262–64
  rights and freedoms, 248
  women activists and moral debates, 255–62
PPP. *See* Partai Persatuan Pembangunan (PPP); Phak Palang Prachachon (PPP)
Prachatham, 307n48
pre-Obama Democratic Party, 282
Presidential Advisory Council, 225
Presidential Resolution, 232
Prevention of Misuse or Desecration of Religion, Law No. 1/PNPS/1965 on, 221, 237

print capitalism, 56, 61
Prophet Muhammad, 194
  and Allah, 224, 227
  biography of, 74
Prosperous Justice Party, 10, 248, 251
Protestants, 39
psychological defences against terrorism, 357
public caning, 115
PULO. *See* Patani United Liberation Organization (PULO)
puritan Islamic reformist movement
  cooperation with Thai Government, 291–92
  educational and religious structures, 289
  kenduri, 288
  Maulid an-Nabi, 288
  Salafi characteristics, 289
  Thai preference for, 292–93
  traditional heterodox form of Islam, 287
puritan reformist movement, 297, 301
puritan reformists, 302
pusaka, 20
Putrajaya, developments of, 133–34

Q
Qadiyaniah, 218, 223
Qardhawi, Sheikh Yusof, 366
Qur'an, 222, 237, 252, 261, 265n3, 288
  Ahmadiyah teachings based on, 219

R
racialism in Malaysia, 150
racism, Islam and, 195
radicalism, 364, 366
  problem of, 343–44, 359
radical political Islam, 344
Ramadan, 305n21

Ramaji, spiritual advisor to Hindraf, 143–47
Rancangan Undang-Undang (RUU) Pornografi, 247
 liberalized version of, 257
Rasadorn (People) party, 286
Rashtriya Swamysevak Sangh (RSS), 145
rationalist Muslims and extremist Muslims, 343
Razak, Najib, 141, 163
rebellion, 20
 Islamic, 25
Red Shirts, 310n83
Regent of Bandung, 51
regional autonomy of Indonesia, 249
Regu, leader and co-founder to Hindraf, 140–43
Relative Deprivation Theory, 280, 305n25
religion, 3, 39, 262–64
 arguments in favour of, 208
 concept of, 4
 and democracy, 206
 dispute in, 42
 functions in human societies, 39
 gender and, 253
 nationalism and, 200
 and politics, 6, 192
 pornography debate in Indonesia. *See* pornography debate in Indonesia
 relationship between state and, 196
 role of, 192, 197
 and secularism, 4
religion conversion in Malaysia, 125
religious activists, 19
religious authority, 19, 24
religious classes, part-time, 364
religious diversity, 254
religious education, 71
religious elite, 18, 25

 authority of, 41
 claims, 43
 definitions, 26
 disputation among contending, 42
 general pattern of, 38–39
 in Indonesia, 26–34, 38
 Muslim community impact, 360–63
 Shi'ite, 33
religious freedom
 for Ahmadiyah, 218
 claim of, 235–38
 in Indonesia, 218, 230
religious hegemony, 254
religious orthodoxy, 33
religious pluralism, 9
 in Indonesia, 10
Religious Rehabilitation Group (RRG), 361–62
religious schools, 88n13, 366–368
religious teachers, accreditation of, 360–61
reverse patrimony, 151
Reynolds, Craig, 30
Rida, Rashid, 200
Ridwan, Kholil, 226
ring-fencing
 homogenization and, 105
 Muslim subject, 119, 122–26
Risalah, 365, 366
Risalah for Building a Singapore Muslim Community of Excellence (2006), 365
Rizieq Shabib, Habib, 229
Roman Catholic Church, 45n15
Round Table Conference 1949, 204
RRG. *See* Religious Rehabilitation Group (RRG)
RSS. *See* Rashtriya Swamysevak Sangh
Rufaqa' Corporation, 77, 81
ruling elite, 28, 300

S

Sabah
  authorities in, 166
  Chief Ministers of, 164, 168
  Chinese immigrants to, 169
  conditions of Islamization in, 166–68
  education in, 166
  ethnic and religious constitution of, 9
  ethnic composition in, 173–74
  ethnicity by, 172
  ethnic state of, 180
  High Courts in, 162
  illegal immigrants in, 173–76
  indigenous people in, 165
  Islamic leadership in, 170
  Islamization in, 159, 166–68
  Malaysian administrations in, 177
  non-Muslim communities in, 168
  policies in, 169
  politics in, 159, 171
  population in, 173
  remote villages in, 169
  two-year rotation system of, 171–73
Sabah politics, federalization of, 172–78
Sabah Progressive Party (SAPP), 176
Salafi, 308n60
Salafism, 87n4
Salafi-Wahhabi movement, 291
sangha
  reformation of, 29
  religious objectives of, 31
Sarawak
  High Courts in, 162
  indigenous people in, 165
  non-Muslim communities in, 168
Sarekat Islam, 196
Saudi Arabia, 287
  ban of Ahmadiyah in, 220
Saudi purification movement, 259

Sayyid, Ayatollah, 32
Second Malaysian Plan (1971), 91n30
secular bureaucracy, role of, 125
secularism, 158–59, 180, 208
  religion and, 4
secular law, 265n3
secular state, 158, 163
  principle of neutrality in, 161
Selangor
  Administration of Muslim Law Enactment 1952, 114
  syariah laws in, 115
self-rationalization in Malaysia, 134
self-validation Appiah, 314
11 September (9/11), 335–36, 346, 356–57
  culturalist approach, 337–44
Serat Yusuf, 21, 23
sesat, 220
shahadah, 227
Shah Alam
  developments of, 133
  Hindu temples in, 137, 142
  land use patterns in, 135
Selangor State Government Secretariat in, 136
Shah Sibghat Allah, 31, 39
Shariah Court in Singapore, 76, 89n16
shari'ah law, 19, 26, 249, 265n3
Sheykh ul-Islam, 291
Shi'ite group, 31, 33
Shi'ite Sacred Law, 33
Shinawatra, Thaksin, 280, 283, 300
  People's Power Party, 285
  Tak Bai massacre, 279, 284
short story writers, formation of, 316–21
Siamese democracy, 284
Siamization, 282–83
Singapore
  Arab Muslims in, 88n11
  attack by Muslim aggressor, 340

Aurad Muhammadiah
  congregation in, 74–77
British colonial rule in, 369n1
Chinese population from, 167
ethnic relations, 335
federal-state relations in, 168
Islamic education in, 75
Muslim minorities, 11–12
political harassment in, 74
Rufaqa' Corporation in, 77, 81
Shariah Court in, 76, 89n16
tudung, 370n15, 370n17, 370n18, 370n19, 370n20
Singaporean Muslims
  conflicts for, 341
  minority community, 364
  religiosity of, 346–56
  sentiments of, 342
Singapore Government, 352
Singapore Malay National Organisation, 348
Singapore Muslim identity project, 364–66
Singapore Religious Teachers' Association, 348, 351
SKB. *See* Surat Keputusan Bersama (SKB)
SKP. *See* Surat Keputusan Presiden (SKP)
slametan, 307n53
social cohesion, 356–58
social contract, 163, 178
social defences against terrorism, 357
Socialist Party, 25–26
social order, 86n1
socio-economic reality in Malaysia, 153
Soeharto, 191–92, 247, 249, 251
  pornography debate, 250
Soon Singh A/L Bikar Singh V Pertubuhan Kebajikan Islam Malaysia (PERKIM) Kedah & Anor (1999), 123

South Asia
  Brahmin in, 29
  Buddhism in, 29
Southeast Asia
  Brahmin in, 29
  diffusion of Aurad Muhammadiah in, 70–74
  Islam in, 6, 66–68
  Muslim population, 5
  profile of, 66
  prominence of Islam, 5
  religion and politics, 4, 12
  Sufi orders in, 68
  transnational Sufism in, 67–70
Southeast Asian
  hajj, 48–49, 60
  Muslims, 50, 56
  pilgrims, 48
Southeast Asian Islam, 67–70
south of Thailand
  assimilation policies, 272
  constitutional set-up of, 280
  cultural assimilation, 272
  foreign jihadi groups, 281
  Malay Muslims. *See* Malay Muslims in South Thailand
  martial law in, 272
  1988 parliamentary elections, 282
  political participation and accommodation, 281–82
  separatist groups, 272
  suicidal mission, 277
  TJ. *See* Tablighi Jama'at (TJ)
South Sumatra, ban of Ahmadiyah in, 233, 243n54
Special Assistance Plan (SAP) schools, 353–54
"Spirits in the Box" story (Sadain), 326
state authority, 19, 24
state-controlling elites, 17–18, 39, 40
  authority of, 41

state elite
  comparative primacy of, 41
  general pattern of, 38–39
  and religious elite, 27–28
state-society relations, 105–6
  centralization, 108–9
  contestation, 106–8
  expansion, 109–10
  marginalization, 106
statist Islam, 104, 108–9
Sufi movements, 7
Sufi practices, 276
Sufism, 21, 67, 85, 87n3, 90n26, 126
  influence of, 87n4
Suhaimi, Muhammad Fadhlullah, 74–75
Suhaimi, Muhammad Taha, 76–77, 81, 89n16, 90n24
Suhaimi, Sheikh, 70–78, 80, 86, 88n11, 89n19
suicide attacks in Aceh, 277
Sukarno, 9–10
  arrest of, 193
  and characteristics of Western democracy, 199
  and democracy, 211
  Five Principles/Pancasila of, 201–2, 207–8
  Guided Democracy, 198, 205–7
  idealization of Kemal's rule, 197
  and Islam, 193–94, 199, 211
  and Natsir, 192, 197–99, 203–5, 209–11
  opposing Western democracy, 199
  separation of religion, 196
Sukarno's National Party (PNI), 193
Sulong, Haji, 283
Sultan Agung of Mataram, 18–19
sultanate of Patani, 303n3
Sultan Ibrahim II, 31
Sulu Islands, violence in, 328
Suluk Garwa Kencana, 21, 23

Sunan Bayat, 21
Sundanese account, 56
Sunnah, 265n3
Sunnah Wal Jammah, 119, 126
Sunni Islam, 119, 126
Surat Keputusan Bersama (SKB), 232
  government's critics of, 233
  government's decree, 232, 237, 239
Surat Keputusan Presiden (SKP), 232
Susuhunan, 22
Syaikh Daud, 49
Syamsuddin, Din, 235
Syariah and Civil Technical Committee, 112
Syariah Court, 8, 110, 112–13, 166
  "cautious" tolerance, 126
  elevation of, 113
  institution-building process, 113
  Islamic banking and finance, 117
  Islamic religious laws, 105
  jurisdiction of, 123–24
  legal institution for Muslims, 109
  levels, 112–13
  procedures, 114
  public caning, 115
  punishments, 113
  strengthening of, 109
syariah crimes, laws on, 114–16
syariah criminal enactments, 115–16
Syariah Criminal Offence Enactment (Takzir), 124
  Section 25 of, 129n12
syariah judicial process, 111
syariah laws, 105, 112, 119
  in Kelantan, 115
  in Selangor, 115
syariah legal system, 110–11
syariah legislations, 114
Syariah Lower Court, 112–13
syariah system in Malaysia, 116
"system of symbols", 4

Index

T
Tablighi Jama'at (TJ), 11, 279, 293, 301–2
  administration of, 298
  followers from Pakistan and China, 295
  in India, 297–98
  Islam, 296, 299
  khuruj, 294
  Malay Muslims, 296
  organizational structure of, 298
  puritan reformist movement, 299
  in South Thailand, 296
  Thai Government, 296–97
  violence in South Thailand, 296
Tadzkirah, 222, 227
Tahlil, 89n18
Tahrir, Hizbut, 226
Takaful (Islamic Insurance) Act of 1985, 118
Tak Bai massacre, 11, 278–79
  Chulanont, Surayud, 285
  Thaksin's credibility, 284
Tale of Hang Tuah, 49
Tamil community, 8–9
Tamil folklore, 151
Tamil Hinduism, 151, 154
Tamil protesters, 143
Tamils in Malaysia
  Batu Caves temple, 142–43
  demolition of temple in Shah Alam, 142, 145
  economic marginalization of, 135
  Hindraf, 138–40
  "Makkal Sakti" campaign, 142–43, 145
  Ramaji, spiritual advisor to Hindraf, 143–47
  Regu, leader and co-founder to Hindraf, 140–43
tariqahs, 69, 71, 85
teachings of Islam, 348, 360

"Termites" story (Mustafa), 323
terrorism, 339
  and radicalism, 343
  social and psychological defences against, 357
terrorist organizations, 35
terrorist violence in Thailand, 11
Thahir Ahmad, Mirza, 224
Thai Buddhist legal system, 272
Thai Buddhists, 279
  police arrest, 279
Thai-Buddhist state, Malay Muslims and. *See* Malay Muslims in South Thailand
Thailand
  Bali bombings, 292
  electoral politics participation. *See* electoral politics participation, Thailand
  ijtimas in, 295
  Malay-Muslim politicians in, 281
  martial law in, 272
  Muslim students, 292
  1988 parliamentary elections, 282
  puritan Islamic reformist movement. *See* puritan Islamic reformist movement
  puritan reformism in, 289
  south of. *See* south of Thailand
  terrorist violence and separatist ambitions, 11
  Theravada Buddhism in, 30
Thai Muslims, 11
  politico-religious influences on, 273
Thai parliament, 283
Thai police, 278–79
Thai political system, 281
Thai politics
  Democrat Party, 282
  by Malay-Muslim politicians, 281
  1988 parliamentary elections, 282

Thai security forces, 275–76, 279
Thai security services, 292
Thaksin's Thai Rak Thai (TRT), 283, 285–86
 anti-Thaksin coup, 285
Theravada Buddhism in Thailand, 30
Third Javanese War of Succession, 24
Threat of Terrorism, parliamentary debate on, 346
Tiamson, Alfredo T., 325
TJ. *See* Tablighi Jama'at (TJ)
Tohmeena, Den, 283
tok guru, 307n55
"Toleransi Sosial Masyarakat Perkotaan" survey, 243n48
"tomboys", 129n11
Toqueville, Alexis de, 39
traditional culture of Indonesia, 257
Transnational Sufism, overview of, 67–70
tudung, 347, 370n15, 370n17, 370n18, 370n19, 370n20
 ban on, 353
 in school, 349–50, 353
 theological opinions on, 351
Tuhfat al-Nafi, 50
Tukku Paloh, 69
Twenty Points agreement, 170

U

ulama, 19, 21, 25, 35, 69, 76, 277, 296, 307n54
 MUI and, 37
 from Muslim organizations, 221
 politics, 34
 religious elite of NU, 27
umma, 341, 342
ummah, 66
 concept of, 86n2

United Malays National Organisation (UMNO), 79, 103, 136, 142, 144, 165, 171, 173, 175, 179
 institutionalization of Islam by, 126
 Islamic moderation, 104
 lawmaking and policymaking, 104
 legitimacy, 104
 state promotion of Islam by, 110
 statist Islam, 108
United Pasokmomogun Kadazandusun Murut Organization (UPKO), 177
United Sabah Islam Association (USIA), 169
United Sabah National Organization (USNO), 168–69, 173
United states, 11 September (9/11), 335–36, 346, 356–57
Unity Development Party, 233
UPKO. *See* United Pasokmomogun Kadazandusun Murut Organization (UPKO)
USIA. *See* United Sabah Islam Association (USIA)
USNO. *See* United Sabah National Organization (USNO)

V

van Goens, Rijklof, 22
Vejjajiva, Abhisit, 286
Verelendung, 300, 309n81
Vienna Convention on Diplomatic Relations, 304n13
violence
 in Indonesia, 249, 257
 on Islam, 339
 in Muslim stories/lives, 326–29
violence in South Thailand, 292
 economic situation, 280
 escalation in 2004, 292, 294

Malay-Muslim struggle, 274
security forces, 278
Tablighi Jama'at (TJ), 296
violent confrontations in South Thailand
    Al Furqan incident, 279–81
    extrajudicial killings, 274
    Krue Se incident, 275–78
    Malay Muslims and Thai-Buddhist state, 275
    Narathiwat province, 274
    separatist groups, 274
    Tak Bai incident, 278–79
violent jihadi movements, 275
Vishnu Hindu Parishad, 145

W

Wahab, Ahmad, 287
Wahdah, 300, 305n30
Wahdah, Thai politics
    New Aspiration Party (NAP), 282–83
    separatism, 284
    Tak Bai massacre, 300
    TRT, 285
"Wahhabi", 87n4
Wahhabi-Salafi, 67, 80, 84–85
Wahhabism, 87n4, 259, 266, 308n60
Wahid, Abdurrahman, 224–25, 258
Wahid, Hidayat Nur, 35
Wahid Institute, 236, 239n1, 242n35, 242n41, 243n52
Wali Songo, 68
Wan Nor, 300, 306n35, 306n37

Western Christian societies, 28
Western democracy, 206
West Irian, 204–5
Wirjosandjojo, Sukiman, 26
women activists, pornography bill in Indonesia
    aurat, 256
    debates in parliament, 255
    demonstrations, 255–56
    Internet, 255
    in Muslim political parties, 257–58
    public outcry, 256
women's rights in Indonesia, 251–52, 257–58, 263
    individual freedom and, 262
Wood, Leonard, 317
World Mosque Council, 223

Y

Yala Islamic University, 289–91
Yellow Shirts, 310n83
Yeo, George, 343
Yeong Yoon Ying, 372n31
yoga, ban of, 126, 129n11
Yogyakarta, 220
Yongchaiyudh, Chavalit, 282
Yudhoyono, Susilo Bambang, 34, 37, 40, 218, 224–25, 238
Yusuf, Mawlana Muhammad, 296

Z

za'im, 27
zakat, 197
zuama, 25, 27, 43

www.ingramcontent.com/pod-product-compliance
Lightning Source LLC
Chambersburg PA
CBHW070300010526
44108CB00039B/1344